HUNTING THE DANGEROUS GAME OF AFRICA

HUNTING THE DANGEROUS GAME OF AFRICA

JOHN KINGSLEY-HEATH

SYCAMORE ISLAND BOOKS · BOULDER, COLORADO

Hunting the Dangerous Game of Africa
by John Kingsley-Heath

Copyright © 1998 by John Kingsley-Heath

Publisher's Cataloging-in-Publication
(Prepared by Quality Books, Inc.)

Kingsley-Heath, John.
        Hunting the dangerous game of Africa / John Kingsley-Heath.--
1st ed.
        p. cm.
        Includes bibliographical references.
        ISBN: 0-87364-958-3

        1. Big game hunting--Africa. 2. Wildlife management--Africa.
        I. Title.

SK251.K56 1998   799.2'6096
                                  QBI97-41215

ISBN 0-87364-958-3
Printed in the United States of America

Published by Sycamore Island Books, a division of
Paladin Enterprises, Inc., P.O. Box 1307,
Boulder, Colorado 80306, USA.
(303) 443-7250

Direct inquiries and/or orders to the above address.

Illustrations by Hugh Kingsley-Heath.

TABLE OF CONTENTS

FROM THE PUBLISHER

Sir Richard Francis Burton, famous African explorer, big-game hunter, and gold medalist of the Royal Geographical Society, wrote:

'The world is a great book of which those who never leave home have read but one page.'

John Kingsley-Heath has read a great many pages and perhaps more than one book.

—Peder C. Lund

FROM THE EDITOR

Having spent 20 years in the U.S. Marines—in the infantry, reconnaissance, and special operations at that—I was convinced upon my retirement that I had enjoyed the most thrilling and daring of lives, which no one could possibly surpass or even lay equal claim to. However, now that I have spent two weeks in John Kingsley-Heath's home and three months editing his book, I realize that I was mistaken.

—Bob Newman

ACKNOWLEDGEMENTS

Above all to my wife, Sue, who has faithfully produced the manuscript, learned and battled with the computer, and at the same time contrived to look after everyone providing the kind of sustenance and support without which this book could not have been written.

To my life-long friend Dick Ayer, godfather to one of my sons and financial advisor to me and many of my fellow professional hunters, must go an inestimable vote of thanks. Many, many times a client on safari and always a friend, Dick typically kept his help and advice low profile, when in fact both were of inestimable value. The hospitality and kindness extended to me by both Dick and his wife, Norma, on every one of my visits to the U.S.A. these 45 years are unforgettable and forever appreciated.

The friendship and loyalty of one man in Africa made possible much of the success I was fortunate to experience. Lionel Palmer was fairly and squarely with me in all our decision making. His wise advice and unfailing sense of humour, coupled with his wife Phyllis's dedication to our business and everyday work, will always be something that I shall respect and cherish. His loyalty has remained to this day, and our joint endeavours and life together are a source of great mutual satisfaction.

I must acknowledge the contribution and encouragement of my publisher, Peder Lund of Sycamore Island Books, without whose advice and guidance this book would have been poor by comparison to its original form. Particularly, thanks go to Bob Newman for his care and diligence in editing the considerable quantities of manuscript and photographs. His friendship in this task has been a pleasure to experience. A combination of the U.S. Marine Corps and the Brigade of Guards has been the best motivation for us!

To my friends and clients who have dug deep into their records to find photographs, dates, and other information.

To the late Jack O'Connor and his son, Bradford. To the former for all his help and encouragement in my literary attempts, and most particularly for impressing upon me that I simply had to write up my experiences and beliefs in the use of firearms and of hunting the big game of Africa. To the latter for making available hitherto believed lost records of photographs, experiences, and encouragement in my task.

My thanks are also due to the directors and members of the Dallas and Houston Safari Clubs, the latter most particularly so and with whom I have enjoyed a close and lasting association in the furtherance of wildlife conservation and the continuance of sport hunting.

The late Rene and Jo Jo Babault, the former a life-long friend with whom I shared some wildly exciting moments of my life.

Pauline Loveridge and the late Joel Loveridge, the latter being the most loyal and supportive friend a man could possibly experience, both of whom offered me the hospitality of their home in St. Louis. So, too, did Brian and Debbie Skeels in Houston, Ardiebelle Draeger in Orinda, Alex McGrath in Portola Valley, Chuck and Karen Bazzy in Detroit, and many other kind and hospitable people all over the U.S.A.

To Joe Cougan, whose advice, unfailing support, encouragement in finding an agent and publisher, and whose always 'being there' whenever I needed his sound judgment on my prose was most helpful. A man could have no better friend.

To Roger Mitchell of Holland & Holland, Simon Clode of Westley Richards, and Paul Roberts of Rigby, I am indebted not only for the help and support their firms have given me over the years, but also for the information and displays in the gun chapter of this book. I trust they will forgive me for not being able to afford their fine and superbly engineered rifles. If I win the national lottery I should be knocking on their doors at once!

And to Tom Spang, who introduced me to my publisher and who spent many days in Africa with me around some memorable campfires, and to whom, now that my task is done, I must devote my encouragement to write also.

I am eternally grateful also to my fellow members of the East African

Professional Hunters Association (E.A.P.H.A.) in East Africa and to all my loyal and trusted friends with whom I shared many campfires in Botswana.

Last but not least to my gunbearer, the late Edward Alimao, a Makonde from the Rovuma River on the southern border of Tanzania, with whom I shared all the hopes, fears, and dangers of my daily life for more than 40 years. We were together before I was married, and after I was, he treated my children with such kindness as if they were his own. To him and all the African staff, be they from Kenya, Ethiopia, or wherever, I am eternally grateful for their humour, hard work, and companionship.

Photographic and illustrative credit and thanks go to the following people:

- Douglas Van Howd from Auburn, California, for the drawing of an elephant.
- Hugh Kingsley-Heath, my youngest son, for all the line drawings of the many different species of animals used in the book.
- Mark Green of Plymouth, Devon, U.K., for photography and restoration.
- W.H. Winter of Nairobi for a photograph of a leopard.
- James Mellon of New York for a photograph of a pair of elephant tusks in Murchison Falls National Park Museum, Uganda.
- Baron W. Von Alvensleben of Portugal for a Mozambique poaching photograph.
- Peter Jenkins, M.B.E., of Nairobi for a photograph of Ahmed of Marsabit.
- Wildlife Department, Tanzania.
- *Outdoor Life* for photographs of and quotations from the late Jack O'Connor's articles, 1953–78, and a quotation from *Survival* by Ben East, an *Outdoor Life* book with drawings by Tom Beecham.
- Bradford and the late Jack O'Connor for permission to reproduce some of their own safari pictures.
- The late Mohammed Iqbal for his collection of elephant tusk photographs.
- Paramount Pictures Inc. for photographs from the set of *Hatari*.
- Keith Scheir of Houston, Texas, for safari photographs of hunting in Bechuanaland and Kenya.
- Dallas Safari Club for photographs from the late Herb Klein's records.
- Dr. R.S. West, D.D.S., from California.

- The late Frank Miller.
- Lionel Palmer and his wife, Phyllis.
- Alex McGrath, Ardiebelle Draeger, Dick and Norma Ayer, J. del Savio, and many other kind persons.
- Bob Newman, U.S. Marines (retired), for photographs of John and Sue Kingsley-Heath and J.K.-H. with the skin and skull of his black leopard.

INTRODUCTION

The bullets of the Turkish Mausers fired by the hands of Arab brigands ricocheted off the steel bars of the windows, pockmarking the walls and showering me with dust and plaster. The door of the bedroom burst open, and Lieutenant Colonel William Dobbie, in one swift movement, grabbed me and disappeared under the bed. It was 1929, and my father was leading repeated baton charges against the Arab rioters at the Jaffa Gate in Jerusalem, the first such action since the mandate for Palestine had been given to the British.

For me, a very small boy at the time, it set the dreams of life flowing in my imagination. It was sheer and utter excitement, and I craved it forever afterward and even to this day. When my friends tell me that I have led a remarkable life, I have to admit that I stand guilty of having done my best to make it so.

The information contained in this book is drawn from my hunting experiences (financed by the most meagre resources) in Ethiopia, Kenya, Eritrea, Sudan, Somaliland, Tanganyika (Tanzania), Uganda, and Bechuanaland (Botswana) between 1949 and 1978. It does not include my travels and experiences in Arabia and the Middle East, nor the years during which I held wildlife administration and warden appointments or was supervising the direction of wildlife conservation funding. Much of the statistical information and observations on wildlife, rifles, and cartridges have, of course, come from present-day sources. Such experiences as are related here are largely unrepeatable

To see a world in
a grain of sand
And heaven in a wild flower,
Hold infinity in the
palm of your hand
And eternity in an hour.

—William Blake
Auguries of Innocence

When my friends tell me that I
have led a remarkable life, I
have to admit that I stand guilty
of having done my best to make
it so.

—J.K.-H.

1

Eastleigh Airport, with an Ethiopian Airlines Convair about to take off. Clearly the 'old days!'

in today's Africa—and certainly not for the same cost. Alas, the environment has changed radically, and little can now be done to bring it back. Enormous increases in human populations have denuded the land of its assets—its forests and its water resources and, above all, its valuable wildlife. Subsistence economies have seen to that. To be fair, there was little or no alternative. Few, if any, of the African countries granted independence from colonial powers were prepared for the responsibility of government in such a short time, and they were without the infrastructure to plan for the future.

Sometimes I am asked if my conscience bothers me about hunting animals. Quite definitely it does not. My hunting was done in accordance with the laws of the land. At all times one presumed that the government, which permitted hunting, knew what it was doing and that its acts and permissions were based upon facts that supported its wildlife policies. However, as time went on, one began to suspect that this was not so. That time came for me in 1978. I awoke in my little house by the bridge over the Thamalakhane River in Maun, Botswana, to the noise of aero engines. At 5.30 A.M. This was very unusual. I jumped into my car in my pyjamas and slippers and beat it up to the airstrip. There I found two twin-

2

engined Piper Aztecs loaded with insecticide about to take off to spray the Okavango Swamps, with the object of eradicating the tsetse fly.

There had been no consultation with our company regarding this exercise. It just happened on this day. It was shattering. It was at that moment, as I sat in my car at the airstrip, that I realised that the existing wildlife and its habitat would give way to expanding populations of human beings and domestic stock, and that the process was irreversible. It was time to make a change, and I did so.

Recently, I revisited the area where I farmed on the slopes of Mount Kilimanjaro in Tanzania. The forest that had come to within 100 yards of the house was gone. The rainfall was down from 31 inches to 8 inches, and the huge ice cap on the summit of Mount Kilimanjaro had largely disappeared. Lava rocks were plainly visible from the lower slopes to the peak of the mountain.

Top: The snows and ice cap of Mount Kilimanjaro in 1960.

Above: Mount Kilimanjaro in 1996. Where has the ice cap gone?

1970 flood in Maun. Our house is below the bridge in the grove of trees. Note the backup of water behind the house. Such a flood has not been seen for the last 15 years.

In 1996, the president of Botswana made a speech in the United States of America. He stated that 'Botswana's resources are under pressure from overexploitation and unsustainable utilisation because of land degradation, a depleting ground water reserve, and decreases in wildlife species and indigenous grassland resources. There is increasing concern as to the ability of these resources to sustain themselves'.

For the last 15 years the water from the Angola rains that feed the Okavango Swamps has more or less failed to materialise. The swamps have shrunk. Lake Ngami and the Botleitle River have no water. The cattle in Ngamiland have contracted a lung disease necessitating the slaughter of 240 000 head. The enormous overpopulation of elephants is causing the destruction of their own habitat. Time-honoured migrations of animals from the Kalahari Desert no longer take place due to the installation of veterinary fences that are rigidly maintained and constantly extended.

Elsewhere, in Uganda and Angola—ravaged by civil war—there was total destruction of wildlife and its habitat, as was the case in Somaliland and Sudan. Wildlife has been plundered in Ethiopia, Eritrea, and Zambia. Huge populations of elephants have disappeared from both

Tanzania and Kenya, leaving virtually no chance of seeing big ivory. In the last 15 years, tens of thousands of animals have been destroyed. Hunters of my kind have played no part whatsoever in this.

A giant baobab tree, a meeting spot for lunch.

In a recent interview, I was asked if I had one regret that I could express concerning the preservation of wildlife. My concern was that the hunter, professional and indigenous, whose very life and living depended upon his knowledge of wildlife, its habitat, and the appreciation of the weather cycle that made up the environment, had in most cases never, in reality, been consulted. I am convinced that had this not been the case, far stricter and more meaningful conservation policies would have resulted. Giving hunters responsibility and a part to play in conservation would have produced a balanced team, rather than one entirely composed of officials and scientists who had seldom visited the environment and seen the wildlife for which they were legislating. It is a fact of human nature that where one's daily bread is in jeopardy, a way of jointly safeguarding it is usually found by those who need it most. Participation by those whose very lives depended on the abundance of wildlife would have made an enormous difference to what was left for posterity. To deny responsibility to genuine and honest people is to run the risk of turning

Above: Poachers are the antithesis of fair chase and are responsible for tremendous destruction of wildlife assets.

Following page: Despite poachers and other problems, scenes like this can still be seen, almost entirely thanks to the work of ethical professional hunters and caring wildlife administrators.

friend into foe. Once a 'them and us' situation is created, wildlife is always the loser.

FAIR CHASE: AN OBSERVATION ON TODAY'S SPORT HUNTING

For much of the period covered by this book, game animals were plentiful everywhere. Reference should be made to the appendices, which clearly show that the plentiful numbers of animals permitted to be hunted gave no excuse for poaching or overshooting a licence. The ethics and conduct of professional hunters was strictly controlled by the East African Professional Hunters Association. The E.A.P.H.A. seldom had cause to discipline a member for poaching animals, overshooting a licence, or acting unethically. The filming of any dying or

Try telling this fellow about fair chase.

wounded animals for any purpose was illegal everywhere. Any person so doing would have lost his licence and probably his immigration status immediately. Most professional hunters in East Africa were honorary game wardens, and the governments of the countries in which they resided relied on their judgements as caring conservationists who upheld the law and supported the control and conservation work of the game department.

This statement is made because the ethics and conduct seen today in several of the eastern and central African countries leave a great deal to be desired and in no way should be tolerated by any fair-minded sportsman. The almost total eradication of wildlife, even in reserves set aside more than 40 years ago, is unbelievable. The wounding of animals to provoke a charge and thereby make a sensational film is unethical. Hunting at night with spotlights from cars and tree platforms cannot by any stretch of the imagination be regarded as sporting. (This does not

The king of beasts surveys his fair chase area.

Fair chase was employed by G.C. George to get this good Botswana maned lion.

include the game management areas where overpopulations need to be reduced quickly and by any means the authorities deem desirable to save the habitat from destruction by the particular species at risk.)

Blame for the deterioration in ethics and respect for the law is easy to appreciate in the poorer countries of Africa, where subsistence economies still prevail. However, the cosy conservationists who are resident in these countries, practising their wildlife conservation policies whilst living in style without vehement objections to corruptive practices, only serve to convince their hosts that they can more or less do what they like. Now it is too late to object. Future generations will realise that nothing was done and that all too few people, in reality, stood up for the animals of Africa and upheld the principles of fair chase, which was the essence of being a professional hunter in Africa. Professional hunters played a vital role in the utilisation of the wildlife resource so that its survival was assured for future generations.

Today this statement probably wins me no friends amongst those outfitting big-game hunts in Africa, but it is time that the truth was faced and

ethics were put back into a sport that has, in my opinion, suffered griev-
ously from the corruptive practices of the guardians of African wildlife
and those who have done little to draw attention to this sad situation.
Nearly all professional hunters in business today would welcome a return
to ethics in sport hunting if they no longer had to face the unfair competition from the few whose contempt of the law is inevitably creating contro-
versy over one of the inherent instincts of man. The modern interpreta-
tion of this instinct is that sport hunting is the tool that controls wildlife
populations where it is needed. The income arising from such control
helps to pay for ensuring that the wildlife resource continues and that it
lives within its inevitable boundaries decreed by ever-increasing populations and domestic stock.

—John Kingsley-Heath

CHAPTER ONE

GATHERING EXPERIENCE

In 1949, when I was stationed in Tanga, a small port on the north-east coast of Tanganyika—now Tanzania—as a district officer for the provincial administration, sailing was my stimulus to life. I built a 12-foot 'sharpie' (a small Bermuda-rigged vessel) with a dagger board and sailed it to Pemba Island, 18 miles off the coast, and was caught in a frightening electrical storm on the way back. After that, I turned my attention to dry land.

I was sent on a 10-day safari up to the north-west corner of the district to the Umba Steppe (an area of thick bush and small glades with the Umba River running through it) in order to attend to government business. Walking along one day, I inadvertently passed upwind of a small herd of elephants. Having got my wind, they decided to come looking for me. If I had not run like the proverbial stag, one old cow would have hoisted me somewhere into the heavens. This event taught me a valuable lesson. The ratio of weight between a human being weighing approximately 190 pounds and an elephant at five tons is considerable, to say the least. One light touch of the trunk is sufficient to break several bones and render you unconscious. I determined that elephants could raise the adrenaline and that it would be exciting and challenging to hunt them.

About this time I met up with R.K.M. (Keith) Battye, a former Indian Civil Service officer, then a game warden recently appointed to Tanga. We became reasonably good friends in a short time, and then I was transferred right across Tanganyika to Kigoma, the port on Lake

I have seen people killed in war, but never such a grisly sight as a person who has been tusked and knelt on by an elephant and the smashed body of the victim used as a fly whisk.

—J.K.-H.

Tanganyika. I was in the Tabora Club, a European club for all resident members, when an acquaintance of mine asked if I had heard about Keith Battye.

'No!' I said. 'What happened?'

'An elephant got him!' was the reply.

'Where?' I asked.

'On the Umba, I believe', was the answer.

Living just outside Kigoma on a small estate was an elderly gentleman called Ted Millership. He was a kindly person and offered to sell me his .350 Rigby Magnum for £10, and I would get 30 rounds of ammunition as part of the deal. I bought it on the 'never-never', paying him £4 down and £3 a month thereafter. Shortly afterwards I was sent on safari—by the District Commissioner to collect tax and survey the alignment of a new road, transfer prisoners, and check licences—to Lagosa, southwards down the lake at the foot of the Mahali Mountains, arriving in Lagosa after a vile passage on the district boat, the *Imara*. She was nar-

Arrival in Nairobi, 1949. The plane is an Avro York, a modified Lancaster bomber from the 1939–45 War.

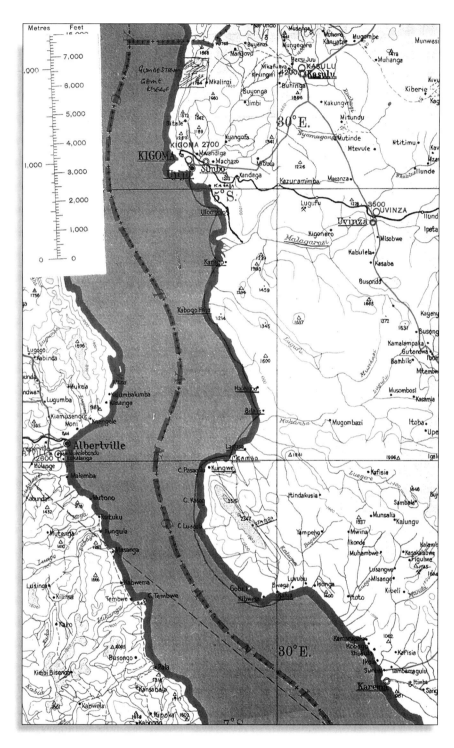

Map of Lake Tanganyika showing the route of the Imara *and our land routes (1949).*

15

row in the beam and wallowed like a hippo. We had a following wind, and the old Kelvin diesel engine smoked incessantly. Gerry Swynerton, the game ranger in charge of the area and afterwards chief game warden, was away on leave.

I was met at Lagosa by ashen-faced natives, who told me that two of their number had been killed by elephants that had been raiding their cultivations. When we reached the spot there was little doubt of the immense power of the bull elephant that had ground and smashed to pulp the two natives. I have seen people killed in war, but never such a grisly sight as a person who has been tusked and knelt on by an elephant and the smashed body of the victim used as a fly whisk. Hunting elephant would never be one sided.

Taking the local game scout and my .350 Rigby with us, we followed up the elephant and found him standing under a tree, waiting for the sun to go down, when he would return to the cultivations. Keeping downwind and taking the game scout with me (with his .404 Jeffery), we gave the bull two quick bullets in the heart followed by two more. The old bull turned so quickly I hardly had time to react, but at 25 yards I had time to give him another in his forehead. He stopped, shook his head, and then the heart shots told and he quietly collapsed.

His flanks were covered with the blood of the two natives he had killed. The whole village turned out and cut up the carcase, and in 24 hours there was nothing left. In this tsetse-fly-infested area there were no domestic stock, save a few scrawny goats.

I made a careful study of the anatomy and bone structure of the head for future reference. My frontal shot had been too low, and I could see why he was a rogue elephant: his right tusk cavity was full of maggots where he had broken it off and exposed the nerve. He must have been in the greatest agony, and, needless to say, I felt no sadness for his passing.

My safari was complete when I walked up onto the spine of the Mahali Mountains, climbing Mount Kungwe and viewing Lake Tanganyika from 8000 feet. Looking away south-westwards, I could see the Katavi Plains in the distance.

The fishing for yellow-bellied tilapia off Kibwesi Point was fabulous, but the journey back in the bloody *Imara* was unpleasant. We ran out of fuel off Ujiji (where the Stanley and Livingstone Memorial is situated) and finished the remaining five miles back home in a trade truck.

At the club that evening, catching up on local gossip, I was informed that a beautiful young girl had arrived and gone to the Gombe Stream

Game Reserve, about 50 miles north of Kigoma on the lake side, to study the chimpanzees. Her name was Jane Goodall.

Six weeks later I was off on safari—on foot—with 25 porters. I was soon up to my neck in buffalo, hippo, crocodiles, and the problems of feeding the porters as we travelled (having to hunt at midday for something for the porters to eat, with the animals hidden in deep shade and it being 100°F, was difficult). The .350 Rigby kicked like a mule, but it worked, and I had obtained some more ammunition. Three weeks later—assisted by the game scout, with eight elephants down that had been raiding the cultivations, and after a closer look at the Mahali Mountains and the chimpanzees there—I returned to find that I was to be transferred elsewhere. But the 'bug' had taken root.

Elephants were very exciting, and so was everything else, including the leopard that drank my washing water one night in the Mahali Mountains and the buffalo that scattered the porters and disappeared into the bush with a canvas wash basin on its horns! Great stuff. This was the life, and I rejoiced in physical fitness and the feeling of exploration.

Being single, I was lucky, as I was always able to travel. It became well known that I was interested in hunting and control work, and several game rangers were kind and went out of their way to enable me to do control work and gain experience. I shot my two elephants a year, and the resulting cash for ivory bought me a short-wheelbase Land Rover and a new battery of rifles: a .404, a .318, and a 12-bore shotgun all by Cogswell and Harrison in a good, strong wooden safari box with compartments for ammunition and cleaning equipment. No telescopic sights were used at the time, it being generally regarded as unsporting. My new battery of firearms had cost me half a year's salary, but as the income from ivory easily equated to a year's salary, it was affordable.

Colonel D.C. Branfoot, a recently retired British Army officer, was at that time hunting in Tanganyika, having bought his own truck and camping equipment. He was most kind to me, allowing me to use his camp when he was absent. This gave me a base from which to hunt and do control work.

I also struck up a friendship with Basil Reel, who was working as a veterinary department game observer. Rinderpest, a virulent cattle disease, had decimated native herds of cattle some years previously. It was Basil's job to observe constantly any disease from which game animals were dying; this kept him permanently in the bush. Basil was well over 70, but he walked continually for months at a time all over the uninhab-

The .465/.500 H & H Royal Grade (1951).

ited parts of western and central Tanganyika. Leave being due, I was asked to accompany him on safari on the condition that I would shoot nothing. Having a good deal to learn, I agreed. We were gone for a month, during which time I probably learnt more of bushcraft and the habits of game than I did in all the previous years put together.

Basil had a double-barrelled .470 'Army and Navy' rifle, not expensive but effective. After a month with Basil I determined to find one. He also had some sophisticated camera equipment. Some months later, when we were sitting over a drink at the Tabora Railway Hotel, he took me to his room saying he had something important to show me. Opening his box of personal possessions, he produced an envelope that contained the pictures of nine enormous tusked elephants.

Swearing me to secrecy, he told me that in the last two years he had photographed each of them and that to the best of his knowledge they had not been shot. I could not believe my eyes. Gazing at the pictures, I tried to record in my mind each and every elephant. It was, of course, impossible, but I believe I did remember five of them. I could not bring myself to ask him if he would let me have a copy of the pictures, but I thanked him for his confidence and promised that I would never tell a soul. Years later, I felt certain that I had shot one of them and accounted for most of the others from information that I gathered from various sources.

Some time later Basil Reel passed on. His friend who looked after him at the hotel, Mrs. Goodrich (the accommodation manager), handed me a small packet: it was the photographs. He had wanted me to have them. Fate decreed that they would be stolen from my personal effects some time later without copies having been made, but by that time I had several more opportunities to memorise the look of that incredible collection of ivory. I have faithfully kept Basil's secret until now.

Moving farther south (I was on leave and had taken a temporary job), I got to know George Rushby, the senior game warden at Mbeya. He soon realised how keen I was on hunting and went out of his way to encourage me. We did a number of safaris together, and he became a father figure to me. His stories of 'the old days' when he arrived in South Africa penniless, boxing in booths for his supper in the mining areas, and his frequent exploits hunting ivory in the Lado Enclave (an agreed no-man's-land between the Belgian Congo, Sudan, and Uganda) were enough to excite anyone with a spirit of adventure.

Fringe-eared Oryx.

It was whilst hunting with George on the perimeter of the Buhoro Flats (the flood plains of the Ruaha River) that I came to grief with an elephant. The old bull, a 90-pounder (the approximate weight of each tusk), was standing behind a low thorn bush within a few yards of a large rain puddle. With that unforgettable, wry grin of his, George indicated that he would take a grandstand view of the 'expert' shooting an elephant. I had approached to within 10 yards, concealed by a low thorn bush, when in an instant I found myself cartwheeling through the air, landing in the rain puddle and the mud. The elephant had grabbed and thrown me!

As I hit the water there was a deafening explosion. George's .577 roared out, and down went the elephant, brain shot through the ear. I was so embarrassed at my failure and had so much pain in my dislocated shoulder and strained neck that I had little to say.

George took me to Iringa Hospital where my shoulder was put back in place and I was strapped up. I also had four broken ribs and could not breathe without difficulty. It took me about three months to recover, and for a time I learnt to shoot from my left shoulder. The experience convinced me that a double-barrelled rifle was needed.

As luck would have it, Mr. Halliwell, the administrator of deceased estates, was holding an auction. One of the items was a double-barrelled .465/.500 Holland & Holland Royal Grade gun. I went to the auction and bid £55 for it, but it was withdrawn. Afterwards, I made a deal with the administrator and purchased it for £65, together with six rounds of verdigris-encrusted ammunition. I had no money but was still able to buy an elephant licence by arranging a bank overdraft of £30.

I despatched Asumani Kaduga, my gunbearer and tracker, forthwith to the Idodi area to see if he could find any elephants. By the following Monday, at 10.00 in the morning, I had to have the cost of the double in the hands of the revenue officer. On Friday afternoon I left for Idodi. At 4.00 that Sunday afternoon we sighted four bulls. Three heart shots at a 70-pounder secured a fine pair of tusks. We had 30 miles to walk to the car and the tusks to remove. I made it to the Iringa ivory dealer, Mohammed Shivji, by 9.30 the next morning, and at 10.00 the revenue officer had his money.

The first shot at the elephant was a 'hang fire'. The second and third were apparently good. Closer inspection revealed that one had 'key-holed' (when the bullet tumbles and hits the target sideways because of a worn-out barrel) into the elephant. I was lucky! I mentally chalked it up to experience and determined to sell the rifle. Shortly after I did for £80.

A close friend of mine, Bill Bindloss, had had his parents attacked by the Mau Mau terrorists in Kenya. After hearing his story, I decided to move back to Kenya to offer my assistance, but not before I had shot my second elephant that year, a prize 130-pounder whose tusks are with me to this day. I believe it was the only one of Basil Reel's elephants that I ever saw.

Masailand in north central Tanganyika is a huge area into which it was possible to escape for a few days' hunting. Whilst in the Arusha area in Northern Province, I went hunting deep into what was then totally uninhabited country. I visited the grave of A. Spurrell, who in the early 1930s had been killed by an elephant near Kibaya. My old friend and subsequent partner Frank Miller, who was with the veterinary department at the time, knew Masailand as well as

Thompson's Gazelle

anyone and was also a dedicated elephant hunter. He had the misfortune to be sharing a camp with a friend who, when out hunting one day on his own, was also killed by an elephant.

In Kenya, after plenty of control work on forest elephant and buffalo, and having enjoyed many reunions with old friends of my family, I took a job that launched me into Ethiopia, Eritrea, Somaliland, and Sudan. In these countries there were no friendly game wardens or government rest houses where one could stay. There were, however, unrivalled opportunities for exploration and hunting, and I made full use of them.

In Ethiopia I hunted the Danakil (a depression in eastern Ethiopia) and the 'Awash', which is a basin adjacent to the Danakil. I shot a magnificent mountain nyala (like a greater kudu but found at high elevations) in the Arusi Mountains and a black leopard in the forests south of Shashamane.

I hunted the Tacasse Valley and the Semien Mountains, visited Gondar, and met up with Ras Kassa, who had been at the same school as I had in England many years before. I passed via Jimma in south-west Ethiopia and hunted the bush country between the Omo River in the west and the Ethiopian Mountains in the east. I hunted the Dilla Plains and the plains to the north of Lake Stephanie and northwards back to the Omo. I shot Swayne's hartebeest, oryx, lion, lesser kudu, and many other species of game.

In Eritrea I spent some time in Keren, the scene of the crucial battle for Eritrea between the British forces from the Sudan and the Italian forces defending Ethiopia. Here I shot greater kudu and leopard.

Farther north, on the Red Sea littoral, I collected the Red Sea ibex near Karora. Gazelles abounded in the Wadi Mansour in western Eritrea at that time, and I made a trip to the Setit River in the Sudan.

Gerenuk

In Somaliland on the Dibra Wein I came across the last indication of elephant. The elephant dung was a year or so old, but I believe it marked their very last visit. I shot *dibatag* (the Somali name for Clarke's gazelle) and beira antelope, the latter in Erigavo on the Horn of Africa, and made a three-day visit to the island of Socotra off the Somali coast (where modern-day pirates still exist). In the 'Haud', that waterless and uninteresting piece of country shared with what used to be British and Italian Somaliland and Ethiopia, I shot gerenuk, dibatag, and lesser kudu.

Stationed on the Webi Schebelli River at Mustahil, I had a field day with lions that had become unmanageable, killing herdsmen, camels, cattle, and goats in considerable numbers. Daily my camp was visited by

parties of Somali tribesmen pleading for me to come and put an end to their nightmarish existence. To some extent I obliged, shooting some man-eaters (more than 30 lions in all), but I have never had much love for these people, whom I consider to be the most avaricious and untrustworthy that I have ever met. The police officer in charge at Belet Uen, the Somaliland border post, gave me a bit of a hard time one day. He was none other than the later-to-be-infamous Mohammed Farah Aidid, the Somali warlord of 1994 and 1995.

In 1955 I bought a one-and-a-half-ton, four-wheel-drive Austin truck in pretty good condition. I loaded it with all the camp kit that I had and set off for Nairobi by road from Hargeisa, the capital of British Somaliland. It was the day that they gained their independence from Britain and we were lucky to get out alive. I had given a lift to Geoff Best,

an actor who was making his way overland to Kenya. He was a good companion, and we set out in good style. Driving down the newly cut border between British Somaliland and Ethiopia, we came to a village called Duruksi. We had had vaporisation trouble with the carburettor and stopped to cool off the engine.

Out of the corner of my eye I saw a man with a rifle disappear behind a hut. Time to go! Alerting Geoff, we jumped into the truck. Luckily she started on the first try and kept going. We had gone 50 yards when we heard the bullets thump into the back of the truck. Fortunately, the two huge spare wheels mounted behind the cab protected us. We kept going in spite of the fact that a herdsman deliberately drove his herd of goats across the road, several of which met their end as we thundered on, not stopping till we got to R.F. 'Fungi' Smith's camp at Bohotle.

We all vacated 'British' Somaliland at 6.00 the next morning and headed for Galcaio in the former Italian Somaliland, and from there, via Mogadiscio and Garrissa in Kenya, we headed for Nairobi.

Above: Looking across the flooded plain of the Webi Schebelli River in southern Ethiopia from Marshall Graziani's rest house (1955).

Previous page: Lion country in southern Ethiopia along the Webi Schebelli (1955).

23

Here I was in Nairobi, fresh from all stations north, and it was getting expensive. As luck would have it, there was a job guiding a photographic safari to Uganda, so packing my truck once again I set off for Entebbe in Uganda, where I was to meet my clients. Finishing the trip that covered all the major national parks, I once again set out to do some private hunting, visiting the Sese Islands for sitatunga.

I hunted the Pian Upe, Bokora, and Mathineko (on the Kenya-Ethiopia border, an area that looks like much of Arizona and Utah with massive rock outcroppings) for leopard and lion, and after spending a few days in Moroto set out for the Kidepo Valley.

Negley Farson's book *Behind God's Back* brought other words to mind. Kidepo was 'God's own country'. It was a garden of Eden, a part of Africa created in one's dreams. Animals of every kind abounded. From several small rocky hills I spotted hundreds of elephant daily. In 1958 the area rightly became a national park. The local people, the Karamajong, were more or less friendly, but it did not take very long to realise that there was little love lost between them and the surrounding tribes of the border with Sudan to the north.

Time passed, and the rains of Uganda were upon me. I took the long road back to Nairobi in the hopes of finalising my future. Little did I realise at the time that 35 years later I would return as chief park warden of the Queen Elizabeth National Park and subsequently as assistant director of national parks, to find but 350 elephants left out of 45 000 and that 98 percent of the game animals in the country had been killed. It was impossible to fully understand the complete and systematic destruction of wildlife that had taken place in the intervening years. It was likewise impossible to forget that the life's work of so many game and national park wardens to preserve wildlife for posterity had been for naught.

In 1951, I obtained a professional hunter's licence in Tanganyika and had accompanied a few people between times on their hunting safaris, but had not hitherto considered this form of employment as a permanent one. Now somewhat satiated with my experiences in Ethiopia, Eritrea, Sudan, and the Somalilands, and with the passage of years, I began to feel that perhaps I should behave more normally!

My oldest and best friend at that time was Rene Babault. We met one day in the Long Bar of the New Stanley Hotel in Nairobi to discuss our future plans. Rene was all for joining White Hunters Ltd. (as it was then called; it later changed its name to Hunters Africa Ltd. for obvious reasons). I, with connections through both my father and uncle, was in favour of joining Ker & Downey Safaris. Myles Turner, another old friend, was keen on my doing so, and Syd Downey had offered me a base at his home near Hoppy's Hotel on the Ngong Road on the west side of Karen, a suburb of Nairobi. Rene and I decided to go our own ways and compare notes in a year's time. We both did well and had the very greatest enjoyment out of life.

Once again ivory gave me a start. The money from my first and second elephants bought me my first hunting car, which had been the property of Syd Downey and meticulously maintained. Two years later, I was appointed a director of Ker & Downey, and my career as a P.H. was safely launched. I felt confident that my experience by then was sufficient to take care of my clients, for to this day I have been fortunate never to have had any client injured on safari. For myself it was a different story, but that was part of the job.

The accrual of the knowledge of languages had been an essential part of my gathering experience. I was fortunate to have been brought up learning Arabic in my childhood and a little later Swahili. I found Arabic to be of some considerable value in East Africa, as most of the far outlying villages had a shop owned by an Arab. In the coastal villages of Lake Tanganyika this was especially the case. In Tanganyika's Western Province, one of the centres of the slave trade, there were still many Arab shopkeepers and traders who, when spoken to in their own language, made me most welcome and were the source of much useful information. In Ethiopia and Italian Somaliland I learnt a smattering of Italian, and throughout the area a working knowledge of Somali proved useful. For much of the time I was entirely on my own with no recourse to my own language. It was the best way to learn, as in emergencies I needed to speak clearly in the native language to the people I was with at the time.

On reflection, I am struck by the very genuine sense of friendship and the feeling of responsibility for each other that we all felt during times of adversity. Of course, it was inevitable that there were a few on the periphery of the profession who did not come up to standard, but they mostly, in due course, found something else with which to occupy themselves. There was no animosity or excessive competition between us. We helped each other and spent Christmases at the coast together

In the den of my old friend Dick Ayer reading Jack O'Connor's story of his safari with me. We had all 'gathered experience' by then!

with our families and friends. Later, the insecurity of the future of the countries in which we lived destroyed much of the camaraderie and friendship, as each person was forced to fend for himself and his family. Necessarily it became a battle to survive. Competition became fierce whilst wildlife populations dwindled, and when Kenya shut down professional hunting it was the end of an era. Corruptive practices, nationalisation of hunting safari companies, poaching, and war quickly brought to an end the lives of millions of animals. My experiences were unrepeatable and gone forever.

CHAPTER TWO

ELEPHANT HUNTING

The Big Tuskers

KENYA

When I joined Ker & Downey Safaris it was run by a triumvirate of Donald Ker, Syd Downey, and Jack Block. Ron Stephens, who was a trained chemist who had decided that wildlife was more interesting than a life of patent medicines, had joined the Kenya National Parks. After a stint there he had joined the company as the manager. He and his wife, Marlies, were a very efficient team. The company had, however, taken a severe knock after eight of its professional hunters walked out and set up their own organisation after the directors refused to make them shareholders. In some ways it was an opportune moment to join, but at the same time, as most of the professional hunters who had left had taken their safaris with them, there was not a lot of work about and I was the new boy. Eric Rundgren, Bill Ryan, George Barrington, Kris Aschan, and Roy Home were, however, well established, and Syd Downey and Donald Ker were exceedingly well known. I did a couple of safaris as second hunter to Syd Downey and rapidly got myself organised.

I soon realised that both Eric Rundgren and Roy Home were inveterate elephant hunters with great experience. I was not so worried about shooting the elephants as finding them. I also had to find the right clients to hunt them.

Kenya at that time was divided into hunting blocks, and the head-

'Ready! Fire!' he said. Both bulls staggered and both rifles were reloaded in a second. 'Fire!' he said again. . . Our guns roared.

—J.K.-H.

27

Top: Fly camp for elephant in the Northern Frontier District north of the Tana River (1963).

Bottom: The short-wheel-based four-wheel-drive Land Rover with hunter's modifications: four jerricans and room for three spare wheels (1968).

quarters of the Kenya Game Department controlled the booking of areas. No area could be booked without evidence of deposit, and the area booked was exclusively for the use of your own safari. I decided to publicise the point to my own contacts and sent out a newsletter. It read as follows:

Kenya is a country very nearly the size of Texas. A large part of it is above 5000 feet. It is mainly between the coast at sea level and 4000 feet that most of the elephant populations live. Years ago elephant roamed over most of the country. At the turn of the century the population of Kenya stood at two million people, now it is in the region of nine million. Game populations are not as great nor can they roam at will wherever they choose. The government of Kenya has established huge national parks so as to safeguard

the wildlife which by its very presence generates for Kenya an enormous income from the tourist industry. This is composed of people from all over the world who come to see the animals of Africa. It is generally agreed that Kenya's national parks are the finest of their kind in the world.

Surprisingly enough there are more elephants in Kenya now than at the turn of the century. In the Tsavo National Park it is believed there are some 25 000 and the country as a whole may have an elephant population of up to 45 000. The animals are no longer shot or poached for their ivory as in previous years. Approximately 100 licences to shoot an elephant a year are issued by the game department to visiting sportsmen. Residents account for a further 100. In the last two years no less than 22 elephants were shot with tusks of over 100 pounds in weight in each or single tusk. Contrary to general belief, elephant hunting in Kenya has not deteriorated. This is due to the assumption that as other game populations have decreased so also has the elephant pop-

Not everyone shot 100-pound-tusked elephants. There were many other trophies to be hunted. These two Southern gentlemen, Bob Card and Dr. Wayne Gilley, gave me as much fun as they had themselves (1968).

ulation. The elephant population in fact continues to grow, and presents problems of control of a considerable magnitude. The ever increasing numbers of elephants in the national parks continue the depredations of their habitat caused by their choice of food. This in turn causes them to migrate into other areas in search of better food with the result that there is an immediate conflict of human and animal interest, competition for water, grazing resources, etc.

Genetically speaking, big ivory breeds big ivory. Locked into a huge park, unmolested, it follows that big tuskers breed undisturbed for many years, therefore the park-born elephants should, given time, grow as big ivory as their forebears. This is undoubtedly the case, since so much big ivory has been shot in the vicinity of park borders.

Weather controls the movement of the huge herds of elephant in Kenya. Generally speaking, the short rains start on November 15th and end on December 20th. The long rains start on April 5th and end during the last week in May. The advent of the rains causes substantial migrations of elephant population. This is because food and water become readily accessible both in and out of the parks and the competition with human agencies for both these items is reduced to nil. Cattle populations in Kenya are very considerable. The semi-nomadic tribes herding huge numbers of cattle often deny elephants access to water. The elephants in time are forced to retreat into the national parks where they can feed and water undisturbed. Like human beings, elephants become dissatisfied at being forced to remain in a single place. Oft-browsed bushes on which they subsist become distasteful so that when rain falls, grass and bushes sprout forth anew, and water becomes plentiful everywhere, they set forth on migration into the country surrounding the national parks which is still sufficiently large as to have huge tracts, under prevailing conditions, disused by both cattle-tending tribes and ranchers.

This is the moment that the elephant hunter has a prime chance to pick out a huge bull elephant carrying heavy ivory that has emerged from a national park into a hunting area. Very careful planning and booking of hunting areas is required, together with real, and expert knowledge of the country and elephant migration routes. This is normally achieved by bearing in mind the following facts:

1. Selecting the professional hunter with a requisite knowledge at least one year in advance and commencing the necessary correspondence.
2. Making the required deposit at least nine months in advance, without which no areas can be booked.

Following page: Ahmed of Marsabit. Photographed and by courtesy of Peter Jenkins, warden of the Marsabit National Park.

30

3. Authorising the professional hunter to make an aerial reconnaissance of the country several days in advance of the commencement of the hunt. It is forbidden to search for elephant by use of an aircraft 48 hours or less prior to commencement of a hunt.

4. If at all possible, give the professional hunter and yourself some latitude in dates of commencement of the hunt. This means that if the rains come a week late the professional hunter can contact you by telephone from Kenya and arrange for you to come earlier or later as the case may be.

There are three main areas of Kenya that elephant hunting for big ivory are by proven results best:

1. The north-western part of the Northern Frontier District.
2. The Tana River area that stretches to the Somalia border.
3. The circumference of the Tsavo National Park and the known migratory routes to the south-east, to Tanzania and the north-east to the west of the Tana River and the coast.

Here is a short description of each hunting area:

The North-West of the Northern Frontier District

The hunting blocks under the control of the game warden of each sub area are in some cases restricted so as to preclude the use of motor vehicles. Camp is made by using a vehicle to reach the campsite. Hunting is then carried out on foot with the use of camels and horses. The best country lies mostly at the foot of the Mathews Range. This area is not far from Marsabit where the fabled Ahmed (150-pound tusks a side?) lives within the confines of the Marsabit National Park. This is country strewn with lava boulders and therefore volcanic in origin. Its appearance is reminiscent of parts of Arizona, being broken up into rocky hills interspersed with dry watercourses. Very occasionally a spring of water causes a small elephant population to centre in the area. The height of the rocky outcrops enables one to spot and study elephants from considerable distances. This area is not so much affected by rain as the other two, and hunting is generally good throughout the year. The weather is hot by day but not humid. The charm of the evenings on safari in this country leaves perhaps one of the most indelible impressions of Africa on one's mind. Of all my own recollections of Africa in which I have spent most of my life, this is the area that I remember best. The sand grouse shooting and other bird shooting can only be described on occasions as fantastic.

The Tana River Northwards to Somalia

Tana River ivory is famous for its unblemished length. Hunting is mostly in motorable flat country and is relatively easily accomplished. The local people, the Somalis, provide guides and information. Rain makes all the difference to hunting in this area, and it is advisable that the area is viewed from the air so that the incidence of rain showers can be recorded and the areas where vegetation flourishes can be visited. Generally speaking, one sets forth from camp each day prepared to spend a night or two in a fly camp, ending the day wherever the day's hunting takes one. The country is low, 800 feet above sea level. February is the hottest month of the year when temperatures rise to over 100 degrees at midday in the shade. It is humid. Base camp is normally on the Tana River under heavy shade. Camp is spacious, comfortable, and equipped with the luxuries of life, iced drinks, etc. An excursion on the river by boat is a welcome diversion. Many a good tusker has been obtained on more than one occasion by this method. It is customary on occasions in this area for big elephant bulls to establish residence in a thicket of choice food close to the river. The Tana River has a belt of sometimes impenetrable forest of up to half a mile on each bank. This area is hunted from a boat and when a landing is made the hunt continues on foot. Teams of local people acting as scouts are employed to locate sizeable elephants and bring in information to a prearranged rendezvous. The Tana is reminiscent of Kipling's 'great, grey, green, greasy Limpopo River', except that it is coloured reddish brown and heavy with sediment. There is excellent bird shooting and crocodiles are frequently seen. Hunting blocks, 14, 14A, 13, 10, 16, 16A, etc. make up this area. About 7-10 days in a block are required to make a thorough hunt. Hunter's hartebeest and Hagard's oribi can also be hunted.

The Circumference of the Tsavo National Park

This park contains an estimated population of 25 000 elephants. These elephants are sometimes seen easily, often by the thousand, from the air. I will always have an ever-present picture in my mind when flying a light aircraft, of the rain squalls falling on the precincts of the park, normally in the late afternoon, viewing almost at the same time the heads of the elephants visible below wheeling toward the falling rain. One is usually able to tell from the weather reports where the most rain is falling. A look in this direction will almost certainly be fruitful. The area is a vast one and should in turn be divided into at least three parts. The principles of hunting are much the same as for Tana River hunting. Most of the country is motorable though there are some patches of thick bush. There are also some remarkably good observation points from which, sometimes, several thousand elephants can be seen at one time. It is, however, more essential in this area to be at the right place at the right time, than in either of the other two areas mentioned. It is hot but not too humid over most of this area. The west bank of the Tana River is hunted for the most part in a similar fashion to the east bank. The area where the Thowa/Lak Galole Rivers flowing from west to east and for most of the year totally dry, runs through block 33, 15, and 17 into the Tana at Galole is not in reality part of any of the three areas mentioned. Some of the best hunting there takes place in September and October before there is any rain at all. Elephants here are normally a few old bulls who obtain water from the bed of the dry sandy bottom of the Thowa or Lak Galole by slowly digging with their trunks in the sand until they strike a sufficiency of subsurface water. They drink only once every 2-3 days at night. Tracking them, which can only normally be done on foot due to the presence of thick bush, is a physical experience for which one has to be fit and capable. One may well walk 30 miles in a day!

In all areas there are other game animals to be hunted, buffalo, leopard, oryx (callotis and beisa), gerenuk, grevy zebra, dik-dik, lesser kudu, and waterbuck, to name a few. For one who wishes to shoot a big elephant, however, other hunting must be placed second. Hunting for big ivory takes a great deal of hard work, persistence, and perseverance. Its rapidly changing fortunes elates and depresses one in turn but remains always a really genuine, never to be forgotten hunting experience.

For a few golden years it was one of the best experiences of my life, to be with a superb bunch of kindred spirits who all had great loyalty to the firm. Management and equipment were excellent. The company built up a quite remarkable reputation and began to handle film contracts such as *Hatari* and *Sammy Going South*.

I was able to expand my hunting area to southern Tanzania and Uganda. I had obtained a pilot's licence and had correctly surmised that if I could maintain myself in the bush in southern Tanzania—

Top: Standing, l to r: P. Becker*, K. Aschan, S. Rabb (company secretary), B. Ryan*, A. North, J. Cook*, F. Bartlett, G. Barrington, T. Archer, J. Dugmore, T. Mathews.
Sitting, l to r: R. Home*, J. Kingsley-Heath (director), S. Downey* (director and founder), Jack Block* (managing director), D. Ker* (director and founder), E. Rundgren* (director), R. Stephens (general manager).
* Designates deceased.

Left: Dick Ayer and me with a 90-pound tusked elephant shot at Galole, Kenya.

Dick and Norma Ayer with a beautiful matched pair of 90-pound tusks (1967).

where there were no block-booking systems—I could simply fly my clients in one after the other by commercial air charter and cut costs drastically. Careful management of safari date made this possible. Of course, there was a hidden benefit, for at the end of the last safari it gave me time to shoot my own two elephants, and that meant we could look forward to a good Christmas on the coast without having to worry too much about the cost—and female company was almost guaranteed!

I was a professional hunter (and director and shareholder) of Ker & Downey for seven years. Throughout that time the company kept a list of big ivory shot by their clients called the 100 Pounder Club, in which my name was fortunate to be recorded a number of times. This list includes elephants shot between August 1957 and January 1967.

Hunter—Location—Professional Hunter—Tusk Weight (Each)

1. Dr. Paul New—Kenya—Roy Home—117 & 120 lbs.
2. Mr. Pat de Cicco—Kenya—Fred Bartlett—100 & 110 lbs.
3. Judge Russel Train—Kenya—George Barrington—106 & 102 lbs.
4. Mr. Jim Shirley—Kenya—Peter Becker—112 & 109 lbs.
5. Mr. Wilfred Heinzel—Kenya—Peter Becker—107 & 101 lbs.
6. Mr. Vern Walston—Kenya—Eric Rundgren—102 & 100 lbs.
7. Mr. Raymond Guest—Kenya—Tony Archer—109 & 117 lbs.
8. Mr. Raymond Guest—Kenya—Tony Archer—108 & 111 lbs.
9. Mr. Ed Wilson—Kenya—Fred Bartlett & Peter Becker—112 & 110 lbs.
10. Mr. Dennis (Woody) Krieger—Tanganyika—Eric Rundgren & Bill Jenvey—110 & 123 lbs.
11. Mr. William Holmes—Tanganyika—J.K.-H.—103 & 104 lbs.
12. Mr. Erwin Wilson—Kenya—Terry Mathews—101 & 110 lbs.
13. Sr. Guillermo Torielli—Kenya—Eric Rundgren—111 & 103 lbs.
14. Mr. Charles Rumsey—Kenya—Eric Rundgren—101 & 107 lbs.
15. Mr. Richard Kriete—Kenya—Terry Mathews—111 & 105 lbs.
16. Mr. F. Asche—Kenya—John Fletcher—114 & 108 lbs.
17. Mr. F. Auerbach—Kenya—Reggie Destro—119 & 114 lbs.
18. Mr. C.L. Mitton—Kenya—J.K.-H.—101 & 100 lbs.
19. Mr. C.C. Gates—Kenya—John Sutton—115 & 118 lbs.
20. Dr. H.S. Misner—Kenya—John Sutton—125 & 111 lbs.
21. Mr. Yates Powers—Kenya—J.K.-H.—100 & 103 lbs.
22. Mr. Gary Leader—Kenya—Mohammed Iqbal—120 & 116 lbs.
23. Mr. A.W. Frederick—Kenya—Mohammed Iqbal—102 & 105 lbs.
24. Mr. A. Karmark—Kenya—Terry Mathews—102 & 103 lbs.
25. Mr. Eric Ridder—Kenya—John Sutton—118 & 122 lbs.
26. Mrs. Marcia French—Kenya—John Sutton—117 & 121 lbs.
27. Mr. Lim Po Hein—Kenya—Mohammed Iqbal—115 & 111 lbs.
28. Mr. J.R. Mustek—Kenya—Mohammed Iqbal—110 & 104 lbs.
29. Mr. J. Iverson—Kenya—John Dugmore—122 & 119 lbs.
30. Mr. J. Iverson—Kenya—John Dugmore—133 & 126 lbs.
31. H.R.H. Bernhardt, the Prince of the Netherlands—Kenya—Eric Rundgren—101 & 102 lbs.

One of the largest set of tusks I ever saw. The estimated weights were 140 pounds a side. I had no licence, and, of course, I was tempted. Poachers got him shortly afterwards when he moved back into the Meru National Park.

This represents a total of 31 elephants with tusks of more than 100 pounds, of which only two were shot in Tanganyika. This indicates how little Tanganyika was hunted for ivory at that time by professionally conducted safaris, and that it lay relatively undiscovered by the larger Kenya-based safari firms. The main reason for this was that the distances involved and the consequent cost of travel, wages, food, and other expenses made it much easier to operate in Kenya whilst such success

was possible. The Tanganyika areas were also infested with tsetse fly, whereas the Kenya areas were not.

The huge numbers of elephants in Kenya, variously reckoned at 45 000 based upon the huge areas demarcated as national parks and game reserves, ensured that this taking of heavy ivory was but a fraction of what was being reproduced by the national herd.

Not for long was Tanganyika to escape the attention of Kenya-based firms.

It must also be remembered that the previous list of elephants shot by the professional hunters of Ker & Downey was but a small part of the total shot by the clients of other safari companies, such as White Hunters Ltd., Safariland, Lawrence-Brown Safaris, and many others. S.I. Hassan, operating out of Mombasa, was also conspicuously successful. Also added to the total should be those elephants shot by resident hunters.

My reader will have noticed in the list of elephants shot by Ker & Downey Safari clients the name of Raymond Guest, who shot two 100-pound-tusked elephants with Tony Archer (numbers 7 and 8). Raymond was the scion of a Welsh steel family and an American citizen (his mother, Amy Phipps, was American). He not only shot two 100-pound-tusked elephants on the same day, but the following day won the Epsom Derby with his horse, Larkspur. He was one of the most success-ful racehorse owners England has seen, winning the Derby again in 1970 with Sir Ivor and the Cheltenham Gold Cup twice (in 1970 and 1971) with L'Escargot, and the Aintree Grand National with L'Escargot, which also came in second to Red Rum the previous year.

Raymond's brother, Winston Guest, took a notable part in the set-ting of a hunting precedent in East Africa. Hunting in 1938, he wounded an immensely tusked elephant carrying 196 pounds and 198 pounds a side. After an exhausting follow-up, he had to turn back for want of food and water. The gunbearers, however, continued the search. Meanwhile, the elephant was found dead, but it had been appropriated by a South African hunter who sought to pass it off as his own, but who was discovered by the game warden to have actually only found it. The tusks were confiscated by the district administration. Winston claimed the tusks and in

Perhaps no African hunting book is complete without a drawing of an elephant by renowned international artist Doug Van Howd.

the resulting court case had his lawyer come to Kenya and stay long enough to achieve a residential qualification to enable him to represent Winston. The case was lost, and thereafter the precedent was set that once the chase is abandoned by the licence holder, the trophy becomes government property. The tusks were sold at the Mombasa auction rooms and cut up for ivory carvings. They were never recorded in the record books.

As I have mentioned elsewhere, Rene Babault was a great friend and we were somewhat kindred spirits in those days; anything a bit hare-brained—but with just a chance of success and adventure—appealed to us. I recall one time when we were both temporarily employed by the Desert Locust Control Organisation in the northern frontier of Kenya. When I arrived at Garrisa, where Rene was camped, I knew the moment I shook his hand and saw that puckish smile on his face that we would get up to something!

A message had come over the radio that the First Secretary of the British Embassy at Addis Ababa, Mr. Killick, was driving down via Mogadiscio (Mogadishu) in Somaliland to Nairobi via Garrisa. This meant he would cross into Kenya via the border post at Belescogani. After telling the authorities that Mr. Killick was mad, as the rains were about to break, we hoped he would postpone his trip. He did not and kept on coming! We were asked to go and meet him but had no idea when he would arrive and, because we had already decided that the advent of the rains would make an admirable joint elephant-hunting opportunity, we left, ostensibly to look out for Mr. Killick. A few days later the rains came heavily and with a vengeance. The country flowed with water, and the water holes were soon overflowing. The elephants left the safety of the thickets on the Tana River and headed out into the *barani*—the wide open spaces on the two countries' borders.

We saw a lot of elephants but no 90-pounder, on which we had set our hearts. We were using one short-wheelbase Land Rover, which had four-wheel drive and only one spare tyre. A square wooden box of food we had contained beans and soup. Rene had a .375 and I had a .404 (neither of us had been able to afford a heavy double). After four days we had but one day to go before having to return to pick up more fuel. We checked the incoming road from the Somali border at Hagadera to see if there were

The Cogswell & Harrison battery, my first. L to R: .318, .404, 12-bore shotgun. Mauser actions. Room for a fourth gun plus ammo and equipment. £185 delivered (1951).

41

any tracks of vehicles, but none were there. Due to the rains, all traffic had ceased. Next day the rains lifted, and the sun shone with great intensity. We decided on one more big arc across country and a return the next day.

That evening we camped at a sizeable water hole some 30 yards across. It had two anthills on the edge of the water nearest our campsite. We did not have much of a campsite. We parked the car behind a bush and stretched the tarpaulin from its roof using the part not used to lie upon under the shaded section. We had a mosquito net and a *lungi,* or *shuka,* for sleeping gear. This is best described as a wraparound half sheet. The one native Somali with us slept on the front seat of the car.

About two o'clock I was awakened by the unmistakable stomach rumblings of an elephant and the splashing of water. It was a brilliant moonlit night. Rene soon woke up and together, after first donning our trousers and shoes and picking up our guns, we crept out of our hiding place. There before us were two huge elephants, their tusks now washed clean and gleaming brightly in the moonlight.

'We better clobber them', I said.

'Certainly', said Rene. We did our best impersonation of a couple of crocodiles and crawled up behind one of the convenient anthills.

Both elephants carried big ivory. Tana River ivory was long, so care had to be taken to confirm its thickness and that it was not simply long and thin. Even allowing for the poor visibility of semidarkness, there was no mistaking the fact that these two elephants were carrying 80- to 90-pound tusks and none of the tusks were broken. Moreover, as they stood at the edge of the water, the reflected light off the water made it a certainty that this was the quarry for which we had been searching.

As we watched, both bulls turned and ambled off. Giving them a few minutes, we set off after them. They were feeding, moving slowly from clump to clump of sanseveira and small bushes. After following them for a mile or so, they stood together sideways onto us, offering us the best chance of a good heart shot. This was what we had been waiting for, as a brain shot would have been just a little too uncertain in the poor light.

Rene did the countdown. 'Ready! Fire!' he said. Both bulls staggered and both rifles were reloaded in a second. 'Fire!' he said again. Both bulls took a second shot in the lungs as they wheeled away from us. Our guns roared out again as we attempted to anchor them with spine, hip, or pelvis shots.

We were now running after the elephants, and both animals slowed.

'Let's back off and reload full magazines', I said. Sprinting back 50 yards or so, we made sure that both our guns were full with one up the spout before we returned to the fray. As we approached, one elephant fell over, and the other raised a blood-curdling shriek and turned in our direction. Dropping to our knees, we gave him a total of four shots between us into his chest as he raised his head. This was more than he could stand, and, falling backward, he collapsed by his friend.

We sat for half an hour on an old log and made sure they were dead. As we did so we realised that we could not follow our tracks back to the car in the moonlight, as there was just not enough light.

We examined the ivory. Using a handkerchief, we measured the circumference of the tusks where they protruded from the lip to get some idea of their weight. If the corners of the handkerchief did not quite meet, it was somewhere near 85 pounds, and if they did not meet by some two and a half inches, then one was looking at a possible 100-pound tusk. Our measurements indicated that we had nearly 400 pounds of ivory. We waited some distance away for dawn.

As dawn broke, we tracked our way back to the water hole, finding a worried and lonely Somali sitting on the roof of the car. A large brandy was drunk for breakfast as a starter, followed by more lacing of the tea to wash down the last of our supplies. Three men, two axes, and four knives worked hard till the tusks were broken free, with help from the car and a rope. The little Land Rover was heavily loaded, since we did not have time to chip off the bone sheath of the tusks. We set off across country heading north-east to cut the road from the Somaliland frontier about 10 miles south of Hagadera.

We were nearly there when the first back tyre went flat. The spare tyre was flat, too, and we discovered that we had no hot patches. We filled the tyre half full with water, using the foot pump filled with water to fill up the inner tube with the valve removed. It took hours. Finally, replacing the valve, and with the wheel jacked up, we spun the wheel until the hissing of escaping air stopped. It was only then that we knew that the water was between the air in the tyre and the punctured inner tube. As soon as this was the case, we blew the tyre up with as much pressure as we could get in it. The car was let off the jack with a bump, and we took off as fast as we could. This had the effect of keeping the water circulating within the tube and preventing the air from escaping.

The second back tyre gave in, and after a similar procedure involving both back tyres, we made it back to camp at Garrisa at 3.00 in the morning. It had been a long day. We had 385 pounds of ivory between us. (We had a good Christmas!) Mr. Killick duly got stuck and was rescued and, I believe, subsequently became the United Kingdom's ambassador to the U.S.S.R. I hope he did not take the Russians' advice during his term of office.

Rene and I had several other adventures, one of which involved going out of sight of land off Mombasa on the Kenya coast, hooking a sailfish, and having it taken out of our hands by a shark whilst getting it into the boat. The boat was 15 feet long, and we had a 20-horsepower Mercury outboard for power. We got back to Mombasa on a gasp of petrol left in the tank, but that is a fishing story and not for this chapter on elephants.

Rene Babault was to me one of the great people of my life. The world was, quite simply, Rene's oyster. His father, a Frenchman, had built a beautiful home behind Isak Dinesen's 'Karen House' in the Karen suburb of Nairobi. In 1956, he sold it to Syd and Cynthia Downey and moved to Mombasa to a nice home overlooking Kilindini Harbour. Rene, and I with him on occasion, used the house as a base for whatever we were doing at the time. It was from here that Rene planned his safari to Arabia with Lord Hambledon. Whilst there, he sent me a card headed Hunters Africa (Arabia) Ltd. When he was 18 years old Rene had joined the Desert Locust Survey and was posted to Arabia. Both of us knew southern Arabia and the Persian Gulf well, and we spoke sufficient Arabic to make progress anywhere we wished.

For Rene there was always another place as yet unvisited. It is a tragedy that he and his wife, Jo Jo, were both killed in separate appalling accidents. When he was killed, he was flying down from Mombasa to Mafia Island off the Tanzania coast, where he had rented his camp to an oil-prospecting company. Rene was found some distance from the crashed aircraft and must have made some attempt to save himself. The aircraft flew into heavy weather and broke up; quite simply it should not have been flying through such incredibly stormy conditions.

During this period, there were some very large elephants shot on the periphery of Tsavo National Park, the largest shot at Darajani by Mohammed Akbar and having tusks of 172 and 164 pounds (see Chapter 5, 'The Man-Eater of Darajani'). David Allen, accompanying his party in close proximity to camp at Kibwezi, spotted a huge-tusked elephant for his client, Brian Trafford. The tusks weighed 142 and 140 pounds. No lesser person than Tony Dyer, the president of the E.A.P.H.A., also secured a fine matched pair of tusks of considerable

length, weighing 119 pounds and 114 pounds, for his client, Mr. Vogel, which were obtained in the Northern Frontier District of Kenya.

Charles Mapes, the owner of the Mapes Hotel in Reno, Nevada, achieved some notoriety when he shot Oginga Odinga, so named after the vice president of Kenya at the time, the large-tusked elephant normally resident in Amboselli National Park. Oginga Odinga, due to heavy rain falling outside the park, had forsaken his usual haunts in favour of fresh pastures. His tusks weighed 129 and 107 pounds and rapidly made their way by air freight to Mapes's home in Reno prior to

Top: Probably the best 22-day safari I ever undertook for elephant. Six of the tusks weighed more than 100 pounds each.

Bottom: One better! Mohammed Iqbal's seven tusks weighing more than 100 pounds each. 'Bali,' as he was known, was the best (1962).

the outcry of a 'park' elephant's being shot. The elephant was shot quite legally on licence, a line being a line just as it always had been. Buffer zones, which were zones where no shooting was allowed within 10 miles of a park boundary, were believed to be unworkable, and they were eventually dropped.

Many other professional hunters were significantly successful, but they are too numerous to all be named. One such person, Mark Howard-Williams, whose experiences will go down in history as almost unbelievable, had his client shoot an elephant, which dropped like a stone. Together they walked up to the elephant and inspected the tusks, which were a good 90 pounds a side. Before returning to the car, they cut off the tail. After a walk of two or three miles and a cool drink at the car, they made their way back to the elephant with the car by cutting a track.

The elephant had departed. Though they tracked it for all of 24 hours, they never caught up with it. The tail proved the story.

No discourse on elephant hunting in East Africa would be complete without mentioning several notable personalities and events. Foremost amongst these were the exploits of Mohammed Iqbal, known to us all as 'Bali'. Bali was an Asian born in Kenya of Pakistani stock. He was a huge man with a big heart and was the life and soul of any party. He was an inveterate and very successful elephant hunter. Apart from this fact, he was the most accomplished mimic and possessed a wicked sense of humour, which those who attended his occasional 'Indian curry parties' in the off season will remember with great satisfaction. As a genuine friend he was trusting to the point of naiveté. Food and drink were his passion in town, but in the bush he was intuitive in his movements and clever in his design to obtain the best trophy for his clients. He also possessed a remarkable gift for obtaining the best information that was locally available from guides and residents, which enabled him to score some big ivory. The fact that he was an Asian in European company never fazed him, nor did it mean anything to his friends—his education had taken care of that. Alas, the strain he had put upon his heart proved too much some time later, and he passed on, never to be forgotten.

About 1970, things in Kenya began to change, and the code of conduct became suspect. Independence had come. Quite a lot of things in the administration of the game department had altered radically. Money began to talk. One or two professional hunters hired themselves to clients at reduced rates on a six-month basis simply to look for big ivory, calling their clients by telephone when it was located. No fewer than 16

Above: Frank Miller, far right, views a pair of 109-pound tusks recovered by the Kenya Game Department from poachers (1966).

Left: A successful hunt for a 100-pounder (1964).

pairs of 100-pound tusks were obtained by one person in this way.

By this time both Ronnie and Marlies Stephens had retired from Ker & Downey. New management arrived, and whilst Eric Rundgren and I were on safari, arrangements were made to take back most of the professional hunters who had left the company in 1955. We gave it a year or two, but after having put the company first in my plans, I, with several others who were by now highly reputable professional hunters, very regretfully decided to go it alone. Tanganyika and Bechuanaland beckoned, and a higher level of anticipated excitement, endeavour, and exploration was upon me. For 14 more years it was so.

Frank Miller, my old friend from early Tanganyika days who had also joined Ker & Downey, and I left together and formed our own safari company in Kenya and Tanganyika, styling our company with our own names: John Kingsley-Heath and Frank Miller Safaris. We did well. Several more big-tusked elephants came our way, and we successfully established ourselves in Bechuanaland with Lionel Palmer, who had just registered his company, Safari South (Pty.) Ltd., and partnered him in our company. Lionel Palmer and Doug Wright both came up to Kenya with us, and for a few years we ran a highly successful operation, dovetailing the two seasons in each country together so that we almost had a full 12 months of work. We had such good hunting experiences and so much fun together that none of us will ever forget those halcyon days.

When Frank Miller and I set up our own business in East Africa, we had of necessity to hunt separately. Our volume of business was such that we had to handle two safaris simultaneously, no matter what their size. To keep our clients convinced that our firm was the best, and that should they wish to return, then, of course, we had Bechuanaland to offer them. Additional hunters were employed on an ad hoc basis. During this time, most of the clients who wished to hunt elephant did so with me. The following list documents my clients who shot elephants with tusks of more than 100 pounds.

1. Jim Gray—104 & 106 lbs.
2. John Morrill—134 & 132 lbs.
3. Richard Martin—116 & 119 lbs.
4. Stanislaus Palaski—109 & 114 lbs.
5. Arthur Coates—110 & 114 lbs.
6. Garfield MacNamara—116 & 112 lbs.

The Morrill Elephant

My tale has not mentioned the technicalities of elephant hunting so far, except to refer to the importance of the weather and the seasons. Every professional hunter of my era undoubtedly dreamt of hunting successfully an elephant with heavy ivory. Some dreamt of tusks weighing 190 pounds or even 200 pounds, but most of my dreams were more realistic at 150 pounds. Regretfully, I never made it to this weight, but this is how I came close to it.

John and Ginny Morrill came into correspondence with me by referral from a client who had previously hunted with me. John was a hard-working chief executive of a large American company with a schedule that tried to turn a 24-hour day into a 48-hour one. A month's break had, however, been set aside no matter what. An African safari was going to take place. Our correspondence was crisp and to the point and the deposit handed over at the time I requested it, well in advance. John wanted to hunt as much as possible—all the time! Reviewing the correspondence, I thought with a wry smile what other professional hunters must have thought on occasions: *This guy thinks the trophies grow on trees and that we shoot all day and travel all night to the next shooting gallery.*

John, thankfully, proved to be not quite like that. Being only recently married, I suggested that my wife, Sue, come along to keep Ginny company.

I decided to hunt the north of Kenya near the Meru Game Reserve first. At that time there was still a huge area of Kenya that stretched east of Mount Kenya, then south to the Tsavo National Park. This area was fed by numerous streams off the mountains and forests of Mount Kenya. In the Meru area, an unusually large number of mountain streams and springs flowing out of the lava rock passed into the Meru Game Reserve. Between Mount Kenya and the tribal lands of the Meru people there was still a large uninhabited area. Although the Meru National Park was well demarcated by a 30-foot-wide track made by a large D8 bulldozer, most of the species of animals took little notice. There were some large thickets of bush in the hunting area lousy with buffalo, and there were plenty of leopard and other animals, which provided meat for the pot. When elephant hunting takes place, silence is essential. The sound of shots, even in the distance, will bring memories to the minds of old bulls, and they will soon be on their way. The area was hunted only occasionally.

Having met John and Ginny at Nairobi Airport, I despatched the lorry with the camp to Meru that day as soon as I knew they were safely in the country. We met for dinner, and I explained the plan for the safari. We left

Nairobi the next day and arrived in camp in the late afternoon. Early the next day, utilising the park border cut, we headed south-east into the prevailing wind. Ginny came along with us in the car, leaving Sue in camp. A local tribesman with his mind in his stomach informed us that elephants were to the south of us. Simultaneously, I sent two trackers to the north-west back up our road of entry to check if any large elephants had passed behind us. The country generally was higher to the west of us than the east, so by climbing the smaller foothills to the west it was possible to glass the country for 180 degrees, from the north on your left to the south on your right, with your back facing west.

A bull elephant's front foot of the kind we were hunting in Kenya had to be 20 to 24 inches across to be worthy of consideration. This does not mean to say that there were not elephants shot with small feet and heavy ivory, but one generally used this as a yardstick, and we had a stick literally in our hand cut to 21 inches as a guide.

We stopped often, as there were a lot of elephants about. We spotted several cows moving up the banks of the shallow streams running into Meru Game Reserve, and there was nothing much better than the odd bull carrying 40 pounds a side of ivory. I made sure we took a close look at one or two to give John the experience of being in close proximity to such an enormous animal, so that when we did see one we wanted he would be less overawed by the sheer size of the elephant. He would also have a clearer understanding of the target area at which he would be required to shoot.

We left camp at seven o'clock in the morning, and it was now nearly nine o'clock. Seeing a good hill to the west of us that would take a short walk to climb, I headed the car through the light bush toward it, being careful to come up behind the hill from downwind. My two gunbearers, Edward and Musioka, were with me, but a third man was left to guard the car in case some of the natives decided to pay it a visit. I had promised Sue that we would return about midday to question the scouts, who had gone off to look at the tracks on our road of entry. Taking a flask of tea and a packet of biscuits, we set off for the summit of the little hill. It was a good observation point. In the far distance, we caught glimpses of the park boundary track where it crossed some small open plains. Here we saw plenty of plains game—zebra, impala, waterbuck, etc.

Below us was a large, very thick patch of bush with a little glade in the middle of it, in the centre of which was a big tree often used at midday for shade by elephants.

Watching approximately 90 bull elephants, one of which was John Morrill's big tusker (1968).

For half an hour or so, we saw very little until, through his binoculars, Edward saw an elephant moving on the edge of the thicket. It had ivory and was a bull. By this time, John had very nearly become bored with glassing, but now at least something was happening. Questions poured upon me: 'How long will it take to get down there? What if the wind changes? Is it big enough to bother about? Should we not move on somewhere else—elephants cannot exactly hide in this stuff, can they?'

'Wait', I said. 'Be patient. I think this is one of the leaders of the herd of bulls coming up from that low ground that we cannot see'.

By 9.45 we had some 25 bulls in view, and by 10.30 we had 50. John was looking at his watch but said nothing. I sat looking steadily through my binoculars, wondering what the hell was my best course of action. It was not going to please anyone if I did nothing. At that moment any decision was taken out of my hands. Out of the thick grey bush came an elephant on whose tusks the sun shone, flashing light from huge white ivory. We all saw him at the same time. For a second no one spoke. John said, 'That one in the middle is a good one, isn't it? It seems to have long white tusks!'

I replied, 'I think, John, that this is the biggest elephant I have ever seen, certainly with a beautiful long matched pair of tusks like that'.

Excited conversations took place in English and Swahili. The burning question was asked by John: 'So what are we going to do?'

'I shall have to give it some serious thought', I replied. 'It's not something upon which one can make a quick decision. I think a cup of tea would calm my nerves and help my British mind to come to the right

John Morrill and me with the big bull down with 130-pound tusks.

decision!' There was no hurry, as the elephant did not appear to be going anywhere and had obviously chosen the patch of bush in which to rest during the heat of the day. We were quite safe where we sat, as there was little if any chance of the elephants getting our wind.

More elephants came into view, and I estimated that there were probably 80 to 90 bulls now below us. Two other elephants drew my attention, and I delegated each of the gunbearers to watch one: either elephant might have made 100 pounds a tusk, but the patriarch by the big tree was the best. There was no way we could get anywhere near him. We were going to need an awful lot of luck to be in the right place at the right time when they moved off. This then was my task, to determine what the elephants were most likely to do and position ourselves accordingly. Summoning all my memories of the behaviour of elephants, I felt reasonably sure that our big elephant would not wish to feed in the wake of others, and that he could reasonably be expected to head out of the bush first or come to one side or the other so that he had the first choice of foliage. It was likely, too, that he would have on either side of him his 'minders'. Old bulls often have one or two other elephants with them, probably 10 to 15 years younger, who appear to act as additional eyes and ears for their revered elder statesman.

Descent from our hilltop to a level area of thick bush would give us great difficulty in keeping our position relative to the big bull. Ninety bull elephants all munching and moving about in thick bush cause the utmost confusion in one's mind as to where they are and who is in close proximity. Furthermore, now time was an important factor. We were two

The great elephant safari. John Morrill and me.

hours from camp and had said we would be back by midday. No way were we going to meet that deadline, and certainly nothing would make us return with the prospect of this huge elephant to be hunted before us.

I discussed my views with John and then my gunbearers. We would leave as soon as the elephants started to feed, descending to the downwind side of the patch of thick bush, and then it would be a question of luck as to whether we could winkle out the big one.

Time passed, and we continued to study the elephants. Occasionally one or two trumpeted or together broke down and stripped a tree of its bark. By one o'clock most were dozing in the limited shade that was available to such a huge animal. Our big tusker continued to monopolise

53

the tree. After several long hours, I formed the opinion that he did not really look like a very old bull, but I would have to find that fact out for myself shortly. It was now very hot and there was no wind. I began to realise that it was by no means certain that when the wind did return it would blow in the same direction. What if it changed and blew towards the elephants? If it did, we might be faced with a fast run of a mile to get to the opposite side of the patch of bush.

At 3.15 the crucial period had arrived. There were stirrings amongst the herd. One or two began to stretch their legs and feed, and by 3.45 they were nearly all moving. It was essential that before we left the hill, we got some idea of the direction in which the big bull set off. He was still under the tree and was the last to move.

It was 4.15 now, it would be dark at 6.30, and we still had to descend from the hill and get close to the elephants. At 4.25 the bull turned and headed for the side of the patch of bush nearest to us. I took one last long look and mentally said a small prayer.

'Off we go', I said. We were ready—inaction had been boring and made us tense. I made sure as we passed the car that the assistant skinner knew what he was in for if 89 bulls passed in close proximity after they had heard our shots. As Ginny was staying with the car, I also made sure that he was not, under any circumstances, to leave the car.

Taking some water bottles with us, for it was hot and thirsty work and our mouths were dry from excitement, we set out. The wind had come back and continued to blow from its original quarter, but not sufficiently to hide the noise of our footsteps, as there were several of us.

'Always lightly tread', I said to everyone and reminded myself to do the same. A 20-minute walk and we could hear the elephants feeding. I divided the gunbearers to my left and right and instructed them to report what they saw. I calculated that we were in about the right spot where the big bull should break cover at the edge of the thicket.

I carried an old sock full of wood ash. Shaking it, I was able to tell quickly and with accuracy which way the wind was blowing and also at what speed. Simultaneously, signals from both gunbearers indicated that both were in sight of bull elephants. John grabbed my arm.

'What's that gurgling and rumbling noise?' he whispered.

'That's the elephant's stomach and digestive system', I replied 'But they also make a slightly similar noise when they are alerted and smell danger'.

We were now within 20 yards of some 12 bull elephants. None so far as we could see were the big tusker. *Time to retreat—pray heaven they don't get our wind from our tracks*, I thought. We reassembled a short ways away. Four bulls came closer and passed across us to our right; we were facing due south and the sun was rapidly fading to our right in the west. I realised that the light was going to go a bit earlier, as the sun would go behind the hills and so give us less light just when we might need it. More bulls came past. We were now in danger of those that had passed getting behind us and thus getting our wind. Another retreat, this time a further 50 yards.

Looking through my binoculars, my attention was drawn to one elephant whose tusks I could not see but who appeared to be rooting something out of the ground. He was immediately in front of me.

Raising my binoculars, I made out the shape of a big bull. At the same time I saw something move in the bush in front of him. For a moment I thought it was the tail of the elephant in front of him. Searching closely with the binoculars amongst the grey sticks of the close-packed branches I saw that it was the end of a tusk. Could this be the big bull? The end of his tusk was a long way in front of him. My gunbearer nudged me.

'Bwana, there are more elephants going off to our left—they may get behind us', he said.

'OK', I said, still looking at the elephant in front of me. At that instant I saw his whole tusk and the other behind it. It had to be our bull—they were enormous.

'Ready', I whispered to John. 'Our bull is here in front of us'.

'Where?' John asked.

'Come with me and I will show you', I replied. 'It will be an ear or heart shot sideways on'.

Together, with Edward and Musioka behind us keeping a nervous lookout to our rear, we crept forward. The bush was thick—it would be difficult to avoid the chance of a ricochet. John had to get a clean shot, and so did I if the bull did not go down on the spot. At that moment the bull moved and John and the gunbearers saw the tusks clearly. We were 25 yards from the big bull. He took a few steps forward and stopped again, partly hidden—no chance of a shot.

'Damn it', I said. 'We cannot hold this position for long; we will be surrounded'. The bull moved nearer across our front, but once more he was covered.

'OK, back everyone', I ordered. 'Slowly, don't make a noise'. We retreated some 15 yards, leaving the elephant some 40 yards in front of us. The bull moved forward, and this time his head and tusks came out and there was a gap in the bush behind his shoulder.

'Come on John', I whispered, 'in and bang this time'. Moving carefully, we reduced the distance to 25 yards. John placed a bullet squarely in the ear hole and I one in the heart for good measure an instant later. Slowly the great bull toppled over onto the opposite side to that from which he had been shot, and all hell was let loose.

'Stand still', I commanded, 'don't shoot until I do, John'.

Both gunbearers stood close to us. I suddenly realised that it was getting dark. Elephants whizzed by 20 or 30 yards away, fortunately desperate to get out of our way. There must have been more than 20 elephants that had nearly got our wind whilst we were trying to get into position.

It was a good five minutes before we could move to examine the bull's ivory. It was a perfectly matched pair of tusks, which looked as though they would go a good 120 pounds a side. *Who sees tusks that big every day of the week? Not I*, I thought. He was a prime bull in good physical condition and did not look particularly old.

One of the gunbearers had the camera. After a quick picture in the rapidly fading light, I sent Musioka, who could drive, to get the car. Having first cut off the tail of the elephant and leaving a white handkerchief to mark the spot, I gestured to John and Edward to follow me. I had heard the elephants tear off, but after a few minutes the noise had ceased abruptly, and I felt certain that they were not far away. I wanted to be sure that we had shot the biggest. After telling John of my interest in following up the herd, we set out at a brisk walk. It wasn't long before we came to the end of the patch of bush. Rounding the end of it, we saw an unforgettable sight: roughly 90 bulls en masse in a small short-grass open glade, all with raised heads and trunks testing the wind. With the elephants so positioned it took four pairs of eyes but only a second to determine whether there was a bigger pair of tusks than our bull. There was not. The two other bulls I had seen were there. One was certainly carrying 100 pounds of ivory on each side; one other might have made that weight, too. A second or two later they must have heard the car coming towards the fallen bull, for they all wheeled and tore off in a huge cloud of dust, trumpeting and screaming their disgust.

Weary, we returned to the elephant, but our day was not done yet. We were not about to leave such an immense pair of tusks in the bush overnight for some poacher to take home. We needed three axes, but we only had one, and by the time we had finished chopping we had blisters on our hands. The task of cutting out the tusks, however, was eased by the fact that their length gave us greater purchase when extracting them from the skull. Working like Trojans, we took all that was required from the carcase, and by 11.00 that night we finally turned the car in the direction of the boundary track and set off for camp.

'Are you thinking the same thoughts as I am?' I asked John as we negotiated the ruts and rocks of the bush road.

'I have a lot of thoughts in my mind at this time', he said. 'I am not at all sure to which one you are referring'.

'A large drink', I said. 'I also think Sue may be a little worried as to what's happened to us. We are about 12 hours overdue'.

'I must admit I had not given the latter a thought', replied John. 'Elephant hunting is very exciting. It lasts for hours. God, yes, I could do with a martini!' An hour later when we arrived, a worried Sue discovered where we had been. A group of Meru tribespeople camping out collecting palm nuts had decided to have a party not far from camp. Their drum beating was difficult to interpret to the uninitiated, and thoughts of missionaries and cannibal pots had stirred Sue's imagination! Next day, when the tusks had been cleaned and washed, we learned that we had a pair of 130-pound elephant tusks. We left camp early and took along a local guide who had been helpful when we had first arrived, so that we could fulfill our promise that he and his family should have first cut at the carcase.

Common Waterbuck

The 'bush telegraph' worked overtime. By the time we arrived—Sue with us this time—there was a large crowd of Wameru waiting patiently to start work.

Four hours later there was nothing left, and all went to good use. We moved on a few days later and had a great safari, and the Morrills and Kingsley-Heaths have all been good friends ever since. Such is the friendship that African safaris breed.

The Hunt for Bakuli

The MacNamaras were coming on safari. I had been their guest in Flagstaff, Arizona, the previous winter when I had sat down and planned the hunt. It was to be a father and son safari. Jimmy MacNamara had been fortunate enough to make a tidy sum of money

The access to water dug by an elephant's trunk in the bed of the Thowa 'sand' River.

bidding on oil exploration leases on the North Slope of Alaska. He was proposing to spend some of that money on an African safari, and I felt no reticence in helping him. I had been present one day in his office when the results of the bidding had come through. Jimmy had been smart enough to hire a former government geophysicist well before the leases were offered, thus securing a person's services who had an excellent idea as to what the likely value of the areas that came up for lease might be. These ideas resulted in a handsome profit, there being enough money as a result to pay for a substantial number of safaris. Jimmy's son, Garfield, was the fly in the ointment. At age 18, he looked as though he was 14. He couldn't have cared less about his dress and food and was brash to a degree. I felt sure that I would have difficulty stomaching his demeanour on safari. *He'll end up eating 'posho'*—the native maize meal—*with the staff*, I thought.

Jimmy was happy to follow my advice, since all he wanted was a real break from business and home. Mrs. MacNamara was a kind and hospitable person, but outdoor pursuits were the premise of her men and not to her liking. She told me the boys could 'go do their thing' and that she had plenty to do at the country club.

'Just make sure they come back and don't get sick', she instructed me.

Naturally, I promised that they would have a great time. Looking at their beautiful stone fireplace in the central hall of their large, commodious home, I remarked to Jimmy that a pair of 100-pound elephant tusks would look good on either side of it.

'Great idea', he said, 'let's do that; let's have that as the safari target'.

Now that the seeds of an elephant hunt to my liking had been sown, the plans were easily made.

On my return to Kenya, I put out the word to my Wakamba contacts in the Mutha area of the Upper Thowa River in eastern Kenya that I wanted information on any big tusker. Of course, half the professional hunting fraternity were doing the same thing, but as a young man I naively believed that the local Africans of that part of the country would be more loyal to my organisation than others. The Upper Thowa River area came under the control of Barry Chapple, the game warden in charge at Kiboko, who was a close friend. Partly on my advice he had learnt to fly, and he had been at school close to me in England, so we had many mutual friends. Barry confirmed that an elephant of huge body size and heavy but curved ivory had been seen by a game scout on the Upper Thowa River.

Three weeks before Jimmy and his son were due to arrive, I went down to the Thowa River to have a look at the country and assess the chances of a successful hunt. After I spent a few hours chatting to local 'experts', it became clear that there was indeed a big elephant in the area who was called Bakuli, which in Swahili means a saucer or shallow dish. This was because his right front foot had a swelling in the centre, so that when he left a footprint in the sandy bed of a river, he was easily recognised by the indentation in the centre of his print. We duly set out to see if we could find his tracks and thereby have some idea as to the route he used to come in to water.

The Thowa River was one of sand, with no water being visible above the surface. Every two to three days, elephants would travel to the river at night from 20 to 30 miles away to drink. Arriving at the river at about midnight, they would stand in one spot for hours, having whisked out a small hole in the sand with their trunks until the seeping water formed a small pool. Carefully and meticulously, they would suck up into their trunks this small quantity of water, until after two to three hours their stomachs were full. An average elephant could carry nearly 30 gallons of water in its stomach. The moisture content of the foliage that the elephant consumed determined the frequency of its desire to drink. In the conditions in which our hunt was to take place, at the height of the dry season, our friend Bakuli would undoubtedly drink every other day.

Before completing my reconnaissance, I chose two Wakamba tribesmen who were local residents to be my *kiongozi,* or guides. All I asked them to do was patrol the sand river for a distance of some 15 miles downstream for the next three weeks, marking on a rough map of the area the spot where Bakuli was seen to drink most frequently, which they did.

On that spot, I chose a campsite for the safari and partly cleared it so that it was ready when the truck arrived with our camp. I had booked the hunting blocks in which the Thowa River lay—the river was the northern boundary of block 33—and in order to hunt both banks of the river, it was necessary to book the north bank as well, block 33A. On production of evidence of the deposit of the MacNamaras, this was done at the headquarters of the Kenya Game Department in Nairobi. All was set for the hunt for Bakuli.

The MacNamaras duly arrived, and the truck was sent off the same day. As I expected, young Garfield looked like a tramp. During the long drive out from Nairobi, Garfield announced that he was 'bored as hell!' On arrival in the camp he exclaimed, 'Gee! Is this the camp? It looks like a spike camp'. Since all the equipment was brand-new, I was not amused.

Like my father before me, I liked to get things done. Some of my contemporaries who liked to get things done on the basis of 'tomorrow perhaps', known colloquially as *bado kidogo*, had given me the unwarranted nickname of 'Prickly Heath'. (It only lasted a while until, a few years later, it was changed to 'Uncle'.) On this day, and following Garfield's remark, I was decidedly prickly! Jimmy planned to spend the first week of the safari in camp, taking a long rest whilst we hunted elephant. In the late afternoon, he would go out up the track from camp to shoot some game birds, thereby keeping us fed with a good meal when we returned to camp.

Camp meat was the first priority. Taking the hunting car, we set out on the incoming road to collect some guinea fowl, francolins, and dik-dik. Garfield was a good shotgun shot; he could run and was athletic, which I was glad to see.

Next day, collecting our guides, we set out at dawn to search for Bakuli's tracks. We soon found them and, buoyed up with the hope that it might be a short and successful hunt, we set off in hot pursuit.

Bakuli and a pal had put their best foot forward. They travelled a straight 10 miles before we even noted that a leaf had been disturbed, never mind a half-eaten branch. The dung was cold, cold; we were hours behind them. At two o'clock, with the sun burning down upon us, I decided to turn back for home. We would have to rethink the whole plan and see if there was an alternative.

Garfield continued to infuriate me. He had announced—wearing white gym shoes, white trousers, and no hat—that he was ready to shoot the elephant. Politely I tried to explain to him the problems of blisters and thorns that would assail his feet and that the colour of his clothes should blend in with the foliage. At least they should be khaki coloured. How did I know whether elephants could recognise colour, he demanded. Anyway, he could walk all day in gym shoes, he informed me. *Stupid little bastard,* I thought. *We will have to carry him home one day, without doubt.*

Wearily, we returned to camp with a 25-mile walk under our belts. We started earlier the next day, but Bakuli had not come in for water. We chose another set of reasonable-looking tracks and set off through the grey bush and featureless country once more. I was not particularly hopeful, but at least it kept us busy and we might just be lucky.

At 11.30, we came up to four bull elephants who were casting around for a shady tree under which to spend the heat of the day. Always mindful of the unexpected and having no wish to shoot an elephant with small tusks in self-defence, I sent Edward, my chief tracker, off to have a quick look. After 20 minutes he returned with the information that one might go to 50 pounds a side.

These elephants are just college boys, I thought to myself. The wind was good, blowing strongly from the elephants to us. Now was the time to give Garfield a quick lesson on where to put the bullet if we came into contact with Bakuli. Taking care that his white shirt was kept out of the elephants' view by staying outside their limited eyesight of some 25 yards, we squatted under a convenient bush with a pair of binoculars and commenced lesson number one.

For once Garfield was receptive to my conversation, probably because he realised that his life might depend on the information that was being imparted to him. I explained the heart shot and the ear shot in some detail, and he was able to study with the binoculars the precise spots on the elephants where the bullet should be placed. After some 10 minutes we pulled out and headed back to the river. Garfield decided that we were walking far too slowly and set off at a fast pace by himself. I exchanged a knowing glance with one of the guides, who set off after him. It would be just our luck for Garfield—without a gun—to run into a herd of cow elephants or even Bakuli himself on his way back to the river, particularly as Garfield had no desire to carry his own gun.

When we arrived back at the river, the car came to meet us, driven by my driver, whom I had left in camp. Garfield had driven himself home and sent the driver back to collect us.

Whilst I was sitting in camp, having a welcome cup of tea and recounting the day's events to Jimmy, I was surprised to hear Garfield's description of his encounter with the elephants. He was thrilled to bits and seemed determined to pursue Bakuli.

Once again we set out early, and by seven o'clock we were on his tracks. Bakuli had drunk that night, but this time we were sure it had been in the early evening. I had three choices. Firstly, I could give up, knowing that by this time he had gone too far for us to catch up on foot. Secondly, I could send Edward and a guide to track them until they were found, and then to return for us. However, they would almost certainly run out of daylight, so this plan had little merit. Thirdly, I could call off the day's hunt and take two porters to sleep on the tracks the next time.

The third alternative appealed to me. We were all able to walk a lot farther than we had the first day. We felt fitter now that all the memories of the flesh pots of Nairobi were both mentally and physically a thing of the past. There was one additional problem, that of time, which would run out if we exceeded the allowed seven days for an elephant hunt. Although there were easier areas in which we would hunt for other trophies later in the safari, the chances of getting a big tusker in these areas were remote. A very disgruntled Garfield returned to camp. As was his custom, Bakuli did not drink that night. Four days had passed.

The following day we were well prepared. Seven of us set out, suitably equipped with five gallons of water distributed amongst us, and sandwiches, a bottle of soup, matches, and a light blanket and mosquito net each. The staff had a cooking pot, a little bag of posho, salt, tea, tinned milk, sugar, and some dried meat. We found Bakuli's tracks and what joy—he was late drinking! Full of hope, we set off over the red dirt and in the dry 90-degree heat under a blue sky, with cicadas singing and the hornbills making their repetitive, mournful cry.

Bakuli and his pal had chosen a well-worn elephant path, and for two hours we marched along at a good pace. Edward was the chief tracker, for he was in his element, being, quite simply, a genius in this sphere of hunting. Even so, I was at pains to remind him every so often to be sure to keep an eye open for any deviations from the main track that Bakuli might have made. I was already impressed with our adversary's performance, and, as usual, I underestimated Edward's dedication to the task at hand. He had, by now, as firm an imprint of Bakuli's peculiar track in his mind as was in evidence in the tracks on the ground. Realising this, I looked carefully once again at Bakuli's track. There was just the faintest suggestion of a twist in the fine sand as his right foot left the ground. This was not always evident, as the back foot sometimes covered the front foot's tracks. Bakuli's pal was leading, which was fortunate.

By 12.30 we had covered some 20 miles; now something should happen. Would they start feeding? Would they start looking for shade? We estimated that we were some two hours behind them. Our walk had, so far, merely kept pace with the elephants. Within a few minutes of these thoughts occurring to me, the elephants began to feed—a few odd branches at first, and then, by 1.30, we came upon a place where they had stood, breaking up bushes and dropping dung for some time.

Our relief at catching up with them was short-lived. Back they went onto the elephant path, and off they went again, with us in pursuit. After a mile or so, we paused and had a general discussion. Had the elephants got the wind from some other itinerant party? It was at that moment that we heard the cattle bells. Quickly we found the Galla herdsmen. Had they seen any elephants? No, but they had heard them trumpet in the distance. There were five Gallas in all, and they were proposing to camp halfway to the river, taking their cattle to the river the next day. One of them insisted that he knew the country and could help us, and we took him with us. It was uncharacteristic to find these people so far west of their normal grazing areas, but the season was so dry that they had come farther west for both grazing and water.

On we went at a fast pace. It was hot—incredibly hot—and I was anxious for our water supplies. At three o'clock I called a halt, and I noticed that Garfield was in surprising shape—the walk did not seem to have fazed him at all. However, he had added to his unacceptably conspicuous appearance by tying the four corners of his white handkerchief into a knot and placing it on his head.

Seeing a tall and isolated acacia tree, I dispatched one of the guides to climb it to spy out the flat country ahead. I made a point of telling him to look carefully at any shade tree. Five minutes later the white handkerchief I had given him waved from the top of the tree: it was the signal that the elephants had been sighted. Our tiredness and disappointment evaporated. The guide was sure he could see two elephants a mile ahead, so I held a conference with Edward.

We had hunted crafty elephants on a number of occasions, several without success. At three in the afternoon we knew the wind was fickle. Approaching the elephants would be tricky, time was passing, and they would be leaving the shade as the sun died in its intensity. We had to get there before that happened.

Taking Edward, Garfield, and one guide and leaving the rest of the party under the prominent acacia tree from which one of our guides had spotted the elephants, we set off. Within 200 yards the elephants had turned upwind. Edward and I exchanged glances. We both recognised at once what the old elephant was planning to do for his own safety: the duo was going to execute the 'question mark' tactic. Imagine a question mark lying on its side with the bulge downwards and the elephants ending up in the centre, and the reader will quickly understand that if any hunter was following their tracks he would quickly give the elephants his scent as he passed upwind of them. At that moment the elephants would be gone and the hunt over.

We set off in a direct line to come up behind them from a downwind position. The brush was thick, thorny, and difficult to traverse; it took longer than expected and the heat continued to be intense, but soon we could see the backs of the elephants partly hidden by the grey bush in which they were seeking shade from the sun. They were headed directly away from us. It was immediately obvious that one elephant was far bigger in body size than the other. He had to be Bakuli—or was he? He must be Bakuli. I nodded to Edward, who set off to check. Within a very short time he was back; that broad, filed-tooth smile of the Makonde—whose tribesmen had heavy facial tattoos, muscular, lithe bodies, and who were expert hunters and carvers with an innate sense of art—was all that I needed to get my adrenaline flowing: it was big ivory. Quickly I enquired if both tusks were okay.

'Yes', he replied, 'but very curved, but big—*mkono tano na zaidi ya mia*' ('five arms' lengths and over a hundred'), he said. Arm's length was measured with a clenched fist and thence up to the elbow and not to the armpit.

Tearing the white handkerchief from Garfield's head and telling him to take off his shirt, as he was a reasonably tanned lad, we set off. We were using two double-barrelled rifles: my own .470 Westley Richards with full metal jacket (F.M.J.) Kynoch bullets, and Garfield a .450/.400 Manton, also with F.M.J. Kynoch bullets. I realised at once that we were going to have a difficult shot, as we would not be able to get square to the elephant. The wind, although in our faces, varied to the left and right, and coming up square with the elephants made this too much of a risk. The shot would have to be taken from behind the shoulder, angling forward into the heart. It was impossible to get between the elephants, as they were standing too close to each other. Slowly we crept forward. The wind was no friend, and several times I feared we had given our scent to Bakuli, but fate was on our side. I could see the tusks quite clearly now coming out in a great and acute arc from his head.

The body of the elephant was immense—he was one of the largest I had ever seen, fully two and a half feet higher at the shoulder than his pal, whose tusks I now saw for the first time and who appeared to be carrying 75 pounds a side. Inch by inch we crept closer until, at 35 yards, I judged we had best take the shot without taking any more risks with the wind and possibly losing the elephant. I touched Garfield on the shoulder, and we both slowly raised ourselves to full height.

'OK, now', I said. The .450/.400 roared out, the bullet striking Bakuli behind the shoulder but fractionally too high. I let go both barrels of the

.470 Westley Richards, being certain that Bakuli was not going to die as a result of Garfield's shot. My first shot hit dead in the right place, the second, as the elephant staggered, a little far back for choice.

'Eject and reload', I said, as I did so myself. Bakuli and his pal took off into the wind. I expected this of a heart-shot elephant, but at 60 yards his pal turned and faced us. 'Lower yourself to the ground slowly', I whispered to Garfield, who by now was trembling like a leaf in his excitement. As we disappeared behind the low bush, the elephant raised his head and trunk and gave a fearful scream, trumpeting and swinging his head from side to side. I made ready to brain him if he came, but at that moment, hearing Bakuli disappearing in the distance, he wheeled and followed him as fast as his legs could carry him.

Edward came up with the guide, and we examined the spot where Bakuli had been standing. Walking slowly back to the position from which we had fired, we checked the foliage for any damage caused by a deflected bullet—we found none. We could clearly see from the tracks where Bakuli had been standing that the bullets had shifted him forward and sideways, almost to his knees. I sent the guide to bring up the rest of the party. If Bakuli was by now dead, it was too late to head for camp— we were out for the night and a long day tomorrow.

When we had all gathered, I sent the Galla back to his cattle with instructions to come to the acacia tree with helpers by 11.00 the next morning or, if he didn't do that, to go to camp with a note to the effect that we had shot an elephant and were following it. He decided to meet us at the acacia tree the next day with two of his men, returning my note and making a welcome addition to the labour force.

We set off on the tracks of the wounded Bakuli, Edward in front followed by myself, then Garfield, and some distance behind, the rest of the party. Within 30 yards we came across bright frothy blood—the unmistakable sign of a lung shot. *It could well be a long walk*, I thought. On we went for nearly half an hour. Both elephants had torn up the bush in their headlong flight, and then quite suddenly they began to walk. Edward turned to me and said, 'Bakuli is wobbly'.

'He should be', I replied, 'he has three bullets'. At that moment, we heard a tremendous noise of breaking trees and bush and thrashing foliage.

Moving to my right with Garfield and making sure that I had a good field of fire, I waited. The wind was fresh in our faces and it was 4.30—getting late. The noise continued, punctuated by groans—it was Bakuli in extremis. Telling Edward to take Garfield back to the others, I crept forward, seeing no point in putting Garfield, or anyone else, in a position of risk. Then I saw a sight that will be with me for the rest of my life. The two elephants were side by side—Bakuli could go no farther and was smashing every bush within reach to the ground in his frustration and pain, and his pal was propping him up. My initial reaction was one of total sadness and guilt, but this was quickly overcome by the necessity to put Bakuli out of his misery. I had to do this with one shot, as I had to have one left to take care of his pal, who was well able to seek his revenge on me.

I moved into position at 35 yards, and, resting one arm on a convenient branch, I dropped Bakuli with a brain shot in the ear.

The immense size of the elephant was staggering. He fell into his pal, nearly bringing him down with him. Secure in the knowledge that Bakuli was down forever, I rapidly beat a retreat. From half a mile away we kept watch until the light faded, seeing Bakuli's pal move off into the distance just before sundown.

'When are we going to see what I shot?' Garfield asked.

'Tomorrow', I said, happy that I could make him wait.

We walked a half mile downwind to a suitable shade tree. I decided to camp well away from the carcase and out of harm's way from hyenas and lions. We were all tired and needed a good night's sleep. We had three and a half gallons of water left, and we needed at least one and a half for the next day. We made just enough hot, sweet tea for all of us, and the rest of the water for that day went into the staff's posho. Our sandwiches were a bit soft, and I would have given an arm for a beer, but the happiness resulting from a successful and exciting hunt soon overcame my thoughts of alcohol. I explained to Garfield how to set the blanket and little mosquito net, instructing him to use his knife to cut the little pegs and tie down his net. I was reminded of Bakuli as I made a little cup-shaped hole for my hipbone to rest in as I lay on my side. It was comfortable. After trying it, Garfield took up the blanket and did the same.

That night I lay awake some time after the rest of the party had fallen asleep. Looking at the stars and hearing those familiar noises of tree frogs and crickets, I wondered just how long it would all last. Would it really be possible to continue to live to the fullest one's life in these circumstances? It was almost too good to be true.

Ten years later, there was not an elephant track to be seen in the country in which I eventually fell into a deep and happy sleep. I had, that day, seen the best of it.

The next day, two axes and five knives made short work of removing the tusks, the Galla and Wakamba herdsmen having arrived at 10.30 (the Wakamba wanted the meat). We had forgotten to bring a camera.

We examined the carcase carefully. The acute angle that we had been forced to adopt in shooting Bakuli had misled us. A .450/.400 and .470 bullet had passed through the lungs but missed the heart, and we had, on reflection, been fortunate that sufficient damage had been done to bring Bakuli to a stop. The tusks were an ugly pair—thick ivory, but very curved. We knew they were a good 100 pounds each and later, when weighed, they proved to be 116 pounds and 112 pounds. I examined the *bakuli* in Bakuli's foot. It was a rock-hard cyst that encapsulated a stone about the size of a chestnut. At some time he must have cut his foot, and a stone must have entered the wound and lodged within the pad of the foot; as skin slowly grew together, it covered the stone. Garfield was delighted with his tusks and 'cock a hoop' as to how 'easy' it had all been. *Do words of wisdom really come out of the mouths of babes?* I wondered, as it became my turn to take station and helped carry the tusks back to the river. We walked 35 miles that day with the tusks, and even

The tusks of Bakuli. L to R: The Galla, Edward, two guides, two staff. I am in the chair.

67

Garfield was quite done in by the time we all threw ourselves down on the wet sand of the Thowa River at 6.30 that night. Hunting an elephant like Bakuli was an unforgettable experience but one tinged with regret that it had not been a clean kill.

For obvious reasons, the names and addresses of these clients are fictitious.

TANGANYIKA (TANZANIA)

Tanzania is a third larger in land mass than Kenya and, pro rata, has a smaller population. Large areas were infested with tsetse fly and well-populated with game animals. Different species of game occurred in profusion. Moreover, it encompassed the staggering populations of game animals of the Serengeti Plains and Ngorongoro Crater. The elephant population was considerable and much in excess of that of Kenya. The vast Selous Game Reserve in the south-east, totally uninhabited by humans, was the largest protected game animal area on the continent of Africa and contained huge herds of elephant and many other species of game. Roads were poor and access to hunting areas difficult. Some Nairobi safari operators had penetrated the easier hunting areas on the Ugalla River for sable antelope in the Western Province.

Local safari companies, such as Russell Douglas's Tanganyika Tours & Safaris, were prominent in the northern part of the country, and there were very few individual operators. Only some of the heavily game-populated areas were subject to controls. To cut down the distances and consequent loss of time and increased cost, I opened Ker & Downey Safaris (Tanganyika) Ltd. on behalf of the parent company. We located in Arusha, 178 miles south of Nairobi, under the towering 10 000-foot Mount Meru.

I based myself in Arusha for several years. Because Arusha was at 5000 feet and had such an equable climate, it was a joy to live there. The volcanic soil, well supplied by mountain streams, made fresh vegetables and fruit available in large quantities. Resupplying safari camps when clients flew in by charter aircraft was therefore easily achieved. For a time the company flourished, and was even

Previous page: Tanganyika as I remember it. A photograph taken from the road running alongside the Ruaha River—the green hills of Africa where elephants roamed at will (1958).

East African Sable Antelope

69

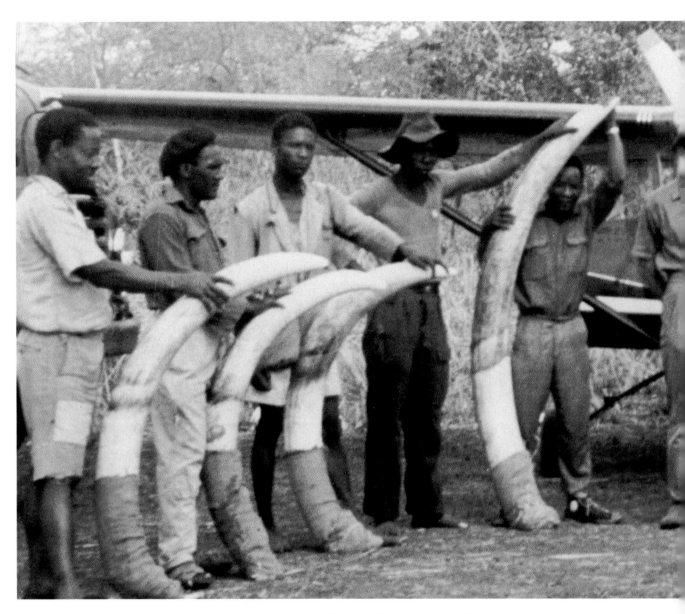

The 'Five on a Licence' safari. My client, Bill Holmes, shot the big one. The aircraft was the charter plane piloted by John Tuckwell, who came to take Bill back to Nairobi and who also took the picture on Nguala airstrip (1962).

hired to arrange selected action footage for the films *Hatari* and *Sammy Going South*.

My safaris in southern Tanganyika went well, and I enjoyed a very successful few years. During this period, the game department became concerned that too many hunters were picking out the big tuskers and so introduced an elephant licence to encourage the shooting of smaller-tusked bulls. The licence permitted you to shoot five bull elephants, but the combined weight of the tusks should not exceed 300 pounds. If it, through no fault of the hunter, did so, then a cession of so much a

pound as declared at the time would be assessed. Initially the 'cess' was lowly calculated and declared. On first examination this system appeared to be straightforward. However, one memorable evening—over a few beers—it was decided that there was a loophole in this system. Discreet enquiries were made, and it was discovered that this was so. The loophole appeared to be that as the licence was written there was nothing to stop a hunter from shooting ivory totalling, say, 298 pounds and then shooting a 100-pounder and paying the penalty on it.

Frank Miller and I decided to test this out, and we were not the only

Top: Both elephants had the same size ivory, 120 pounds each side, shot on the same day 50 miles apart. Frank's was on the Piti River, mine near Nguala Lukwati Controlled Area.

Bottom: My long-time friend and partner Frank Miller, now passed on. He wrote on the back of this picture, 'To John, in memory of all our happy days together'. He was a great person (1964).

Left: Bill Holmes and me at the Nguala airstrip in Tanzania, waiting to fly clients into camp without the safari staff, trucks, and equipment returning to base.

Above: These are the tusks of the elephant shot legally by a Tanzanian policeman who lost possession of them when his trophies were confiscated for shooting a leopard without a licence. The government of Tanzania then became the owners of the tusks (1971). Courtesy of Tanzania government.

wise guys to do so. Within the next few months all the well-known private hunters, such as the Van Rooyen and De Beer families, had departed for the bush en masse. When the day came to register the ivory, the point was proved amongst much rejoicing. Needless to say, the new licence deal was duly revoked the following year. In fact, no damage had been done, as the national herd was vast.

Frank Miller and I departed for the Lukwati area in the Chunya District of Southern Highlands Province. Frank camped on the Piti River and I at Nguala. We had one of the finest hunting experiences of our lives, and it was from this point that we had serious thoughts of making our own way in the safari business, which within a year or so came to fruition. Sometime afterwards, Frank sent me a picture of an elephant he shot on the Piti River with the note: 'To John, in memory of all our happy days together'. It is a note I treasure to this day, for it was very true and special.

Whilst hunting Southern and Western Provinces of Tanganyika, I always had in the back of my mind the pictures that Basil Reel had taken of those huge tuskers between approximately 1950 and 1954 in Western, Central, and Southern Highlands Provinces, but I never had the good fortune or, more importantly, the time to find them. Nevertheless, slowly but surely they all came to be hunted and shot.

Edward Sundae lightheartedly pretending that this elephant was shot with a bow and arrow. This one was definitely one of Basil Reel's. The tusks weighed 180 pounds and 167 1/2 pounds (1960).

The list of Reel's elephants that were probably—and I say *probably*—shot, is given as follows:

1. Edward Sundae—west of Uyowa, Tabora District—180 & 168 lbs.
2. Saleh Nassoro—west of Uyowa, Tabora District—142 & 147 lbs.
3. Oliver Milton—Rujewa, Myeya District—162 & 158 lbs.
4. J.K.-H.—west of Idodi, Iringa District—136 & 134 lbs.
5. Frank Miller—Piti River, Chunya District—120 & 116 lbs.
6. J.K.-H.—Nguala, Chunya District—119 & 117 lbs.

7. W.T. Yoshimoto—west of Kisigo, Manyoni District—127 & 123 lbs.
8. Mrs. C. Antonidis—Ugalla, Tabora District—153 & 149 lbs.
9. Tanzania govt. policeman—north of Madibira, Mbeya District—194 & 196 lbs.
10. A.N. Other—Moyowosi, Tabora District—141 & 140 lbs.

It is a matter of considerable uncertainty as to the exact ownership of much of this ivory.

The huge Rungwa Game Reserve was a refuge to most of the large tuskers. Not till they emerged, probably due to weather conditions, did they stand a chance of being hunted. It is possible that they remained in the reserve for several years, but Basil Reel's travels knew no boundaries.

In my earlier days in Tanganyika, when I was allowed two elephant licences for myself, there were many who, to my certain knowledge, registered heavy ivory with the government. In the particular area in which I hunted, there were many other private hunters who also shot elephants with 100-pound tusks, but I do not think they were in excess of an additional 10 individuals. Some of them were game wardens who took a local leave of absence to do so, as they were not permitted to hunt on licence during the course of their duties.

These are some of the elephants known to have been shot between 1950 and 1954 in Southern Highlands Province of Tanganyika. All of these hunters were known to me personally. Much of this ivory was sold, perfectly legally, through the hands of Mohammed Shivji, the ivory dealer in Iringa.

1. Quirce Van Rooyen—between Idodi and Madibira—103 & 105 lbs.
2. Luis Van Rooyen—between Idodi and Madibira—111 & 113 lbs.
3. Issak Van Rooyen—between Idodi and Madibira—105 & 109 lbs.
4. A. Joubert—between Idodi and Madibira—101 & 110 lbs.
5. Peter Shepherd—between Idodi and Madibira—103 & 106 lbs.
6. Ali Nassor—between Idodi and Madibira—110 & 116 lbs.
7. J.K.-H.—Nyamasagaha, Iringa District—101 & 103 lbs.
8. J.K.-H.—Ruaha River, south bank—107 & 109 lbs.
9. Lt. Col. J.W. MacKenzie, D.S.O.—Rujewa—111 & 108 lbs.
10. Jack Bousfield—Lake Rukwa East—109 & 103 lbs.

Top right: A poachers' camp in southern Tanzania.

Above: The .450 Martini Henry and muzzleloaders used by the poachers.

There were many more elephants with tusks weighing more than 100 pounds shot in this and adjacent areas after 1954 until approximately 1984, when their slaughter by poachers, some of whom were organised gangs of Somalis, almost eradicated the elephants in that part of Tanzania, as the country came to be called after independence was granted.

This is not to say that elephant and other game poaching was not present at all times. Poison arrows were the main cause of death. The deadliest of these poisons was that made from acocanthera bark and twigs. This was done by placing the bark and twigs in a small pot and leaving it to boil away all the moisture until a sticky black substance was left. This is deadly poison for which no antidote is known. The poison in most cases is applied to the shaft of the arrow just behind the arrowhead. To an elephant weighing five tons, death comes within 20 minutes.

In 1995 in the region of the Longido Controlled Area on the Tanganyika-Kenya border, I witnessed the death of an elephant poisoned by this deadly potion, which had been administered by a weighted spear dropped from a tree above the elephant's back. The most popular type of acocanthera used is the *muriju* (*Acocanthera longiflora*). This comes from an easily recognised small bush that has dark green leaves and purple berries. Prior to the berries appearing, the bush blossoms with white

The late 'Red' Harvill with 94-pound and 84-pound tusks. The elephant was shot within 25 minutes of our making camp at Nguala (1958).

trumpet-like flowers. The poison has to be fresh and used within six months of manufacture to be potent. Thereafter its effectiveness fades with exposure to the elements. The poison acts by paralysing the systolic artery of the heart and, in the case of an elephant, causes most violent vomiting, urination, and defecation. The hunting clan of the Masai—the Wanderobo—were masters in the production of this and other poisons used in hunting.

My narrative would not be complete without a comment on the Van Rooyen family, with whom I enjoyed two safaris for elephant's ivory. The family farmed at the southern base of Essimingor Mountain, between Arusha and Lake Manyara. The old man, or 'Baas' as he was known, was a General Smuts-like figure, tall and straight as a ramrod with a little pointed beard. He did not suffer fools and kept the family busy at all times. Only once did I see him smile. He spoke no English and was a die-hard Boer who had trekked up from South Africa in 1919. To him, Africans were *kaffirs!* I never discovered why he permitted a *rooinek* like me to join him, except that I got on well with his three sons (Quince, Luis, and Issak), who were all licenced professional hunters and had conducted many very successful safaris. Like many South Africans, they were brought up with 7x57 Mausers in their hands and were crack shots with open sights. However, the serious business of collecting eight ele-

*"Ah, there, Piet! be'ind 'is stony kop
With 'is Boer bread an Biltong, an
flask of awful Dop!
'is Mauser for amusement an 'is
pony for retreat,
I've known a lot o' fellers shoot
a damn sight worse than Piet."*

—Rudyard Kipling
Piet

77

phants with tusks over 100 pounds annually was a monumental challenge that the family finances demanded, so they had invested in British heavy double rifles.

Baas was in his 70s, and the sons collected his two elephants for him. He sat by the fire in camp, contemplating the environment and making sure all was ready on our return from the bush. We hunted in pairs: Quirce and I, and Luis with Atti. We camped on the Ruaha River at Makuluga. Daily we drove out some miles, west or east, and on finding tracks that crossed the bush road we would set out on foot to follow them. The two hunts we made were very successful, and as a result I came to know the family reasonably well, calling in occasionally at the farm. I am told that there were nine consecutive registrations of 100-pound tusks, mostly shot by the Van Rooyens.

Baas had an old Ford 'box body' car. Every week, one of his sons drove the stern figure of Van Rooyen to Arusha to see to the farm's business. The only occasion he ever smiled on me was when I opened the door of the Standard Bank of South Africa for him. I think it suddenly occurred to him that to have a door opened for him by an Englishman was just the sort of day it should be!

The Van Rooyen family were no fools. After the old man died at Essimingor, Luis took over. One day, shortly after independence, I called at the farm. I noticed as I drove up to the house that a long strip of grass had been planted through the fields and that it had been rolled. It looked to me to be an airstrip. I was always careful not to ask questions of the Van Rooyens, leaving them to do the talking—they were silent on the matter of the airstrip. As the disagreements over the policy of apartheid intensified, the South African community in Tanzania came under government scrutiny. One day a chartered DC3 from Rhodesia landed at the farm. The Van Rooyens had quietly packed their bags, and not an item was left as they took off and headed into the welcoming skies of Rhodesia. Everything had long since been sold and the money moved elsewhere. I knew then for certain the purpose of the long strip of grass. Vertrek once more my boetie!

Very few safari clients at the beginning of the 1950s shot heavy ivory in Tanganyika, except perhaps in Masailand south of Arusha, which was more accessible. One of the better-known persons who in fact spent a great deal of time hunting large elephants was Donald Hopkins of Spokane, Washington. His wife Marjorie also hunted for long periods of time, sometimes with her husband and sometimes without him. Both hunted with Stan Lawrence-Brown for periods of three to six months. Whilst they both saw elephants that had tusks of over 100 pounds, Donald refused to shoot anything with less than 150-pound tusks, but Marjorie did shoot several over 100 pounds a side.

I admit to this next little story being part hearsay, but, shall I say, hearsay in 1950 is better than hearsay all these years later. The facts are, I am sure, authentic.

The district commissioner (D.C.) in Same (a district in the north-east of Tanganyika) received a letter to the effect that all Tanganyika Public Works Department (P.W.D.) stores of explosives were to be checked against their ledgers, a perfectly normal annual practice. Sending for the lowly placed road foreman, the D.C. informed him that the check would take place in a few days' time. The following day the road foreman appeared with excuses as to why the date set was difficult to meet. He explained that he had a lot of work on at the time and wished to check his outlying stocks. The D.C., a busy man, put off the date for 10 days and forgot the matter.

A week later, arriving at his office early one morning, he was confronted with a policeman and two scruffy natives.

'What's all this about?' he asked. 'I'm very busy'.

The policeman explained that both natives had an odd story to tell. It appears that while they were cutting out a bees' nest from a baobab tree to obtain the honey, they had heard a dull 'boom' in the distance. Shortly afterwards they heard the pitter-patter of something falling about them. After a search they found two small pieces of flesh. The D.C. was concerned and alerted the Tanganyika Civil Aviation Department, requesting a report as to whether any aircraft were in the area, thinking that one might have crashed. Calling in the Indian subassistant surgeon stationed there, Dr. Alukar, the D.C. asked him to examine the now dried-up piece of flesh the size of a sugar lump. He placed the natives in custody and turned to his busy day's work.

The day came for the board of survey to be done on the P.W.D.'s explosive stores. The foreman appeared with more excuses. After agreeing to a further delay, the D.C. paused for thought. Picking up his telephone, one of only 10 subscribers, he dialed '2' for the police station. Yes! The foreman had a firearms licence. Next he dialed '5' for the revenue clerk. Yes! The foreman had an elephant licence. Next he dialed '8' for the dressing station and spoke to Dr. Alukar. The doctor had looked at the flesh in his microscope—it was not human flesh. He sent for the Indian police inspector in charge at Same. After some consultation, he decided to do a check on the P.W.D.'s explosive stores. This he did, accompanied by many protestations from the road foreman. Having completed it, the D.C. returned to his office and called in the head game scout. Duly instructed, the scout went on safari accompanied by a police corporal and the two natives who had brought in the flesh. Three days later they returned.

'Effendi', reported the police corporal, 'we found a hole that was big enough in which 10 people could hide and even a small car!'

'And what did you find?' asked the D.C., addressing the game scout.

'I think an elephant has been destroyed', he replied. 'Here, I have found the toenails of its feet', he added, producing them from a small bag.

When the road foreman arrived at the D.C.'s office he was under no illusions as to his predicament. After faithfully stating each part of the evidence, the D.C. asked him what he had to say.

'Sir', he said, 'it was an accident. I shot the wrong elephant with the small tusks. I am a poor man and do not have the money to buy a second elephant licence, so I destroyed the first one so that I could find a second and sell the ivory'.

The road foreman was duly punished and left the service of the government. So far as I know, this was the only case in which too much powder was used, resulting in the total disappearance of five and a half tons of target material. Perhaps even too much gun for Elmer Keith!

Perhaps the most unusual elephant 'hunting' in which I took part occurred in Tanganyika. Paramount Pictures was to make the film *Hatari*. The fact that it was working with its chosen outfitter, Ker & Downey Safaris Ltd., of which Eric Rundgren and I were directors, was almost entirely due to Eric. In the initial stages, Eric was attempting to keep his own safari contracts going and give time in between safaris to Paramount's requirements. This did not work, as Paramount was very demanding of his time. Matters came to a head when Howard Hawks, the director, demanded that the second unit, under the direction of Paul Helmick,

Coke's Hartebeest

photograph a herd of elephants tearing through and destroying a safari camp. This was no easy matter, for Eric had to interview John Owen, the newly appointed director of Tanganyika National Parks. The characters of both men were such that the chances of them seeing eye-to-eye were nil. However, a fee of £5000 was agreed to be paid by Paramount to Tanganyika National Parks for the privilege of securing this footage within the perimeter of the Lake Manyara National Park, which lay about 60 miles due west of Arusha in northern Tanganyika.

The money had been paid, and the second unit had three weeks in which to get this shot. A spot had been chosen on a riverbank where the water flowed off the escarpment on the western boundary of the park due east into Lake Manyara. On the northern bank of the river stood the camp, below which ran the 30-yards-wide shallow waters of the river. On the south bank was a hurriedly constructed concrete pillbox containing the cameraman and two assistants. The idea was that a small herd of elephants was to be found and driven panic stricken through the camp in the hopes that they would destroy it totally. This was to be done by using professional hunters and their gunbearers and trackers, equipped with 'thunder flashes' (small explosives), who would form a 'U' around the herd and push them towards the camp, the escape route chosen for them.

The day before this took place, Eric Rundgren fell out with John Owen and left to continue his safari programme. John Owen, who had, on arrival in Tanganyika, stayed with us in our home in Arusha whilst his home was being made ready, asked me to come and see him. I was asked to take over and get the job done as quickly and cleanly as possible and then get out of the park. John was already experiencing criticism for letting the national park to a film company. He in fact had little alternative—the parks were strapped for cash.

I left for Manyara, and next day we tried the plan. It was as hair raising as could be possibly imagined. The elephants had minds of their own. Twice they broke back through us, and accidents were narrowly avoided. One gunbearer made a lucky escape by climbing a huge acacia tree. An irate cow elephant tore the lower branches off the tree until a well-aimed thunder flash changed her mind. Everyone knew that if an elephant was shot in the park it would spell the end of the career of the P.H. involved.

The next day we tried to refine the method. 'Softly, softly' was the order of the day—move them very slowly and then, when near the

East African Impala

camp, push them hard. On this occasion we very nearly succeeded, but as soon as they saw the canvas tents, back they came over us. We tried once more but to no avail. We had taken some serious chances with everyone's life expectancy, and it was time to call a halt to the plan. Regretfully, I gave the order to pull out. John Owen was happy: he had his money, and we all had assured futures as professional hunters. However, when the news got back to Howard Hawks we all knew who was going for the proverbial 'high jump'.

To say that I was wracking my brains for an alternative is an understatement. I had one bit of luck—Hawks was away. Everyone was busy on the film set at Momella for several days, with the first unit and all the actors headed by John Wayne. On the evening that we pulled out, I sat down with a helpful special effects man and discussed things over a few beers. Between us we came to the conclusion that with the help of Willie de Beer, the animal trapper who had all the tame animals for use in the film, we might do the scene in miniature.

We hurriedly had little tents made, about five feet high. We mocked up beds, basins, and towels. A visit to Willie de Beer—a nicer and more helpful fellow never existed—secured the help of the elephants.

Willie decided not to feed the 11 little elephants till next day. Their staple food was fresh cabbage, and a rattle of the bucket brought them in a headlong gallop towards us. The camp was between the elephants and the fresh cabbage. All was set and the camera ready. Willie de Beer rattled the bucket, and here came the elephants through the miniature camp, trampling it to pulp. One washbasin did a graceful cartwheel over an elephant's back. It was perfect.

Secrecy as to what was in the film can was strictly imposed. It was imperative that no one knew we had succeeded. Howard Hawks returned and heard the news that we had left Lake Manyara without getting the shots. Someone was going to get the chop. The next evening the 'rushes' were to be shown at the Safari Hotel, the hotel in Arusha that had been 'taken over' by the film company. Ben Benbow, the owner-operator, was a good friend to all of us and ran a first-rate organisation.

I knew that I would be asked what I had to say about Manyara. Howard Hawks was held in awe by all his staff. He did not tolerate fools gladly and took some enjoyment in making people squirm under his questioning. The first rushes were shown and then it was my turn. 'Well J.K.-H.', Hawks said with a stern countenance, 'what have you got to say for yourself?'

'Would you like to see the rushes?' I asked.

With obvious surprise he said, 'Come on now. There aren't any, are there? You failed, didn't you?'

'Oh no!' I replied. 'Sit down and you will see some remarkable film.'

Totally mystified, he sat down, and the rushes came on. Up in the air went the washbasin, crack went the tent poles as they snapped under the weight of the little elephants with their massive tusks, put in place by my friend in special effects. (This had been done by putting harnesses with white plastic tusks attached over the heads of the elephants and spraying the whole thing with paint the colour of the elephants' hides.) The effect was sensational. When the film came to an end there were cheers all round—everyone was smiling. After a struggle with himself, Howard Hawks smiled. I had escaped censure. Later in the evening he came over to me.

'I want a word with you', he said. 'Why did we spend £5000 on the national park?'

Choosing my words carefully I said, 'You have invested in the future of African wildlife. I believe that as the future develops, Paramount's image will greatly benefit by this generous donation'.

He smiled. 'Stick around', he said. 'I can use people like you'. The word 'use' described his methods quite neatly, and I made a mental note that in the future I would take great care never to be 'trapped' again. Strangely and disappointingly, our sensational film was never used.

A great deal of fun was had by all the professional hunters on this contract, and Ker & Downey Safaris Ltd. made considerable profits, thanks to the sterling efforts of Ron and Marlies Stephens, the company's managerial staff. (Our further exploits are recorded in Chapter 3.)

No description of elephant hunting in Tanganyika would be complete without a mention of Bob Foster. A quiet Scotsman who seldom discussed his undoubted prowess as an elephant hunter, he shot more than 100 elephants that had tusks over 100 pounds. He knew the whole of East Africa's elephant haunts as well as any man living at that time. I was privileged to see quite a lot of him as he frequently visited his brother, a dentist, who was my next door neighbour when I lived in Arusha. Of an evening, he and I would meet at his brother's or my home and share a sundowner of the proverbial malt. Inevitably the conversation would drift to hunting, and I enjoyed the rare experience of listening to an expert telling his tales of adventure. Sadly, both Bob and his brother suffered from heart disease, and both passed on shortly afterwards—within a year of each other—still in their early 60s.

Also a pioneer at that time was Brian Nicholson, who, with the famous C.J.P. Ionides as his mentor, had not only managed huge elephant control measures on the borders of the Selous Game Reserve, but also sensibly brought into focus the enormous potential that the Selous Game Reserve had for controlled elephant hunting and thus income for the government.

The debt that posterity owes Nicholson has not been fully appreciated. Under his tutelage, the management of this huge area became cost effective. Had this not been so, much of it would have disappeared into the hands of a rapidly expanding elephant population and its unique and original habitat lost. His battles with authority were long and complex but eventually successful—though they did involve his banishment and reinstatement. His experience in controlling excess elephant populations was unrivalled, but he would not tell you that.

When I first arrived in Tanganyika, there were approximately 400 animals on a resident's game licence, which cost roughly £10. There had been virtually no hunting since before the 1939-45 War, and the country had been largely 'mothballed' economically due to the fact that every asset, financial and otherwise, had been devoted to winning the war. Elephant control had been limited to emergency cases, and no safaris of the kind that we know today had taken place. It took several years for Britain and its colonial staff to reassert themselves and address the pressing economic needs of the African colonies. It was therefore not until 1948–49 that newly qualified and trained colonial senior staff arrived on the spot. I was one of them.

Shortly after independence, the new government in Tanganyika decided that private enterprise in the safari business was best controlled by the Tanzania Wildlife Development Company. By the late 1960s this had taken place. Existing safari companies shut down, and, as the colonial officials left and economic conditions deteriorated, poaching became rife. The era we knew was gone, never to return. By 1963–64 Frank Miller and I had moved to Bechuanaland. We continued to return to East Africa as long as it was feasible, which was only for a few more years.

UGANDA

On my return to East Africa after the war, Uganda, with its history of big-game hunting, was a country that had to be visited and explored. The

train to Uganda passed only a few yards from the front of the Norfolk
Hotel in Nairobi. It was the effort of a few quick strides to board it and so
be on your way to the country that Churchill described as the 'jewel of
Africa'. There were preferential tariffs for government servants to travel,
and so it was relatively inexpensive when taking local leave to obtain a
travel warrant and move across East Africa cheaply. The train from
Nairobi took you over the high plateau of central Kenya and slowly
descended into eastern Uganda, where the altitude averaged about 3500
feet above sea level. Alighting at Namasagali—the port on the Nile before
the river flowed into Lake Kyoga—one could take the lake steamer that
travelled west down Lake Kyoga to Mazinde Port. From here it was a
short ride to the Mazinde Hotel where the traveler usually spent the night.
The next day, another short ride to Butiaba on Lake Albert put you upon
the lake steamer that sailed north up the lake, rejoining the Nile, which
flowed into the lake from the east out of the Murchison Falls National
Park. The boat then followed the Nile to the north to Nimule on the
Sudan border. The Nile continued to Egypt and the Mediterranean.

This route had some significance, for it took one to the most sought-
after areas of the ivory hunters at the turn of the century. The West Nile
District of Uganda and the Lado Enclave, together with the enormous
open, rolling grassland plains of northern Uganda stretching into the
Sudan, were the home of many, many thousands of elephants.

Uganda was a rich country. The land was fertile, and cotton growing flourished. Fish in huge quantities were readily available, together
with fresh fruit of all kinds, as the land was supplied with an abundance of water. The railway was (and still is) Uganda's lifeline to the
East African coast at Mombasa, Kenya. The climate, however, was not
as equable as elsewhere in East Africa. It was hot and humid; malaria
was endemic, and diseases of many different kinds flourished in these
conditions. Tribal wars had kept human populations to a minimum
until the turn of the century. Many an ivory hunter suffered from
malaria, dysentery, and blackwater fever, and many succumbed.

After the war, Uganda was open to safari hunting by East African
companies for a shorter time than is generally realised. The formation of
the Uganda Wildlife Development Company prevented outside interests
from using the assets of Uganda. The company had for a partner a well-
known firm of taxidermists in the U.S.A., the Klineberger brothers, who
made sure their special relationship and assets were well protected.

Most of the successive chief game wardens of Uganda were them-

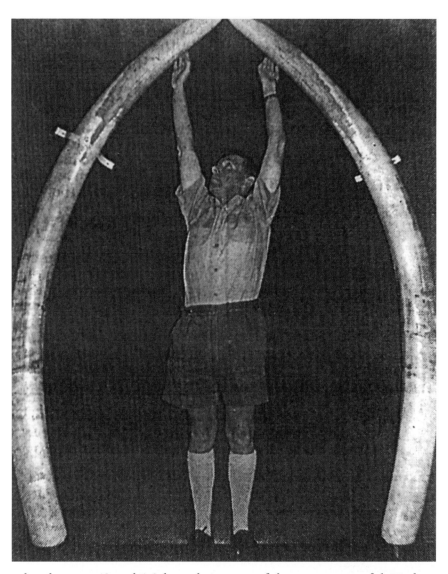

'Sandy' Field, O.B.E., with his 134-pound tusks, a fine matched pair, shot north-west of the border of Murchison Falls National Park, Uganda, circa 1960.

selves hunters, 'Samaki' Salmon being one of the most successful. Under his tutelage the country's game populations had been well managed and preserved. He was succeeded by C.R.S. Pitman, who was followed by Major B.G. Kinloch, M.C. Kinloch was also interested in hunting and secured a fine set of tusks that weighed 134 and 131 pounds from an elephant he shot in Kenya.

There were several well-known ivory hunters in Uganda at that time, one of the most noteworthy being E.A. Temple-Perkins, a former district commissioner and game warden. I spent some time with him and listened carefully to his advice. He was a remarkable man, surviving blackwater fever twice and living to the age of 93.

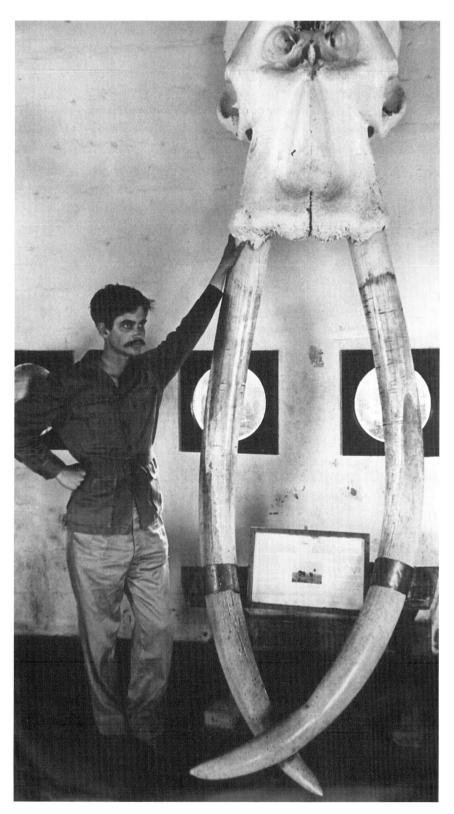

J. Mellon alongside the huge tusks in the museum at Murchison Falls Park Headquarters. Note the skull and entry to the brain. These tusks weighed more than 150 pounds each but disappeared during Idi Amin's regime (1962).

P.A.G. 'Sandy' Field, O.B.E., a provincial commissioner in Uganda, was also a keen elephant hunter, obtaining a fine pair of tusks weighing 134 pounds a side. Sandy subsequently became a good and kind friend. He became chief park warden of the Serengeti and park warden of the Ruaha National Park, the scene many years beforehand of my initial elephant hunting. He was also a wonderful host, but if you mentioned elephant hunting, you had best resign yourself to going to bed at four in the morning. For me, I made certain I had an afternoon nap before going to dinner with him. He donated his beautiful matched pair of tusks to the Powell-Cotton Museum in England, where they are the second largest pair of tusks (the heaviest being shot by Powell-Cotton in the Lado Enclave and weighing 198 and 174 pounds, the second largest pair of elephant tusks ever shot).

Tony Henley, a former professional hunter at that time, was game warden in charge at Moroto and had under his control the whole of the Karamoja area northwards to the Sudan border and eastwards to the Kenya border. He was not only most helpful to all of us safari people, but was a born naturalist and conscientious warden. I was to see a lot of him in later life when he returned to professional hunting. Wardens of his capabilities were rare.

The hunting areas in proximity to the large national parks of Uganda were the main areas where safari elephant hunting was concentrated— the Queen Elizabeth National Park, Murchison Falls, and Kidepo National Park. The Murchison Falls and Kidepo National Parks presented the best opportunities. Because I was based in Kenya, only a few safaris were possible, the logistics difficult, and the costs considerable, which resulted in my having to charge a higher price to my clients to cover the cost of fuel and wages to get into position prior to their arrival. Whilst we secured good trophies in most respects, finding an elephant that had tusks of 100 pounds was exceedingly difficult. By the early 1960s it was pretty obvious to me that the days of big ivory in Uganda were past. There seemed to be some considerable strife between its national park authorities and the game department, and I had the impression that they were not a happy lot. However, the good-natured attitude, hospitality, and humour of some of the individual game officers that one met in the bush more than made up for any problems.

On one occasion when visiting the Murchison Falls National Park, presided over by the redoubtable Lieutenant Colonel 'Bombo' Trimmer, I chanced to be a spectator when the local 'tame' elephant known as 'The Lord Mayor', on seeing a Volkswagen 'Beetle' arrive with two young

Germans, spied a bunch of bananas in the back of the car. Sauntering up to the car, he first investigated with his trunk as to whether it might enter the car through the window. The occupants promptly rolled up the windows. Quite slowly and deliberately The Lord Mayor rolled the Beetle onto its back. Within seconds the elephant was showered with stones, ashtrays, and everything that came to hand and sensibly moved off. We rolled the car back on its wheels and helped the occupants recover their senses.

But The Lord Mayor was not done yet. Nodding his head and swishing his trunk about, he ambled round to the back of the lodge where the kitchens were situated. Here there was a truck being loaded with supplies for a distant ranger station. Behind the open window of the kitchen, the cook was busy making bread and kneading it in a large basin. The Lord Mayor walked up to the truck and punctured a bag of flour, sucking up several pounds into his trunk as if it were dust to spread on himself, but with a swift turn of his head he put his trunk through the window of the kitchen and blew the flour all over the cook. I never saw an elephant with a better sense of humour! Alas, his exploits became intolerable, and he was destroyed.

Whilst hunting beyond the park I was struck by the vast numbers of elephants in the open grasslands. The grass was seven feet tall, and one could well imagine 'Karamoja' Bell climbing on the backs of his gunbearers to obtain a view of a big tusker. Like so many other hunters, game wardens, and naturalists, I was captivated by Kidepo National Park. Forty years later I returned to see that the country had not changed, but the wildlife was destroyed. There was, so long as the civil war and poaching continued, absolutely no chance of its return to its former state. In the short time that I was assistant director of national parks in the early 1990s, I made every effort to focus international attention to the appreciation of this unique wildlife habitat. Alas, it was doomed to failure. Security was a huge problem, and the consequent loss of confidence of investors made sure that no progress in Kidepo's recovery would be made. The appalling corruptive practices of the Uganda National Parks officials further made certain that the wildlife of Uganda would continue to be plundered. The civil war in Sudan made certain that Kidepo National Park bordering on the Sudan was plundered for the meat it could supply to hungry insurgents.

Generally speaking, my generation was born too late for central Africa ivory hunting. Abundant literature exists telling of the adventures of those who were fortunate to have enjoyed such experiences, and my library of 'Africana' bears testimony to the appreciation that I have for their efforts.

Nearly all the professional hunters of Kenya made safaris to Uganda. Several whose roots were in Kenya remained there for some years. Prominent among these was Nicky Blunt, whose father, Commander D.E. Blunt, was an elephant hunter and game control officer of some note in Kenya and Tanganyika. Commander Blunt's book *Elephant* is of considerable value. Nicky, who started hunting at a very early age, was one of the youngest licenced professional hunters of his day. He is without doubt, in my mind, one of the most ethical and careful professional hunters that I have known. Moreover, he has managed, in spite of the political upheavals in East Africa, to hunt continually from the late 1950s to the present day. Brian Herne also turned to Uganda for a considerable period of his hunting life. His book *Uganda Safari* tells the story of his life there.

It should be recorded that between 1958 and 1961, Uganda's tourist industry and wildlife assets reached a state of development unsurpassed by neighbouring countries. The rapidly increasing stream of tourists who came to view the Queen Elizabeth National Park and Murchison Falls Park ran into the tens of thousands, and Uganda's wildlife assets made a huge contribution to the economy. It should also be remembered that this occurred without the asset that the gorillas have provided to tourism in the southeast of the country today. The access roads in Uganda were better than in any of the other neighbouring countries, and the air communications were excellent—nearly all the smaller towns of Uganda had a weekly air service. The Baganda, the largest of the ethnic groups of the country, were progressive and intuitive traders. All were devoted to further education, with Makerere University being the first of its kind in East Africa. Uganda was one of the first of the colonial territories to have its own doctors, lawyers, and many other qualified professionals. It had all this until the advent of Idi Amin. Thereafter, a suitable epitaph would have been the sign that some disconsolate ivory hunter placed at the Gondokoro (Juba) Nile crossing to the West Nile and Lado Enclave: 'Abandon Hope All Ye Who Enter Here'.

After my experiences in Kenya and Tanganyika, it was difficult to mount a realistic effort to sustain and maintain a continuous level of safaris in Uganda. Elephants of heavy ivory were certainly not so numerous, although they were there. The wishes and physiques of my clients were not necessarily compatible with what was on offer there. Uganda

Uganda Kob

kob, Jackson's hartebeest, sitatunga, and world-class waterbuck were the main species peculiar to the country.

In the ensuing years Uganda's wildlife suffered the greatest devastation of any East African country. The corrupt practices of its officials of today continue to give little hope for the future, more particularly, when it becomes necessary to build a zoo in Entebbe.

BECHUANALAND (BOTSWANA)

During 1962–63, I wanted a new horizon to hunt and explore. I hit the jackpot when I arrived in Bechuanaland, as it was unknown. Several others had arrived there at the same time, and one or two had preceded me, but all, including myself, were unaware of the real potential that the country held.

Bechuanaland was a vast country with seemingly no people. Little more than half a million people lived there, which is the size of France, and most of them lived on the eastern border. There was one game warden, Pat Bromfield, who lived in Francistown on the railway that connected South Africa with Rhodesia, which later became Zimbabwe. Bechuanaland had no capital, and it was with some amusement that it was realised that the country could not be given independence without one! Gaberones was chosen to be the place. Out of virgin, sparse thorn bush arose the parliament building, and nearby a dam was constructed on a small sand river so that the capital had a water supply.

Not one resident in Bechuanaland at the time had the least idea what a safari company was or how it was organised. There were no roads— tracks would be a better description of what was meant to be a road. Furthermore, the roads were filled with deep sand, making it impossible to use them without a four-wheel drive vehicle. The sand, however, was no disadvantage when tracking elephants, showing clearly the bull track that was singled out for attention. Elephant hunting was not, however, in the same class as in the East African countries, where the terrain was more varied and interesting. Hunting elephants was best in the Okavango Swamps in crocodile-infested water, and the added excitement of a malevolent hippo eyeing one's canoe most of the time added a new dimension to elephant hunting, as did tracking and shooting elephant when up to one's waist in water. The cutting out of the tusks and their removal from the swamps by the flimsiest of canoes were hazardous, to say the least. The boldness of the crocodiles increased with every few minutes spent cutting out the tusks of the elephant. In these cases it was

Top: The late George Bates (left) with his client's (John Bryant) 94-pound tusk. The other tusk weighed 84 pounds. The elephant was shot in the Okavango Swamps in 1970.

Right: Three of the famous team enjoying life. L to R: Doug Wright, Simon Paul, and Cecil Riggs with the tusks of Simon's 100-pounder on the outside.

Following page: Such destruction of their habitat by elephants, compounded by their radically increased numbers, has given the government of Botswana a serious problem. Imagine what the elephants can do to cultivations (1974).

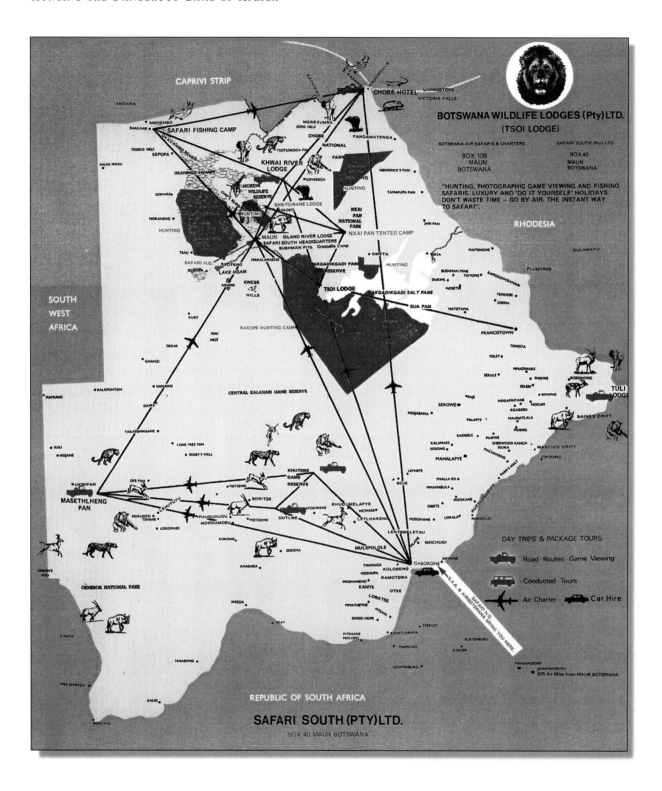

94

difficult to alert the Mamakush, the tribe resident in the islands of the swamps, of the availability of so much meat. When they were present, sheer force of numbers ensured that little was wasted and the crocodiles kept at bay.

The alternative to hunting the swamps was hunting the mopane forests. These areas of forest were not thickly wooded, and it was easy to perceive one's quarry at more than 100 yards. In April, May, June, and July, the major water holes still provided an adequate water supply, so hunting was a question of checking these water holes and determining from the tracks the size of the bull elephant you chose to follow.

Bechuanaland ivory was disappointing when compared with East African ivory. The tusks were short and stubby, but the specific gravity of the ivory was greater. The movement of the elephants from west to east and back again annually further increased their numbers by the elephants from the Wankie National Park in Rhodesia; when subjected to culling, these elephants moved into Bechuanaland by way of escape. To the north and west the war in Angola had the same effect on the elephant population. Considerable numbers of elephants moved into the Caprivi Strip, the tongue of land north of Bechuanaland, part of Namibia, and thence into the Linyanti swamps of the Chobe River, a major tributary of the Zambesi. In effect, this put more elephants into the Savuti area on the north-eastern side of the Okavango Swamps, and from there they spread out into the islands of the swamps. Because of the lack of length of the Bechuanaland ivory, few, if any, clients took the trouble to shoot an elephant unless the opportunity was easily presented. However, in Bechuanaland each tribe had a tribal council that issued licences to members of their tribe to hunt in their tribal area, and as ivory was ivory to them and the price was right, considerable numbers of elephants were shot each year by local people. Very few 100-pound-tusked elephants were shot.

One such elephant was collected by Kenny Kays, a redoubtable professional hunter who, before becoming one, was my guide and interpreter when I first arrived in Maun, the town from which our company, Safari South (Pty.) Ltd., operated. The Kays family was synonymous with that part of Botswana. Without them little could be done. They were friendly and helpful, and it was fun to be in their company. Their part in my life in this part of Africa is mostly told elsewhere in this story.

My godson, Simon Paul, who came to Botswana with me when he was a young man, had developed a desire for elephant hunting, and he,

Previous page: Map of Botswana showing Safari South concession areas.

95

too, found a fine elephant with 100-pound tusks. He made himself a fine reputation as a professional hunter.

George Bates, who had been one of the first clients of my famous partner, Lionel Palmer, some years before, later obtained a concession in the middle of the Okavango Swamps and succeeded in shooting some fine-tusked elephants.

The elephants in Bechuanaland were some of the largest on the continent, sometimes standing more than 13 feet at the shoulder. They were once described by one of my clients, with whom I had hunted elephant in East Africa and who had obtained some sizeable tusks there, as 'all-American college boys with toothpicks'.

During my final years in Bechuanaland there was some poaching of elephants by Europeans. This was due to the shortage of foreign exchange because of the escalating state of hostilities in Rhodesia. The eastern part of the Caprivi Strip was somewhat of a no-man's-land due to the action of insurgents in Angola. Two Europeans, thinking to take advantage of the fact that little wildlife law enforcement would be practical there, decided to go elephant poaching and met their end on a land mine. There were reports of maimed and wounded elephants that had suffered this fate entering the northern hunting concessions in Bechuanaland. One other infamous character, Bob Madison, also tried his luck by flying directly into the Okavango Swamps and out with his poached ivory. So far as I know he was never brought to justice, but he was on the run for some time. Nature, however, took its revenge, for he died prematurely of a heart attack a short time afterwards.

Today Botswana is overrun with elephants, and the Ministry of Natural Resources has a serious problem. Its forested areas are being destroyed by huge herds, and the delicate balance between desert and foliage-covered land and consequent rainfall is in jeopardy. If ever there was a case of utilisation of the wildlife resource, this surely must be it.

MOZAMBIQUE

Mozambique, which was under Portuguese administration until 1975, attracted a considerable number of safari clients, the major safari outfitter being Mozambique Safarilandia Ltd., which was owned by the Arbreu brothers. Their general manager was none other than the redoubtable Baron Werner Von Alvensleben. Werner was a 6-foot-2-inch-tall, well-built, blue-eyed, blond-haired, good-looking German. He looked and was

Baron Werner Von Alvensleben (left) and Harry Manners after a good day against local poachers in the Save River concession, Mozambique (1963).

every inch the part he portrayed. The scar on his left cheek came from his duelling whilst a student at Heidelburg University. In Hitler's 'putsch' in 1938, he had escaped, making his way to northern Rhodesia. He made a rough living by elephant hunting and looking after absentee landlords' estates. During the 1939-45 War he was imprisoned as a German alien in northern Rhodesia. Again he escaped, making his way through the bush to Mozambique.

Ker & Downey Safaris had asked me to make a survey of Mozambique Safarilandia Ltd. with a view towards buying into its stock holdings and setting up an associated company to which its repeat business could be directed. I was therefore given full treatment on arrival. I spent some three months with Safarilandia and enjoyed everyone's company enormously. I flew up to the concession on the Save River, passing over Gorongoza National Park. There were lots of elephants about, but few, if any, in the Save that I saw. On the Save I met Walter 'Wally' Johnson Sr., Walter Johnson Jr., Harry Manners, and several of the better-known Portuguese hunters, including Ruis Quadros and Ardelino Peres.

I was struck by the leadership that Werner gave the whole operation. He was a tower of strength and tolerated fools not at all. Antipoaching operations were in full swing when I arrived, and I joined them at once. Werner, with a red bandanna round his head, his Land Rover stripped of its upper hood windows and windscreen, and his 7x57 Mauser cradled in his lap, had scant consideration for anyone who was caught. Huge quantities of wire snares were removed. Poachers who were caught were removed to another part of the country, hundreds of miles from their homes, and told to walk back. This was a lot easier than taking them to court, which was a very time-consuming procedure. I had several opportunities to talk with Harry Manners, who had in the early days known John 'Pondoro' Taylor, and had spent his earlier life hunting for ivory. So, too, had Wally Johnson and his son Walter, who was 17 when I met him and spoke fluent Portuguese and who had spent long periods hunting for ivory in Mozambique. Naturally, I listened carefully to what these great hunters had to say.

It appeared that decent ivory in hunting areas in the north and centre of the country was in short supply. The best remaining area was between the railway from South Africa to Lourenco Marques (now Maputo) and the Kruger National Park, which lay adjacent to the frontier between the two countries. This area comprised a concession area granted to Sr. A. Sarnadas. Sarnadas had built a fine little rest camp of several rondavels under the big thorn trees on a sand river not far from the nearest railway station. Wally Johnson and I used this camp with the intention of making a survey of the area for elephant and other game. A line of water holes ran roughly north to south and parallel to the border some seven miles into the concession, to which large bull elephants came from the Kruger National Park. It was while on this exercise that I saw what has always been to me the largest bull buffalo upon which I have ever set eyes. We saw some good bull elephants, too, and the concession, when married to the game in the Save, had good potential.

It was whilst here in camp that I met once again Don Hopkins of Spokane, Washington, still looking for his 150-pound-tusked elephant. Don was not at all happy to see J.K.-H. there! He complained bitterly to Wally Johnson and Harry Manners that he was sure I had come for one reason only and that was to shoot the big elephant that everyone had told him was there. Over a beer that evening Wally explained Don's fears to me. Choosing an appropriate moment, I explained to Don my true intention for being in Mozambique. He seemed reassured, but I believe he still nursed a lingering doubt in his mind. Harry Manners, with whom he was hunting, had some years previously shot an elephant that had tusks weighing 190 and 189 pounds. Wally Johnson, who also spent many years ivory hunting, also shot two elephants that had tusks of more than 160 pounds each.

By the time I arrived in Mozambique, those days were gone. The uncertainties of the country did not convince me that Ker & Downey Safaris would be right in making an investment there—too much depended on Werner. Later, both Wally and his son Walter lost everything in the civil war in Mozambique and joined us in Botswana. More is told of our exploits together in other chapters. The elephants of Paturi returned to the Kruger National Park, and today they are restricted from entering Mozambique by ditches and fences.

OTHER COUNTRIES

I did not seriously hunt elephants in Ethiopia, Somaliland, or Sudan. There were none in British and French Somaliland. In Italian Somaliland, there was a considerable population on the lower reaches of the Webi Schebelli near Brava, and also farther inland and between the south-west bank of this river and the Kenya border.

Foremost in Somalia as a professional hunter was Belli del'Isca, an Italian. Belli had a fine record of obtaining big ivory, some of which ran well over 120 pounds a tusk. I discussed at some length the possibility of doing a safari with him on the Somaliland side of the Kenya border, and at one time my close friend Rene Babault and I had nearly finalised arrangements to do so, but the transitional government of Somaliland scuppered our plans. Shortly afterwards, the Somalis and their newly imported AK-47s saw the demise of virtually the entire elephant population. Slowly but surely, this influence spread into the Northern Frontier District of Kenya, removing by 1990 all but a few elephants north of the Tana River.

For a brief period, I had some exciting times in the southern Sudan, but here, too, a war between the north and the south was developing, and security became a problem. No ivory of any great size was easy to come by. Poaching was rife and had been for some considerable time after the departure of the British administration. However, by air and with Rene Babault on board I made a reconnaissance into the eastern Congo. (I have often been asked where I think the largest-tusked elephants are left on the continent of Africa. Without doubt it is in the huge canopied forests of the Congo.) For a brief few minutes, Rene and I flew round a small clearing in the forest on our epic trip. We saw two elephants with enormous tusks, long and thick, standing at the edge of a water hole in the clearing. Both Rene and I had at that time been hunting elephants on safari continually for many years. We were well accustomed to reading the weight of ivory on elephants with some accuracy and in all sorts of conditions. Both elephants had tusks of a size that we had never seen at any time in our careers. Try as we might, we could find no place where we could put the plane down to refuel and keep looking at the country, so regretfully we had to turn for home.

On our return to Nairobi, Rene, whose father was French and who also had an uncle who was coffee farming in the Congo, went to the Congo to see if it was possible to get permission to hunt in the area that we had seen from the air. Rene spoke fluent French and was able to communicate well with the various government officials. Security in the areas was, however, nil, and his report on his return was dismal. Shortly afterwards other professional hunters of a mind to try the Congo tried to establish themselves there. The results were disastrous, and they lost all their equipment to government thievery. I have no doubt that if it is made worthwhile—and I am sure that it has been—there will be a trickle of ivory from these great forests for some time to come.

Many years later, when Peter Frazer flew a Cessna 206 out to East Africa from California for me, I asked him on his arrival at Entebbe what had been the worst part of the journey. He told me that if he had gone down at sea he had a life raft, signalling equipment, flares, and some chance of being spotted. If he had gone down into the forest canopy of the Congo he would have disappeared without a trace. A very true statement, since only in recent years has a complete Lancaster bomber been located that was lost in the Aberdare Forest of Mount Kenya for more than 20 years. The same fate had overtaken 'Sandy' Field, who disappeared in his aircraft in bad weather in the same area.

I made a somewhat halfhearted attempt to hunt elephant in Ethiopia. At that time, it was an exceedingly difficult task to obtain a licence, but with my family's connections with the Ethiopian royal family (who had been our guests in Palestine when I was a boy) I managed to do so. Even all those years ago, the elephants with acceptable ivory were locked into the very thick forest in the south-west areas of Ethiopia, which were inaccessible. My finances did not permit me to sustain an expedition of the size and scope that was required. The Gambella area (later to prove such a

At home in 1996 with the tusks of an elephant I shot 46 years earlier in Southern Highlands Province of Tanganyika, weighing 136 pounds and 134 pounds.

prime elephant area, yielding some huge tusks over 120 pounds a side to Ray Petty while on safari there) was inaccessible to me at that time. Moreover, there was more insecurity in the area than there is even today. I looked over a lot of frightened, scruffy, and persecuted elephants on the upper reaches of the Ganale Doria River in southern Ethiopia, but they had also been poached heavily for their ivory.

I found Ethiopia, a country run on feudal systems, an absorbing and beautiful place, its heights and many abysses unsurpassed, and its people, most of whom have been Christians for as long as we have in the Western world, fascinating. It had the one background missing from so many other African countries: a sense of history in fact, implied and visible. When I went to meet His Imperial Majesty, The Emperor Haile Selassie, Lion of Judah and King of Kings, I passed between the two huge, male maned lions chained at the palace gates. They looked at me with eyes that bored into my body, seemingly asking the question, 'Are you a hunter of us?' I gritted my teeth and walked between them. Their chains strained as they moved toward me, but there was 10 feet between them and me on either side of me, so I was safe. Smiling wryly to myself as I walked on, I wondered if the gateway to hell or heaven would be like that and what questions I would be asked.

I would not have missed my time in Ethiopia. It was a great experience. The two years I spent there were like a few months, so fast did the time pass.

CHAPTER THREE

BLACK RHINO HUNTING

The Unpredictably Tempered Beast

GENERAL OBSERVATIONS

Whilst rhino were more than plentiful in East Africa, they were not north or south of East Africa to any great extent. In the early 1950s Kenya, Tanganyika, and Uganda were literally, in some parts, stiff with rhino, and many rhinos were shot on control when molesting innocent people. In reality less than 50 percent of visiting sportsmen shot them.

The idea of 'I want the "big five," of course' had not arrived, but towards the end of the 1950s and during the 1960s it certainly did. As the fame of East African safaris led to safari clubs being formed in the Western world and America, 'performance' by a sportsman became more desirable and attracted greater esteem from his peers. Rhino as a trophy became more popular. For me, I seldom had the yen to shoot a rhino, except on control when there was good reason to do so. Rhino amused me with their uncertain temper and their attempted impersonation of a steam train releasing its brakes. They did, however, cause some alarm when they were stumbled across en route to a different quarry.

In my travels in Ethiopia, Somaliland, and Eritrea, I saw none except on the west bank of the Webi Schebelli in its lower reaches near Brava. These few rhino were an extension of the population on the Kenya side of the border. They soon disappeared, as did those on the Kenya side, with the advent of Somalis equipped with AK-47s. In southern Ethiopia I came across several rhino near the Kenya border in

The game scout—partly assisted by the rhino—flew over some large boulders to his right and up a small tree.

—J.K.-H.

Five rhino together on the Masai Mara.

the vicinity of Farole and the Mega Escarpment. There was also a scattered population south of the Doua Parma River to the Kenya border, in the area of the water holes at El Dere and Dembeldero. By the late 1950s they had all disappeared. I found no evidence of them elsewhere to the north, excepting the dwindling population in Sudan. In the early 1950s, there were still substantial populations of rhino in northern Uganda, and some white rhino still existed in the West Nile District. Twelve years later the rhino's distribution had contracted to mainly Kenya and Tanganyika.

Rhino were easy meat for the poacher; being creatures of habit and territorially inclined, they readily advertised their presence by defecating regularly in the same spot. For a poacher, it was easy to pick up fresh tracks from one of these sites and come up with the rhino. A convenient tree usually rendered the poacher safe, which was not often the case when following elephant for its ivory. Somehow rhino had my sympathy, mostly because of their unpredictable behaviour, but there was more than one occasion when my ideas were rudely disputed.

No discourse on rhino hunting would be complete without reference to the 'Itigi thicket' in central Tanganyika, south of the railway line from Dar Es Salaam to Kigoma. This area of some 300 square miles grew the thickest bush imaginable. Inside its twisting, turning paths it was heavily populated with black rhino. In the years immediately after the war it must have contained several hundred black rhino. It was so consistently thick with thorn bush and creepers that it was impenetrable to humans. Even so, the sparse human population surrounding it slowly but surely reduced its extent over the years. Today it is hardly recognisable, and the rhino have gone.

Until the early 1970s, it was possible to obtain a permit to shoot forest-living rhino in Kenya, some other countries having protected the species by then. (Previously, in the early 1960s, if one's client wanted a good rhino, the Aberdares or Mount Kenya was the place. This was hard hunting on foot at high altitude.) It occasionally happened that one's client was forced to shoot a charging rhino that was not the trophy desired. In this case, the rhino had to be taken on licence, and no further licence was issued. The forest rhino's horns grew long, and in most cases the female's horn was longer than the male's. Providing that the female was without a calf, the shooting of females was permitted. When a fine trophy was required, five out of ten shot were females. Naturally, there were areas in Kenya other than forested areas where good rhino were found, but as rhino populations in this era were being reduced quite rapidly, the areas where they were available were inevitably difficult to access.

In the years before the war, Tanganyika provided some sensational lengths of rhino horn, George Rushby himself taking a rhino with a 52-inch horn in the mid-1930s. It was also my privilege when visiting Sir William Gordon Cumming, Bt., in Scotland to see the 62-inch horn that his forebear, Roualeyn Gordon Cumming, shot in South Africa in the 1860s.

KENYA

A Hunting Accident with Rhino

Ker & Downey employed two old hands with pre-1939-45 War experience, Roy Home and John Cook. Both became good friends of mine, and we did a number of safaris together. John Cook had to be one of the most generous Scotsmen I ever met. Always the life and soul of a party and the last to leave, he was a most friendly person. He had taken out a group some months previously when we had met up on safari with our respective clients. His clients were returning, bringing with them other friends who needed a professional hunter to accompany them. John asked me to come along.

Three famous mentors of mine. L to R: Sydney Downey, Myles Turner, and Jack O'Connor.

John chose one of his favourite hunting areas: Bura on the north bank of the Tana River in the Northern Frontier District of Kenya. The country north of the Tana River stretched for about 100 miles northwards to the Somalia border. It was largely flat and featureless, but the vegetation provided the habitat for most dangerous game, for which the Tana River always gave access to water when the usual water holes became dry.

Camp was set up on the river in typical safari style. We set off hunting with our clients, each of us going in our chosen and agreed directions. At first we had great success, returning each day with a good trophy. After a few days, John's client became a little irritable at his lack of continued success—no fault of John's, as the man was plain unlucky. John and his client set off in the morning, with his client quite determined that he was going to shoot the first thing he saw. This was not an easy situation for any P.H. to handle.

Fortunately, they were not able to catch up with the one or two poor trophies seen, but at midday they spotted a rhino with a 14-inch horn that was quietly dozing under a thorn tree. The second horn was smaller. John was reluctant to have his client shoot such an average trophy because, since we were on a 45-day safari, there was ample opportunity to shoot a better one later. This did not suit his client who, for the purpose of this tale, I will call Bill.

Bill was a huge man, standing six feet four inches and weighing 300 pounds. He had been a colonel in the U.S. Marine Corps and was accustomed to having his way. He was going to shoot the rhino no matter what. Whilst this conversation was taking place, the rhino became uneasy and suspected that something was not quite normal. Realising

106

that he had little time left, John got everyone in line and started to stalk the rhino. There was not much cover, and the shot would have to be taken at 10 yards. Bill and John were side by side, Bill with his .458 Winchester Magnum Model 70 and John with his trusty .475 No. 2, each being more than adequate to put down a rhino. Behind them came a gunbearer with a double-barrelled .465/.500 Holland & Holland Royal Grade rifle, which was Bill's second gun.

The rhino, by this time, had become suspicious and sensed the direction from which danger was approaching. The tick birds, normally attending closely, flew upwards and departed. Before John and Bill could halt and take aim, the rhino charged, churning up dust and small sticks as he came.

'Take him past the head and into the shoulder at the neck', said John firmly. Bill fired and kept firing. Three rounds went in the direction of the rhino in quick succession.

The rhino had to make slightly more than 30 yards during this time and was hit only once, the bullet going through the fleshy part of his left front leg. Bill threw down his .458 and turned to take the .465/.500. At that moment there were two simultaneous explosions. John shot the rhino with his .475 No. 2 and killed it stone dead 10 feet from them. The gunbearer behind Bill, who had squatted down behind them, panicked, and as Bill turned for his gun, the gunbearer fired, hitting Bill just behind the right side of his pelvis. The bullet passed through him and exited just in front of the left side of his pelvis. Bill and the rhino hit the ground at the same time.

For a moment no one realised what had happened until Bill spoke.

'I've been hit!' he shouted. Bill was bleeding but not badly. Luckily no artery had been damaged, but he could not move his legs. This was an ominous sign. The car was brought, and he was gently lifted into it and driven to the Garissa police post 55 miles upstream from Bura. The rhino was naturally abandoned. The police called in an aircraft from Nairobi, and Bill was flown to hospital.

John returned to camp to find my clients and me having an afternoon siesta. We were all shocked at the news. Gunbearers with guns in tight corners were always unpredictable. Poor John was beside himself with worry. He had been a founding member of the E.A.P.H.A. in 1934 and had had a long and distinguished career as a professional hunter, during which he took H.R.H. the Duke of Gloucester and many other notable personalities on safari. He took the incident as a personal failure, but he eventually was completely exonerated and soon returned to his normal self. I arranged for the rhino to be retrieved, and John packed his car and headed for Nairobi, where we joined him a few days later.

Bill, to whom a miracle had happened, was making a good recovery. The .465/.500, 500-grain solid Kynoch bullet had entered just behind the thigh bone on his right side but incredibly had arced round behind his stomach and through his body cavity, doing no damage, and exited in front of his thigh bone on his left side. There were two clean holes and no internal damage. The doctors and surgeons could not believe their examinations. The force of the bullet had shocked the sciatic nerves of both Bill's legs, but the left leg soon came back into use. Although he had, in the first two weeks of his recovery, some difficulty in raising his foot from the ankle down, he soon recovered from this and within a month he was walking normally.

After a day in Nairobi, my party and I continued with our part of the safari, which was completed successfully. We all met on our return, Bill having been released from hospital, and ensured that the celebration party was a good one. John Cook saw to that matter in his own inimitable way. There were no hard feelings, and both John and I were booked to take everyone out again the following year.

Shortly after everyone had departed for America, I learned of an amusing sequel to Bill's hospitalisation. Bill was most concerned in hospital that his virility had been impaired by the accident. Just before he was due to be released he could stand the uncertainty no longer. He therefore decided he simply had to 'test the equipment'. He asked his wife, who had not been with us on safari, to come early to visit him in hospital. His wife, a much admired woman of charming disposition, duly arrived at the hospital and went to his private room, where together they put Bill to the test.

Nairobi Hospital had on the staff a redoubtable ward sister, Brenda Towson. Woe betide any patient who was not as good as gold when Brenda was on the prowl. Brenda was a large lady and well made, standing all of 5 feet 11 inches. She was a South African, but behind her formidable exterior she was as kind and understanding as any nurse could be. This particular afternoon she paused outside Bill's door and tried to open it. It was locked. Brenda's hackles were up—no one locked patients' doors. 'Open up at once!' her stentorian voice boomed. No answer came. She rattled the door handle vigorously. 'Open up immediately!' she shouted, putting her ear to the door to see if she could hear what was happening in Bill's room.

After a few seconds she heard a small voice answer, 'Just be patient. We will be ready in a few minutes'. The effect of this statement on Brenda had to be seen to be believed. The blood rose to her face, and she became very angry and fearsome to behold.

'What?' she cried. 'In this hospital? Never!' Not quite sure what to do, she stormed up and down the passage for a moment or two. Quite suddenly the door opened, and there was Bill's wife looking sweet and beautiful as always.

'Did you need to talk to Bill, Sister?' she asked charmingly.

When Brenda, an unmarried woman, entered Bill's room she was firmly put in the picture by Bill—the former U.S. Marine Corps colonel, you will remember—in graphic terms. For once in her life she was speechless. Being the good and kind person she was, however, she soon saw the funny side of the matter.

I was to meet Brenda and her staff of the MacMillan Ward of the hospital a year later under very different circumstances (see Chapter 5).

Sadly, a few years later Bill was killed in an aircraft crash. Fate has odd ways of manipulating us. John Cook continued to hunt very successfully for many years. Generous to a degree, full of stories, and a die-hard hunter, he was one of those that many hunters of today try, but fail, to emulate. I was fortunate to speak to him on the telephone in South Africa a few days before he died in his 80s.

The Rhino That Did Not Like Elephants

Arthur Santomo, who hailed from Pittsburgh, Pennsylvania, was a short and stocky man of Sicilian-Italian extraction. We had met in the U.S.A. at a soiree given by some friends of mine in Pittsburgh, and he had booked a 30-day safari with me in the hope of collecting as many trophies as possible. He was an excellent companion and enthusiastic hunter. Arthur wanted some good ivory, and, as luck would have it, it had rained on the eastern border of the Tsavo National Park and a migration of elephants in search of new pastures was imminent.

We were booked into block 21A in Kenya, which was a 250-mile drive from Nairobi down the main Mombasa Road. At MacKinnon Road, the scene of the old British Army supply dump of the 1939–45 War, we turned north-east and followed the park boundary to the Galana River, where we camped.

A few miles before reaching the Galana, we passed two hills on the east side of the national park boundary. These hills were small and easily climbed within a few minutes. The surrounding country was flat, and from our observation post a fine view of the area was possible.

The soil was red, the reflected light from the small water holes easily spotted. Big, red mud-encrusted elephants stuck out like sore thumbs. Our little group of spotters saw little this day, so, returning to the car, we headed back up the border cut, heading south-west on the road by which we had entered the previous day. We crossed over the Garibete flood plain and decided to stop for a cup of tea. Sitting on the roof of the car, we immediately spotted a large bull elephant on his own heading out of the park into the hunting area.

The wind was blowing strongly from east to west, so turning the car round to face north towards camp we sat and watched. The bull was carrying good ivory that I estimated to be in the region of 80 pounds a side. He crossed out of the national park and kept on heading east within the hunting area. After giving him a mile within the hunting area, we collected our rifles and water bottles and set out after him.

Art Santomo and gunbearer on top of the elephant (1967).

About an hour and a half later we came up to him browsing on some

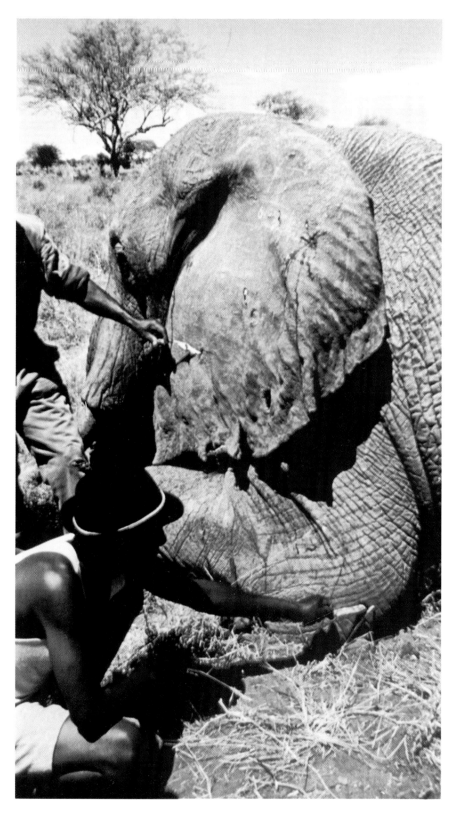

Left: Counting up the number of holes made by the rhino's horn in the elephant.

Following page, top: The view from the elephant to the spot where the rhino died.

Following page, bottom: The reverse view.

newly grown vegetation. An ear shot with Arthur's .458 Winchester Model 70 killed the bull immediately and left him sitting bolt upright. After taking a few pictures and leaving Arthur and Edward, my gunbearer, by the elephant, I set out to return to the car, carrying my trusty .470 Westley Richards double-barrelled rifle.

The country was open and easy to traverse on foot. I hit the road and turned left towards the car, which I could now see clearly on the brow of the rising ground. As I got nearer, a large animal, that at some distance appeared to be a rhino, moved across in front of the car. Rhino were totally protected in the area, and I had no wish, therefore, to provoke it, which is easily done. From the lie of the ground I decided to make a long detour within the hunting area and come up to the back of the car with the wind securely in my favour. The rhino seemed unconcerned and continued to stand by the car as if it was guarding it. The detour completed, I approached to within 20 yards of the car, keeping it between me and the rhino's head. I made it to the car, climbing onto the roof from the back and diving down through the observation hatch in the roof.

Musioka, the other gunbearer whom I had left to look after the car, was squatted down in the back trying to make himself invisible and scentless. As I climbed into the car the springs squeaked, and the rhino was alerted and snorted. Leaning over I switched on the ignition and blew the horn. The rhino—duly startled out of his wits—took off. Thankfully, we had seen the last angry rhino for the day—or so we thought.

Setting off in the car in the direction of the elephant, we had hardly gone three-quarters of a mile when we heard a fusillade of shots. We stopped and glassed the country, but saw nothing. More shots—they were coming from the direction of the elephant, Edward, and Art. Quickly I decided on the direction in which they were firing. Incredibly, I saw them sitting on top of the upright elephant through my binoculars. Driving to my left, I approached the elephant from the opposite direction to which they were regarding an enemy unseen by me. On my arriving a few yards from the elephant, Edward pointed out a rhino not 30 yards from them, apparently dead and sitting upright.

My .470 in my hands, I got out of the car.

Immediately I was treated to a tirade of complaints from Arthur. 'You abandoned me in the bush to my fate!' he shouted. 'And I am lucky to be alive!' He was the epitome of an excited Italian. It did not take me long to obtain the story of what had happened.

113

Both Arthur and Edward had sat on the ground with their backs resting against the elephant, watching me walk away into the distance. Shortly after I had disappeared they felt the elephant move behind them. Edward stood up and climbed onto the elephant's foot to look over its back.

There, not five feet from him, was a rhino. There was no tree in sight, the only refuge being on top of the elephant's back. Grabbing Arthur's arm and putting his fingers to his lips, Edward coaxed Arthur onto the elephant's back.

Arthur was speechless and petrified. The rhino backed off, snorting.

'No shoot! No shoot!' said Edward. (He knew rhino were strictly protected in the area.) The rhino, hearing Edward's entreaties, charged the elephant and repeatedly horned its carcass, causing the elephant to rock uncontrollably. This was understandably unnerving to the two elephant jockeys perched on its back. The dialogue continued: 'No shoot! No shoot!' said Edward. The rhino continued its altercations, and the carcass of the elephant rocked dangerously, threatening to spill Arthur and Edward onto the ground in front of the rhino.

Finally my Italian-American friend could stand it no longer. By now there were more than 30 holes in the elephant's carcass made by the irate rhino. His .458 Winchester deterred it somewhat, but not until it had charged twice more was Arthur able to get a fatal shot into the rhino, so unsteady had become his perch on the elephant's back. Heart-shot, the bull rhino lumbered off a few yards, where it collapsed and died, sitting upright, just like the elephant. The rhino's horn measured 14 inches.

After everyone had cooled off, we had a predicament on our hands. We had shot a rhino in a protected area without a licence in the most bizarre and unbelievable circumstances. There was only one thing to be done: the matter had to be reported to the game department. I carried in the car at all times a radio telephone with its 50-foot wire aerial. Operated by the car's 12-volt battery, this had a range of more than 500 miles. I set up the radio and made the call.

As luck would have it, David Brown, the newly appointed chief game warden, was in and prepared to take the call. As I described what had happened with some embarrassment, I could well imagine the look of incredulity creeping over his face.

'Strange things happen, stranger than fiction', he said. 'All right, John. Carry on with the safari; bring in the horn, headskin, and feet, and if the facts that you have reported can be substantiated we will see about Mr. Santomo keeping the trophies on payment of the licence fee'.

I was very relieved to hear this outcome of what could have blown up into a difficult matter. At the end of the safari, we duly presented ourselves with the trophy to David Brown at game department headquarters in Nairobi and, after talking to the gunbearers and Arthur and me, he duly settled the matter. The elephant's tusks were a nicely matched pair, each weighing 85 pounds.

A day or two later we left the area. In so doing we passed another safari camp just before we reached the main Mombasa-Nairobi road. The camp was some 50 yards off the road. As we approached, a European in safari clothes strode out and stopped us. Without the perfunctory greetings, he demanded to know where his professional hunter was.

I wished him good morning and told him I had no idea.

'He's gone off with my companion—a lady', he said, 'and has not come back since yesterday lunchtime'.

'OK', I said, letting out the clutch and beginning to move the car forward, 'I'll stop and send him to you post haste if I see him'. At that moment I remembered where I had seen that only too familiar face. It was none other than Stewart Granger. 'Yes', I thought, 'most unaccustomed to losing a lady friend. Stewart Granger of all people'.

When hunting a female rhino with an impressive horn of 30 inches, with Austria's Duke of Rotibor, I had a narrow escape. The duke had, it was believed, heart-shot the rhino, but she had a calf nearly as big as herself. (It was permitted to shoot a female if the calf was of this size.) The calf covered the female rhino, which did not go down, preventing further shots. She had been hit in the lungs. We had, therefore, to wait. As there was an easily climbable tree nearby and I had no wish to shoot the calf in self-defence, I told the duke to climb the tree, which he did with consummate ability. At that moment both rhino charged.

As the tree was occupied, I positioned myself behind a small thorn tree no bigger than myself and had no alternative but to hope for the best. I knelt rooted to the spot without a movement. The rhino parted on both sides of me, the calf within two feet on my left and the cow to my right. As the cow passed a great gout of pink blood gushed from her side and saturated me from head to foot. They rushed blindly on, the cow falling over dead 100 yards beyond. I was a sorry, stinking sight when the rest of the party converged on me, and I was forced to travel in one

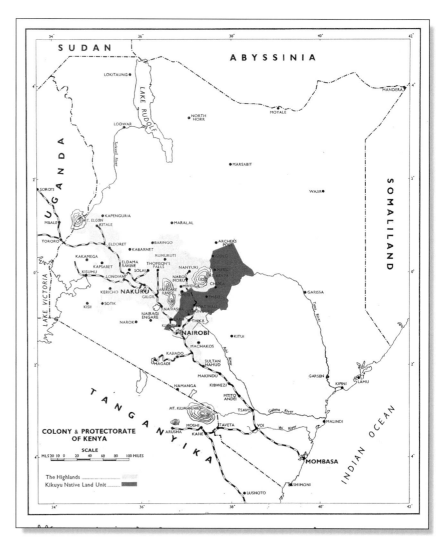

Kenya showing the Mau Mau area shaded darkly. The lightly shaded area shows where a permit to travel and hunt were required due to terrorist activity, and the unshaded areas were unaffected, making booking a hunt possible.

car by myself whilst they all piled into the other. I took the hot water first that evening, washing with the best Austrian perfumed soap.

It is interesting to note that professional big-game hunting continued in Kenya in spite of certain areas being out of bounds to all persons. The Northern Frontier District, Masailand, and eastern Kenya were unaffected. From 1952 to 1956, 11 503 terrorists were killed (many by their own people), 1035 were captured and wounded, 1150 were captured in action, 2714 surrendered, and 26 625 were arrested.

At the same time security forces casualties were as follows:

Europeans: 63 killed and 101 wounded
Asians: three killed and 12 wounded
Africans: 101 killed and 1469 wounded

Local civilian casualties were as follows:

Europeans: 32 killed and 26 wounded
Asians: 26 killed and 36 wounded
Africans: 1819 killed and 916 wounded

The total cost of the Mau Mau rebellion at the end of 1956 to all parties was £55 585 424 ($2.83 to the pound sterling).

A total of 37 500 privately owned firearms, almost entirely sporting rifles, were deposited in the Gilgil Firearms Repository between 1952 and 1956, a veritable Aladdin's cave to firearms collectors and entrepreneurs. The redistribution of these firearms after the end of the emergency can well be imagined. For some seven years, there was no hunting permitted in the Aberdare Mountains and the mountains and forests of Mount Kenya, but considerable game control measures were carried out by Kenya Game Department staff, many of whom were acting in the dual capacity of game warden and member of the security forces.

Whilst only 63 Europeans were killed in direct action by Mau Mau terrorists, the world's attention was particularly concentrated by the media on the political use of witchcraft and oath-taking in primitive societies in regards to the Ruck murders. Mr. Ruck was beheaded and cut to pieces by machetes, as were his children, one of whom escaped by hiding. His pregnant wife was forced to watch and then disembowelled of her child and left to die. Such incidents evoked the strongest sentiments of revulsion and revenge in all races in Kenya. My father (Commissioner of Police and sometime Attorney General of Kenya, Colonel A.J. Kingsley-Heath) had repeatedly warned the then governor of Kenya that the Mau Mau movement was developing as early as 1943, but his warnings went unheeded. Significantly, it was my father's long-time brother officers from the Palestine police who were called upon to stamp out the Mau Mau rebellion and who knew well that he had appraised the problem correctly.

Whilst operating in Botswana as well as Kenya, my partner Lionel Palmer came to East Africa during the Botswana 'off' season to help me in conducting safaris there. Doug Wright also joined us. On one occasion, we had on safari Peter Alport, the then owner of 'Norm Thompson', a large U.S.-based mail order company. He and his friend Arthur Rasmussen (a Mercedes car dealer from Portland, Oregon) wanted to hunt elephants in the Meru area of northern Kenya.

We had spotted a big tusker we thought would go to 100 pounds a side. The grass was long, and it was very hot. To get to the elephant, the stalk involved a walk over rough ground and through long grass. Peter, whose heart was suspect, decided that discretion was the better part of valour and called off the hunt. We returned to the small rocky track that led back to the road and the car, walking single file. A gunbearer led the way, followed by our clients and then me. Behind me walked Lionel and, bringing up the rear, a game scout. The next thing I knew there was a shout from the game scout and a rattle from an empty aluminium water bottle. Sensing that danger was imminent, I threw myself to the left into some long grass under a small bush. Lionel had the same inclination, and, shouting a warning to the clients, we ended up in a heap together. Past us charged an irate rhino that had come up unsuspected on the game scout at the rear. The rhino had hooked his horn under the game scout's belt, snapping it and releasing the empty water bottle, which clattered amongst the rocks. The game scout—partly assisted by the rhino—flew over some large boulders to his right and up a small tree, where he clung for dear life, looking like an over-ripe apple about to fall off at any second. The rhino charged on, leaving us all cursing his name.

TANGANYIKA (TANZANIA)

The Hombolo Rhino

On another occasion in central Tanganyika, when hunting with my old friend Dick Ayer, the game department had directed us to put an end to an irate rhino that was terrorising women who were going down to collect water from the Hombolo dam. The dam was some two acres in extent and the water development department had made sure that the local people were not allowed to cut down the thicker bush to the north and south for fear that the ground would become eroded with the heavy rain, and so depreciate and eventually destroy the dam. The rhino lived in the thick bush surrounding the dam, from which, from time to time, it could proceed to other areas. The dam was its only source of water.

Dick and I made a reconnaissance of the area, during which the rhino indicated that it was present but invisible in the thicket.

'We are about to become involved in some "postgraduate" hunting', I informed Dick. We both had heavy double-barrelled rifles. We decided that between 11.00 in the morning and 4.00 that afternoon would be the time to try and get the rhino. This would be his siesta time, when he would have most likely sat down in his usual resting place in some shade. A rhino's oft-used midday resting spot in the dry, arid bush of East Africa is under a euphorbia tree, or *Euphorbia candelabra*. It is, as its name implies, a tree reminiscent of an aerated umbrella. It is a cactus type of tree that exudes a white, milky sap when the branches are broken. There were a number of these trees in the thicket.

Having consulted with my gunbearer and made sure that no one from the village would collect water during our war period, I posted both of our gunbearers in different positions up trees to see if they could locate the tick birds that would undoubtedly be accompanying the rhino. About midday the agreed signal was given: a waving white handkerchief. The birds—and hopefully the rhino—had been spotted. We gave it another half hour to make sure there were no other birds in other trees, telling of another rhino.

We entered the thick and thorny bush on all fours, dragging our heavy double rifles by the barrel over our right arms and checking the safety catches frequently. Very slowly we headed in the direction of the tree, which we could not see. After we had been crawling for half an hour, leaving behind us a giant drag mark in the dust as though a huge python had passed that way, I stopped for a whispered conference. Very slowly, in a small gap in the bushes, I stood up.

The tree was 35 yards away and slightly to my left. The wind still blew well from the rhino to us, with occasional gusts that rattled the dry bush around us and concealed the noise we made as we proceeded. We commenced our final approach.

Having gone another 10 yards, I found my face within 18 inches of a large puff adder snuggled down in the sand ahead of me. Bringing my beret over my face to protect myself as best I could, I began a slow retreat. Dick, being about six feet four inches in his socks, which made crawling about in the thicket difficult, was somewhat put out, but slowly we retreated without provoking the snake. It was a near thing. Puff adders, though sluggish in movement, strike fast, and their bites are mostly fatal. A whispered conversation took place, and we changed direction.

Soon we were within 15 yards of the tree. Moving slightly to my right, I saw the huge bulk of the rhino sideways to us. There was just

Crisp work for heavy doubles. At left a Holland & Holland .465/500. At right a .470 Westley Richards. Note the fine camera at left.

room for us, lying closely side by side, to get a shot into the heart behind the shoulder.

Up came our double rifles. This was it. Dick, who had spent most of the war in the U.S. Marine Corps, gave me a look as though he was about to go over the top in Okinawa and bent to his aim. I followed his shot instantaneously. Under the circumstances two bullets were better than one. Clouds of thick, red, choking dust arose from around us, brought about by the explosions of two shots of heavy-calibre rifles fired

so close to the ground. We could see nothing, let alone each other. The rhino hit the bush full tilt, and it was a second or two before we realised that it was, thankfully, going away from us. Thousands of guinea fowl, which had been dust bathing beyond the rhino, flew into the air squawking and screeching. As the dust began to clear there was a crash some distance into the bush beyond us, followed by a noise as though bushes were being flattened and a pig-like cry. He was down.

We stood up and made our way to the euphorbia tree. We looked at

Me and Dick Ayer with the Hombolo rhino reported to have killed a woman and injured others (1957).

each other—we were filthy but victorious, and it had been pretty exciting. Everywhere around there were signs of the rhino. He had used the spot as a siesta haven for some considerable time. Slowly we followed the rhino's tracks, and 75 yards on we came upon him lying on his side, very dead. A few minutes later we heard the clinking of cans and the noise of metal upon metal. The shots had told the village that meat was now available. Men, women, and children arrived ready to carry home much-needed protein. After I shouted to my gunbearers to mobilise the local gentry, they cut a path to where we stood and cleared a large circle round the rhino. After pictures and the removal of the horn, some hide, and the feet, which took two hours, nothing was left except a wet spot in the sand. A menace had been removed.

Paramount Rhinos

Eric Rundgren, who was a co-director of Ker & Downey Safaris, had been staying with his old friend Woody Krieger in Los Angeles and was introduced to Howard Hawks and his associates, who were contemplat-

Conferring as to the best way to produce the rhino for the film (1961).

ing making the film *Hatari*, which is the Swahili word for danger. Eric persuaded them to send over a reconnaissance team to East Africa, which he took on a tour of all the possible sites and introduced them to the directors of national parks in Kenya and Tanganyika. The team was very impressed and, having met Jack Block, the managing director of Ker & Downey Safaris (and the leading businessman and hotelier of Nairobi), decided that Ker & Downey was the best available company to handle the business.

Arusha, Tanganyika, was chosen as the headquarters for all operations. Backup came from the Ker & Downey office, where Ron Stephens, the company's manager, proved equal to the daunting task of handling all the problems and supplying all that was needed. As I lived in Arusha, it was decided that I should be in charge of the wildlife side of the film company's requirements. Eric was required to keep the safaris going, as the company could not afford to abandon its normal business. The wildlife operations required eight professional hunters, not all of whom were company men, who were hired into the scheme on a daily basis with their hunting cars.

The task facing me, required by the film company, was to present wild animals of the company's choice to the camera in circumstances that suited the script. Naturally, the animals had not read the script! The film was the story of a wild animal trapper and his crew. The stars consisted of John Wayne, 'Red' Buttons, Hardy Kruger, Elsa Martinelli, John Cabot, Michelle Gauderan, and several others. The actors were all involved in the first unit's filming at the ranch at Momella, where the story unfolded. The second unit was responsible for obtaining action pictures with a local animal catcher's staff doubling for the actors. Willie de Beer, who had a thriving wild-game trapping business near Arusha, was well versed

Top: The camera car and catching car set out.

Middle: The rhino puts its best foot forward.

Bottom: The camera car and catching car get into position.

Top: The rhino has other ideas

Middle: The noose is over the rhino's head.

Bottom: The action goes on record in the camera car.

125

Keith Mousley on the set of Hatari, *flying the Piper Tripacer.*

and able in this profession, which is why he and his staff were chosen. I had to work closely with Willie.

The second unit was located in a large tented camp for more than 50 people in the yellow fever trees on the north-east corner of Lake Manyara, a mile or so outside the park. In front of the camp was a large open plain, and within 100 yards was a smooth green patch of short grass that served as an airstrip.

A small air charter company, called Wilken Aviation, had recently been formed in Nairobi. It employed three pilots: George Hodgkinson, John Falconer Taylor, and Keith Mousley. Each flew a Tripacer aircraft. Mousley was the second unit pilot, and I spent long periods flying with him game spotting. After some initial experience, we found some of the flying rather tricky in this type of aircraft because of its design and handling: it was difficult to push an animal out of thick bush into an open area to be photographed. After some consultation over a few beers one evening, we devised a plan.

Keith, through contacts in Kenya, managed to find a Piper Super Cub with a 105-horsepower engine and double (one behind the other) wheels. This aircraft in the hands of Keith, who is still a brilliant pilot, was the nearest thing to a helicopter! The double wheels, of which the rear contained a braking gear, enabled him to land and at the same time, with the nose partially raised and the brakes on, to literally stop the plane within 40 or 50 yards. It was therefore easy to make almost instantaneous airstrips wherever we were.

For my part, I lined up five of the eight professional hunters and had painted all the roofs of their cars, each with a different colour. Each hunter had a radio, which enabled me to call from the air each car according to its roof colour. Keith took care of the flying whilst I called each car by its colour into position round the rhino that we wished to push into the flat plain, where it would be caught by the catching car and filmed from the camera car. The camera car had more than 80 shock absorbers with a large, heavy Mitchell camera mounted in the centre. Once Keith and I had spotted the rhino, we would land and brief the hunters in the cars. They got into position based upon the direction of the wind. Keith and I would take off and call them into position, approximately into a rough 'U'. The 'U' gently pushed the rhino into the open; however, not all the rhinos were cooperative, and occasionally a hunter's car would be severely mauled, which necessitated that a recovery vehicle come to his aid. The film company stood the bill for repairs.

Daily, the convoy of some 35 vehicles would set out at seven o'clock in the morning for the chosen operating area. Paul Helmick, the director of the second unit, luckily was a reasonable person and realised that we were attempting something that had never been done before, even though all of the professional hunters had considerable experience with dangerous game. Fortunately, we had early success, so Howard Hawks was able to see some progress early on. He was impressed, so we secured some breathing space. Initially, we concentrated on the Mtu-Wa-Mbu area near Lake Manyara and worked the floor of the Rift Valley heading north to the Nguruka Depression. The country was open thorn bush strewn with lava boulders. If driven through by one car, there was little dust, but when 30 vehicles followed the same tracks, the volcanic dust rose heavenward for all to see for some 20 miles. Any following wind made it impossible to avoid the dust, and the camera crew had to devise all manner of gadgets to keep their equipment clean. There were plenty of rhino, and on one occasion we pushed four into the camera car area. Rhino are notorious for having minds of their own, and two of them submitted to the attention of the catching car, but the other two decided that the camera car would be easy meat. Only the intervention of Keith with the Piper Super Cub at zero feet saved the camera car, which had 'bellied up' on a lava rock.

The second area tried was in the region of the Amboselli National Park on the Tanganyika side of the international boundary. There was a large rhino population there in the thickets of yellow fever trees, which were surrounded by dry alkaline pans on which a car could travel at considerable speed without a whisper of a bump. Airstrips were everywhere. We also had success there.

On one occasion I decided to do a stint of ground work, so Keith had the radio's microphone. He called me up to a small patch of bush in which he had seen a rhino—a good bull with a substantial horn. The rhino declined to move out. I proceeded in the car, pushing the bush down in front of me until I was in the centre of the thicket. The rhino did not like his privacy disturbed. Such was the density of the bush that the next thing I knew the rhino was hitting the front wheel and lifting the car on its side, precariously close to turning over. As the car returned to an even keel I shifted my position into the centre seat—not an instant too soon. The rhino struck the bottom of the door, missing the petrol tank by a few inches—the horn stopped six inches from my leg. Luckily, he did not push his head upwards; had he done so, he would have whipped off the steering wheel with his horn.

The radio came in. 'How are you doing?' asked Keith from his safe and lofty perch.

The rhino answered by hitting the front wheel again.

'Did you hear that noise?' I asked Keith. 'That was the rhino murdering my car!'

'Sorry', he said, 'I can't see you from here'.

'If I'm not out in half an hour you better try to rescue me', I said. 'It will be dark in an hour's time'.

Keith flew off. My shotgun was now in my hands and I fired both barrels just past the rhino's ear. He didn't like it and left. I heard later that he had appeared from the rear in the wake of the other hunting cars, which had found a rhino and were just about to launch it into the area for the camera car.

Chaos ensued. The camera car went to photograph the first rhino, closely pursued by the second. The driver of the camera car by this time had a little experience and, by using a little intuitive driving, left the catching car sandwiched between two rhino. Willie de Beer, who was driving the catching car, managed to handle it, but the two rhino then proceeded to fight each other, not realising that their mutual quarry had escaped. The camera car had a great day, and my car had independent suspension on both front wheels.

I returned 'upstairs' the next day. We spent more than two months dealing with rhino, buffalo, and elephant in similar fashion. No animal or human being was injured, and all the animals caught were successfully returned back into their environment.

CHAPTER FOUR

BUFFALO HUNTING

The Mean Ruminant

GENERAL OBSERVATIONS

In almost all the areas described in this book, there occurred the southern race of Cape buffalo (*Syncerus caffer caffer*). Only in western Ethiopia and the Sudan did I encounter the smaller 'red' type of buffalo known as the northern race (*Syncerus caffer aequinoctialis*). There were no buffalo of either race in Somaliland or Eritrea, but both races occurred in Uganda and southern and western Ethiopia. However, in the area between the Kenya border and the Duwa Parma River in southern Ethiopia, I believe the southern race has disappeared, thanks to systematic poaching and the use of Italian carbines 'rescued' during the 1939-45 War. Certainly, this was the case when I hunted buffalo there in the early 1950s.

As Rowland Ward declares in the latest edition of *Records of Big Game*, the African buffalo is probably the most challenging trophy to sportsmen. Certainly the several pages of entries in the record book indicate this to be the case. At the risk of disagreeing with my contemporaries, I believe that the real measurement of a trophy buffalo is the outside width measurement of its horns. Furthermore, in my era, a buffalo that had horns that were soft where they came together at the centre of the head, was not regarded as a mature buffalo and, therefore, the horns were not a real trophy. Such a head invariably had long curly horns culminating in a hook backwards, with the tips

With only a split second of warning, there came an outraged buffalo—1500 pounds of sheer fury—tearing down the path, leaving me no time to move. The hook of his horn caught the uppers of my desert boot . . .

—J.K.-H.

129

Top: 'I know you are there.'

Right: Massive body, tremendous curl, soft on top—yesterday's immature bull; today, 'Shoot him, Merana, him big one!'

pointing to the ground. In all my experience over the years 1949–78 and afterwards, I never saw a case of a human being mauled or killed from an attack by this type of horned buffalo. Quite the reverse was the case with what I humbly regard as the genuine trophy buffalo. A buffalo with a heavy, hard, seasoned *boss* (the part where the solid horn meets at the centre of the head) has invariably worn down his horns to wicked-looking sharp tips that curl slightly inwards. The mature buffalo, being older and wiser than the younger bulls first described, has learned to use his weight and horns to earn the position of a senior

130

breeding bull in a herd. Therefore, to be attacked by a beast of this description is more often than not fatal. These are the bulls that become experienced at being hunted and are capable of trapping their pursuers by leading them on in circles and then lying in wait as they unsuspectingly pass by. When such a situation occurs, one's back is against the proverbial wall and shoot to kill is the order of the day—and one's passport to survival. The chips are down!

Perusal of the record book shows that most of the largest and most impressive heads come from the areas between 5000 and 8000 feet in

Top: Bill Wetzel hunted this buffalo with great 'boss' and wicked hooks with Lionel Palmer. The horns were 46 inches wide (1968).

Bottom: Me with a similar buffalo with horns 45 inches wide. Note the hooks and solidly formed bosses of both buffalo, indicative of those generally found on the islands of the Okavango Swamps.

131

elevation, and nearly all are from Masailand in both Kenya and Tanzania. In the high forests of the Aberdares and Mount Kenya there were great opportunities for hunting huge trophy heads of buffalo. Many of these were shot on game control in the wheat fields of surrounding farms. This also occurred in the west Kilimanjaro area of Tanzania. Whilst farming there in the early 1960s, buffalo that came out of the canopy forest into the wheat fields in the evening were shot regularly. The veranda of the house sported five buffalo heads with horns more than 48 inches wide (outside measurement), the longest being 54 inches across. So, too, to this day does the veranda of my old friend, professional hunter, and former game warden Bill Winter in Nairobi.

In Botswana, where the country was hunted for trophies in the early 1960s, there were some of the greatest concentrations of buffalo in Africa. Alas, no more.

I regularly flew my aircraft over the Okavango Swamps to the various camps that our company maintained. In October of each year, just before the advent of the rains that normally commenced in mid-November (when the waters of the swamps had retreated after a long, dry few months), buffalo herds would number several thousand in each herd at a time. Occasionally, two or three herds would graze in close proximity to each other, giving the impression that from 800 feet the whole country as far as the eye could see was covered with buffalo. As the first rain fell, the herds moved to the periphery of the swamps to the west and east. If the rain was sufficient to fill the dried up water holes, they would leave. Not till the following year did they concentrate once again.

Within the herds were some fine heads, but I found that many older bulls did not take off with the rest of the herds at the time of the normal migration brought about by the coming of the annual rains. These buffalo we called 'island buffalo', because within the Okavango Swamps were thousands of islands. There was plenty of water and a varied diet for buffalo. Many of these older buffalo grew massive bosses to their horns, as did their East African relatives, and were equally impressive. Pro rata, I had the impression, however, that there were greater numbers of wider heads in East Africa than in Botswana, and so our trophy results proved. Interestingly, the same concentrations of buffalo herds occurred in southern and western Tanzania in October in the regions of the Katavi Game Reserve, Lake Rukwa, and the upper reaches of the Malagarasi River in the Myowosi swamps.

KENYA

In 1949 the human population of Kenya was approximately 5.5 million. In 1996 the population was approximately 30 million. The explanation for this increase is best described by this little story.

On my return to Kenya from the Botswana season with my Kenyan staff, I had a pay parade for them all. Their contract was for payment for every day they were absent from Kenya plus food, clothing, and tips from visiting clients. On this occasion one person, a gunbearer, was missing. The other staff were paid, and back into my pocket went the missing man's wages. Early next day, I was about my appointments in town when a touch on my arm brought me face to face with my absent gunbearer.

'Where the hell have you been?' I asked.

'You see, Bwana', he said with a grin from ear to ear, 'whilst I was away each of my three wives gave birth to a child, and so to be sure what to do with my money I decided to visit with them first. I am sorry for inconveniencing you!'

The vast pastures of Kenya bush no longer exist for much of the buffalo population, but in the early 1950s I well remember a buffalo's being shot on a coffee estate that was almost where downtown Nairobi is today. Buffalo were very common and in large numbers. The best heads could be hunted in Masailand and on the high forested slopes of Kenya's mountains. Much of these areas were bounded by farms, and large numbers of buffalo were therefore shot as crop raiders. On nights with a full moon many a raider met his end. Buffalo horns 50 inches wide were not uncommon in these areas, and many a veranda or 'stoop' of a farmhouse had a monster set of horns on display. In Nanyuki, a town in central Kenya between the Aberdare Mountains and Mount Kenya, the game department had both a game control officer and a game warden.

Quite a number of East African professional hunters gained experience in hunting dangerous game by taking up employment as temporary game control officers. The game department had its headquarters for some time in game warden Myles Turner's family home, which had been purchased from his family. Here the department kept a pack of dogs that was used to hunt buffalo in the thick forest, into which they retreated after raiding crops. Elephant, buffalo, rhino, leopard, and lion all

133

A good example of three fine bull buffalo with heavy boss meeting well in the middle of the head. Note the bull at far right with head up—it has big curly horns but is not mature.

occurred in the area, and in some cases the poor pack of dogs got more than they expected by way of opposition.

As Kenya developed its agricultural assets after the war, pressure to eliminate marauding animals that were damaging cultivations became greater. It was always possible for a hard-pressed game warden to direct hunting safaris into the area where marauding game and rogue animals had to be eliminated to take trophies. In the early days, Nanyuki was the main headquarters from which these arrangements were carried out. Game wardens Fred Bartlett, Don Bousfield, and Rodney Elliot ran this operation with great success. They were followed by Jack Barrah.

During the Mau Mau emergency, these wardens and many others were also heavily committed to antiterrorist operations. On one occasion

Don Bousfield, whilst on an antiterrorist patrol, was hit in the chest and ribs with two bullets from a Sten gun, which knocked him down. Fortunately, he was wearing a shirt with large pockets that contained maps that had been folded many times over like a wad or a book, which slowed the bullets down appreciably. When asked if he was all right, Don said yes and attempted to walk. However, after taking a few steps he noticed blood coming out of his trouser leg and passed out.

Don recovered completely. Alas, fate decreed that, in later years, of all things he was to be run over by a train in the early morning mist at Karatina whilst travelling down to Nairobi in his car to take out a safari.

Perhaps the best remembered game warden at Nanyuki as the Mau Mau emergency came to an end was Bill Winter. No one could have had

Top: Buffalo in the bamboo forests of Mount Kenya. Note the body size: looks like a bad-tempered bastard.

Bottom: The 'Bailey' bridge over the Tana River at Garissa, Kenya, built by British Army engineers for the campaign against the Italians in Somalia and Ethiopia during the 1939–45 War (1954).

a better game-control organisation going than he did. He was incredibly helpful to many, many hunters with their clients, but woe betide the hunter who traded on his good nature and flirted with the law.

Game wardens in those years were paid a pittance. Any warden who was married and had a family could not afford to live on his government emoluments. So Bill Winter joined the ranks of professional hunters, for a time running his own safari company. He became a long-time and revered friend and visited us in Botswana on several occasions. His son, also Bill Winter, runs the best photographic safari in Kenya today.

Farther west in Kenya Masailand the country was more open, and here the buffalo sometimes numbered several hundred in a herd. Here,

too, groups of bulls were sometimes found in open country. The list of record heads shows that by far the largest and widest buffalo heads in Africa came from this area.

Posterity has to be grateful for the outstanding conservation work of Major L. Temple-Boreham, M.C., the game warden in charge of Masailand, who was based at Narok. The strictest rules were enforced upon visiting professional hunters. If a dirty campsite was left, it was invariably found by 'T.-B.'s' Piper Super Cub patrol, which he flew by himself. The offending hunter could be banned from Masailand for months. T.-B., however, never bore a grudge, never had a favourite, never varied his rules, and was rightly respected by all with whom he came in contact.

Towards the east of Kenya the land descended from the 5000-foot plateau to sea level at the coast. Here the country was dry, receiving a good deal less rainfall than elsewhere. Temperatures and humidity were

Ed Quinn, then senior vice president of the Chrysler Corporation of America, with a fine 45-inch buffalo shot in the shadow of Mount Kilimanjaro, Kenya (block 66) in 1964.

much higher, and lush vegetation was seasonally limited. The trophy heads were less massive and narrower in width. Sometimes, as if to prove the theory, there were exceptions, but this was seldom the case. The buffalo population of Kenya was mostly static and did not migrate as it did in parts of other African countries. During this period, if one was asked to plan a hunt for trophy buffalo for a month's safari, one would, in all probability, choose first to camp in an area of some attraction and beauty, where plains game was available for camp meat. Such an area might be east of Kilimanjaro at Loitokitok, in western Masailand, south of Narok, or well north in the Maralal area on the Lerogi Plateau. If no trophy buffalo were to be found, perhaps the next 10 days might be spent—when both one's clients and oneself were a little fitter—in either the Aberdare Forest or an area on the slopes of Mount Kenya. Game department officers were invariably most helpful, and perseverance usually brought about the obtaining of a trophy head between 40 and 43 inches wide.

It was unusual for a client who wished to shoot a trophy buffalo to go home without one, but it was inevitable that there were casualties amongst both hunters and game wardens. Bill Winter himself, after becoming a professional hunter some years later, had a buffalo fall across him after he had shot it dead at point-blank range. Someone thought that the buffalo was still alive, and another bullet was put into it. It smashed Bill's lower leg. After many painful graft operations, Bill made a better-than-expected recovery. Not so fortunate was Tony Catchpole, who was caught with too small a calibre rifle and ammunition—he was killed. Glen Cottar was badly raked about the legs and was lucky to make a remarkable recovery. Reggie Destro was knocked down but uninjured. Game scouts particularly suffered injuries and death from buffaloes wounded by poachers and rogue buffaloes as well.

TANGANYIKA (TANZANIA)

Most people in the Western world of today have no idea what the phrase 'subsistence economy' means in real terms. In the parts of Africa covered by this book, there are no supermarkets or malls—99 percent of the population grow their own food. They are therefore 'subsistent economists', and today's Western way of life has not reached them. Probably 75 percent of those living in Tanzania attempt to grow all or part of their diet. In plain and simple language, this means that a person must clear a piece of ground—cutting down trees and foliage and prob-

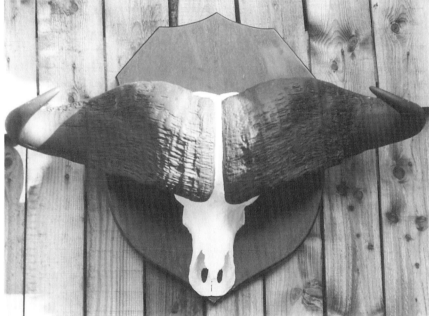

ably burning it—and till the ground. A seed must be planted, rain must fall, the sun must shine, and the seed or fruit must grow and then be harvested. Once the land has been used once or twice for this purpose, a new plot is cleared.

But the consumption of the environment does not end there. The produce has to be cooked. Heat has to be produced. Trees must be felled, as wood is the only fuel available. No thought is given to saving for fuel the trees cut down when the land for cultivation is first cleared. As the population multiplies three times in 40 years, so does the attendant stocks of cattle and goats. This incredible consumption and destruc-

Top: A 50-inch Tanganyika buffalo.

Bottom: These 42 1/2-inch horns with heavy boss came from a nasty buffalo shot on Mount Kilimanjaro.

Top: A buffalo caught and anesthetised on the set of Hatari.

Right: Bringing back the 43-inch-wide head of Arnie Garza-Vale's buffalo at Lake Rukwa.

tion of the environment continues today, gathering in momentum. The competition for water resources is intense between humans with their stock and wildlife.

No greater demonstration of this can be seen than in Tanzania. In the period covered by this book, there was probably the greatest population of buffalo in Tanganyika of any country in Africa. Huge areas of the country were pristine wilderness. No better examples of this existed than the Selous Game Reserve and the Serengeti Plains.

The main hotel in Arusha in the middle 1950s. My hunting car is on the right.

Hunting for buffalo in Tanganyika in those years was not worthy of prime consideration when planning a safari, for buffalo existed in nearly every area a safari was likely to visit. Unless a hunter wished to specifically hunt buffalo, one simply collected a good trophy in the area in which one happened to be hunting at the time. Normally, if a record class head was required, western Masailand would be the area in which to plan such a hunt. In the early days covered by this discourse, there was no extension of the Serengeti National Park northwards to the Kenya border. This area was known as the Serengeti Partial Game Reserve. Only lion and leopard were protected here. From this area (on either side of the Kenya-Tanganyika border) came such record heads that Andrew Holmberg secured many years ago and are recorded in Rowland Ward's *Records of Big Game.* The largest of these heads was 58 inches in width between the horns with a boss of 14 inches in width. Three of the first six entries in the record book came from this area.

The largest recorded horn spread of a bull buffalo from here came from Maswa, a few miles farther south but in exactly similar country. Derrick Dunn, an old friend and my next-door farmer on the slopes of Mount Kilimanjaro, had his client shoot a head of 59 and 5/16 inches wide, which won the Shaw & Hunter Trophy for Derrick for a record second time.

On one occasion, when hunting in the region of the Nesheshaw rock outcrop close to the Kenya border, I saw and photographed an enormous bull buffalo that could well have been of record size. Our licence had been filled, and although we hunted for that buffalo several times later, we never saw him again. There were several buffalo on licence, and of course they made excellent lion and leopard bait. The Loliondo area of

141

north Masailand, which was bordered on the north by the Kenya boundary and ran west until the Mara River entered Tanganyika from the north, provided a very favourite hunting area by many professional hunters. Attention had been drawn to this area originally by Al Klien, an American resident of Kenya in the 1920s and 1930s, who gave his name to the present-day Klien's Camp. When I first visited the spot in the early 1950s, the walls of his rondavel still stood and traces of his vegetable garden were still evident. His practice was to come down by road in his Model A Ford safari car, accompanied by his truck, and camp for the season in this spot, bringing his clients in from time to time. The country, having an average altitude of 6000 feet, was beautiful, open grassland interspersed with heavily wooded, small watercourses. Huge piles of basalt rocks occurred, providing wonderful hiding places for cats and roosting spots for numerous olive baboons. One of my clients described his hunting experiences here like this: 'Gee, John, I never thought hunting would be like taking candy from kids'.

Masailand Bushbuck

Most often I camped on the Bologonja Stream, an idyllic site in the deep shade of some huge, old olive trees and a favourite spot many years earlier of Stuart Edward White, an American explorer and hunter. On several occasions, I walked out of camp into the sunlight and saw buffalo grazing peacefully no more than 40 yards away.

Sometimes we (myself, clients, and staff) looked over as many as 100 bull buffalo before taking one. At other times we decided to have a little more fun. Perhaps in hindsight we were a little misguided in our attitude towards buffalo, but at that time we always made an effort to improve our sporting experiences. This took the form of beating some of the bigger watercourses, with all the staff on foot armed with every available saucepan and tin can. I stationed a client with a gunbearer at strategic points on either bank where they had a clear field of fire and a convenient tree to which retreat could be made. I often had an apprentice with me, whom I stationed with the beaters and armed with my .404 Cogswell & Harrison if he did not have a gun. I myself found a position in the middle of the watercourse bed, usually on a fallen log or low tree trunk that gave me a little height so that I could see over the bushes in front of me and get some idea of what was coming.

After studying the tracks on both sides of the watercourse, we had some indication of what might be in the thickets. However, there were always surprises. After synchronising our watches, the din began. It was easy to tell when an animal was sighted, for the cans were beaten faster and the shouts went up an octave in tone.

I remember two occasions when the beats were very successful. The first occurred when four good bull buffalo came belting up a little valley towards me. I hitched myself a few more feet up into a tree and shouted and waved my hat at them. They split, two going out of the bush and up the bank to the right and two to the left. Each client, therefore, had two buffalo coming towards him.

The fire zone had been agreed upon. As with wild boar shooting in Europe, the buffalo had to pass to the rear of the shooter before a shot could be fired. This gave both clients a shot behind the shoulder of the buffalo diagonally towards the opposite shoulder. Both pairs of buffalo passed within 25 yards of each client, and both clients made excellent shots, being able to choose the biggest head quite easily. Two buffalo with horns of 45 inches resulted. (This method was also ideal for collecting bushbuck and reedbuck.)

On the second occasion, I was beating for buffalo with only one client when the most magnificent maned lion appeared. It was a mercy he did so, for he had a broken leg and would have been pulled down by hyenas within a few days.

These beats, as can be well imagined, were not without incident. On one occasion a young vervet monkey fell out of a sapling as one of the beaters passed by, landing on the beater's shoulder and neck. It seemed to think it was in familiar surroundings and refused to let go. The beater stopped, and peals of laughter ensued. At first he was petrified, believing that he had been seized by a python, as he was not able to see what animal had fastened upon him. He had his leg pulled unmercifully by his companions thereafter.

On another occasion, I was standing on a log some five feet above a game path that ran below and parallel to me. With only a split second of warning, there came an outraged buffalo—1500 pounds of sheer fury—tearing down the path, leaving me no time to move. The hook of his horn caught the uppers of my desert boot and took the shoe off my foot in an instant—a lucky escape. Two or three inches nearer and it would have taken my leg and ankle off. Scarcely more exciting times were possible.

On one occasion, when leaving the Loliondo Controlled Area on completion of a particularly successful safari with Dick and Norma Ayer, we came across an empty hunting car parked by the side of the

Bohor Reedbuck

143

track. At that moment, two shots of a heavy rifle went off amidst much crashing and shouting in a large patch of bush 200 yards from us. Taking my .470 and Edward, my gunbearer, I walked towards the patch of bush. As I arrived at its edge, there came two gunbearers carrying my old friend Owen McCullum.

'John', Owen said, 'we've had trouble with a buffalo'. Fortunately he was only shaken, but the buffalo had rushed past him, knocking him headlong into a thick olive tree. The last two shots that I had heard had finished the buffalo.

Right behind Owen out of the thicket came a good-looking girl, no less a person than Virginia Kraft. We set Owen down and gave him a stiff drink before going on our way.

Rather extraordinarily, a year later we were once again on our way out of Loliondo, when almost exactly the same thing occurred not far from the same spot. On this occasion we met John Cook and his client having an altercation with a wounded buffalo. The combined efforts of a .458, .475, .470, and .465/.500 put paid to the buffalo in quick time, and after a celebratory tot we were on our way.

In 1949, the Tanzania game licence had more than 400 animals on it, with 20 of all the common game species, including 10 buffalo. In the early 1950s, the game killed on these licences were used to feed the labour on the sisal estates, particularly in the Northern and Tanga Provinces. It was soon realised that this removal of animals was excessive, and in 1951 the Fauna Conservation Ordinance was drafted, and the number of animals allowed on a license reduced. With this came the reexamination of the whole wildlife structure of Tanzania. The Serengeti Partial Game Reserve was added to the Serengeti National Park, and similar conservation measures took place in Kenya, where the Masai-Mara Reserve tied in with the Serengeti National Park on the other side of the international border. Shortly after this came the gazetting of game-controlled areas. As big-game safaris increased, so too did the controls of their activities.

One of the largest concentrations of buffalo on the African continent today remains in the Selous Game Reserve. As already stated, this vast area was cut into many blocks and was fed by a huge river system in totally uninhabited country. It will for many years preserve the existence of the buffalo, thanks to a great extent to Brian Nicholson, the major architect of its future. The buffalo heads from the Selous were not wide or massive—very occasionally a good one was found—but then, comparatively speaking, very few were seen, so vast is the country in which the buffalo live.

BECHUANALAND (BOTSWANA)

Bechuanaland had vast areas of buffalo country. Nearly all the buffalo were of a migratory disposition and moved generally east and west across the northern part of the country. They seldom, if ever, were seen south of the Francistown-Maun road, which ran east to west. The huge area of the Okavango Swamps was an exception.

Strangely, Bechuanaland achieved interest from the hunting fraternity simply because regulations in East Africa and changes in company staff made a number of the more adventurous hunters look for new pastures. Their journeys south included visits to Rhodesia (now Zimbabwe), where their enquiries attracted interest and offers of association.

The breakup of Selby & Holmberg Ltd. had a particular influence on me and my ambitions. When a number of those who had, as I understood it, left Ker & Downey in the lurch in 1955 returned to the fold rejoicing and were issued valuable shares (which the staff of Ker & Downey Safaris Ltd. had, by their efforts, made valuable), it caused many of the newer professional hunters to reconsider their position. Economics also played a large part in their discussions, and many were forced to consider going into business on their own. Andrew Holmberg, the former partner with Harry Selby in Selby & Holmberg Ltd., did not return to Ker & Downey Safaris Ltd. and was probably the first to make a move to recce Bechuanaland. He was, however, closely followed by Harry

Top: Buffalo in Botswana's Okavango Swamps massing before the rains in October-November 1966.

Above: Kenny Kays, youngest member of the famous Maun family, P.H., guide, and interpreter to all of us who came down from East Africa. A kinder or more willing person could never be found (1963).

145

Top: A hunter's job is never done. Frank Miller talking to Phyllis Palmer on the radio after hours (1966).

Bottom: L to R: Me, Elizabeth (Elsie) Miller, Lionel Palmer, Frank Miller, and Mr. and Mrs. Jorge Palleja (1966).

Selby, who had persuaded the board of what was now Ker, Downey and Selby Safaris Ltd. to invest in safari operations in Bechuanaland. Neither Eric Rundgren nor I attended the board meetings when these decisions were made. Eric also had been in contact with the Henderson brothers of Rhodesia and was interested in establishing a hunting safari company in eastern Bechuanaland. Jack Blacklaws of Hunter's Africa Ltd. and John Lawrence, its managing director (and a long-time professional hunter as well as president of the E.A.P.H.A.), moved into the northern part of Bechuanaland and based themselves at Kasane. Jack Blacklaws, like me, was a pilot, and both of us were convinced that flying between camps in

146

country so inhospitable to vehicles was the answer to the economics of operating there.

These moves covered the period of 1963–65. In opening up Bechuanaland, finance was a huge problem. Aircraft, four-wheel drive trucks, and hunting vehicles were very expensive. Staff were totally untrained, and radio communications had not reached the standard of reliability that they have today. Sleeping sickness was ever present, and medical facilities were very poor.

By the end of 1965, having experienced the indifferent treatment that the new management meted out in spite of advice by both Eric Rundgren (rather forcefully) and me (perhaps a little more tactfully), we both left the company. Eric set up in eastern Bechuanaland, where he and the Henderson brothers, assisted by Mike Cameron, had their own company. I joined Lionel Palmer and Frank Miller in Safari South (Pty.) Ltd.

Suffice to say that at the age of 36, to be given a concession area for four years covering 50 000 square miles, to develop both for the country and your partners, was the challenge of a lifetime that can seldom be experienced by any man. My partners and I spared nothing to ensure success, and we were, on reflection, amply rewarded, without a casualty of any sort and with our reputations unsullied. Moreover, our relations with other safari companies were good. When necessary we helped each other, and we were all thankful to escape the vicissitudes and intrigues that were becoming commonplace in East Africa. In short, we settled down to a period of 10 years of wonderful hunting and companionship, flying some 15 000 hours between us without mishap and leaving, so we thought at the time, a secure wildlife population for posterity.

Of course, there were casualties, and one of the most tragic was that of Jack Blacklaws of Hunters Africa Ltd., who succumbed to sleeping sickness. Jack was a burly, fair-haired man, a bundle of energy and entrepreneurial ideas. I always enjoyed talking to him, and we were good friends. One day when he passed by via Maun, our headquarters at the southern part of the Okavango Swamps, he came into the office looking very haggard. He was convinced he had malaria and was accompanied by Captain Page-Smith, the senior pilot for Pan Am who was hunting with him. They had Jack's plane, a Cessna 180, at the airstrip. I insisted they go to the hospital at once for a blood test, but Jack refused, saying he was certain he had malaria and was taking medicine for it.

Jack was stubborn, and I became very concerned, feeling we should

Keith Scheir with a typical island buffalo of 45 inches in width. Keith was hunting with Frank Miller (1966).

literally manhandle him to the hospital. He maintained that the anti-malarial drugs he had taken would mask the blood slides examination. He spent the night at Riley's Hotel and flew off next day with Captain Page-Smith, but not before both Lionel and I had convinced Captain Page-Smith to fly direct to Victoria Falls and put Jack into hospital. Much against Jack's will, Captain Page-Smith did so, but five days later Jack died of sleeping sickness. The seventeenth day of infection had passed—after that there is no recovery. It is a moot point that if he had had a blood slide on arrival in Maun and then been flown to Johannesburg, he might just have recovered. It was quite simply a tragedy. Thereafter, all our clients and staff had a mandatory blood test at the end of their safari and another three weeks after they returned home.

My story would not be complete without mention of my old pal, 'Ace' Christmas, who, alas, recently passed on. Ace was a quite unforgettable character and had he been born 50 years earlier would have undoubtedly been a famous African hunter in the 'Karamoja' Bell mould, for he was the finest and most accurate shot I have ever seen. Ace came on safari regularly. An obvious no-nonsense man, he would simply pick up a small bag with a change of clothes and his gun box with two guns and walk right out of his ranch in New Mexico onto his international flight to Africa—boots, jeans, cowboy hat, rope, and all else. He was quite unconcerned and oblivious to the many curious eyes that beheld him at the airport or elsewhere. On one occasion, when signing the register at the Norfolk Hotel, a boy of some 10 years approached him.

'Excuse me, sir', he said, 'but are you a real cowboy?'

'Sure am, son', said Ace with his inimitable cowboy drawl. 'All the way from New Mexico'.

Ace was a kindly man who liked talking with children and loved shooting buffalo. On his last safari with me in Botswana, we decided to do something exciting and unusual. We did not need much encouragement.

My safari with Ace was the last of the season. We had plenty of buffalo left on our quota, and it was our practice to shoot one for the Botswana staff party at the end of the season, only this time we decided to rope it first. Ace produced the rope—the real McCoy—fashioned into a lariat, just as he used on most days of his life on the ranch. We duly found a buffalo, but, of course, we had no horse in this tsetse-fly-infested area. We used the hunting car, and had it not been for a quick-thinking member of the party, we might have come to grief.

We came alongside the buffalo, and Ace's whirling rope settled beautifully round the base of the horns. Cheers echoed from all of us. But to what part of the car was the rope to be tied?

The buffalo was heading for the trees, and it was inevitable that the car was going to go on one side of a tree and the buffalo the other. Quickly the rope was passed up out of the hatch, and as it dropped outside the car, a quick half-hitch was made round the nearest mopane tree. Brought up short, the buffalo did a somersault, and the tree held. Ace was out of the car like lightning and killed the buffalo with one shot.

Ace and I, on another occasion, found ourselves shooting an elephant at 25 yards in Kenya, when suddenly both gunbearers appeared very close to our sides and told us that there was a rhino immediately behind us. Turning round I saw the rhino no more than 20 yards away.

'I'll shoot the rhino, you shoot the elephant', I said to Ace.

'Right', Ace replied.

'Shoot now', I said. Our backs were almost touching each other as we fired. Ace brained the elephant—an 85-pound tusker—with a frontal shot and I shot the rhino, more by good fortune, just above the eye, which killed it instantly. Ace shot the elephant with a .458, and I shot the rhino with my Westley Richards .470.

Ace was also a target shooter with an unbelievable collection of shooting medals. On one occasion, he asked me to strike a log with an axe and place a playing card in the resulting crevice, the narrower end of the card pointing towards him. With a .22 and a scope at 25 yards he split the card right down the middle—leaving the two pieces still in the crevice—not once, but five consecutive times! Ace never missed a shot in Africa. He was one of the finest companions with whom a P.H. could wish or hope to share a safari experience.

Whilst my reader reads on for information on buffalo hunting, I nevertheless believe it is both important and interesting for a reader to understand the background of the endeavour, the hope, and the fear that are behind the exhilarating run up to hunting a big bull buffalo. Bechuanaland still provides one of the best areas in Africa to hunt buffalo. Quite a few, at 48 to 50 inches, figure at the top of the record books. Bill

John J. McCloy, American elder statesman, on safari watching his son hunt in Botswana (1970).

Gottwald, hunting with Lionel Palmer, shot one at 47.5 inches. Miss B. Mecom shot one of 50 inches in 1964 hunting with Harry Selby on one of the first safaris conducted by Ker & Downey Safaris in Bechuanaland (although this buffalo head had the widest horns on record for Bechuanaland, it did not score so highly in the new points system).

Buffalo Adventure Extraordinaire

New and unexplored country and the challenge of hitherto unseen huge trophies to be obtained, coupled with the sheer excitement of living in the wild, have motivated hunters for centuries to take extraordinary risks.

The professional hunters who were with us in Safari South (Pty.) Ltd. were all adventurers. One such P.H. was Mike Cawood, with whom I had a great deal in common. We loved hunting and the challenge of unexplored territory, and we were also accomplished bush pilots, Mike more so than I at that time.

On this occasion, we had a large party of very well-known and highly respected Americans. John J. McCloy was the senior member of the party with his wife, Ellen, his son, John II, and his wife Laura, and John Sr.'s daughter, also called Ellen. John II was of the same age and inclination as we were.

We were hunting our company's western concession area—Matsibe—and had camped by the Mobatu airstrip. One evening, over a few beers after a successful day's hunting, we decided to do something special. Mike and I had often discussed the capabilities of the Cessna 172 STOL with oversized gear. Each of us had flown the plane under very adverse bush conditions and found its performance remarkable. Most particularly, with just two persons on board, we found that with 20 percent flap, nose up, at 35 miles per hour we could land and stop within 100 yards, provided we were headed into a light wind. The plan we hatched was that we would fly to a big island we had seen in the centre of the western side of the Okavango Swamps and land on a completely untried piece of ground and then undertake a full day's hunting on foot, flying out in the evening when the heat had gone out of the day and the aircraft's performance was thereby enhanced.

Mike and I put it to the younger John—he would do anything we would was his rejoinder. We correctly surmised that we could fly in with a full load, but we would have to fly out in possibly three trips, as the surface of most of the islands was sandy. Taking Mike's gunbearer—who rejoiced in having the ridiculous name of 'Dangerous'—we loaded our

guns, ammunition, two machetes, an axe, and a spade into the plane. Each of us had a packet of sandwiches. There was no problem with water, as the swamps' water was crystal clear and eminently drinkable. The plan was that Mike and John would hunt whilst Dangerous and I would improve the strip. Once that was done, Dangerous would guard the plane—from elephants tipping it over and lions chewing the tires— and I would make a recce. John, being a highly ethical hunter, was anxious that we did not hunt any game that we had seen from the air, and rightly so, since such actions are unsporting. The aircraft was equipped with a radio, an emergency beacon, and a first aid kit.

The plan was a secret among the three of us. Very early in the morning, just as dawn broke, we arrived at the spot where Alpha Two Zulu Fox-trot Charlie was parked a mile or two from camp. As far as anyone else in camp knew, we were going on a recce for next week's hunts.

Both Mike and I could fly the plane from our respective seats. We tossed a coin for the left-hand seat—Mike won and flew the aircraft. Five minutes' flying brought us over the huge mass of water of the Okavango Swamps. We could just make out the western edge of the swamps stretching away into the distance. We flew over a number of islands that were mostly too small and then saw a rather bigger island with a white pan in the middle of it. We estimated we could walk the circumference of it in a day. The island was completely inaccessible except by boat, and

Top: Cecil Riggs and Mike Cawood on the McCloy safari in 1970. Tragically, Mike was killed in an accident 15 years later.

Above: McCloy father and son bathing in the Tamalakhane River at the bridge at Maun on the edge of the Okavango Swamps (1970).

even then the task of navigating the innumerable lily-choked lagoons linked by miles of twisting little channels would have been a daunting task. There was a good chance that a human being had never stood upon the island that we now had in view, certainly no one such as us. The island was completely surrounded by thick, impenetrable papyrus swamp growing out of permanent deep water.

No game was evident. Maybe it would be blank. We concentrated on looking at the obviously open spots. A long final approach over water was not a bad idea. This enabled us to touch down early without coming in high over trees and then having to cut power, making the aircraft lose altitude very quickly, and to catch the landing with engine power as we touched. After making several dummy runs on the best-looking spots, we chose one where we could come in low over the water. The landing would require a little kick to starboard to straighten up and touch down. At this point I agreed with Mike that I should cut the switches as we touched the ground. So far as we could see when we touched down we would be into long grass for 150 yards—whether or not there were spring hare or antbear holes and anthills was unknown. Cutting the switches would reduce fire risk and ensure that the engine was not running if we hit an obstacle. We circled some distance away, had a conference, and decided to give it a try.

Motoring in over the water—so far so good—we headed into the wind, which was light but on the nose. Slowly we lost speed as we came to within 50 yards of the touchdown spot. At that instant, out of the corner of my eye, I saw them 50 yards away: a herd of elephants on the edge of the trees, trunks raised for the wind.

We were committed with no chance of aborting the landing.

'Cut', called Mike. The switches went to 'off'. The next second we were into the grass, the last revolutions of the propeller thrashing it about like a windmill in a wheat field. Mike dragged the stick back to his chest to keep the nose wheel off the ground and dug his toes forward on the main gear brakes. A final wobble of the wings and we were down and stationary.

'Elephants, Mike!' I shouted, opening the door and craning my head in the direction I had last seen them. The grass was five feet tall, but a cloud of dust advertised their presence.

All was silent. Moving off our flight path, I climbed an anthill and looked at the small herd of elephants with my binoculars. As I did so, they thankfully moved off into the trees.

We all looked at each other and laughed. The tension of landing in the unknown had been felt by each of us. Mike and I shared the same thoughts: How do we get out? Can we get out? We checked the aircraft, and all was well—a bit of grass here and there. We checked the air intakes, which were fine.

The next priority was hunting. Mike and John set off, and Dangerous and I started work on laying the grass back to the point of takeoff. After two hours of continuous work, laying the grass over the sand in the flight path, we had a good 200-yard-long and 50-foot-wide strip. It was soft, and I was concerned that it would hold down the aircraft, so we set to work on another 150 yards that had some small trees but was a little harder. After that, if we were not airborne, then we were in the swamp.

We had nearly finished this chore when we heard two shots with a fair interval between them. Near the plane was a 'sausage tree'. This was a tree on which hung heavy seed pods that looked like sausages. I climbed quickly to the top and, using my binoculars, looked out to the centre of the island where we had seen the white sandy pan. Soon I saw two little figures walking along with their guns over their shoulders— Mike and John were on their way back. Shortly after, Mike arrived, having left John in the middle of the pan with a good tree to climb if necessary. They had shot a fine bull buffalo after an exciting stalk, which Mike estimated would go 42 to 43 inches. After collecting Dangerous, Mike returned to cut off the head and the tail.

My own hunt was not possible, as I had to guard the aircraft. I waited in the shade of the wing. It was hot, being midday, but by one o'clock Mike, John, and Dangerous returned with the buffalo head.

We decided that there would have to be two trips off the island. Mike, John, and Dangerous would attempt to get off first, and then Mike would come back for me and the buffalo head. We turned the plane around and pushed it into position for takeoff. Mike gave it 10 percent of flap, stood on the brakes, applied full power, let off the brakes, and off they went—no doubt praying to get airborne.

The little plane made it at 220 yards. I sensed that Mike had given her a touch of flap as she lifted and gained speed, disappearing out of sight. As the noise died away I became conscious of the utter silence of the island and my whole environment. I was very much alone in the bush—a long way from anywhere. I looked at the reassuring presence of my .470 Westley Richards and felt the 20 rounds of ammo that was in my pocket.

G.C. George of Spokane, Washington, with a record-class buffalo with horns of 48 1/2 inches and superb boss and hooks from the Okavango Swamps.

Having spent some time in previous years in the desert areas of Saudi Arabia, Trans-Jordan, and Iraq, I had learned by experience that one does not simply drift off on some ill-prepared adventure. I came to be grateful for this experience now. Before leaving camp I had wrapped round myself some 20 feet of half-inch nylon rope. I had put a military prismatic compass in my pocket and packets of antibiotic pills and matches. I also had remembered a piece of invaluable equipment that was to prove most useful: a signaller's reflective mirror.

As we had pushed the plane down to the takeoff point, I had suggested that the buffalo head be left on the island with us to load next time. Dangerous had hooked the horn and head into the crotch of a tree some 20 yards away. I walked back up the strip and checked it again for holes and sticks. Finding none, I went and sat down with my back to the sausage tree. I calculated that Mike should be back in 45 minutes, maximum.

Being conscious of my solitude, I was wide awake. I thought I heard something move behind me. Peering round the bole of the tree I found myself looking at the swishing tail and backside of a large lioness not 10 feet away.

I have always laughed at the rapidity with which the natives of Africa can climb trees in an emergency. Believe me, at that instant I impersonated them most ably. There was no time to climb with the .470—that stayed leaning against the tree. At 15 feet above the ground with plenty of sausages to throw, I felt pretty safe. In fact, the lioness was one of a pride of five, including a fair maned lion. A few shouts and sausages and they moved out, no doubt surprised that the local baboons were so vociferous and accurate.

Time passed, and it had been an hour since Mike had left. I descended from my perch after first checking with my binoculars that the lions had not moved to the tree in which the buffalo head was hanging, but the wind was right and they had picked up no scent.

Dimly, I became aware of the noise of an aero engine. Almost as soon as I had heard it, it faded away. This happened several times, and I realised that it must be Mike looking for our island and not another aircraft flying a course of its own. I whipped out my reflective mirror and commenced flashing an S.O.S. in the direction of the noise of the aero engine. Nothing happened for 15 minutes; then the aero engine noise came nearer. I realised that Mike had missed the island and was squaring the area. I continued to flash the mirror.

A few minutes later in came Mike. When he came to a stop and opened the door he said, 'God John, I thought I had lost you. If it had not been for that flashing thing you had I would have had to turn back'. I showed him the mirror, the rope, and the antibiotics. Round the campfire that night I explained how nylon rope strands could be used as sutures and the rope unravelled to tie splints in place, quite apart from its other obvious uses. Mike had had a good flight back, but the western sun had been straight in his eyes on his return, and this had made recognition of the island difficult, as so many of them look the same.

After loading the buffalo head into the back, we took off and rose above the swamps. This time I was flying, and I took a turn over the island. Elephant, lion, buffalo, and several other animals were all now in plain view in the evening sunshine. 'Goodbye, paradise', I said to myself as I turned east towards camp and the celebratory beer. It had been a great adventure, one which John and I have toasted many times since. Nothing ventured, nothing gained. We never went back, but I am sure we provided the lions with a good meal off the buffalo carcase. I was also pretty certain that the strip would not take another takeoff—the wheels were breaking through the crust of the sand.

Sitting round the campfire of an evening, John Sr. would recount the events of recent history as though they had happened yesterday. He had been an advisor to four U.S. presidents, chairman of the Allied Commission for the Reconstruction of Germany, and chairman of the Chase Manhattan Bank. He had held many other senior and very important appointments. He was a truly great and remarkable person—the finest person I ever met. He was a great student of imperial history, as I was, and we were both intensely interested in each other's experiences.

He knew personally all the great Allied commanders of the forces in the 1939–45 War and had interviewed all the German war criminals. When he died at 93, his wish that I be informed, wherever I was, was faithfully carried out by his son, John.

Going off that morning on our island adventure, I felt rather sneaky at not having kept John Sr. fully in the picture. On my return I apologised, but he said with that unforgettable twinkle in his eyes, 'John, I had a pretty good idea what you were doing. If I'd been 30 years younger, I would have come with you. People like you come back more often than not!'

The Indestructible Buffalo

With the kind permission of *Outdoor Life*, the following is the abridged story of Jack and Eleanor O'Connor's and my experience in the Okavango Swamps of Botswana that was originally written by Jack. Let me hasten to add that this was an embarrassing experience for me to some extent. No professional hunter wishes to kill a buffalo with anything but a shot resulting in a clean kill. However, I would be economical with the truth if I did not admit that sometimes things do not go as planned, and I am sure that my compadres, in reality, have had similar experiences. The unexpected is the essence of hunting; coping with the unexpected is the essence of being a successful professional hunter. To me, Jack O'Connor was a father figure, and his mastery of the pen was inimitable.

Round the campfire one evening, I asked Jack what it felt like to be at the apex of his profession. He said he was to some extent humbled by his success. He wrote because he took great satisfaction from expressing the true facts of the tale he was telling and the events he was describing. Above all, he was in awe of what his pen could describe, and he was certainly aware of the part the media would play in time in our education and understanding of the world, as it does today and will do, undoubtedly, even more so in the future. By the campfire he composed this verse:

The power of the pen has the power of a gun,
The power of the gun is death over life.
The power over life with your wife brings life once again.
Beware the power of the pen!

—Jack O'Connor
Matsibe, Bechuanaland (Botswana), October 1966

ntil midafternoon it had been a pleasant but not exciting day there in the Okavango Swamps country of remote Bechuanaland. I had shot a sassaby, a rather homely antelope closely related to the East African topi and about the size of a large mule deer. It was no great trophy, but the camp needed meat.

We had seen a good deal of game—some kudu cows and calves, dozens of warthogs, many swamp-dwelling red lechwe, some zebras and wildebeest, and a herd of about 30 giraffes. We spent most of our time looking for lion sign and found the remains of some old lion kills— skulls and horns of antelope, whitened buffalo bones—but nothing fresh.

But we had run against a great deal of buffalo sign and encountered one herd of very smart and cautious buffalo. We glimpsed the last of the herd of perhaps 30 or 40 of the big, black cattle as they disappeared into a very dense thicket about a quarter of a mile in diameter. They had fed and watered and they were planning to lie up for the day in the cool seclusion of the brush.

'I don't think it will be hard to get them out of there', said John Kingsley-Heath, our outfitter and white hunter. 'We'll get out and wait here. Then I'll have Musioka, the gunbearer, go around on the far side of the thicket, and make a noise. When the buffalo come out, you and Eleanor can knock off a couple if they are worth shooting!'

This sounded very simple. We got out of John's hunting car, and Eleanor and John took a stand behind one tall anthill and I behind another. Eleanor had the Winchester Model 70 .30/06 she had used on tigers in India the year before and I a restocked Winchester .375 I had carried on many hunts in far countries. She was loaded up with 220-grain solid bullets and I with 300-grain solids. John had his life insurance—an old Westley-Richards .470 double-ejector rifle.

In a few minutes we heard Musioka making one hell of a racket. The brush cracked, and we saw the vague shapes of buffalo moving around just inside the thicket. But they wouldn't come out. Apparently they knew that if they came out in the open they stood the chance of getting bushwhacked.

So next we tried going into the bush after them. The thicket looked to be a favorite resting place. The ground was tracked up, filled with beds and droppings. It smelled like a corral. As we sneaked along, we occasionally could catch a glimpse of buffalo as they moved away, but it was difficult to make out sex and the size of the

Warthog

157

heads. It quickly became apparent that the buffalo wanted to stay in the thicket and were moving around behind us.

As we emerged from the thicket, we discovered that two bulls had come into the open. They had crossed the open meadow and were just about to disappear about 200 yards away into the thick brush on the other side. We could have hit them, but it would have been almost impossible to get in a well-placed shot. We didn't shoot. Long ago I found out that a buffalo is hard enough to kill even when he is hit just right.

So we drove on, still looking for lion sign. Around noon we knocked off, found some shade where the wind kept tsetse flies away, ate our lunch, and reminisced.

My wife Eleanor and I had known John Kingsley-Heath ever since 1959, when he had been a white hunter for Ker & Downey. That year we had a fantastically lucky trip with John and shot lion, sable, puku, zebra, an enormous bull eland, and other lesser trophies as well as a 60-inch kudu, one of the best heads ever to come out of East Africa.

Since then John and I kept in touch with each other. He had spent a couple of Christmases at our Idaho home when he had been in the United States. It was there that we made plans for this Bechuanaland hunt. John had resigned from Ker & Downey and had started another safari company with a partner, Frank Miller, who had also been a Ker & Downey hunter. The two hunt part of the year in Kenya, then take their vehicles and crew south to their Bechuanaland operation, known as Safari South, with headquarters in Maun.

We had flown the Atlantic from New York to London on Alitalia, the Italian airline, and had picked it up again in Rome to fly to Johannesburg. At Rome we had met our friends Richard and Sarah Jane Harris from Atlanta, Georgia, and their 10-year-old son Boyd. When we'd rested a day in Johannesburg, we chartered a twin-motor plane that flew us to Maun, Bechuanaland.

An enormous, dry, and thinly populated plateau the size of Texas, Bechuanaland Protectorate, which has recently become the independent Republic of Botswana, is about as flat a country as can be found on this earth. Except for half a dozen or so low hills a few hundred feet high, no part of the country is more than 50 feet lower or higher than any other part. Located in the north are the famous Okavango Swamps—thousands of square miles of shallow water, low sandy islands, brush, palm trees, and tsetse flies.

There are lions in the Okavango, about the biggest and meanest in

Africa. There are also elephants, giraffes, hippos, thousands of buffalo and strange swamp-dwelling antelope called red lechwe, and sitatunga, kudu, sable, impala, crocodiles, leopards, and warthogs by the tens of thousands.

The lions in Bechuanaland and just to the north in Portuguese Angola are bad tempered. A high proportion of them charge, and they are difficult to hunt and seldom come to baits.

The Okavango leopards never come to baits. The new Republic of Botswana also contains the famous Kalahari Desert, the home of the Bushmen, some of the most primitive members of the human race, and incredible numbers of zebra, wildebeest, gemsbok, springbok, and other desert animals. It is pretty far off the beaten trail, and until the past few years few people have hunted there. That particular day there on the Okavango we took a leisurely rest at about noon. We ate crackers, excellent South African cheese, and cold roast from an impala shot a couple of days before, and we washed it all down with some excellent beer brewed by German brew-masters in Windhoek in what once was called German West Africa but is now known as South-West Africa.

It was the last part of August, winter in the Southern Hemisphere, and the nights were generally cold, even frosty. But it was always warm at midday, and sometimes Eleanor and I took a snooze after lunch. Then the vultures would gather hopefully in the trees to see if we would die.

Along about two o'clock that same day we put lunch things away in the chop box, got into the hunting car again, and took off. Musioka the gunbearer stood behind with his head out the lookout hole in the top of the car. We saw hundreds of warthogs, and also hundreds of red lechwe grazing in the grassy meadows close to water.

We were at least 30 miles from camp, and for 20 miles we had broken trail through the brush. Now we started to follow our tracks back toward what passed for a road—simply a track made by hunting cars and trucks used by Safari South.

Eland

Suddenly Musioka tapped sharply on the top of the car and said 'M'Bogo!' That is the Swahili word for buffalo.

John stopped the car and a moment later said, 'There they are, moving in the brush to the right, a whole herd of them. They're coming this way!'

We were on the edge of a little mbuga, or open grassy space in the brush. It was about 50 yards wide and something over 100 yards long, but all around it the brush was pretty thick.

Slowly the buffalo started to cross the mbuga—cows, calves, bulls. The wind was blowing gently from them to us. We could smell their cowlike odor.

Presently as the rear section of the herd passed, John whispered sharply: 'There's a good bull Jack—that one on the right. I think you ought to take him!' There were two bulls together, one noticeably larger than the other. I had no particular yen for a buffalo, and I have never been an enthusiastic buffalo hunter.

I shot my first one in Tanganyika in 1953 with a .450 Watts, the wildcat predecessor of the .458 Winchester. The first bullet went high through the left lung and flattened against the massive neck vertebrae. I shot this 'dead' buffalo once more—this time through the heart. I ejected the fired case and stood up. As I was putting another cartridge into the magazine, I heard Don Ker, my white hunter, yell at the same time I heard the pounding of hoofs.

That 'dead' buffalo was coming for us. Don and I each shot. The buffalo turned aside, staggered a few yards, and fell. I put another bullet into it. My shots were just where I called them—the first through a lung and flattened out like a silver dollar on massive neck bones, the second through the heart.

The only other buffalo I ever shot was facing me about 125 yards away in Mozambique, a big lone bull. I shot him right in the sticking place with a 400-grain bullet from a .416 Rigby. The handload I used turns up 5750 foot-pounds of energy, but this buffalo fell on his nose, jumped up, galloped 100 yards or so before he died. I wrote a story about the incident and called it 'Buffalo Make Me Nervous'.

I was thinking about all this when I got out of the car, and set off for the buffalo. I switched off the safety on my .375. I was thinking that I didn't want the buffalo particularly but it was a good one and I ought to take him.

The buffalo walked quietly along broadside about 100 yards away. I held the intersection of the crosswires in the Weaver K3 scope right on his shoulder blade about one-third of the way down from the hump, in line with the place his left foreleg joined the body. I hesitated for a second, and then the darned bull started to turn, and I knew that if I was going to shoot this particular bull I had better shoot then. I squeezed the trigger. The buffalo stumbled, almost went down, and started off again, but with the plunging gallop of an animal with a broken shoulder. I quickly worked the bolt and sent a 300-grain solid bullet raking through the buffalo's ribs from the rear. Then the buffalo and his companion, the smaller bull, were in the brush.

'Well', John sighed, 'a wounded buffalo! The way he was hit I doubt if he has gone far. Let's follow him up!' He turned around and extended his hand to Musioka the gunbearer, who handed him his old Westley-Richards .470 double rifle. I filled the magazine of my .375 and put another cartridge in the chamber.

We took up the track. Musioka, who was unarmed, did the tracking. John and I pussyfooted along, watching. We had not gone 100 yards from where we had seen the buffalo last when Musioka extended the flat of his hand towards John and me as a signal for us to stop. He pointed into the brush.

The patch into which the tracks led was very thick, but by getting down on our knees we could see the front feet of a standing bull and a formless black mass that was the wounded bull lying down. They were not over 30 feet away.

John put his lips to my ear. 'Better not shoot again until you know which way he is facing', he whispered. 'He's down and sick but still very much alive'.

How long we stayed there I do not know. It seemed like a long time, but it may not have been over 15 minutes. The buffalo were rock still. They were watching their back track, hoping to ambush whatever had hurt one of them.

What moved them I cannot say. Musioka thought he had figured out which end of the buffalo was which and was trying to tell John. Maybe the buffalo heard him. Perhaps he heard us breathing. Maybe the slight breeze had shifted a bit. Anyway, the wounded buffalo suddenly floundered to its feet, and both buffalo thundered away through the brush. John raced after them.

Now, John is almost 25 years younger than I am. He was badly mauled by a lion a few years ago, but he is still pretty spry and can run much faster than I can. Anyway he shot around the brush and out of sight with me galloping clumsily behind him. I hadn't travelled more than 50 yards when just ahead of me in the thick brush I hear John's .470 bellow twice.

'Well', I thought, 'John has shot the wounded buffalo!' I turned around to see Musioka behind me. 'Kufa—finished', he said in Swahili, grinning.

Just as he said that, I heard the thump of hoofs and crashing of brush to my right. To my astonishment I could see the plunging shadowy form of the bull with the broken shoulder. I threw up my .375 and gave him a high lung shot through the brush. He disappeared.

In a moment Musioka and I found John standing beside a dying buffalo.

'Hell, John', I said, 'that's not the wounded one. He passed me at 40 yards or so, and I took a poke at him'.

'I know it', he said. 'I should have had a good shot at the wounded fellow, but this bloke here came for me when I was about to shoot his pal. I had to let him have it. Look, he's beginning to stir. Let him have another. I'm not too well fixed on cartridges'.

I gave the second buffalo a finisher and we went off after the bull with the broken shoulder. He was very sick and had not gone over 50 yards from the place where I had put that last bullet in him. He was lying down again in brush watching his back track.

I finally made out enough of the buffalo so that I felt I could shoot him in the neck close to the head. I was about to touch off a shot when John punched me.

'Don't shoot', he whispered. 'I just heard the car moving with Eleanor in it. She's right in line with the buffalo. It would absolutely make our day if you put a bullet through the buffalo and it then went through the motor block, a tire, or maybe Eleanor!'

We tried to work around to get another angle, but the buffalo detected us. I heard him flounder to his feet, but I could not see him. John could. He put in two shots from his double. We heard brush crash for a second or two. Then all was quiet once more.

We were not far from the car, so the three of us went over to see how Eleanor was getting on. We found her perched on the top, her .30/06 in her hand. She had a 220-grain solid in the chamber and her right thumb was on the safety. Her face wore the look of one who is resolved to die bravely.

'He went over there and stopped!' she said, pointing to a thick patch of brush about 60 yards away. I couldn't really see him, but I could hear him and see the brush move. 'What in the world has been happening? All this shooting and running around. Can't you people hit anything?'

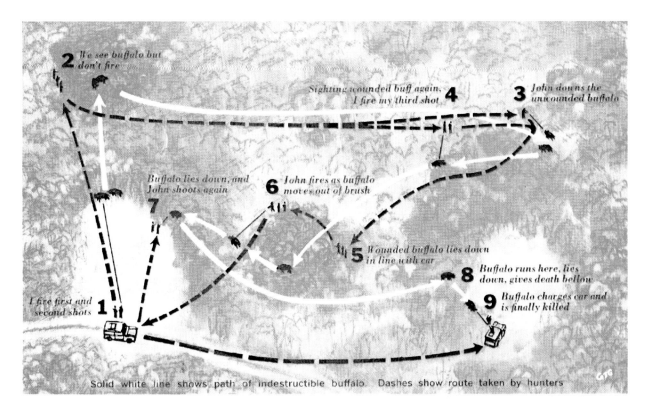

2 *We see buffalo but don't fire*

Sighting wounded buff again, I fire my third shot 4

3 *John downs the unwounded buffalo*

Buffalo lies down, and John shoots again 7

6 *John fires as buffalo moves out of brush*

5 *Wounded buffalo lies down in line with car*

8 *Buffalo runs here, lies down, gives death bellow*

9 *Buffalo charges car and is finally killed*

1 *I fire first and second shots*

Solid white line shows path of indestructible buffalo. Dashes show route taken by hunters

'I had to shoot the buffalo's pal', John said. 'The unwounded one came for me flat out, and I had to let him have both barrels'.

'I had a good shot at him once', I said, 'but the buffalo was in line with the car, and we thought I might hit you!'

'Poof!' she said. 'I don't think I was in much danger. If you two characters can burn up $100 worth of expensive ammunition and still can't kill a wounded buffalo at 20 feet, I don't think you could hit anything you couldn't even see! I wish you had shot and got this silly business over with!'

While we talked, Musioka had sneaked down to the end of the mbuga toward the spot where Eleanor had marked down the wounded bull. He crouched low and peered into the brush. Then he signalled that he could see the bull.

'You wait here', John whispered. 'One man makes less noise than two'.

I stood by the car and watched him sneak up beside Musioka. Then I saw him kneel down and aim. A moment later I heard the .470 roar and saw it rise in recoil. Then he shot again. Once more I heard the wounded bull go crashing through the brush. Then there was quiet. It had either fallen or had stopped about 60 or 70 yards away.

An overhead schematic of our encounter with the indestructible buffalo.

163

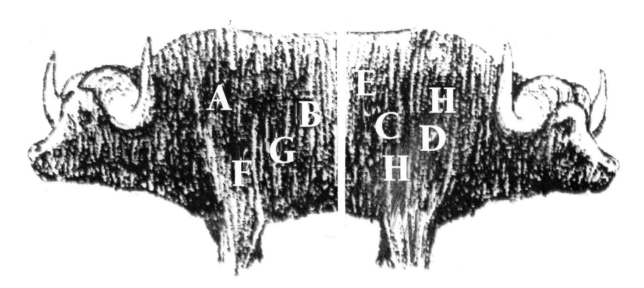

Position of shots on the indestructible buffalo.

A moment later John and Musioka joined us.

'Well', said John, 'hope I got him. I had a pretty fair shot at the lungs'.

As he said that, we heard a mournful, strangling bellow—the same sound I had heard four years before on the Save River in Mozambique when the last buffalo I shot was dying. 'That's his death call', said John. 'He is finished!' He handed his .470 to Musioka and said something in Swahili.

'Hop in the car', he said to Eleanor and me. 'Let's take a look'.

We drove around and came to the spot where we'd heard the bull give his last bellow. I saw him lying inert in a little opening ahead. 'There he is!' I said. 'Dead as a mackerel'.

An instant later that damned bull was on his feet and charging, bouncing along on his one good front leg, blood streaming out of his nose. The car was still moving when I jumped out. The scope was full of buffalo head when the .375 went off.

Jumping from the moving car had me off balance. One foot went into a warthog hole, and I started to fall the instant after I had shot. As I was falling, I could see that the buffalo was also falling, and at the same instant I heard a shot.

I can remember thinking as I fell that I hoped I could get to my feet and get in another shot before the buffalo got up. A second shot followed. I wondered who was shooting.

I looked up as I scrambled to my feet and cranked another cartridge into the chamber of the .375. Musioka had his head and shoulders out of the manhole in the roof of the hunting car. John handed him his .470

Jack O'Connor with the indestructible buffalo.

double. Getting half-eaten by a wounded lion some years ago had made John cautious.

Eleanor and Musioka piled out of the car. John examined the dead buffalo.

'Not bad shooting under the circumstances', he said. 'He's hit twice in the brain and once in the boss of the horn. The bugger is dead. For an instant I thought he was going to knock the car about a bit!'

Somebody had to shoot the damned buffalo before it beat up the car. 'Just think', I went on, 'if the buff had smashed up the car, we'd never have made it for sundowners around the campfire with the Harrises!'

By this time it was getting gloomy there in the brush, but we took a few pictures, counted the bullet holes on one side, turned him over and counted the holes on the other. Excluding the final three head shots, this indestructible buffalo had nine holes in him. We had shot him seven times in the body, and that meant that of the seven solids, two had gone clear through. Every one of those shots either went

Bob Chatfield-Taylor, friend, test pilot, gun nut, and big-game hunter, Botswana (1970).

through the shoulder or the lungs. My first shot at the shoulder had gone exactly where I had called it, and so had my second. What we decided was my third shot, the one I took when he passed me after John had shot his companion, was a bit farther back than I had called it but still well in the lungs.

Apparently my first shot had done little damage to the lungs because of the angle but had broken the shoulder and had then gone up into the neck. The second shot had probably followed about the same route. John's four shots were all good, solid lung shots. If there could be any criticism of the bullet placement, it would be perhaps that all were a bit on the high side yet not high enough to break the spine. However, no lion, tiger, moose, or eland would have lived very long with any of those solid broadside shots through the lungs.

'I don't get it', I said, as we looked the bull over. 'This damn thing should have been dead at least half an hour ago. It strikes me that the only sure way to kill a buffalo is to shoot him a dozen times with a 20mm cannon, take out his guts and bury them, then cut off his head, tie stones to it, and sink it in a lake'.

'Wouldn't do any good!' John said. 'All these swamps are shallow. Water isn't deep enough!'

We hadn't gone very far when the sun went down, and it grew dark. With Musioka picking out our tracks by the headlights, we crept slowly back toward the road and then to camp.

That night when we were getting ready to turn in, Eleanor spoke to me sternly: 'I never want to see you pull another stunt like that!' she said. 'Suppose the buffalo had killed you. I never saw anything so ridiculous . . . at your age . . . and you a grandfather!'

'I know', I said. 'I thought it was a good idea at the time'.

'Something might have happened to you!' she said, starting to sniffle. 'Then what would I have done? I'll admit you're not much, but I am used to you, and you're all I've got! If that buffalo had knocked you off, I doubt if I could do any better and maybe not as well. I'm not very young anymore', she went on drearily, 'and probably not as beautiful as I used to be'.

The .416 Taylor Field Trials

Bob Chatfield-Taylor was a man of many parts. First of all, he was a highly regarded test pilot in the American aircraft industry, working during the 1939-45 War for the Consolidated Vultee Aircraft Corporation.

Almost until his dying day he flew for a small commercial feeder airline in Massachusetts. He was also an accomplished big-game hunter and a total gun nut. He was several times married, once to a famous debutante and heiress. He was a good-looking man and had a way with the fair sex that drew applause from his peers. 'Bob', said one of his friends to me, 'is a first-class swordsman!' I would agree with that statement and add that he was a most amusing, kind, and fun person to be with at any time. He was a friend.

The plot for the .416 Taylor was hatched at a lunch with Bob and some friends, including Jack O'Connor, at the 21 Club in New York, amid much long storytelling. It was then that I invited Bob to come to Botswana as my guest. Bob, being the kind of person that he was, insisted that he should do something in return. We agreed that he would fly our Cessna 320 Sky Night between Maun and Johannesburg when needed. He readily agreed.

Bob had a lot of friends at Winchester and also knew John Olin, the

Top: The second buffalo shot with the .416 Taylor.

Bottom: Bob Chatfield-Taylor and I with the first buffalo killed by Bob with his .416 Taylor. Okavango Swamps, Botswana (1970).

167

Above: Buffalo shot and killed instantly by me with a neck shot with Bob Chatfield-Taylor's 7x57 Mauser (1970).

Above right: Caught napping!

chairman of the Olin Mathiesen Chemical Corporation, the owners of Winchester. John Olin had been on safari with Ker & Downey in East Africa with Eric Rundgren in earlier years. So also had Bob himself, hunting with Harry Selby. Each of them used a .416 Rigby.

Bob called on Dave Carlson of Winchester, who delivered a .458 Model 70 action fitted with a Douglas .416 barrel. The action was chambered to take the .416 Taylor cartridge, which was simply made by necking down a .458 case using, at that time, Colorado Custom Bullet's soft points of 400 grains and Kynoch solids of similar weight. Bob did the necessary tests on the gun at Winchester before he left to join us in Africa. He found that, and I quote, 'I decided to load the .416 with 64 grains of 3031 for a MV of 2250 f.p.s. and a ME of 4500 ft-lbs. The recoil showed 50 ft-lbs. as opposed to the .458's 65 ft-lbs. I achieved great accuracy putting three rounds into a minute of angle at 100 yards'.

On arrival Bob came to stay with me at Buffalo Cottage, my little house in Maun by the bridge over the Thamalakane River. Here we planned our hunt over some good South African wine in company with my partner Lionel Palmer and several other hunters who happened to be in at the time.

Safari South (Pty.) Ltd. had a large concession area called Matsibe on the east side of the Okavango Swamps. At the north end of the sand tongue of land that ran up the centre of the concession area, there were known to be a number of old bull buffalo. We decided that as the area also offered good opportunities for lion and greater kudu, both of which Bob wished to shoot, we would commence our hunting there. I sent up the car in advance, and camp in Matsibe was moved up the sand tongue to a group of *motsaodi* trees, renowned for their shade, at the edge of a big lagoon that was now separated from the main swamps, as the waters of the earlier flood had receded.

The airstrip was made on a nearby *vlei* (an open plain), where the ground had a crust of dried mud. We flew in the Cessna 172. This was a standard 172 with a Robertson STOL conversion and oversized main and nose gear. Bob and I had a lot of fun flying this aircraft.

We set out in the car to look for buffalo. Botswana is a flat country, and the Okavango Swamps are no exception. Normally in open country we could see up to 1000 yards, but seldom more. Before long we spied a black dot on the horizon. Standing on the roof of the car, we made out an old bull buffalo in the vicinity of a mud wallow. This was our first target. We had several buffalo licences between us and plenty on the concession quota.

We set out on foot. The wind was good, so by detouring downwind of our quarry the buffalo almost walked into us. At 25 yards it was decision time. Bob lined up on the buffalo, and at the vital moment I banged a stick on a tree. The buffalo stopped and raised his head, looking straight at us. Bob took him full in the higher part of his chest at the base of the neck. The shock of the bullet set him back almost on his haunches. He turned to the right and galloped a few uneven paces before collapsing dead.

We recovered the solid 400-grain bullet from under the skin in the left hind leg as one would view the buffalo from the front. The heart and lungs were drilled by the bullet, which had passed clean through the grass-filled stomach and the lower thigh bone. Penetration was excellent, and the bullet appeared to have no distortion whatever.

Bob was delighted, and we returned to camp to off-load the meat and to write up the day's experiences. Bob insisted that I should have some fun also, so after a discussion it was agreed that I should try out my admiration of 'Karamoja' Bell's accuracy with a small-bore rifle on big game. I therefore loaded up my 7x57 Mauser, a favourite calibre of both Bob's and mine, and at 3.30 we set out to look for another bull buffalo, but we did not find one until the next day. In the meantime Bob had shot a wildebeest for bait. However, at his suggestion he lent me his

7x57 with 4-power scope to shoot the buffalo. In due course, we found an old bull buffalo sitting in a mud wallow between some palm trees. Bob decided that he would take a grandstand view, so he positioned himself on top of a convenient anthill. I started my stalk.

I planned to shoot at 60 yards, having zeroed the gun in at 100 yards spot on target. The buffalo would have to be sideways on at right angles to give me the neck shot I wanted. When I was 90 yards from the buffalo and not quite close enough, I heard a noise behind me. A warthog that had taken refuge in the anthill on which Bob had perched himself had decided that Bob's fart was too much for it and surfaced for pastures new! The buffalo stood up, apparently unconcerned, perhaps believing that Bob was a baboon, which were often seen in similar positions. I made up ground to 80 yards. The buffalo walked 10 paces and stopped exactly sideways on in front of a palm tree. I took aim for the neck column midway between where the neck joins the head and the point at which the neck joins the body and about halfway up. I had a good rest for the rifle. I fired, and instantaneously the buffalo dropped stone dead.

So much for accuracy. Once again the bullet had done its job well, smashing the vertebrae at exactly the right spot and cutting the spinal column to the brain. Once more we loaded the meat back to camp. Bob and I were thoroughly enjoying ourselves. We needed more .416 experience.

We continued hunting, and Bob collected a fine greater kudu. After another very satisfying buffalo hunt with the .416 Taylor, Bob handed me the gun and suggested I have a go. This time we found a buffalo in thick bush on an island, but there was no surprise—the buffalo knew he was being hunted. I had taken the precaution of firing several rounds of the .416, swinging the gun onto a target that had been put up on some trees, so as to get the feeling of the gun. (Whilst I had used a .425 Westley Richards a great deal, the .470 double-barrelled rifle was something with which I was more familiar.)

We followed the buffalo, which stopped in a thick patch of bush. I sent my gunbearer round to the left of the bush with instructions to make himself safe from a charge by climbing a tree. He was to then throw a stick into the patch of bush. Bob and I would go to the right of the patch in the hopes that the buffalo would come out at us or at least see us when we shot.

The plan worked well. The buffalo tore out of the bush, giving me a quartering shot at the leading edge of the shoulder for the heart. This turned him directly towards us. He saw us, never flinched, and came for us. My second shot hit him at the base of the boss of his horns in the centre of his head and brained him. He nearly turned a somersault and collapsed in a heap.

Neither bullet left the body. The frontal brain shot not only vaporised the brain but went on to break up two of the initial vertebrae in the neck, having been slightly deflected by the skull. The shot into the shoulder hit the heart and was found under the skin in front of the right rear thigh bone—once again it had passed through a full stomach of grass. We returned to camp very satisfied with the .416 Taylor's performance.

Sadly, not much more was done about the .416 Taylor. Subsequently, Bill Ruger had two such guns made for Bob, which were lever-action single-shot guns. One came out to me in Botswana, and my fellow hunters and I used it a good deal and found the performance excellent. It certainly seemed to have an edge on the Rigby .416. Looking back on the experience I realise that I should have rebarrelled one of the .425 Westley Richards that we rebarrelled to a .458 to a .416 Taylor instead. The advantage of the larger magazine holding five rounds with the added performance would have made a top-class buffalo gun. Bob Chatfield-Taylor wrote up his experiences in *Guns & Ammo* in November of 1972 in an article titled 'Buff Buster Supreme'.

Unfortunately, the .416 Taylor single-shot made by Bill Ruger's company did not survive. The gun laws in both Botswana and the U.K. did not permit me to keep many rifles, so it went to the U.S.A. It was eventually destroyed when headspace trouble apparently developed, or so I was told.

Years passed, and the rejuvenation of the .416 calibre arrived. Alas, the .416 Taylor did not figure amongst the .416 Ruger, .416 Remington, and .416 Hoffman, to name a few. I am convinced that it should have.

Bob, alas, was just a little too early in this respect and, sadly, passed away before his time. When I stayed with him at 3 Bridge Street in Manchester, Massachusetts, I had to descend some dozen nasty little steps to his home. In the winter they would, on occasion, become covered with ice, and I particularly remarked how dangerous they were in those conditions. They were to prove Bob's undoing. He was never the same after a severe blow to the head, received when he fell there, and passed on some time afterwards.

But the .416 Taylor story was not over yet, for in October of 1974 no less a person than John Wootters, that doyen of outdoor and hunting writers, came to hunt with our firm. This time he hunted with Lionel Palmer in the same area of Matsibe. Our firm had steadily been improving its reputation, and we had been in business for 10 years. We had successfully accompanied and outfitted a number of clients from Texas, one of whom, Bob Brister, a noted outdoor writer in Texas and shotgunner of championship class, had written most kindly about us.

During our annual visit to Houston, we came into contact with John Wootters, and arrangements were duly made. John's findings were fully recorded in the March/April 1975 issue of *Rifle*. In this article he covered the .416 Taylor very methodically and very honestly, which is his style and that has remained unchanged over the years. He is a person that both Lionel and I hold in high regard.

Generally speaking, he thought the .416 did a good job and in the process made these remarks: 'John Kingsley-Heath may have made the most cogent remark of all about the recoil of this .416 Taylor when he said: "It's a good elephant rifle for ladies". I can assure you it makes a hell of a buffalo rifle for gentlemen.' John ended his 22-day safari with us having shot several buffalo, including a 44-inch of the type that I have described as 'island buffalo' with a massive boss and wicked hooks. He also shot a good lion, elephant, and many other species of game.

When asked for his conclusions on the .416 Taylor after his safari in Botswana he had this to say: 'I think it's a great cartridge, perhaps the single all-around best one-rifle African battery for my next trip on which the emphasis will be on dangerous game, and especially if elephant is on the list. The .416 is distinctly better than the .375 on Cape buffalo. I have developed an enormous amount of confidence in and affection for the rifle. The cartridge is simple to form, easy to load, not temperamental, extremely accurate, quite flat shooting for such a powerhouse, and for me remarkably easy on the shoulder. Given a choice between the .375 Holland & Holland, .458 Winchester Magnum, and the .416 Taylor, I'd pick the .416 Taylor every time. Nevertheless, I must sadly report that I consider the odds on a commercial version of the .416/.458 being produced very low. It could have been one of the all time great ones, but I fear it was born about 15 years too late'.

I'm not sure it is too late, but that's probably a statement influenced by sentiment for Bob Chatfield-Taylor, who was one of those that anyone would wish to be in his circle of friends.

MOZAMBIQUE

Mozambique possessed some prime buffalo country. On my stay there, I saw more than a thousand buffalo in one herd that included sev-

Following page: The Sarnadas concession in south-west Mozambique lying adjacent to the Kruger National Park of South Africa.

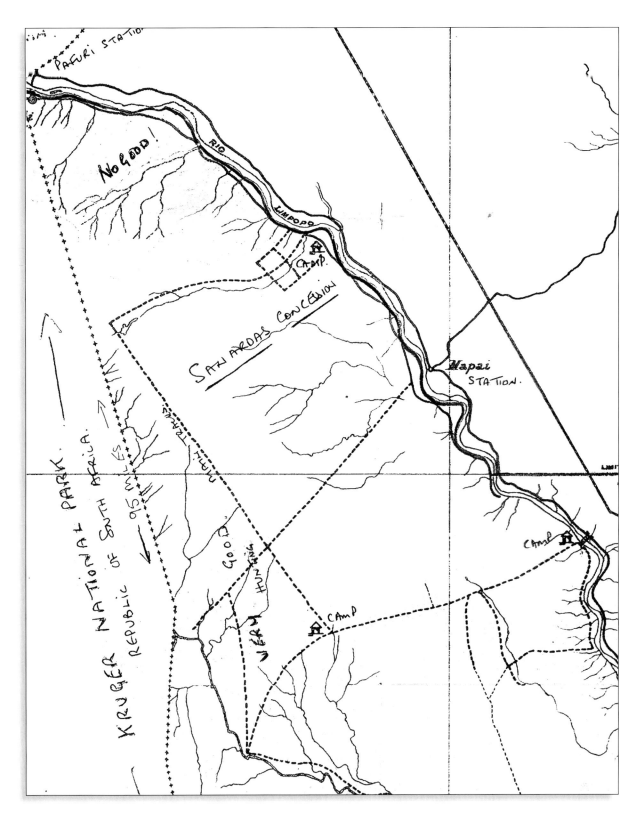

eral heads estimated at between 45 and 47 inches in width in the Gorongoza National Park.

There was, however, considerable variation in the massiveness of the horns. Those that were forest dwellers did not seem to have the heaviest horns, contrary to those in Kenya and Tanganyika. However, the altitude must have played its part, as most of the game country of Mozambique is seldom over 2000 feet, and it is generally hot and humid.

Hunting on the Save River in the Mozambique Safarilandia Ltd. concession was rewarding. Here there was relatively open country, and some fine heads were obtained, one of 48.5 inches in width shot by John Reed and another by my old hunting compadre Ruis Quadros. H.R.H. Prince Don Carlos of Spain, before he became H.M. King Carlos, also shot a fine head with a 45-inch width. All of these heads came from the Save River area. The best of them was shot by the tsetse-fly department of Mozambique and had a width of 49 inches. A bull buffalo shot by F.C. Blasco at Kanga N'thole went nearly 50-inches wide, being 49.5 inches, but I never heard of one shot that was 50 inches wide, although I saw a live buffalo with horns of more than 50 inches on one famous occasion.

I was doing a survey with Wally Johnson of the Sarnadas concession in western Mozambique on the Mozambique side of the border with the Kruger National Park. We were near Mapai Station on the railway and on the western bank of the Limpopo River. We had driven westward towards the border of South Africa. Across the border, inside the Kruger National Park, was the park ranger station near the old Shingwidizi mine. In those days there was no fence along the border, simply a graded border track, and we were within two miles of the border in undulating country, which was relatively open with occasional clumps of short mopane bush. Our vehicle was an open short-wheelbase Land Rover with the windscreen down on the bonnet, and we had two trackers in the back.

Going across country was a rough ride. After finding a good view of a water hole, we stopped the car behind a convenient bush and took a rest—all of us expected to see a fine tusked elephant or two. (See the Mozambique subsection of Chapter 2.) Instead, before us there walked down to the water hole, in unrestricted view, a buffalo with the largest pair of horns I have ever seen in my life. Both Wally Johnson and I studied it with our binoculars.

The buffalo was quite unconcerned. Slowly we compared notes on the horns' length as compared with the length of its ears and other parts of its head. There was no question in our minds that it was 60 inches wide. The boss met well in the middle, and it was undoubtedly an old bull, though still well able to take care of itself and in prime condition. It did not have the massive thickness of the boss of the Masailand buffalo in Kenya and Tanganyika. The horns were longer and thinner but beautifully hooked. It was unquestionably a fantastic trophy.

We watched it for some time until neither of us could stand the suspense any longer. Should we shoot it? Wally had an old and beaten up .458 in the car. We could easily shoot it—it was a sitting duck from where we were—but we came to the right conclusion that if we did, it would cause considerable problems for all of us: we were not in our own concession but in that of Sr. Sarnadas by invitation for a few days, with no permission to shoot any trophies.

We started up the car, and the buffalo, carrying those great horns, never moved as we drove off. My lasting impression of him as he dropped his head to drink once more was that he was probably one in a million, never to be seen again.

Such is hunting all over the world.

OTHER COUNTRIES

Fine heads have come from Zimbabwe and Zambia, though I never did much hunting in either country. Nearly all of the good heads shot in Zambia came from the Luangwa Valley. Very few reasonably sized buffalo heads came from Uganda, although some fine heads did exist on Mount Elgon and further westward. The largest on record was taken by W.T. Yoshimoto at Lake Mburo and had a 49-inch width. It was difficult to find others better than 43 inches in width.

In 1978 I visited Ruanda and Burundi, and there, in the national parks, I saw some typical high-altitude buffalo heads with massive bosses and heavy horns extending to more than 45 inches in width. The national park authorities had put out for tender 10 buffalo bulls at Ghini, and I was asked if I would be interested in promoting safaris for them. I soon discovered, however, that this was a ploy for extra remuneration for national park staff, and I naturally refused to become involved. Little did I realise at that time that the creeping disease of corruption would spread to nearly every African country shortly thereafter.

A number of heads of substantial width came from South Africa in the very early years. Now that wildlife farming has become popular, better heads are beginning to come forward, and no doubt the increasing number of buffalo will show some increase in the quality of buffalo trophies in the years to come.

CHAPTER FIVE

LION HUNTING

The Big Cat

GENERAL OBSERVATIONS

In all the countries covered by this book there are lions of all shapes and descriptions, and they are all formidable adversaries when hunted. Perhaps the fiercest that I encountered were in southern Ethiopia, where they had, after several years of conflict with tribesmen's herds of domestic stock, been in confrontation with human beings for periods of sometimes 18 hours a day. Wherever there was increasing stock and human populations and competition for water amid dwindling game populations, lions were fighting for their very existence. Lions and humans, quite simply, cannot coexist. Furthermore, when they are in declining physical condition they will always pursue the easy option, attacking domestic stock and humans. Much of this chapter is a chronicle of these confrontations.

In my experience there is one great difference between lion and leopard: the lion appears to be less perceptive than the leopard. This is to say that a lion, when confronted with a safari car containing several people—and the car having no enclosed sides—does not appear to be able to see inside the car and recognise the occupants for what they are: human beings. I am quite sure this is not the case with leopard. Although they do not, I believe, see the occupants for what they are, leopard nevertheless recognise that the silhouette of a human is related to their innate knowledge of human beings and their in-born ability to recognise them.

The lion, the lion,
he dwells in the waste.
He has a big head and
a very small waist,
But his shoulders are stark and
his jaws they are grim
And a good little child will not
play with him.

—Hillaire Belloc
The Bad Child's Book of Beasts

I hit the lion over the head with
the barrels of the .470 rifle as
hard as I could.
. . . I struggled on my elbows to
get clear. Too late—the lion was
upon me. . . . I hit him in the
mouth with my right fist with all
the strength I had.

—J.K.-H.

I have had many personal experiences of this. On one occasion, in the Amboselli National Reserve in Kenya, my car failed to start when in close proximity to a pride of lions that my party and I were photographing. Climbing out of the car on the passenger side, I had to continue to keep the bulk of the car between me and the lions. Keeping my beret well over my face and my eyes, I froze whenever the lions looked at the car. In this way I was able to slide my body over the bonnet of the car and open the catch on the side nearest to the lions, and then open the other and raise the bonnet. Fiddling with the battery terminals, I asked my companions to press the self-starter—the engine fired. I got back in and we drove off and secured the bonnet elsewhere. On another occasion the clutch lever linkage became disconnected, the pin and circlip having fallen out. Working underneath the car left me on ground level with lions that were not 10 yards away. I froze when they looked and worked when their gazes were elsewhere. This would never have been possible with a leopard, although 30 years on into the 1990s, leopards have become very tame in some of the long-established parks. Even so, I remain convinced that they are a far more clear-sighted and perceptive cat.

Lions naturally vary in size, mane, and weight all over Africa. Generally speaking, climate makes a considerable difference. A cold climate produces bigger manes and bodies on the males and heavier bodies on the females. In the Southern Hemisphere, and in Botswana in particular, I found the lions to be the heaviest and best maned that I had ever encountered. In southern Africa, where summer and winter are more pronounced (temperatures dropping to below freezing in April and May), lions kill more often and move about far more than in a climate that is more equable. The lions in the Serengeti National Park of Tanzania are fat and do not exert themselves to anything like the extent that the lions of Botswana do, hence the tremendous muscle that the lions of Botswana build into their legs. Living off buffalo to a great extent also presents Botswana lions with a great deal more trial of strength than lions on the plains of the Serengeti, which almost trip over the game, particularly during migration time. In the Serengeti the lion has good ground on which to walk, whereas in Botswana it is sandy in the veld and swampy and wet in the Okavango Swamps (where lions swim strongly when crossing from island to island).

The variation in body weight is also obvious in northern Kenya, Somaliland, and Ethiopia, where male lions have poor manes by comparison but are lean and long in body, brought about by their search for game in thorny, dry bush country that is often waterless for many miles.

In these countries and in the Kalahari Desert I have watched lions sucking up all the stomach moisture from their kill before attempting to eat any flesh. On occasion, this takes hours, as they meticulously lick dry every part of the innards of their kill.

Generally speaking, cattle killers were nasty lions capable of devious tactics when hunted and when surprised. Lions that were constantly hunted also became so. As with many other animals of lesser ferocity, familiarity breeds contempt. There have been many examples of this both within and outside national parks and reserves. Campsites, which contain rubbish (e.g., fresh meat) that has interesting smells to a predator, have often become inadvertent danger points. I well remember a visiting Kenya farmer camping in an official campsite in the Serengeti National Park being dragged from his tent at night. Bitten through the neck whilst he was still half asleep, he died. The tent flap had been left open and pinned back, and he slept without a mosquito net. A mosquito net, whether there were mosquitoes or not, has saved many a life. A lion cannot recognise the profile of the human form when its silhouette is broken up by a mosquito net. On three occasions, I have had a sleeping member of my staff seized from around the fireside at night and dragged off by lions. In all three cases it was a male lion, and in all three cases the man was fortunately wrapped in a blanket and loin cloth, but not within a mosquito net. When the fire dies to nothing and the snores of the assembled sleepers are regular, the lion understands the situation, for it is similar to his own pride's behaviour. On most occasions the lion is not a man-eater but is well fed and simply curious. When the incumbent of the blanket wakes up and struggles, the lion is surprised, but his instinct in such circumstances asserts itself and he naturally feels that he has caught something worthwhile. Very fortunately, none of my staff were injured, but the following night after one of the attacks I noted that the back of the lorry—with the tailgate up—was the dormitory for the night.

I always kept a dozen thunder flashes in my tin trunk containing my clothes. When sleeping rough in the bush, I had one by my pillow with the brazzard. I seldom used one and can well remember keeping some for more than 20 years. Thinking they would be unserviceable and intending to throw them away, I struck them, but all were very serviceable. Thunder flashes were effective against elephant when they strayed too close to camp and when hunting, in the avoidance of shooting other game in self-defence that had been disturbed by the taking of one of their number as a trophy.

Lion hunting can be easy, but it can be both dangerous and difficult as well. In all the days I spent hunting in Africa, I have on more occasions come close to probable death by lions than any other animal. Reflection persuades me that the reason for this is the lion's ability to hide away and conceal itself so well in the long grass and foliage for which its tawny colour provides more than adequate camouflage.

Of all the most threatened species of dangerous game in Africa, I believe the lion is the most likely species to disappear in the forthcoming century. Lions cannot be easily controlled. They follow game, and game follows weather patterns. The meteorology of this world is no respecter of humans and their cultivations. Where game is removed, lions have no alternative food supply and are forced by their desire to live to come into competition with humans and their domestic stock. This puts the king of beasts in enforced retreat. Some of the largest of the national parks are now beginning to experience the long-term effects of the enclosure of wildlife. Either the numbers of dangerous animals build up and spill out of the park, causing serious problems and loss to surrounding human-controlled areas, or they fall almost to endangered species levels. Inbreeding also has its effect. For example, from recent research it seems that loss of immunity from diseases may be the cause of much-reduced lion populations.

SOME FACTORS TO BE BORNE IN MIND WHEN BAITING

I have found the greatest success baiting for lion when following these procedures as far as the geography and environment will allow.

1. Choose a tree:
    - where the cat has a safe, covered approach to it from a 'lie-up' area (normally a river bed of dense undergrowth or similar terrain) and where the wind is blowing from the bait to the lie-up point
    - where, if the lion arrives at the tree and is about to eat the bait, he will be at an exact right angle from the firing point, i.e., broadside on (see final note no. 1)
    - where, if the right angle shot can be achieved, the cat is looking directly into the sunlight when looking at the firing point
2. Make sure you clear a space at the bottom of the tree that can be easily seen from your hiding place, so that when the lion falls and hits the ground the effect of the bullet can be judged and, if necessary, a second shot made.
3. For a short shot, clear one or two lines of approach from the tree to the lie-up area for the cat and block off others. This will confine his approach and escape to a known direction.
4. Make sure the bait is pulled well up to the branch from which the lion will feed and cover it with evergreen branches; a few wait-a-bit thorn branches are also useful. If vultures have seen you hoisting glistening, freshly skinned meat into a tree, you can be sure that only a thick covering of thorns will prevent them from cleaning it out completely by next day. When the bait is hung, make sure

all small branches are cut out from where the cat may lie on the ground nearby, so that no deflection of the bullet occurs on its way to the target area.

5. Choose a site for the hide/blind well out of the prevailing wind so that, as the lion comes up to the tree from the lie up area, there is no chance that he will get wind of those in the hide/blind.

6. Make sure the hide/blind:
    • is thick enough to conceal all internal movement, particularly if no. 4 is not possible
    • has two small holes so that two people can shoot at the same time (professional hunters have to see if the cat is properly shot and also if it is male or female)
    • is as thick on both sides as it is in front
    • has enough view at the back to see if any other animal is approaching, such as an elephant or rhino, and ideally have a third person watching the rear holding a heavy calibre rifle (see 'Mauled by a Lion' on page 216)
    • is a comfortable place to sit, with the floor cleared of sticks and stones, and has enough room for a couple of collapsible stools
    • allows you to have a really good rest when you shoot, so you can rest the right or left elbow solidly and are able to hold the fore-end of the rifle in your hand, thus insulating it from the 'jump' that will occur when wood touches wood. It will lead to a very inaccurate shot if the rifle is not resting in your hand, which acts as an ideal shock absorber.

7. Clear a path of approach to the blind/hide for some 200 yards and ensure in so doing that you are not in sight of the likely lie-up area. Remember also that the lion may be lying near the tree. Check this with binoculars before you set off for the blind/hide.

8. There are a few useful items you need in a blind/hide that can be carried in your pocket:
    • a small pair of garden snippers (to clear your line of fire if drying foliage has fallen into it)
    • a flashlight to enable you to follow the path back whence you came
    • a boiled sweet or two to stop coughing

9. Clothes:
    • Don't be cold and don't be exposed to flies biting your exposed skin so that you have to strike at them and make quick movements and slapping sounds.
    • Wear long trousers and a long-sleeved shirt of a khaki, camouflaged, or dark colour.
    • Don't wear stiff clothes that 'crackle' when you move.
    • Wear a floppy bush hat.
    • Use a camouflage scarf as insulation when shooting and resting the gun before firing.
    • Take advantage of heavy boots. Remember, if you are going to get chewed on by a lion, it is best to have some clothes on!

10. Make sure you have a complete understanding with the staff left in the car as to what they should do when you fire the shot. My practice has always been to carry a shrill whistle, and only when those in the car hear it are they to act as instructed. You do *not* want the car arriving just as you make a second shot or a stalk.

11. If you are in an area of human population or grazing stock, make sure you inform the local people of your attempt to remove a potential danger to them. An individual wandering through the bait and lie-up area is the last thing that is needed.

12. When hanging the bait, throw the major contents of the stomach (partly digest-

ed grass and foliage) all about the tree, the trunk of the tree, and general area below the bait.

13. Drag the carcase about and, if possible, to and from the lie-up position and the tree by the route you would like the cat to approach the tree. You do not necessarily need to drag the bait for miles along roads, tracks, and sand rivers. When baiting in a large sand river and putting up several baits, it is advisable to join the baits with drag marks and to check the drag marks for tracks when en route to check the bait for a feeding lion.

14. If there is a convenient spot where a lion may lie after having fed on the bait, but out of sight of the hide/blind, lightly cover the spot with thorn bushes, thus forcing the lion to lie where you can see it.

15. Most important of all, make sure that the cat does, as far as is reasonable, what you want it to do and lies where you want it to lie at the base of the tree or in close proximity to it.

NOTES

1. Remember that insofar as lions are concerned, the bait should hang downwards so that by standing on its hind legs the lion can feed on the extremities of the meat, and that such meat as is accessible will remain to entice him to return and hold him in the area for several days.

2. Never shoot at a cat with a spotlight: it is illegal and unsporting. However, if a cat is shot in late afternoon, a spotlight is essential to ascertain its death or wounding.

KENYA

The safari industry's clients all seemed to put lion as a high priority on their list of desired trophies. The professional hunters, for their part, were fortunate in being able to bait for lions, which in some other countries was not such an effective way of enticing the big cat within killing range from a concealed position. In essence, therefore, one hunted lions as one hunted leopard, except that the bait was larger and hung lower. The terms and conditions that apply to this procedure are nearly the same as those expressed in Chapter 6 on leopard.

Lion occurred and could be hunted anywhere in Kenya. In the early days they were considered vermin, particularly in the Northern Frontier District (N.F.D.). However, Masailand was the area in which the best trophies were obtainable. The lions there were either great black- or blond-maned beasts. In the N.F.D. the thorn scrub took its toll on the mane hair of the lion, leaving him a rather scruffy fellow that looked at times as though he had been partly plucked like a chicken. Generally speaking, these lions were of a nasty disposition, having been continually chased and hunted by local tribesmen in defence of their stock.

A surprising number of sportsmen, professional hunters, and settlers were killed while hunting lions in Kenya. Perhaps the person I knew best was Henry Poolman, who was shot by his gunbearer when facing a charging lion as he approached a bait with his client. In a scenario similar to that described in 'A Hunting Accident with Rhino' (p. 105), the gunbearer panicked and decided to take part in the action, with fatal results.

In the 1920s, west of Nairobi, the outcrops of lava rock at the base of Mounts Longonot and Suswa in the semiopen country below the Rift's escarpment were the refuges of the lions that lived off the abundant game of many different species on the surrounding plains. Not far away, on the shores of Lake Naivasha and to the north, were some very sizeable estates, and many of their owners were keen sportsmen. On occasion, lions were driven from the plains to their refuges in the outcrops of lava rock, in which lay in wait the local hunters. Considerable numbers of lions were shot in this way, which reduced the number of stock killers. Many of these lions were shot from horseback. As the number of cattle grew, they invaded the wild animals' grazing grounds and came into competition with the game and its predators for water and grass. Naturally, all this increased the number of lion-human confrontations.

Perhaps by compiling some of the more famous episodes into a list including those who were killed by lions in East Africa, I can demonstrate to the reader the serious nature of the problem.

Grant's Gazelle

Europeans Killed by Lions
John W. O'Hara—Kenya—1899
Ungan Singh—Kenya—1899
Charles Royal—Kenya—1900
Two European Railway Line construction workers—1900
Stephen Bagnall—Kenya—1902
George Grey—Kenya—1904
G. Lucas—Kenya—1906
Walter Ernest Stuart—Kenya—1911
D.E. Wattville—Kenya—1914
Fritz Schindelar—Kenya—1914
Paul Rainey—Kenya—1919
Robert Foster—Kenya—1920
George Outram—Kenya—1922
Diana Hartley—Tanganyika—1961
Henry Poolman—Kenya—1967
(shot while hunting a lion)

Total: 16

Africans and Indians Killed by Lions Between 1895 and 1901 between Nairobi and Mombasa

30 Indian railway construction labourers
120 African railway construction labourers
130 African natives living in the railway construction area
26 Africans killed by the man-eater of Darajani
(shot by J.K.-H. in 1962)

Total: 306*

*Note: This figure does not include those killed by man-eaters shot by J.A. Hunter.

Lions Admittedly Shot by a Handful of Professional Hunters and Farmers

Hill brothers—200
Rainey—123
Simpson—365
Stuart Edward White—426

Total: 1114

Note: There are seven victims of lion attacks buried in Nairobi's old cemetery. Add these to the above figures and all those killed in defence of their stock all over Kenya from 1875 to, say, 1990, and you probably have some 1000 people, at a very conservative estimate, who were killed by lions. If you were to take these figures on to other countries in Africa, you would have a pretty good idea of just how well the king of beasts and his consorts performed against high-velocity rifles coupled with the guile of the human brain. Finally, if four well-known sportsmen and hunters shot 1114 lions between them, I wonder just how many were shot in all these years.

Whilst these very sketchy figures are no more than a rough indication of the quantities of lions killed and the casualties sustained in so doing, they do provide a small indication of the risks involved for hunters of that day. Most professional hunters of my vintage and earlier will all say that there were far more people killed by lions than any records could possibly show.

Hunting lions in Kenya was a major part of my safari activity. Although I had no major problems in doing so, nevertheless, as time passed lions became used to being hunted and so learned the tricks of the trade. It became more and more difficult to outwit them, and when baiting in some areas was disallowed to give them additional protection, it became extremely difficult to find them. In the N.F.D., where trophy lions were unlikely to occur, it was easier to track them. In Masailand, where there was permanent grass everywhere (and occasional rain), it was almost impossible. Lions that had been hunted learned to feed at night, and shooting with the aid of a light was forbidden. I do remember, however, on several occasions that odd things happened with lions.

I was camped in the Kajiado District, part of Kenya Masailand about 70 miles from Nairobi. I had taken my clients to Nairobi the previous day and returned to camp. My next safari was not due into camp for three days, so I was looking forward to a quiet day or two in camp to catch up on paperwork. Having marked all the trophies of the departed safari clients and packed them in the back of the truck, I noticed that the carcase of an oryx that had been shot by the now-departed clients had been moved from the tree in which it hung and placed in the back of the truck. In due course, I went to bed believing that the back of the truck would be closed up by shutting the tailgate when everyone went to sleep. However, this little chore was forgotten.

At 2.00 A.M. I heard a scratching noise on my tent and a hoarse whisper from Edward, my gunbearer.

'Bwana, there is a lion in the truck, and it's eating the trophies'.

I had no wish to shoot the lion. My incoming client wanted a lion, and if there was one in the area, it had to be preserved for him. Fumbling as best I could, still half asleep, I got out my thunder flashes from my tin box. Giving Edward my .470 and taking my Purdey Paradox 12 bore, we carefully approached the truck, which was parked on its own some 30 yards from the kitchen. It was a moonlit night, and it was not long before I saw the shadowy shape of a lion rooting about in the back of the truck. The salt on the trophies had captured its taste—for the moment.

It now became a question of timing. If I held on to the thunder flash too long, it would go off before it was pitched into the back of the truck. Striking the brazzard would make a slight noise, and so would the fizzing thunder flash. Choosing a moment when the lion was making a noise, I struck the brazzard and held on. After a calculated pause, I hurled the thunder flash into the back of the truck and hit the lion square on its backside. The lion was now bottled into the truck, the sizzling thunder flash between it and freedom. With a tremendous bang the thunder flash went off. Incredibly, the lion jumped on top of the cab, and at the same time the whole camp came to life. Flashlights appeared.

Frightened and disoriented by the explosion in such close proximity, the lion leapt off the cab and landed on top of a staff tent, which collapsed immediately. The occupants were panic stricken and began shouting for dear life. The lion disentangled itself from the guy ropes and bounded away still unable to get its bearings, for it went full tilt into a large tree and was knocked backwards on its haunches.

I shouted to everyone to keep still—if they valued their lives. We waited silently for some 10 minutes, by which time the lion had taken its leave. A week later we shot a good lion. Although he showed no sign of a singed mane, it was probably our erstwhile truck raider, as he had a distinct bump on his forehead.

On another occasion, when hunting with Ace Christmas, we were driving in the MacKinnon Road area some 60 miles from Mombasa and north of the main Mombasa-Nairobi road. We were bashing along at 30 miles per hour heading for camp when suddenly, out of the bush on the left, a full grown male lion shot into the road like a petrified rabbit. I had to brake to avoid him. He tore off down the road as fast as he could. By this time we had come to a full stop. The lion kept on running until he disappeared from sight. Imagine our surprise when another mile down the road the lion appeared from the right-hand side and performed the same antic. This happened three times before we decided to break up his performance. We passed him doing 40 miles per hour so close that I could have grabbed his tail as I went by. He dived into the bush, and on we went. Our gunbearers were highly amused, but on our return to camp one of our staff, who was credited with some degree of knowledge of the supernatural, was sure it was a 'sign' to us.

We never discovered the significance of the lion's performance, but two days later we were travelling the same road again. Again, we were bowling along at about 30 miles per hour when Edward called out that he wanted us to stop. Backing up, we looked at a small tree some 200 yards away. There, gently rocking in the wind and clinging onto the small branches, was a maned lion. He was about 14 feet off the ground, and no other animal was in sight. There was no kill or any other obvious reason for him to be there. We drove on, and some half a mile later we stopped and discussed the extraordinary phenomenon.

Ace had a lion licence. We walked back to the spot by a circuitous route, getting the wind in the right quarter for our approach. As we reached convenient cover, there, sure enough, was the lion up the tree. At 120 yards Ace put a shot in right behind the shoulder. Slowly the lion fell from the tree. Approaching to 30 yards, Ace gave him a finishing shot. We made a very close inspection of the lion and could find nothing wrong with him whatsoever. After some discussion, we decided to try to backtrack the lion to see if, in fact, he was the same crazy fellow we had encountered previously. To our surprise, his tracks led to a hitherto unsuspected water hole that had water left in it that would last for about two days. Thereafter the tracks led straight back to the road. We decided to return to camp for lunch, after which we would head out in the opposite direction.

When the staff heard the story of how we had found the lion, the skinner, Ndambuki, came to me and apologised for the fact that he could not bring himself to skin the lion. On enquiry it appeared that he and his fellow Wakamba were convinced that the lion was in all probability a man-eater possessed of the brains and souls of his victims. It would have been a mistake to laugh at such people's convictions, the consequences of which could be disloyalty. Edward, being a Catholic, skinned the lion!

No comment on lion hunting in Kenya would be complete without mentioning the traditional methods of lion hunting by the Masai, which took place more obviously due to their stock being killed by marauding lions. However, within the internal relationship of the men of their clan, the warrior section, consisting of those aged between 18 and 30, chose to prove their prowess by spearing a lion. Very naturally this was not always successful, and over the years there can be no doubt that many *moran*, as the warriors were called, succumbed to the wounds they received. In 1953, a full-length documentary called *Masailand* was made for the American Museum of Natural History and was financed by the chairman of the Monsanto Chemical Corporation, Edgar Queeny. This was the last occasion upon which the government of Kenya permitted traditional lion hunting to take place. The safari to provide the guiding and outfitting for the making of this film was one of the first undertaken by Syd Downey and Donald Ker on the formation of Ker & Downey Safaris Ltd. shortly after the 1939–45 War.

There were a number of famous films made of African wildlife, particularly featuring the lion.

Safari, starring Victor Mature, involved the filming of a lion leaping upon the star from a ledge above him. This was achieved by using a dummy lion. Unfortunately, the dummy was a little too heavy and flattened poor Victor!

Terry and Jeanne Mathews, long-time friends, did a great deal to encourage the making of films in East Africa and were closely involved in the making of the film *Lion* in 1960.

Perhaps the most famous film, *Born Free*, starring Bill Travers and Virginia McKenna, was made in Kenya. This was the story of the return to the wild of Elsa, the lioness brought up to maturity by George and Joy Adamson.

The symbol of a lion on Kenya's coat of arms is a natural association with the king of beasts, for if ever there was a natural habitat for lion, Kenya was without question just that.

The Man-Eater of Darajani

Perhaps there is more lion-hunting history in Kenya than in any other country in Africa, firstly because lions were more numerous than elsewhere, and secondly because the population of settlers and English aristocrats inevitably came into contact with them in their farming enterprises and in the general development of the country and its communications. Famous in this regard were the man-eating lions that bestrode the railway line under construction between Mombasa at the coast and Nairobi 300 miles inland at 5500 feet above sea level. Lieutenant Colonel J.H. Patterson wrote at length about these lions in his book, *The Man-Eaters of Tsavo*.

As a preface to this story, it would be well to place it in context with other such occurrences with man-eating lions.

In 1928, Tom Bennett, an engineer and one of the pioneers of the Uganda railways that started in Mombasa, had this to say when writing to the *Daily Mail* (he refers of course to Patterson's immortal tale).

 was stationed at Makindu at the time Mr. Royal was hauled through the carriage window by a man-eating lion. The lion entered the compartment by the door, stepping over one of Mr. Royal's comrades, seized Mr. Royal in his mouth, jumped through the carriage window, carried him into the jungle about 100 yards and devoured part of him.

Mr. J. Costillo and others, including myself, designed a trap with which to snare the lion. A few days later we received a wire from the stationmaster stating that the lion had been captured. When we went to view our prize we discovered that instead of a lion, we had captured two natives, whose intention it was to steal our bait, which consisted of a goat.

We reset the trap and next day received a wire: 'Come at once, lion captured'. We ran a special train from Makindu to the scene of the trap and this time found the lion.

On one occasion I had visited a friend's tent and on my return journey fell asleep. Upon awakening at break of day, I was astonished to see a lion, a lioness, and two cubs within six feet of me. I afterwards came to the conclusion that the lion had licked my face and awakened me.

—T. Bennett, Ipplepen, near Newton Abbot, Devon, U.K.

And Surgeon Rear Admiral C.M. Beadnell, C.B., wrote to the *Daily Mail* on December 21, 1926, as follows:

ne night I was sitting with my twenty Wakikuyu bearers round our camp fire on the banks of the Athi River in Kenya. I can see them now, their swarthy skins greased with evil-smelling hippopotamus fat, glistening in the flickering firelight, in marked contrast with their pointed, white, filed teeth; their hair, matted and clogged with the red mud they love to rub into it, the longer locks hanging from their scalps in a succession of little stalactites; their paunches distended with a recent gorge on rice and zebra; their tongues freely loosened by a great circulating bowl of punch. When one of the stories raised a perfect howl of delight I asked the interpreter to repeat it to me in English. He did so, and I had to join in the general laugh at an infallible remedy for frightening the hungriest of man-eaters.

'All you have to do', said the Wakikuyu, 'is to turn your back on the lion, place your head between your legs, and looking him in the eyes, walk straight at him, whereupon the lion would down head and tail and bound away from the monstrosity'.

In Darajani, Kenya, in 1962, I was better equipped.

Safaris in the early 1960s were not all that plentiful. The costs of maintaining one's equipment and vehicles were high. The economics of the profession were roughly that if you had six 21- or 30-day safaris between June and December, you were on the proverbial 'pig's back'. A good Christmas on the coast of Kenya, and a couple of safaris between January and March, and life was serene. Any little private trip at reduced cost, using a long-wheelbase Land Rover and trailer, was a welcome and profitable diversion, mainly because it kept you out of trouble and gave

Top: *Making a pictorial record for my report to the game department of Kenya.*

Above: *The point at which Mindu Ngui was attacked and dragged into the undergrowth. The drag mark made by his body can be seen beyond the far end of the bow (1964).*

no opportunity for spending unwisely, and also it provided an excellent chance of reconnoitring the country for future safaris.

John Perrott, an oil-pipe-laying expert with Bechtel Corporation of America, had made contact with me with a view toward taking a hunt on the basis of financing my reconnaissance of new areas, the idea being that if we saw a worthwhile trophy he would get the opportunity of collecting it. About this time I had bought my first truck, so John's enquiry suited me well, and I decided to take the truck along, too. Elephant would be our main quarry, so we set off from Nairobi down the Mombasa Road, leaving at about 11.30 in the morning. Using a dirt road, we made it about halfway to Mombasa by dark and decided to camp for the night on the west side of the road a mile or so into the bush, which was sparsely inhabited by local Wakamba people. Three miles to the north-east of us was Darajani Station on the Mombasa-Nairobi railway line, which eventually made its way up to Uganda in central Africa and ended in the shadow of the Mountains of the Moon at Kasese. We were some 60 miles west of the spot where, during the construction of the railway line, 'the man-eaters of Tsavo' rampaged among the 'coolies' from India imported to construct the railway line.

Our thoughts, however, were not of man-eaters but of big ivory. It was raining quite heavily, and some migration of elephants could be expected to come out of the Tsavo National Park that lay to the north and east of the main road. The border of the national park was the Athi River. This left us with an area of some 30 miles north-east of the main

The partly eaten body of Mindu Ngui in the thicket.

road up to the Athi River in which to hunt. To the north of this area was the Msongoleni River, a known haunt of big tuskers. Equipped with a winch, spades, and machetes, we set out into the area. Ahead of us, as we left camp and crossed the main road, was Darajani Station. A small by-road connected the main road to the railway station. We took this road as the fastest and most direct line to cross the railway and head into elephant country to the north-east.

As I drove down the track to the station, I barely noticed a bow and several arrows strewn across the track (in fact, before recognition of the objects dawned on me I had allowed the car to run over them). Bringing the car to a standstill, I called John's and the three gunbearers's attention to this. We all alighted and walked back up the track unarmed. When I came to the bow and arrows, I soon realised that they were in use only minutes before—the poison at the rear end of the arrow head was shining and fresh.

'John', I said, 'we've got a poacher running for his life, and he is so scared he has thrown his bow and arrows away!'

At that moment, Edward, my gunbearer of many years, said, 'Bwana, there is another matter, look! The man has been attacked—there are scratches in the soil like a lion's claw marks'.

Instantly alerted, we examined the marks. Sure enough, a man—the owner of the bow and arrows—had been pulled down and dragged off into the bush. I walked the 50 yards back to the car, Edward took out my .470 Westley Richards double with soft-nosed ammunition, and

I grabbed my camera. John had his .375 Winchester in his hands. We returned to the spot together. I took some pictures and handed my camera to Musioka (my other gunbearer), and Edward and I bent to the task of tracking the lion. Within seconds, we saw the drag mark in the grass where the lion had hauled his victim into some thick and leafy bush. Crouching down on all fours, I crawled along the drag mark.

I was some 10 yards into the bush flat on my stomach, my .470 rifle pointing to my front, when there was the most blood-curdling snarl from immediately in front of me. I could see nothing and could shoot nothing with accuracy, so thick the foliage. Discretion was the better part of valour—I made out the dismembered arm of a human being who could not be alive. Slowly I retreated to more snarls and growls.

Returning to the road, John and I made a complete circuit of the area. The spot where the lion was laid up was completely surrounded by cultivated, cleared land. In the middle of the patch of bush in which the man-eater was chewing upon his unfortunate victim was a tall tree with a good crotch in it—an ideal observation point.

Leaving Musioka to watch the area and Ndambuki (the third gunbearer) up the road to stop all the traffic, the rest of us jumped into the car and went down to Darajani Station itself. The stationmaster was asleep, having attended to a passing train at three o'clock that morning. On being woken and brought to us, he was told of our find. The effect of this news was electric.

'Oh my God', he said in a scared whisper, 'it's the one. It's the lion that has eaten many people. It uses the noise of the train to grab them here at the station'. After further discussion and reassurance, he calmed down and gave us a full account of the activities of the man-eater.

I sent John and Edward back to camp to collect all the staff, leaving only a guard in camp, and to bring the empty truck to a point on the road before arriving at the spot where we had found the bow and arrows. There the truck was to stop, and Edward was to recruit as many able-bodied locals as he could. They were to be armed with sticks and stones and should ensconce themselves within and behind the high sides of the truck. In the meantime, the stationmaster agreed to send an urgent telegram to the game scouts stationed at Kibwezi 30 miles up the line. This is the text of the telegram:

Urgent Game Kibwezi: Have isolated man-eating lion in small patch of bush at Darajani near station. I intend destroying lion immediately. Suggest you inform warden at Makindu and come here to assist if possible. Am professional hunter and honorary game warden. John Kingsley-Heath.

From the stationmaster's story the lion had consistently taken people at night, almost always on the north-east side of the line. So often had the lion done this that when a goods train came in with no passengers, the stationmaster had taken to the roofs of the carriages to communicate with the guards' van, dropping off at his station door as the train passed up the line. In those days, the train burned wood fuel and stopped at Darajani for water, but the stationmaster had reached an unwritten agreement with the train driver and fireman that in the darkness they must replenish supplies further up the line because of the risk of being taken by the lion.

'Surely', I had said to the stationmaster, 'you must have reported this'.

'Yes', he said, 'but they don't listen, as they do not want to come at night. This lion is very, very clever—he has all the brains of his 26 victims now, and he will never be caught. He has learnt exactly what to do when a train comes. He is not afraid of the train. He even put his feet on the footplate of the engine, and only hot coals from the fireman make him leave'.

Outwardly, I kept a concerned face. Inwardly, I was smiling to myself at the thought of a lion with the brains of 26 people, albeit uneducated ones at that.

I set out to return to the scene, walking the short distance and meeting up with John at the car. Quickly we mapped out a plan. The best idea we conceived was that the lion should be persuaded to break into open ground in front of me, where it would be shot. To persuade the lion to conform to this plan, we left the hunting car on the road in close proximity to the arrows with two camp staff who, when the signal was given, would blow the car's horn and make as much noise as possible. On the north-east side we placed the truck, and on the west, on a prominent anthill, I placed myself with Edward. I was armed with my .470 Westley Richards double-barrelled rifle (with ejectors) with 500-grain soft-nosed bullets. As a second gun Edward held for me my Purdey Paradox double-barrelled, 12-bore, self-opening shotgun. In the right barrel was loaded a cartridge of lethal ball, in the left barrel an aptly named Italian-made *cartuccia gigante*, which contained 12 large, spherical steel shot.

Y = John Perrott's perch in the tree with the .375 Winchester Magnum. X = man-eating lion in bushes. The tree was approached from the right by Perrott and me.

The man-eater with a porcupine quill nine inches up its left nostril.

John Perrott had the sticky spot. He went up into the crotch of the tall tree not more than 15 yards from the lion. To do this he and I gingerly moved through the bush, keeping the tree between us and the estimated position of the lion. The tricky part came when John had to put down his .375 Winchester Model 70 (loaded with 300-grain soft-nosed bullets) against the tree whilst he climbed into the fork. At the same time, I had to bend down so that John could use my back as a stepping-stone to hoist himself upwards. A snarl from the lion ensured that we did not dally! John, now being safely in the tree, was to shoot the lion irrespective of my signals if he got a clear shot.

Having retreated to cleared land, I took up my position on the anthill. The signal to start operations was the raising of a white handkerchief on the end of a stick. Edward had the stick in one hand and the Purdey Paradox in the other. On my instruction he raised the stick with the handkerchief, and all hell was let loose. A veritable torrent of sticks and stones descended on the spot where the lion lay. The Wakamba tribesmen in the truck—in their impregnable position—were unafraid and gave full vent to their feelings in no uncertain manner. Several stones must have hit the lion for it snarled several times. Each time it did so there was an answering crescendo from the lorry and the hunting car.

The lion could stand it no longer and moved out.

'He's coming out!' John yelled from his tree.

The lion, hearing John's voice in close proximity, merely hastened his exit. As he did so, he presented John with a raking shot across the right side of the lion's body, angling forward into the heart and lungs. John's .375 roared. It was no easy shot, fired relatively unbalanced from the

crotch of the tree, and John hit him a fraction too far back. This swung him directly facing me. The impact of the bullet jerked the lion's hindquarters so that it changed direction 90 degrees. Now I was faced with a frontal shot and not a sideways shot, which we had planned.

The work of a man-eating lion.

In a second the lion saw Edward and me on the anthill and came bald-headed for us, snarling, his mouth open and bloody, a patchy, mangy mane—he was in a terrible condition—but he was coming. *It's like shooting birds*, I thought as I raised my double .470.

The bullet from the first barrel hit him just above the left shoulder; the second hit him low in the chest—he was still coming, now 10 yards away. The guns changed hands, and by the time he was 15 feet away he took the lethal ball from the Purdey full in the head and the second barrel full in the chest. He died right there, 10 feet in front of us.

'*Tayari!*' we shouted. ('He's finished!') Cheers echoed from the truck, and John jumped out of his tree and came over to us. No one descended from the truck.

David Ommanney and I with Jim Rikoff of Winchester and a lion shot with .375 Winchester Magnum Model 70 (pre-1964) at Hell's Gate, Kenya, in thick leleshwa bush (1963).

We examined the carcase of the lion. Jammed up his nostril was a porcupine quill nine inches long. Only the tip of it was visible. What agony the lion must have experienced. Every time he went to eat something it merely pushed the porcupine quill farther up his nose.

Our plan had worked well, and John, the gunbearers, and I rejoiced in our success. The Purdey Paradox's work had been sensational. Within the skin covering the lion's skull the bullet had literally vaporised the skull bone. You could pat the lion's head into any shape you chose. I had often used the Paradox as a trap gun, but this was one of the few occasions I had seen such evidence of its effectiveness.

We walked over to the bush where lay the body of the man who had been eaten by the lion—a third of him was gone. I had the gunbearers clear the bush round him, and slowly the people of the area began to gather. Gradually they began to realise that they were at last rid of the man-eater and his terror. They began to shake John's and my hands. Already there were some hundred people present. I detailed off Musioka, who was of the same tribe as the local people, to take the women and children to see the lion where it had fallen and point out that the lion was not bewitched but had a porcupine quill up its nose, which was the cause of its behaviour. Whilst the rest of the staff loaded the lion into the truck, John and I sat down under a tree to learn the background of the unfortunate man.

His name was Mindu Ngui, a Wakamba tribesman who lived by hunting and poaching. He had been returning at break of day from a hunting trip when he was set upon by the lion.

At this point the game scouts from Kibwezi arrived. After they had examined both the body of the lion and that of Mindu Ngui and expressed their joy and satisfaction at the dispatch and end of a job that none of them would have relished, they added to the story of Mindu Ngui's nefarious activities. It appeared that near Kibwezi there was a hotel called Bushwhackers, a well-known spot to stop and spend the night when driving from Nairobi to Mombasa and vice versa. The Stantons, who owned the place, had had a pet rhino, which had been kept since it was a calf, had been very tame, and had been full grown with a sizeable horn. One night it had been killed by poisoned arrows and was discovered the next morning with the horn cut off. Mindu Ngui was thought to be the culprit. If he was, he certainly got his just desserts.

It was raining heavily, and John Perrott and I moved on to Masailand farther south-west where the ground was not so soft. Here we hunted lion and leopard most successfully. John was rewarded after some hard work with a huge black-maned lion and a leopard.

At the end of the safari I called into Hunters Lodge at Kiboko some way beyond Kibwezi towards Nairobi, which was now the home of J.A. Hunter. J.A. listened to my story with interest and stated that it was his considered opinion that from the days of the commencement of the construction of the railway, it was quite probable that some 900 people had met their end at the claws and teeth of man-eating lions between Nairobi and Mombasa. That left 876 after deducting the tally of humans amassed by man-eaters.

Twenty-five years previously, J.A. Hunter had recalled in his book, *Hunters' Tracks*, the following:

 telegram from the District Commissioner Makindu: 'Most urgent. Man-eating lion creating havoc in Darajani. Three native victims. Deal immediately'. With a trap gun set the lion was shot. We skinned the beast and it then became clear why she became a killer. Porcupine quills were deeply imbedded in the muscles of her forearms, in her throat and in the tendons of her hind legs. There was nothing in her stomach except the remains of a native's scalp.

When I discussed the end of the man-eater of Darajani with Syd Downey and Donald Ker, both were adamant that far more human beings were killed by lions than most people thought possible.

TANGANYIKA (TANZANIA)

Loliondo, Tanganyika, adjacent to the Serengeti National Park in the late 1950s. One saw probably three to four lions of this quality daily.

To give my reader a little historical background, I will momentarily digress from the business of lion hunting.

In the early 1950s there were five main access roads to Tanganyika from Kenya. In the east, the road near the coast connected the port of Mombasa in Kenya with the port of Tanga in Tanganyika. Then, north-westwards for 200 miles to the east side of Kilimanjaro, the spur of the Kenya railway took off at Voi to the border post at Taveta. A road ran parallel to the railway, both of which were built during the 1914–18 War. West of the Kilimanjaro massif, the main access road south passed via the border post at Namanga to the Tanganyika border post of Longido. This was the axis for the push southwards of the East African Mounted Infantry from Kenya in the 1914–18 War and has now become the Great North Road, connecting East Africa with South Africa. Going west more than 200 miles was another somewhat tenuous connection across the Mara Bay of the east coast of Lake Victoria to the road to Kisii in south-west Kenya. The final connection in the extreme western part of Tanganyika enabled communication between the town of Bukoba north-wards to Uganda across the Kagera River by ferry. My narrative is concerned with the Mara Bay crossing.

The Mara River, which runs almost due west from the Masai Mara drainage area in Kenya, was a natural boundary between what was originally British and German East Africa. As the Mara River runs westwards, the last hundred miles of its course runs through impenetrable papyrus swamps infested with huge crocodiles and large herds of hippo. However, the international border did not follow this natural geographical feature, but was simply a straight line drawn on the map westwards towards Lake Victoria. As a result, a small area known as Tarime was part of Tanganyika on the north side of the Mara River estuary and Mara Bay. To connect this small area a ferry across the bay was a necessity.

In the early 1950s, the district commissioner of this area was none other than Capt. E.C.T. Wilson, V.C., a distinguished soldier. He had won his Victoria Cross in Somaliland in 1941 whilst serving in the East Surrey Regiment defending the British withdrawal to the port of Berbera. Here the British forces were preparing to evacuate their troops in British Somaliland due to the vastly superior forces of the Italian army. Although wounded in both arms and legs, he nevertheless succeeded in holding up the Italian advance for a considerable period with a machine gun until rescued by his comrades. As district commissioner he was in charge

of the tribal area of the Wakuria in Tarime District. A tribe of polyglot
people of mixed Kisii, Watende, and Masai extraction, who were avid
and persistent poachers, lived in this area and were a real and constant
worry to the rapidly growing Serengeti National Park's administration.
They operated most particularly in the Lemai area between the north
bank of the Mara River and the Kenya border. At this point the Mara was
easily fordable as it left Kenya, and their raiding parties began to establish permanent camps in the area and spread south to Mugumu. My
friend and former P.H. Myles Turner described his confrontation with
these people in his book *My Serengeti Years*.

I decided that I would make a recce by boat into the Mara Swamp
and, after discussing it with Myles, I went up to Mara Bay and crossed
over to Tarime to see the district commissioner in whose district the
north part of the bank of the Mara River lay.

The Mara ferry was owned and operated by Mike Cottar, one of the
sons of the famous Charles Cottar, who founded Cottar's Safari Services
in 1924. Mike was probably the best known of Charles Cottar's sons,
Bud being the other. Many years previously, Mike, assisted by Roger
Courtney, had obtained a large luxury motor boat that had been purchased and brought up to Kisumu on a special train from Mombasa by a
member of the Woolworth family. After being used to hunt and fish
around the shore of this huge lake—the source of the Nile—the boat had
been abandoned. With Roger's help, Mike converted it into a ferryboat
and used it to cross Mara Bay, thus satisfactorily connecting the Tarime
and Musoma districts of Tanganyika for the first time in 1937.

Mike had died of blackwater fever in 1940, leaving his wife, Mona,

Top: The 'Moru Kopies King' in the Serengeti National Park, about the finest maned lion it is possible to see in the wild (1956).

Right: Lions kept in captivity in a cold climate grew manes over half their bodies.

to continue to run the ferry. Mona was a determined and forthright woman, who was assisted by a bottle of gin that always stood on the office table. She did not tolerate fools or inefficient Africans gladly. In spite of her small size it was obvious who was in charge. Bill Stapleton had been working the ferry, and with him she developed a satisfactory business relationship.

After taking advice from all whom I had met, I set off into the swamp. After a day and a night, during which irritable hippos attacked twice, I gave up and returned to the ferry, realising that a landward approach was the only way to get onto the north side of the Lemai area. It did not appear that any great 100-pound-tusked elephants and 50-inch-wide horned buffalo were hidden within the swamp. It's possible

that in fact they were there, but the risks to health, mind, body, and limb were too great. Several years later, in the back of Myles Turner's Super Cub, we did in fact see a large-tusked elephant that might have had 100-pound tusks, and we also saw some immense buffalo and several lion, but by this time the area had achieved protection.

The battle to control the Wakuria poachers continues. With an ever-increasing population they are dominating the area of the western boundary of the national park to such an extent that one wonders just how long the existing border will survive. Their activities, coupled with the indiscriminate and unprincipled hunting of lion in the areas adjacent to the western boundaries of the Serengeti National Park, have reduced the lion population to a bare minimum, and in my view the area is in

Peace and war in the Serengeti Partial Game Reserve in 1951.

He may be the king of beasts, but he has some equally impressive neighbors.

need of the imposition of far greater controls. Before this poaching occurred, both Eric Rundgren and I had taken several safaris into the Lemai Wedge area, which had been most successful. Soon, however, Wakuria poachers took such a toll on the local game populations that it was pointless to return.

Until recently, there was probably a larger lion population in Tanganyika than in any other African state. In 1950, lion and leopard were considered vermin in most of its provinces. Even in 1960 there were two lions on a minor game licence, and leopard were still considered vermin in most areas.

One day I received a telegram from George Rushby, the game warden at Mbeya, asking me to meet him in a few days in Iringa, some 240 miles east of Mbeya in Southern Highlands Province. When I arrived, George explained to me that a mutual acquaintance of ours, Major David Ricardo, was trekking cattle along the base of the escarpment to the north of Iringa, below which was the valley of the Ruaha River. He was expecting further lion trouble in the area of Pawaga and Isasi. There was a game scout stationed at Isasi who had so far failed to kill any of the stock-killing lions. He invited me to go there with an additional game scout to see what I could do.

After George had given me a letter of authority and informed the district commissioner, I set off for Pawaga. It was a hot and arid area. The riverine bush was thick with *mswaki* bushes (Swahili for bushes that grow on the banks of most East African rivers below 5000 feet) and low 'wait-a-bit' thorn scrub. The plan was to stake out a dead cow and dig a slit trench some 20 yards away in which to hide. There was a full moon. Saidi (the game scout) and I duly hid in the slit trench, and at 11.30 eight lions put in an appearance. The moon lit the scene perfectly, but not enough for me to see my foresight properly unless it was silhouetted against the sky. This was fine until the rifle was pointed at a lion and the sight disappeared against the bulk of the lion's body. We shot nothing that night, and by morning the cow had been finished. By evening, after the attentions of the vultures, it was gone. I was on a learning curve.

After visiting the surrounding cattle areas, we soon persuaded their herdsmen to donate an ancient cow to the lion eradication programme. This time a visit to the local shop at the Ruaha bridge, where the main road from Iringa crossed the river to Dodoma, provided us with two Tilley lamps (similar to Coleman lanterns) and a torch (battery-operated flashlight). We hung the Tilley lamps some distance away and behind us so as to give us a better all-round view. I tied the torch onto the underside of the barrel of my .318 rifle and, in a darkened native hut, tested the sight. The back glare from the torch was enough to light up the foresight. Back to the slit trench we went.

The lions arrived somewhat cautiously at 2.30 that morning and killed the old cow in seconds. Almost immediately, I had a good broadside shot on the male with a scruffy mane and a nasty disposition. He galloped off heart-shot, cannoned into a bush, and collapsed. The rest of the lions hardly paused in their meal. I picked a second—a huge lioness—and she went the same way. Gaining in confidence, I made a stupid mistake. I should have learned from the first shot that when heart-shot, a lion tears blindly off before collapsing. Therefore, taking a frontal shot at a lion facing straight at me could have unpleasant consequences. As I drew a bead on a big lioness facing me, this possibility did not occur to me until I had pulled the trigger and the bullet took her full in the chest and heart. She dropped her head and headed towards us—

there was no time to shoot. Saidi and I dropped to the floor of our slit trench, and the next thing we knew a lioness weighing 450 pounds had landed on top of us in its death throes, spurting blood all over us.

Our panic can well be imagined. Saidi froze—head in the bottom of the slit trench—petrified. My gun with the torch on was pointing skywards. *Let it die completely before you move*, I said to myself. After what seemed an eternity, I decided to chance a movement.

The lioness was very dead. Gradually Saidi and I extracted ourselves from beneath her. This was not in itself an easy task, as Saidi's legs were pinned beneath the lioness's back quarters and legs. I took a quick look at the rest of the lions, who were busy gorging themselves. After some heaving, Saidi got his legs free, and we both sat on the lioness. Saidi's .404 Jeffery was trapped beneath the animal. The lesson learned, I shot one more lioness and called it a day. A whistle blast sent the rest of the lions scurrying off, and a few minutes later the Land Rover and my gunbearer Asumani arrived. In the lights of the car, as we emerged from the slit trench covered with lioness blood, we presented an eerie and frightening sight. The other game scout felt us both all over to convince himself that we were not wounded in spite of our protestations to the contrary. I had learnt a lesson and given George and David a good laugh. If there was a next time, it would be a *machan* (an Indian tree platform) in a tree!

Southern Highlands Province of Tanganyika had some fine maned lions, many of which were located on the Buhoro Flats. Through this area ran the Ruaha River and its tributaries. One of my most memorable successes was shooting a greater kudu with 58-inch horns, a great black-maned lion, and a 100-pound-tusked elephant on the same day. This was an unforgettable experience, not just for the great success of the previous days, but because the sight of that enormous lion has remained vividly in my memory to this day.

At night I slept on a piece of canvas with a blanket to cover me under a mosquito net. My hat was my pillow. In the early hours of the morning a male lion roared and roared persistently till 4.30. He was not far away on the far side of the river. As the night wore on, he moved until I surmised that he must be about a mile upstream from me. At 4.45 I got up and made some tea. Asumani (my gunbearer) and I set out with two rifles—a .318 and a .404—an hour or so later. It was just getting light enough to see a hundred yards or a little more. Slowly we paralleled the river. After going some 400 yards, Asumani saw the greater kudu on our left. He was a whopper, and I knew the instant I saw him that he was bigger than any I had seen. I aimed for the shoulder but pulled the shot and broke his neck, killing him instantly. I stood by the kudu while Asumani sprinted back to the porters to alert them as to the newly acquired meat supply. On his return we walked on, convinced that the shot had probably scared the game out of the neighbourhood.

After the sun was well up at 7.30, we chanced to walk from behind a lot of dead and fallen trees to where we could see the river. There, crossing the river, was an enormous maned lion. We took cover, and I prepared myself for a shot. I had open sights on the .318, and the rising sun was directly in my eyes. I whispered to Asumani to hold his hat and hand over my forehead to shade my eyes from the sun. In a few moments, I experienced the most unforgettable sight of that great maned lion as he climbed the bank of the river and walked up onto the slope of a giant anthill. Before me, for a second, he stood there for all the world like a Kuhnert painting. Then he shook the water out of his mane and skin. As he did so, the water flying from his mane was back-lighted by the sun, giving him an almost ethereal appearance. My heart was beating faster than normal—was I about to shoot a heavenly lion? I squeezed the trigger gently, and the bullet hit exactly where I aimed, as he stood sideways on to me, right through both shoulders and his heart. He took one gigantic leap and stumbled into some broken shrubs, giving vent to the most ferocious and blood-curdling growls, which froze Asumani and me to the spot from which I had fired. We waited, and slowly the growls subsided. The growls ceased. We gave it a little longer and then moved to the anthill from which he had sprung so that we were able to look down upon him.

He was dead. It took us the better part of two and a half hours to skin him and push his carcase down an antbear hole just to make it more difficult for the vultures and hyenas to polish off the king of beasts. Then, with the skin and skull slung on a sapling between us, we made haste to return to camp. Alas, cameras had no place in our equipment in those days, and it was as much as I could afford to employ eight porters.

After a rest and something to eat, I decided to take a stroll in the evening to see what else was about in the precincts of the river. Once more we took our guns, but this time the 12 bore and the .404, as we had enough meat. After leaving camp about a mile away downwind and whilst considering a return to camp, we both heard a noise in the bush to our right. My first thought was that it might be a rhino, with which I needed no confrontation. However, after listening a while, I became certain it was an elephant from the noise of its stomach rumblings and the breaking foliage. I decided that I had better check what sort of tusks it

Top: Delivering a free meal to an emaciated lion. Note the rope slipping through the leg as the car pulls away.

Middle: Bringing the lions to the tree on the Hatari set by dragging a shot zebra on a rope for them to eat off the back of the car.

Bottom: Mission accomplished. The cage above the lion pride with Countess Bisletti in it.

carried just to make sure I was not passing up a really good tusker. Imagine my elation at seeing a magnificent pair of tusks that were well into the 90-pound class. There was no doubt about it—it was my day— the greater kudu, the lion, and now the elephant. Almost fatalistically, he turned to give me a perfect ear shot at right angles from a good rest at 30 yards. He dropped instantaneously, sitting upright—no second shot was needed. We returned to camp, ate, and slept. The next day eight men and six axes had the tusks out by 9.30. The nerve cavity was small, and the tusks made 100 pounds each. With each tusk slung on a sapling, we set off to walk the five miles back to the track where I had left my short-wheelbase Land Rover nearby with two Wahehe of the local tribe to guard it.

I also particularly remember that day's hunting, not so much for its incredible success, but for the fact that walking out of the area with eight porters, I hit the track at exactly the point where George Rushby was camped. It was 11.00 A.M., and he was sitting in front of his tent drinking a cup of tea.

'Good morning, John', he said. 'I gather you have had a good hunt and some fun'.

'Yes', I said, 'but I could do with being a little less frightened due to my inexperience! How the hell did you know I was here?'

'Well, my job is to know everything about everybody, as you know John!' he said, with that inimitable twinkle in his eye. 'Have some tea. By Jove! This time you found a good one', he said, as he admired the tusks carried by the perspiring porters.

Over a welcome cup of tea, he told me of some of his experiences hunting in the Lado Enclave and of the exploits of Jim Sutherland. He of all people could appreciate the great excitement that I had experienced and he warmed to it. My few paltry days spent nearby were like nothing compared to the privations and physical efforts that he was called upon to make in the many years before in the inhospitable land of the Lado Enclave. By comparison, I had a car and was half a day's journey from town. Even so, I was as excited as a child visiting a fairground. It was an experience never repeated. Not until years later did George admit that he had been driving down the road by complete chance when a native stopped him—thinking that he was me—to cadge a lift into town. He stopped and planned the surprise.

The area drained by the Ruaha and Kisigo Rivers, with which I was by now very familiar, was to provide the setting for my being severely mauled by a lion some 10 years later.

As recorded elsewhere, Paramount Pictures was making the film *Hatari,* and footage of lions was required. This and the other footage needed further negotiation with John Owen. For £3000, permission was obtained to find a pride of lions in the Serengeti National Park in a remote part of its northern extremity, formally the Serengeti Partial Game Reserve. The film company, for continuity purposes, required a pride of lions feeding on a kill. Into the feeding lions below, a steel cage containing one of the central characters of the story was to be lowered from a tree. Knowing the area well from several safaris I had done with Syd Downey, we chose the Kampi Ya Mawe area north of the old Kilimafeza (Swahili for 'mountain of money') gold mine. Here there was space for an airstrip and a small maintenance camp. We had three days in which to get the shots, and I had no difficulty in finding a pride of lions and shooting a zebra for bait. With the zebra tied on the back of the car, I slowly moved the lions the two miles to the chosen tree that held the steel cage in which sat Countess Tschuki Bisletti. The cage was then lowered by winch into the pride of lions below.

The Countess was a brave girl. No one was too sure how much or how far a lion could get a paw through the bars. However, after a few snarls and growls, the lions grabbed the zebra and moved to another tree, but not before the footage had been taken successfully.

Back at Willie de Beer's animal farm, a fatal accident took place during the filming of *Hatari*. How often have we all said to ourselves, 'Never trust a cat?' Diana Hartley had brought down a 'tame' lion from Kenya to be used in conjunction with the film shot in the wild. Whilst preparations were being made for the cameras to roll, the lion, without warning, suddenly raised itself up on its hind legs and bit her through the neck, killing her instantly. The lion was subsequently shot by the Arusha game warden, Tim Pollard. The accident cast a shadow over the whole of the rest of the filming. Actors and animal handlers alike were thereafter exceptionally careful. In view of all the other adventures that we had during the six months of location work involving manipulating animals for the cameras, we were incredibly fortunate not to have had more accidents.

In Northern, Lake, and Western Provinces there were abundant populations of lions. Perhaps the greatest stronghold of the species was in the Serengeti National Park and the high country to the north of it in Loliondo District. This was part of the Masai tribal area. When I first went to Loliondo in 1950–51, the view of that beautiful country left me

Following page: One of the lions of Loliondo (1956).

208

The lions of Castle Rocks. These are the lions of Loliondo feeding on a topi fed to them by our safari. We photographed the lions but did not shoot them. Another day perhaps, but not that day (1956).

with the impression that I had entered another world. There were thousands upon thousands of animals. I camped at what I named 'Castle Rocks' above the Bololedi River watercourse in the same spot as Jim Clark had done some 20 years before when collecting for the American Museum of Natural History. In one day I saw 20 maned lions. For many years afterwards, mostly in the late 1950s and 1960s, I hunted the area very successfully. (Fred Bartlett, in his book *Shoot Straight Stay Alive*, describes one hunt we did together there.) At that time the national park had not been extended northwards. This area was known as the Serengeti Partial Game Reserve. Like so much of Africa's pristine game lands of those many years ago, it is today overgrazed by the Masai. It had been plundered for some years by unscrupulous hunters and leased to oil-rich outsiders. It is now unrecognisable, and the lion population has been depleted to the point of extinction.

At this point it is worth recording a little hunting history. Syd Downey and I had driven down to Castle Rocks by a little-known route to Tanganyika. This had been achieved by heading south after crossing the Uaso Nyiro River 10 miles west of Narok and then turning south, following the track to Morijo and Endasegera. From here, a track along the top of the Nguraman Escarpment, which had been cut out in the 1914–18 War, led to the Tanganyika border and the hunting areas north of the Serengeti. We had made an airstrip at Castle Rocks, and 'Boskie' (Z. Boskovic), the famous Kenya pilot, had flown Edwin Muller into camp. At the end of a successful 10-day experience Ed flew out, and Syd and I were left to find our way home. We decided to go across country to the west via Al Klien's camp and the Bolagonja Springs to the Mara River. After crossing the Mara, we were to head across the Loita and Sianna Plains to approach Narok from the west, thus making the full circle.

All went well until we got to the Mara. Syd's driver, Omari, was getting old in years and instead of driving the two-wheel drive truck with some determination through the sand, he took pressure off the accelerator at the wrong moment; the truck lost power and stuck in the sand. There was simultaneously a nasty cracking noise. Close inspection showed the chassis to be broken between the petrol tank and the forward spring hanger on the rear spring. The truck had to be unloaded and dug out, and a corduroy bridge built of logs and branches so that it could be towed out by the Land Rover. Whilst Syd, I, and a gunbearer took a walk downstream, the staff got on with the job. After walking for some 200 yards, we came across a large piece of channel iron sticking up out of the sand. After I handed my gun to Mbetu, Syd's gunbearer, Syd and I scraped away the sand to uncover an old lorry chassis. We quickly realised that if we cut a piece off it we could bolt it onto the side of the truck's broken chassis and get home safely. Syd was convinced it was a professional hunter's vehicle that had been washed away when crossing the river when it flooded. He could not, however, remember the hunter's name. Whoever it was, he did us a favour. Syd was always well-equipped

Above: We decide to risk it! Edward on top of the truck, southern Tanganyika (1959).

with tools that had been meticulously packed and kept oiled, as I was to discover a few months later when I bought his Land Rover hunting car. Round the campfire with Syd that night, I realised just what his life meant to him. He was full of stories of past experiences on safari. Two such stories have remained clearly in my memory.

Syd was on a three-month safari with Lord Furness and his daughter. Lord Furness was the chairman of the board of the Furness Withy Shipping Company. His forebears had founded the company that went from strength to strength with the growth of the British Empire. Syd had employed as a second hunter, Andrew Rattray, a Kenya farmer who had specialised in attempting to tame wild animals for domestic use. He had crossed zebra with horses, producing what came to be called zebroids. He was an engaging and good-looking fellow. It was not long before a close and loving relationship developed on safari between Mike and Lord Furness's daughter. One day, on Syd and Lord Furness's return from hunting, they found that the lovebirds had eloped and gone to Nairobi. Lord Furness insisted on carrying on with the safari. Some days later a plane flew over camp and dropped a message. It read: 'Daddy, I'm gloriously happy—I'm in heaven!! See you soon, hope the hunting is going well'. When Syd handed Lord Furness the note, he went to his tent and returned with a handwritten reply. It was a short one: 'Go to hell, Daddy'.

The romance did not blossom, and father and daughter eventually left for England together. I was particularly interested in this story, as Lord Furness's son, Dickie, had been awarded—posthumously—the Victoria Cross whilst serving with my regiment, the Welsh Guards, at Arras in France in 1915.

The second anecdote concerned Charles Cottar. Cottar was a law unto himself and well known as an unpredictable and no-nonsense character. However, there were other hunters of equally forthright disposition, one of whom was J.A. Hunter. J.A. was hunting on the Mara and by chance came across a hartebeest hung as a bait in a tree. Calculating that this was probably Cottar's, he stuck a pipe in its mouth and an old safari hat on its head. Concealing his car behind a large bush, he awaited events. After a short time Cottar appeared in his safari car and stopped some 200 yards off to view the bait with his binoculars. On seeing the rakish form of the hartebeest, he was furious. Noticing J.A.'s car bumper sticking out from behind the bush, he grabbed his gun and put a bullet close to the roof of the car. Recognising Cottar's mood, J.A. pulled out!

Next day, with the lorry repaired and whilst the camp was being loaded, Syd and I strolled out of the riverine forest of the Mara River to the edge of the open plains. It was an unforgettable sight. Vast herds of game grazed in utter peace everywhere and as far as the eye could see. Little wonder that from that time onwards Syd did little or no hunting and devoted himself to photographic safaris and the conservation of wildlife.

On the way back to Nairobi we camped east of Narok on the Siyeibei River. Next morning, as we drove out, Syd told me that it was here that he had once met Charles Cottar, who was accompanied by his two sons. Charles was not pleased with his sons' attitude, and after a short argument by the roadside decided to give both of them a hiding. When Syd drew up alongside, Mike was behind the vehicle clutching his head, and Bud was in the ditch.

'Looking for something?' asked Cottar, dusting himself.

'Have a good safari', said Syd and drove on.

Thereafter, most of my safaris were hunting safaris, and although I was living at the Downey's beautiful home, I only saw Syd when both of us were off safari. He had some great stories to tell.

Man-eating lions were relatively common all over Africa during the years covered by this book. Most of them killed people who were defending their stock, and some, as those described in T.V. Bulpin's book about George Rushby's life, *The Hunter Is Death*, were inveterate, committed man-eaters that made many of their kind into man-eaters. It took George two and a half years to account for 22 of them, whilst they had killed and eaten more than 126 people. It is my view, after many years of dealing with man-eating lions on many occasions, that control officers, game scouts, and wardens probably only accounted for 20 percent of the lions that had tasted human flesh. The following extract from an annual report of the Tanganyika Game Department seems to subscribe to this view:

Stock Killers and Man-Eaters

The Tanganyika Agricultural Corporation's ranches at both Kongwa and Ruvu suffered severely from attack by lions. 47 head of cattle were lost at the Ruvu ground and even more at Kongwa where the dense bush made hunting very difficult—and dangerous. Efforts to import trained hounds from Kenya were unsuccessful. Although 3 lions were killed by the Division's staff at Ruvu, the Kongwa lions escaped.

Near Arusha local farmers had to shoot a dozen marauding lions during the year to defend their cattle. In the Northern Region five people were killed by elephant and rhino and, in one case, a herd-boy was kicked to death by a giraffe.

As usual the Southern Region produced a number of man-eaters, all but one of which were accounted for by the Game Division staff. In Masasi District a leopard killed five people and in Mtwara District four others were killed by lions. In Nachingwea town two people were injured by an old lioness which finally took refuge in the Settlement Officer's lavatory where the Game Warden destroyed it. Two more lions which had killed a man had to be shot in Kilwa District, and another which had mauled and killed two children succeeded in escaping.

Tanganyika, for some six years during the 1939-45 War and a period thereafter, had lain idle and underdeveloped. Recovery by Britain from the war brought much-needed interest in this mandated territory.

Another problem was witchcraft. The Germans, whose colony it had been until taken from them in the 1914–18 War, knew only too well what the effect of witchcraft had been when they had to put down the Maji-Maji rebellion.

In the south-west part of Northern Province, Hanang Mountain, rising to 10 000 feet and the last in the line of extinct volcanoes running southwards on the edge of the Rift Valley, was surrounded at its base by the Mangati Plains. Here there was excellent hunting in open country that was sparsely populated by the Mangati, a sub-tribe of the neighbouring Mbulu, Mynoramba, and Mnyatoro. Strong-willed witch doctors had spirited away some youngsters and raised them in the forests of the mountain of Hanang. In due course, at the behest of their mentors, these youngsters clothed themselves in lion skins and at night preyed upon the settlements surrounding the mountain. It appeared that the 'man-eaters' had gone to considerable lengths to conceal their human identity by softening the pads of the lion skins and attaching them to their feet so that the tracks appeared to be those of a genuine lion.

At first not much was done about the reports reaching the district commissioners residing at Mbulu and Singida. Then killings grew in number, and the police and game department began to take an ever-growing interest in the matter. Initially the game department was taken in by the tracks' appearance, but as time passed the police began to uncover, little by little, the background of the matter. An idle word here and there from Africans under the influence of native beer gave the police a clue, but at this initial stage they had no idea of the witch doctors' eventual intention, which was to culminate in their control of the country.

Following page: A mean king of beasts—not to be hunted by the faint of heart.

Meanwhile, there were evident signs of hysteria in the population. Some 24 people had been taken by the lions and tracked to the dense forest of Hanang Mountain. There they were partly eaten, and their entrails were used in ceremonies presided over by the witch doctors, who were thought to number four to five individuals. Before long the media heard of the problem, and, as often happens, the government felt compelled to act with strength and urgency.

Stanley Pearce, an old friend and ex-Palestine policeman, who was the officer commanding the police mobile forces, was sent up to the area. After concerted government efforts, some of the lion men were trapped and the witch doctors prosecuted by none other than John Summerfield (later Sir John Summerfield), the crown council at the time, and duly put away.

Out of curiosity I decided to try hunting on Hanang Mountain, the crater of which had been blown out on the east side. After three days of cutting a foot path, I walked into the most idyllic spot imaginable. At the bottom of the minute crater was a small lake from which ran a beautiful stream. Forest animals and monkeys abounded, and there were good-sized buffalo and some remarkably large leopard and bushbuck. It was impossible to get a car anywhere near this beautiful spot, but on two occasions when I had the right clients we walked into the little crater on foot and spent three or four days hunting there with great success. At night I lay awake wondering about the 'lion men', but we did not see or hear hide nor hair of them. A year or so later, there was a similar outbreak of lion witchcraft in the Mbeya-Iringa District of Southern Highlands Province, but this did not last long with the redoubtable George Rushby in charge of the game department in that area.

According to my records and diaries of my hunting years, I killed 26 lions that I am certain had killed and eaten human beings, and that was but a fraction of them that I had hunted but never succeeded in ending their days.

On one occasion, I was called out to help in a man-eating-lion hunt on a sisal estate in central Tanganyika. A man overcome by alcohol had staggered into the nearby bush to relieve himself and had then succumbed to sleeping it off, lying down nearby. During the night a prowling lioness had sunk her teeth into his buttocks. His cries as he was dragged off awoke the neighbours, who succeeded in driving off the lioness with flaming logs, sticks, and stones.

I had no gun with me at the time and was not expecting a hunt of any sort. In the sisal estate safe in the office was an antiquated

Roan Antelope

216

Winchester Model 70 pre-1964 .375. It had no front sight, and the extractor was broken. I stuck some chewing gum on the end of the barrel and stuck the end of a matchstick in it, and I had myself a temporary sight. A small screwdriver would take care of extracting the cartridge. The ammunition was fortunately new.

We set out tracking the lioness over some burnt ground. Very fortunately we came upon her after about an hour's walk. She was sitting under a bush some 40 yards from me. The first shot rolled her over but did not kill her. By good fortune the screwdriver removed the cartridge and the chewing gum held its place. The second shot finished her.

Southern Masailand, the Myowosi swamps in Western Province, and the northern extremity of Lake Province near the Uganda border at Ibanda all at one time or another provided visiting sportsmen with some magnificent maned lions. Over the years the bordering areas of the Serengeti National Park—Ikorongo, Lemai, Grummeti, Ikoma, Maswa, and Mugumu, to name a few—have surrendered some of the most magnificent maned lions to the safari clients of professional hunters.

Mauled by a Lion

Through my descriptions earlier in the book about my travels in Southern Highlands Province and Central Province of Tanganyika, my reader will recall that I became familiar with the area drained by the great Ruaha River. I had, on one expedition, driven in a short-wheel-based Land Rover down an old German track to the river near Maganzapile and succeeded in fording the river until I arrived at the Ruaha's major tributary, the Kisigo River. The area required some real hunting on foot. It abounded with huge greater kudu, lion, leopard, and elephant. Rhinos of nuisance value were also present when least expected. On occasion I had taken hunting parties into the area, always with success. For some years, whilst I was away in Kenya, Ethiopia, and Somaliland, I did not visit these haunts. In the late 1950s and after I had joined Ker & Downey Safaris Ltd., I revisited the Kisigo and Ruaha Rivers, finding, fortunately, that little had changed.

I entered the area on the north bank of the Ruaha just before coming to the bridge, following a rough cattle track to the west until I arrived at

Greater Kudu

the junction of the Kisigo with the Ruaha. It was an idyllic spot. The campsite was shaded with huge fig trees and *mapogoro* acacias. To the south side of the camp was the Ruaha River, which flowed throughout the year. It was full of several different species of barbel fish, of which the staff took full advantage. On the open plains near camp there were flock upon flock of guinea fowl and francolin. Leopard and lion tracks were plentiful, as were many other species of game, more particularly greater kudu and roan antelope.

Going west, the country changed into the forested *miombo* (Swahili for open forest with canopy) of higher trees. Here it was possible to see sable and Lichtenstein's hartebeest. Elephant and rhino were everywhere. It appealed to me as some of the most promising hunting country I had known. My first professional safari had been here with Richard and Norma Ayer. Needing a greater kudu, we found a monster with 58 1/2-inch horns. I did other safaris again and again with Jack O'Connor, Denis Morchand, Bill Holmes, and many others. Bill Ryan, a well-known and much respected P.H. and member of Ker & Downey Safaris Ltd., was with me on safaris we shared together with Chuck Ennis and Jay Mellon. Always we were successful. During this time I had instructed the camp staff, using the big truck, to clear an airstrip halfway between camp and the main road on a suitable site.

In 1961, I had my old friends back on safari who had been with me when Bill, John Cook's client, had been accidentally shot through his backside with a .465/.500 Holland & Holland (see Chapter 3). This time they had invited a guest for 10 days whose dearest wish was to shoot a leopard. The airstrip, cleared and marked with white-washed stones, enabled everyone to fly in whilst I set up camp beforehand. We had already started the safari in Loliondo, where we had a most successful time. During my move south to the Kisigo River, my clients had taken a three-day break at the Mount Kenya Safari Club.

Due to the advent of additional guests at the last minute, no other regular P.H. from the company was available to take care of the additional person. However, a tall, good-looking Englishman, Kevin Torrens, was found, who had been gaining experience with Hunters Africa Ltd.

Everyone in camp was happy, the bird shooting was fabulous, and the food was good enough for any gourmet, with curried breast of sand grouse being the most popular dish. The safari went along nicely for the first three days, as plains game came easily and the leopard baits increased in number. My client was anxious for his friend to get a good leopard, so when we checked one of our baits some eight miles west and upstream on the Kisigo River, we found a huge leopard asleep in the tree. We returned to camp feeling the job was half done. Not so, for Kevin's baits were also bearing fruit, and he and his client felt that they would prefer to shoot a leopard on their own bait. My client was a little put out by this attitude, as both of us knew that our leopard's size was quite exceptional. After lunch we had a council of war and decided that the client's wife would shoot the leopard.

It was August 12th. At 3.00 P.M. we set out for the leopard bait, arriving in the vicinity about 45 minutes later. I took a little walk on my own until I could see the bait and the tree with my binoculars, but no leopard was to be seen. On my return, Kiebe, one of my gunbearers, drew my attention to some elephant tracks, one of which was of some size. Edward, who was normally with me, had been lent to Kevin, as Kevin did not know the area. Ndaka, who served as a skinner and gunbearer, was with us. I sent both Kiebe and Ndaka off to see what sort of ivory the elephant was carrying whilst I made ready to creep into the blind at the leopard bait with my client's wife. Her husband stayed with the car. She was using a .243 Winchester Model 70 pre-1964 action, and I was using a .300 of similar type. Under normal circumstances, one of the gunbearers would have come with me with my .470 Westley Richards double and taken up a position behind us, looking to the rear whilst we waited for the leopard's arrival. This, of course, was not possible on this occasion.

Softly we crept towards and into the blind. It was 4.15, and all was quiet. At 5.15 nothing had moved, and there was no noise from birds or monkeys heralding the leopard's arrival. I became suspicious and uncomfortable. I turned to look behind me, and there crouched down not 15 feet from me was a huge maned lion. As our eyes met he gathered himself to spring. Instinctively I shot from the hip as I sat on my haunches with the rifle across my knees.

The bullet hit the lion as it faced me at an angle across my line of fire, just behind the lion's left shoulder, raking back through its body and

My desert boot that had been punctured by the lion's teeth and locked into its jaws when it died.

stomach. It instinctively turned, biting at the spot in which it had been hit. Grabbing my client's wife, I knocked out the front of the blind and, taking her by the arm, brought her back to the car at a fast pace.

'What happened?' asked my client. A brief explanation sufficed. His wife was as white as a sheet and obviously quite unnerved. After a brief discussion, during which my two gunbearers returned with the information that the elephant was of no consequence, we armed ourselves with the appropriate heavy double-barrelled rifles. I had my trusty .470 Westley Richards and my client my .450/.400 Manton. Both were loaded with soft-nosed ammunition. Kiebe and Ndaka accompanied us.

We returned to the spot where the lion had been shot. From that point the tracks led to the nearest thicket of *mswaki* bush. The ground was hard, and here and there were patches of reddish sand. The lion was not dragging any feet—he was right in all four legs. In the proper fashion we tracked the lion: first Kiebe looking at the tracks, I close to him so that I could touch him and look over his shoulder beyond, then my client, and then Ndaka.

Very slowly and carefully, at a snail's pace, we followed each pad mark. The light was fading fast. In a small clearing the tracks did not lead on. Looking to my left I saw the lion lying, its head away from us sideways on, breathing heavily. I caught Kiebe by the shoulder, indicating to him the lion on the left. Slowly and carefully Kiebe dropped behind us. My client moved up. Turning to my left, I indicated the lion and motioned to him to step up by my side and shoot. I intended to shoot with him.

I was watching the lion very intently, never taking my eyes off him. Before I realised what was happening, my client, without taking a step forward to bring himself level with me, raised his gun and fired at the same second I fired. The effect was twofold. First, the explosion from his rifle some 18 inches from my right ear threw me to the ground. Second, the lion, appearing unharmed despite my bullet in him, turned towards us. The bullet had taken him just below the eyes, but since his head had been turned down facing us, the bullet had passed out of the underside of his jaws, doing little damage. Kiebe grabbed my client by the arm and tried to propel him elsewhere. I tried to rise but found that I had no balance—my inner ear and equilibrium had been affected by the explosion of the .450/.400 so close to my head.

The lion took one bound of 22 feet and landed between my client and me. If I had shot at that moment the bullet would have passed through the lion and smashed my client's legs. I did the next best thing by hitting the lion over the head with the barrels of the .470 rifle as hard as I

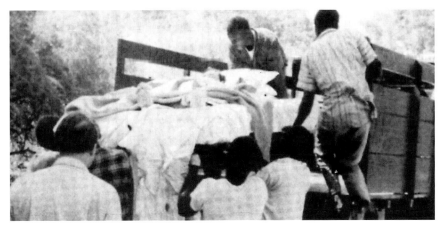

could. The stock broke at the pistol grip. My position sitting upon the ground whilst still entangled with 'wait-a-bit' thorns made hitting the lion no easy task. The lion staggered, stunned. Kiebe removed my client, dragging him by the arm elsewhere, thus leaving me with a rapidly recovering lion and a gun with a stock broken off at the pistol grip joined only by the tang of the trigger guard. I struggled on my elbows to get clear.

Too late—the lion was upon me. I smelt his foul breath as, doubling my legs up to protect my stomach, I hit him in the mouth with my right fist as hard as I could. His mouth must have been partly open as my fist went straight in. Realising that every second counted and believing that help was on hand, I forced my arm and fist down his throat. For a few seconds his mouth closed over my arm, which fitted exactly between his big eyeteeth. He rocked sideways back and forth trying to rid himself of my arm. Then, with a jerk of his head, my arm broke, and my hand and wrist fell from his mouth. Frantically I punched him with my left hand, but he was gaining in strength and purpose and bit my left wrist through, breaking the lower arm and leaving my hand hanging by its sinews. Pushing myself back with my elbows, I put a little distance between his mouth and my neck, head, and shoulders, striking out at the same time with my right leg. He caught my leg above the knee, tearing open a huge hole in the muscles of the underside of my upper leg.

All this time—only some 30 seconds—I was shouting at the top of my voice in Swahili for someone to return and shoot the lion. At last Kiebe and Ndaka appeared. By this time both the lion and I had moved some 10 yards from my gun into the thicket. Picking up my .470, Kiebe calmly broke the gun to see if it was loaded, losing a valuable second! At that moment I kicked out my other foot at the lion, which was moving closer to me. It took my foot and crushed the bones in it by twisting my ankle and held on to me.

Top: Me being loaded into the truck en route to the airstrip. Dr. Brian McShane is on the left superintending operations the morning after 12 August 1961—a date to remember.

Above: Me one week later, after a bad go of malaria in the MacMillan Ward of the Nairobi Hospital and with my scalp back in its proper place! Note the casts on both arms (1961).

This was the first real searing pain that I had felt. Until that moment the noise of my bones breaking in my arms had seemed to come from within my body—a strange and eerie sensation. Ndaka threw himself on the back of the lion, stabbing it repeatedly with his hunting knife. Ndaka then jumped aside to allow Kiebe to put the .470 rifle stock into shape, pull the trigger, and shoot the lion through both shoulders. Ndaka then beat the lion over the head with a heavy log.

The bullet anchored the lion, having severed an artery leading to the heart, so we subsequently discovered. The lion was now dying slowly with my foot firmly in his mouth.

'Another shot', I pleaded. Again Ndaka appeared with the six-inch-thick log and beat the lion on the head. My foot continued to suffer from this treatment, and I called for him to stop.

The lion was now dead, having taken a second .470 into his vitals, and my foot was still locked into his mouth. My client appeared and, carefully taking the .450/.400, he blew the jaws of the lion apart so that my foot could be removed by opening the lion's now broken jawbones. This took a couple of minutes to work out, as my foot's position could not easily be seen within the lion's mouth.

I was then free of the lion and bleeding heavily. I was carried out of the thicket onto a dry, hard spot. Kiebe fetched the car, and I set about giving everyone instructions as to what to do. Tourniquets were in order: one on each arm with the arms kept bent and one on each leg. On the left leg a tourniquet was placed above the ankle, and on the right another was placed just below the groin. A fire was lit and tea was brewed, with a large helping of sugar added. Acromycin antibiotics were broken out of the medical bag, and I took a double dose. It was hot, and dusk had fallen, it now being 6.30. I was shaking uncontrollably, felt cold, and was likely to lose consciousness. I realised that if I did so, I might die.

Both my clients and gunbearers were horror struck and looked for leadership. I instructed them to take off the detachable, light canvas curtains from round the car and wrap them around me and secure them in place with binder twine. Thus trussed up, I was lifted into the front seat of the Land Rover, and we set off for camp. Stupidly, I left the search for the way back to the track to my two gunbearers. In the darkness they quickly got lost. After two hours of bush bashing and some superficial damage to the car, I became angry. It was now 9.00 P.M. I ordered them to stop, light a fire, make some more tea, and fire a shot every two minutes (we had stacks of ammunition of all calibres on board). I was banking on someone from camp coming to look for us. It was pitch black, and there was no moon.

Back in camp my headman, Yulu, supported by Edward, expressed his concern that I had not returned. It was a golden rule of mine that the truck came out to look for me if I was not back by 9.00 P.M. However, Kevin was not aware of this, so another drink and dinner were taken. By 10.00 Yulu, by then, had the truck started up and ready to go, with Edward in charge. Kevin realised that the staff were serious—quickly he gathered his kit and set out in his hunting car, following Edward in the direction that Edward knew we had taken. At 10.00 the first shot was heard; at 11.00 we heard the car, and soon thereafter we were located. Quickly we headed for camp. We couldn't find the tracks that the car had made in finding us. For an hour we searched in vain, until quite suddenly, we came upon the track. It was now 12.30 A.M. By 1.15 we were back in camp.

The staff laid me out on a spare client's bed, a large one. Edward made a splint for my left hand to rest on, and someone else made one for my right arm. Dust and foliage were in every wound, and my hair was matted with blood from a huge gash in my scalp. Urgently I discussed a plan with Kevin. He was to drive to Dodoma some 100 miles from camp, and from there to phone Nairobi in emergency and get a plane and doctor down as fast as possible. At 3.00 A.M. he left for Dodoma. As it happened, I had had an operation on my nose only a few months previously. This was as a result of my being blown up by a land mine planted by Jewish terrorists whilst serving in the British Army in Palestine. My nose had been damaged, and further repairs had been required. This meant that Dr. Goodchild, the surgeon, would have my blood group. I drew attention to this fact in my message to Ron Stephens, the manager of Ker & Downey Safaris Ltd.

In Nairobi, Keith Mousley of *Hatari* fame was ready with his plane to go in quick time. He was joined by Dr. Brian McShane, the doctor with whom the company consulted and who knew me well. Blood was available. They arrived at the airstrip at the Kisigo River at 12.30 in the afternoon. Brian quickly dressed my wounds, disinfecting them as much as possible. A drip was attached to me, and I was given blood. The whole bed on which I was lying was lifted into the truck. The journey to the airstrip just about finished me, as the bumps and the rough ride were agony. By the time I reached the plane, I was on the edge of unconsciousness.

I knew little of the five hours that it took to clean me up under anesthetic and awoke as sick as a dog the next day. Pretty soon I went down with the father and mother of a go of malaria, and for 24 hours my life hung in the balance. I will remember forever the sensation of somehow

The acting governor of Kenya, pre-senting the Queen's Commendation for Brave Conduct to Kiebe Ndana.

being suspended in midair, not knowing whether I was staying in this world or leaving it. I remember, quite clearly, saying to myself that I was staying and not going!

Slowly I pulled out of it. My foot was agony. For some time I complained of the pain, but the doctors did not feel that anything was wrong. Finally, Brian, who was kindness itself, told me that they had agreed that I could have my foot X-rayed any way I wished, if that would make me feel better. The doctor in charge of X-ray had seen a few funny ones in his time, so he humoured me and cooperated. I was convinced there was a bone splinter in my foot. It felt like it. A few days later Brian and Dr. O'Donahue, the surgeon, appeared. 'Well', said Dr. O'Donohue, 'it's not often we have to apologise. You have a splinter of bone loose in your foot at the back of the joint in one of your toes'. Two days later it was removed, together with several other damaged bones that would in time have turned arthritic. I have been grateful for both doctors' efforts ever since and walk with no trace of a limp. I have done so for many thousands of miles, except when accompanying my wife on walks or shopping expeditions. I am a very normal husband.

I have recounted the story of my mauling exactly as it happened. However, I had little or no control of the aftermath of events that followed my accident. The following sequel has never been told.

I was a little surprised when I learned that my gunbearer, Kiebe, had been recommended for a medal. He was subsequently awarded the Queen's Commendation for Brave Conduct. Apparently, whilst I was in

Left: Frontal view of the lion's jaw and teeth. Skin removed showing how eye-teeth lock on either side of jaw.

Below left: The lion's skull (side view) with my arm in its mouth so that the scar on the right arm coincides with the small teeth in the centre of the lion's jaw. This shows my fingers virtually in the lion's throat.

Below: My arm fit between the eye-teeth. Note the scar on my arm coincides with the small centre teeth in the lion's jaw.

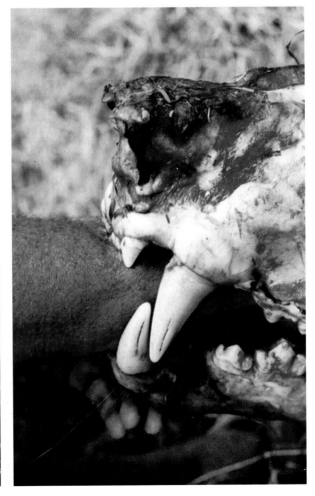

The lion that mauled me, showing the exit hole of the first shot. 'At least, John', said my compadres, 'you were mauled by a decent lion'. (1961)

hospital, a lot of stories had been told as to what had happened, without my being consulted. I well remember Myles Turner when he left Ker & Downey Safaris Ltd. to work for the national parks in Tanganyika asking if I would like to take on Kiebe, his gunbearer. His words to me were, 'John, he's a quite phenomenal tracker and blessed with superb eyes, but don't ever trust him with your gun because he is a runner'. Even so, Kiebe was a brave man, but if he was going to be brave he should have come to my aid a little sooner! That may sound unfair, for no one knows how one will react in a moment of crisis. The moment of advantage to me when the lion was stunned by the barrels of my .470 had been lost when Kiebe left me and took my client with him, and by his actions my client was denied a valuable opportunity to help me.

I was now on the horns of a dilemma. The people involved were not going to change their paperwork or stories when I, on my own, came out with my version of the story. They outnumbered me by 10 to one. Either I remonstrated with them and got the story changed, or I went along with the situation as it stood. I decided that it really did no harm to anyone and so left the die so far cast to continue. I said nothing, but I felt sure that one day Kiebe's true story would be told. It was not long before it manifested itself.

Joel Loveridge, my long-time and respected friend, was on safari with Art Coates. David Williams and I were the professional hunters. We

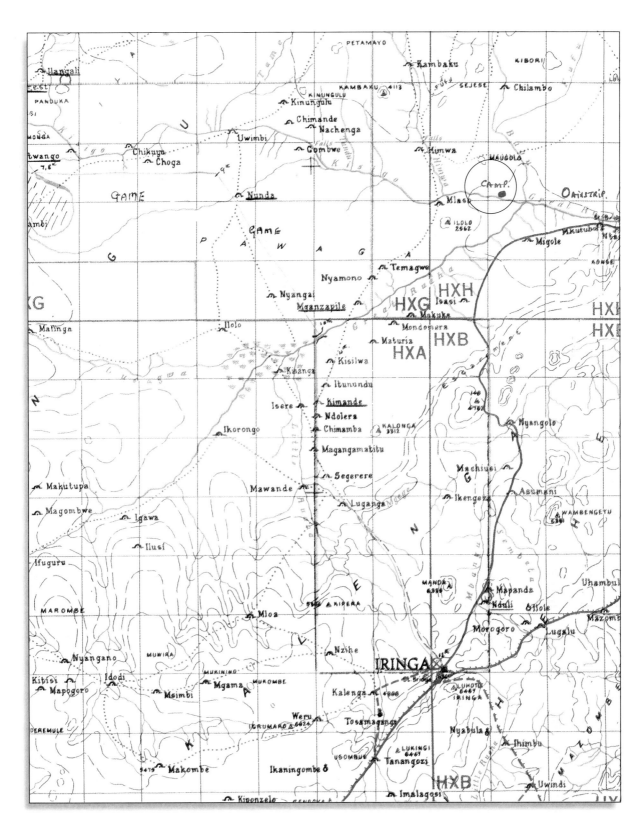

A pair of magnificent lions shot by the Mittons, father and son. The best in Botswana! These two lions are indicative of the trophies taken in Botswana. The exploration and development of hunting there followed my being mauled in Tanganyika.

were hunting the Kajiado area of Kenya Masailand, 70 miles due south of Nairobi. David had a lion feeding on a bait in an acacia tree standing at the base of a large flat-topped rock at the base of a small hill. The lion moved as Joel shot, and David and Joel had a wounded lion on their hands, which went over the flat rock behind the bait and into a small rocky gorge. Leaving a man up a tree, David returned to get me. Quite rightly, he believed combined forces were likely to achieve faster results.

We climbed the rock and looked down into the gorge. Standing between David and me was Joel, and behind us was Kiebe. I moved to

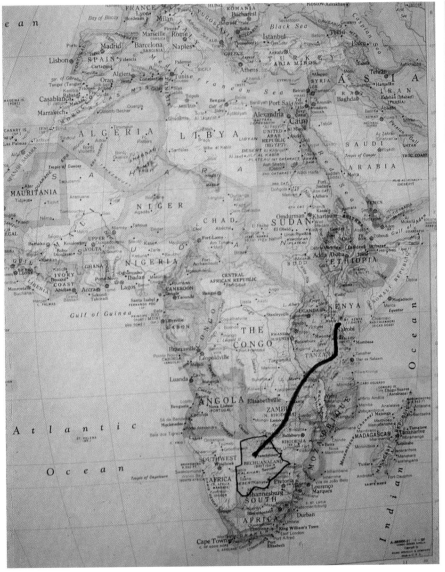

Aircraft played a vital role in the opening up of the safari-outfitting business in Bechuanaland. Roads and tracks were virtually nonexistent in concession areas.

Top: Our company, Safari South (Pty.) Ltd., chartered this Bechuanaland National Airways DC3, re-fuelling at Francistown en route to Maun with 16 clients (1970).

Above: Pointing to Maun in Bechuanaland, showing some of the hunting concession areas in 1965, while visiting in Jack O'Connor's home at Lewiston, Idaho (1971).

Left: 2158 miles from Nairobi to Maun, Bechuanaland.

Vehicles were crucial to moving safari equipment all over East Africa and eventually into Bechuanaland. After Tanganyika, Bechuanaland remained as one of the last safari challenges in Africa.

Top: What joy! We strike the tarmac road near Livingstone in northern Rhodesia (Zimbabwe) on the 2158-mile journey from Nairobi to Maun, Botswana (1968).

Bottom: Loading the truck—weighing at least 10 tons—onto the ferry over the Zambezi at Kazengula to cross from northern Rhodesia to Bechuanaland. A time for prayer. (1968)

the edge of the rock and hurled a large stone into the bushes. This was answered instantaneously by an almighty roar and prolonged snarls. At that moment, Kiebe grabbed Joel by the arm and, much against Joel's will, piloted him back to the car, urging him continuously to leave. The lion stayed where he was.

I turned to David and said, 'I'd like you to take particular note of Kiebe's behaviour. That's exactly what he did with my client when I was mauled by a lion. You now know the truth of the matter'.

Some months later I had a safari cancellation in Botswana. Kiebe and Yulu informed me that the staff were going to strike if I did not pay them double pay for the period of the cancelled safari—once for the cancelled trip and once for the safari that I was lucky enough to find as a replacement. I decided to agree to their demand. I returned the cancelled safari deposit to the client in full. On our return to Nairobi some five months later I duly paid the staff double pay. In front of all the staff Kiebe and Yulu asked me when they should return for the next safari. 'Never', I replied. 'You are all fired. I shall find another crew'.

'You never will', rejoined Kiebe.

'Watch me', I replied. Edward was the only one who had at that time refunded his double pay. During the next three days all except Kiebe, Yulu, and the cook returned their money, apologised, and were re-employed.

Shortly thereafter, Kiebe was arrested by the game department for shooting zebra on the Athi Plains without a game licence or a firearms permit and for having a stolen .375 rifle. He was dead drunk when arrested and sent to jail for five years. Quite simply, the medal and whole incident had all gone to his head and ruined his life. Years later his cousin, Musioka, brought me my Rolex Oyster watch that had been lost at the scene. Kiebe had it. Musioka persuaded him to return it. If Kiebe is still alive he would be nearly 80 years old.

Dr. Brian McShane has remained my lifelong friend. We talk to each other regularly and visit each other's homes. Two months after I came out of hospital, Dick Ayer came over and spent a month with me. He helped me to recover the use of my legs and arms whilst going on some gentle hunts on which we ended up shooting a buffalo or two. After that, still with one arm in plaster and an open wound that I had to dress daily, I took Herb Klein, accompanied by Fred Bartlett and Don Bousfield, down

After tremendous successes in East Africa, Bechuanaland gave our clients the opportunity of a repeat hunt with us in a new and hitherto unexplored part of Africa.

L to R: Doug Wright, Lionel Palmer, and me. For 10 years Lionel and I were the sole partners of Safari South (Pty.) Ltd. Botswana. Doug was our right-hand man. Much of our good reputation can be attributed to Doug's loyalty and success on safari. Much of our initial success must also be attributed to Frank Miller.

231

With East Africa behind me, Bechuanaland beckoned.

Top: Gunbearers Musioka, Kiebe, Edward, and Katara. All smiles now! The lion charged at 25 yards and was hit three times with a .375 Winchester Magnum's 300-grain soft points. The bullets broke the jaw, pierced the heart twice, and ended in the thigh bone and stomach. The lion dropped seven yards from the gun. Two .375s were used. The lions were shot by Frank Draeger (my client) and me (1968).

Top right: Keith Schier and Frank Miller after a successful tracking exercise (1966).

Above: The annual floods of the Okavango Swamps as they were in the 1960s and 1970s.

to the Malagarasi Swamps in Tanganyika in search of sitatunga and whatever else we could find. Sadly, however, my fellow Cornishman, Jack Carlyon, after coming in to see me in hospital, drove into the back of a stationery truck showing no lights on his way back to Arusha. His passing made me realise just how fortunate I was. As for my friend Kevin Torrens, like many of us, he continued till the hunting ban was enforced in Kenya. When I last heard from him, he had qualified as a civil engineer and was working in Botswana. Bill Ryan retired to the Kenya coast and passed on some years ago, shortly before his 80th birthday.

Finally, my clients, well after the first trip when Bill was shot through the backside and the second safari in which I was mauled by the lion, very naturally decided that if worse may be in store, then more safaris were not to be readily undertaken. They were both generous and appreciative of my efforts to ensure their safety, and we remained good friends, enjoying our reminiscences. It is all too easy for a P.H. to talk and criticise from afar, but when a client with absolutely no experience of hunting dangerous game is suddenly in a situation where he has no idea how to react, full responsibility falls entirely on the P.H. and his staff to ensure their client's safety no matter what the cost. This was the unwritten law of the E.A.P.H.A., which in all circumstances was to be upheld, and it was so. I felt that Ndaka had certainly earned a mention. All he had had was his bare hands, a hunting knife, and a log.

For five years thereafter I continued to successfully shoot a lion on August 12th—coincidentally the opening day of grouse shooting in Scotland. I shot a leopard out of that same tree in 1962. After that I felt the jinx had been laid.

Change-over day at Maun. I am at left, around whom is Lionel Palmer, Mr. amd Mrs. Palleja from Barcelona, Spain, Bill Siebert, Janie Joubert, and Frank Miller (1966).

Some years ago, the Mtera dam was built just above the bridge crossing the Ruaha River. Our hunting area was submerged beneath its waters and gone forever.

In the early 1960s the rapidly growing firm of J.H. Minet & Co., insurance brokers in Nairobi under the able direction of Ray Pettit and Murray Mowat, had offered the professional hunting fraternity special accident and life insurance. I took and paid the premiums of both. The first bought me a house in Arusha, the second, 10 years later, a house in the U.K. This advice was well worthwhile, but I would not advise anyone to sustain an accident such as I had as a means for obtaining the cash to buy a home.

BECHUANALAND (BOTSWANA)

On my arrival in Bechuanaland I was unaware of the type and scope of lion hunting that Bechuanaland offered the visiting sportsmen. Lion hunting in Botswana, as it is now called, was always a matter of tracking and seldom one of baiting. The Botswana lions were large, very active, and numerous. They were also certainly not to be hunted by the faint of heart. Considerable physical effort was required to track and follow a lion on foot for several hours at a time. Often, when the tracks were first followed, it was six to eight hours before the chance of a shot was offered. The sandiness of the soil made tracking possible for long distances, but the foliage of the palm tree islands rustling in the wind provoked the occasional bowel movement from one's clients, and even more so when the lion was wounded! Following a wounded lion into a palm

Top: A lion that charged the .375 Winchester Magnum Model 70 (pre-1964) loaded with 300-grain soft points—killed at 20 feet. The bullet hit the bottom of the brain and broke the neck, ending in the stomach (1971).

Above: Phyllis Palmer flies in to see Lionel in camp in Matsibe (1972).

island was probably the most dangerous pastime a P.H. could undertake in his whole career.

I never ceased to admire my long-time partner and friend Lionel for his ability to survive unscathed for so many years. Lionel was quite simply the best lion hunter it was ever my privilege to know. Doug Wright was not far behind, and including Frank Miller among the four of us, we probably had as much combined experience as any four men had anywhere on the continent. When Lionel was hunting lion he often wore a red shirt; whether it was out of sheer bravado or superstition, I never discovered the truth, but he was always successful and left nothing to the imagination when celebrating his achievements. He quite simply enjoyed lion hunting as much as his parties, and together that made up a large part of his life in those never to be forgotten years.

I will always remember our first night's arrival in Maun after we had succeeded in obtaining the old meteorological station building near the airstrip for our new company headquarters. Unbeknownst to us, there was a plague of rats. They were quite literally everywhere and in everything. After we arrived very tired after a long and dusty journey on an almost nonexistent, sandy, rutted road for nearly 200 miles from Kasane on the Botswana border (the end of our annual 2158-mile journey from Kenya), Phyllis (Lionel's wife) and Lionel moved out of their bedroom to allow us a good night's sleep. During the night I felt something on my face. Instinctively brushing it off whilst half asleep, I sent a rat flying off into space, which landed with a thud on the floor. It had been shredding my moustache of the leftovers of the soup we had had for dinner. Shortly afterwards my wife's hand cream fell off the bedside table to the floor. Next morning it was empty—sucked dry by a huge rat! A month or so later they had gone.

There was never a year for many years that we did not kill a snake in the office. One even got into bed with Simon Paul, my godson.

It did not take me long to learn the tricks of the trade. Edward, a Makonde from northern Mozambique, had a gift for languages and soon picked up Tswana. Both he and Musioka, a Mkamba from Kenya, were still serving as my gunbearers, as Frank Miller and I brought our East African staff with us to Bechuanaland until we could train enough local people to take over from them. As readers will discover from their perusal of the appendices of this book, the company of Safari South (Pty.) Ltd. was built up from nothing to the point that from 1970–72 it was handling close to 100 shooting clients a year, approximately 60 percent of whom wished to shoot a lion. Not all did so, as the records show.

Thanks to Lionel and Douggie's efforts, the Batawana tribal council allowed us to use the Chitabe and Makwi areas adjacent to the Moremi Game Reserve. This reserve was named after the wife of the former chief of the Batawana tribe. In the centre of the Okavango Swamps was a huge island some 30 miles long by 10 miles wide known as Chief's Island. This was the private hunting preserve of the chief of the Batawana and was subsequently gazetted a game reserve and joined by a corridor to the reserve. On the perimeter of the reserve, roughly bordered by the Gamuti River, the lions crossed out of the reserve into Chitabe and Makwi and provided our clients with some quite outstanding trophies.

At that time, my good friends the Mittons had successfully completed two outstanding safaris in Kenya, shooting 100-pound tusked elephants and many other trophies. (They came to Bechuanaland for lion and sable.) The game licences in the early 1960s were designed as packages 'A', 'B', and 'C'. On the package 'B', licence holders were allowed two lions, thus with two clients we had the chance for four lions. Many visiting sportsmen took advantage of this for several years, and with hindsight, this should, in my opinion, never have been allowed. Even so the choice was there. Perhaps the finest lion trophy I ever obtained for a client in my whole professional career was shot by Charles Mitton Sr. The size and weight of the lion, at just under 600 pounds, were very impressive.

The hunting conditions were tough. We regularly waded across rivers and swamps, often having to retrace our steps after an abortive hunt. On one occasion, after a long period of tracking, Lionel and his client came up with a lion that was asleep on an island way out in the swamps. It heard them coming and, dashing out of the cover on the far side of the island, it plunged into deep water, swimming strongly. Lionel, thinking quickly when he heard the splash, sprinted through the island. His client shot the lion 50 yards out in the water.

Magao's Lions

The Okavango Swamps contained a small tribe known as the Mamakush. These people had fled to the swamps many years before when their area was raided by the Matabele and other tribes from the east for their cattle and women. Such were the regularity of the raids that some of them stayed and continued to live on the hundreds of islands in the swamps. Fish and game provided a good diet, but the swamps were infested with tsetse fly so no stock could be kept.

One of the first safaris I took to Bechuanaland, whilst I was in my last few months of partnership with Ker, Downey & Selby Safaris Ltd.,

Top right: Michele Pascucci with the first 'Magao' lion.

Above: Enzo Grossi with the second 'Magao' lion.

was with two Italian friends, Michele Pascucci and Dr. Enzo Grossi. Both wanted good lion trophies. I decided that I would break into some hitherto unhunted country to the north of the River Kwai on the eastern side of the Okavango Swamps. In Kenya, bureaucratic new management and devious attitudes were to send most of us into business for ourselves.

It was May and bitterly cold. A frost at night that left ice on the washing water in the morning was a common experience. The unusual phenomenon of the floods arriving from Angola in the middle of the cold season, when the Bechuanaland rains had long since terminated, was an added obstacle. Slowly and with no sign, the water rose. The crystal clear water seeped through the grass across tracks that were presumed to be dry after the previous day's passage. Many were the occasions when, hurrying back to camp, the car was brought to an abrupt halt when it sank to the axles in bottomless mud. A winch was a necessity.

The Okavango Swamps, when full and overflowing in years past, had broken out to the east forming what was known as the Selinda spillway. One of the many rivers formed within the swamps when the Okavango River entered Bechuanaland from the north and broke into many smaller rivers was called the Monachira. The banks of the river were close to some dry grass-covered open plains. This enabled us to camp on the river and gain access by boat to some large lagoons and permanent swamp country to hunt sitatunga, buffalo, and elephant. The plains provided the opportunity for lion, roan, sable, greater kudu, and other trophies. It took us three days of breaking new country to reach the spot. On the way, I had chanced to come across a Mamakush tribesman who had come ashore to collect grass for roofing his huts. His name was Magao. He was a tall, well-built man with a serious demeanour. Through an interpreter and with Kenny Kays assisting, we learned of the best route to follow. Magao agreed to meet us at a spot that he described accurately at 3.30 the next afternoon. We were to fire a shot on arrival.

The next day, after one shot was fired and within 10 minutes, there appeared the familiar figure of Magao, poling his canoe towards us. We placed the canoe on top of the truck alongside the aluminium boat that was already there and set off. At dusk we came to the Monachira River. Quickly clearing a site, the staff needed no encouragement in setting up camp as the temperature fell. After several days of travel, my Italian friends were anxious to start hunting in the morning. By then a good campfire was burning. I asked Magao for his advice. He requested that we bring all the guns, including mine, to him and then he disappeared. We placed the guns on a tarpaulin and waited. Shortly after, he reappeared with a small tin bowl in which there was some white liquid. Squatting down, he bid us all keep silent. He addressed himself to the guns and began a slow incantation in an unknown language.

Picking up the little bowl Magao drank from it and spat the contents of his mouth all over the guns. There was some dismay on the faces of the gunbearers, who were responsible for cleaning them. I personally was not so surprised, as I had heard of this taking place when previous generations of hunters had entered new country. In those days the cooperation of local witch doctors was often sought, resulting in a similar procedure to what now unfolded before us. The guns were spattered with fluid until Magao was satisfied that they were acceptable to the 'spirits'.

After tea was brewed and we had chairs by the fire, I asked Magao what we should do and where we should go next day. He told me that he would have to consult the spirits before he could give an answer. After some half an hour he was ready. In the flickering light of the fire, he sat on the ground, stripped to the waist, cross-legged. In front of him was a small pot covered by an animal skin. I called for silence. Everyone from camp was gathered round in a semicircle. Magao addressed the pot, speaking to it in his own language and placing his hands on it as he did so. His voice rose in a tone of urgency, his hands gripped the pot till it was obvious that he was exerting considerable force upon it. Sweat broke out on his brow, and he became trancelike in his concentration. He continued his talk, now lowering his voice. Suddenly, and without warning, his hands and arms were twisted to the right and back to the left.

Gripping the pot, he became agitated, and his continuing dialogue adopted a respectful tone. Again without warning, his hands and arms twisted under the power issuing from the pot. By now he was pouring with sweat, and suddenly he was silent.

After a few more words he took his hands off the pot and sat staring at it, quite exhausted. You could have heard a pin drop. The faces of the Africans surrounding me were a study in awe and respect—they were unquestionably impressed. I instructed everyone to move away and get on with their work. The cook brought Magao a cup of tea, and after he was somewhat recovered, I asked him what message there was for us. Edward was by my side. 'Tomorrow', said Magao, 'you will go there in that direction and by nine o'clock you will have shot a lion'. I did not have the heart to ask him if it would have a mane!

My two friends and I held a discussion round the fire. I decided to employ an old strategy I had learnt from Roy Home. This involved putting a man on my Land Rover's roof from midnight onwards, placing before him a stick about five feet long. When the man heard a lion roar, he pointed the stick towards the sound. The last roar of the lion before daylight gave us the direction in which we would set out to hunt. After a good dinner we went to bed in anticipation of the next day's events. At 2.00 I awoke. Far away in the distance I heard the unmistakable roar of a lion. Slipping out of the tent, I made sure the man on the car roof was awake. He was, and after last night's visions of Magao, his voice revealed the urgency of his feelings. It was bitterly cold, and I was glad to return to bed and more sleep. At 6.00 we were in the car and ready to go. Magao gave the word. I calculated from the last roar that the lion's position may well have been two to three miles from camp. He appeared to be heading away from us, but Magao knew differently. After following our incoming tracks for a mile or so, he told me to go to my left through some open glades and grassy plains. The gunbearers in the lookout hatch had their eyes peeled. After 20 minutes Edward dropped down.

'Simba', he said. I kept going and drove the car behind an island of bushes. Here we got out and checked the rifles. Edward, Michele (whose turn it was to shoot first), and I set off into the trees of the island to scout out the country. Keeping another island between us and the spot where Edward had seen the lion, we moved slowly into the area where we hoped to catch a glimpse of it. Again we entered the trees of an island and chose a good observation point on the far side on a huge anthill. We sat and waited, with a clear and uninterrupted view of an open plain before us. The wind was set into our faces, and we did not realise that there was a small river some 100 yards away from us hidden by the grass.

The sun was now up shining brightly from a clear blue sky. Slowly, out of the grass in front of us, there rose a huge and beautifully maned lion. Walking to an anthill, he shook the water from his mane and skin and roared. I knew in that second that if Michele did not shoot him quickly he would walk off the anthill into the long grass and that an entirely different situation would present itself.

Michele needed no second telling. He was a good shot, and the soft-nosed bullet of the .375 Winchester Model 70 hit plumb in the right spot, going through both shoulders. The lion sank to the ground. A second carefully and deliberately taken shot made sure he was dead.

Carefully, we approached the lion. His forelegs were as massive as they were impressive. His mane matched his size. Our conversation relative to Magao's predictions can be well imagined as we returned to camp.

Enzo, the doctor, was now in line for his lion. On the second evening, and for the second time, we asked Magao to tell us where to go the next day. Once more the pot was produced, and once more it spoke with consummate energy. Sweat poured from Magao. The African staff were rooted to the spot, mesmerised by Magao's undiluted commitment to his task of communicating with the spirits of the swamps. Now, after his unbelievable demonstration of the previous day, there was a far more respectful audience. With a final twist of his arms he sat back, exhausted by the pot's message. This time he rose and with an imperious indication of his arm pointed to the south of camp.

'There, in that direction', he said, 'you will find a lion at ten o'clock tomorrow'. Silently we all dispersed to our customary positions for that time of day.

I had been warned of the low temperatures that I would experience and, when passing through Johannesburg, I had bought four hot water bottles. I now took them out of the sundries box and gave one to Magao. He had never seen one before and was intrigued by such a simple device. I hardly needed to give one to the man on the roof of the car that night! At 3.30 a lion was heard roaring, but not in the direction that Magao had indicated. At 5.30 we left camp and headed southwards. We stopped for a few minutes to listen for the lion's roar and heard him some way to our left, but Magao insisted we keep on heading south-east. By 9.30 we were some five miles south-east of camp. The country had opened up, and we were into islands of bush and small grass plains, as we had seen the previous day. At 9.40 Edward's hoarse whisper, 'Simba', once again sent the car

Lions at high altitudes in the Southern Hemisphere grow noticeably more mane behind the shoulder.

for cover, and once again we repeated our stalk to the vicinity of the lion.

This time we had a huge fallen tree for cover. For a few moments we saw nothing, until quite suddenly, through my binoculars, I found myself looking at a lion, perfectly camouflaged, sitting in the short light-yellowish grass on the side of an anthill not 120 yards away. One hundred and twenty yards is not really a long shot with a .375 Winchester Model 70 and a 4-power Redfield scope. Enzo was excited, and I sensed that he needed to calm down a little. At that time in the morning the lion was not going to go anywhere, and I felt that time was on our side. Carefully I described to Enzo just how the lion was lying and, therefore, where its vital parts lay. After five minutes of cooling off, he was assured and comfortable in his aim. He had a superb rest on the dead tree with his left hand under the forearm of the rifle, which was insulated from the dead tree by two hats and a coat. He knelt, took a steady aim, and then squeezed the trigger.

The shot was a good one, taking the lion behind the shoulder and passing through the heart. The lion took an almighty leap forward and disappeared in the longer grasses below the anthill.

'Stay where you are', I told everyone. We sat and intently watched the patch of grass into which the lion had fallen. The grass moved once or twice during the first minutes of our observation and once more a few seconds later. Then for five minutes there was no movement.

240

With Enzo by my side armed with a .375 Winchester and me with my trusty .470 double loaded with 500-grain soft-nosed bullets, we approached the lion with caution, but he was very dead. I looked at my watch: it was one minute past 10 o'clock.

We loaded the car and returned to camp. We Europeans were pleased and delighted with our success, but certain members of the staff were quiet, and others were pleased but nervous. That very afternoon Magao asked to be taken back to the spot from which he had joined us. We loaded the canoe on the roof of the car and set out for the rendezvous. I shook his hand and gave him a reward for his help. As the sun went down in a glorious sunset, I shall never forget the tall silhouette against the setting sun of Magao poling his canoe into the Okavango Swamps.

On several occasions, our aircraft took those who, mostly on private hunting expeditions, had the misfortune to be mauled by a lion, to hospital in Johannesburg.

This is a typical story reported in the South African papers:

A hunter told this week how he watched helplessly as a colleague bled to death after a freak accident in northern Botswana. Mr. Japie Nell, 32, of Pretoria, was in a hunting party of six tracking lion in the Nata cattle ranching area.

They were marching in single file when a lion charged. In the confusion Mr. Nell and a guard opened fire. The bullet from the guard's powerful .375 rifle hit local tracker Khomba Mothero in the back, killing him instantly. It passed through his body, hitting the owner of the Gweta Safari Lodge, Mr. Keith Poppleton, in the arm before grazing Mr. Nell.

Said Mr. Nell: 'It was a terrible tragedy. I never for a moment thought Keith would die'. But the professional hunter, who had headed the expedition, bled to death.

The group were tracking a pride of lion which had been killing cattle. Mr. Nell said: 'We left our truck in thick bush and started tracking on foot. The lions were obviously aware of our presence and moved deeper into the bush'.

Belong, a Bushman tracker, was leading the party and after a while he suddenly stopped and started making clicking noises, indicating that lions were close. Said Mr. Nell: 'The next moment a huge lion charged us

Bill Wixley, a strong, determined, top-class P.H. and a proficient pilot, was killed in action on the last day of hostilities in Rhodesia whilst serving in the Selous Scouts (1973).

and Keith shouted "Shoot it!" It came out of the bush like a train and Belong hit the ground on all fours. I didn't even have time to think and instinctually shot it through the shoulder and it let off a tremendous roar. Another shot went off and I saw the lion tumble over. The next second I was down when a bullet hit me in the side'.

The startled man thought his rifle had blown up. 'The bullet must have lost its momentum and only grazed me in the side. I was not badly hurt, but when I got to my feet, I heard Keith say he had been hit'.

Mr. Nell said the tracker, Khomba, was lying dead with a bullet through his back. Mr. Poppleton's flesh had been ripped off his upper right arm exposing the bone. 'I carried him to the shade of a nearby tree, took off his shirt and wrapped it around his arm as a tourniquet; but it didn't help much. Keith said he was OK and told me and Belong to fetch the vehicle and take him to camp'.

After a frantic 12km dash through thick bush with the Bushman, Mr. Nell returned to collect Mr. Poppleton. 'Keith was as white as a sheet and very weak but still alive, although he had lost a lot of blood'.

Driving at breakneck speed all the way with Mr. Poppleton slumped against him, Mr. Nell eventually arrived at the base camp about 15km from where the incident took place. 'I went to get the medical equipment and the drip, but when I got back he was gone', said a distraught Mr. Nell.

The Pretoria businessman returned to the scene of the killing the next day and discovered the lion dead in the bush. The guide alleged responsible for the freak accident was taken into police custody and was held pending investigation.

Mr. Poppleton, a former Selous Scout who has hunted extensively in Africa, is survived by his wife Margaret, daughter Danielle, 10, and son Kyle, 7.

His wife said, 'Keith was obsessed with lion and had a premonition one would take him this season. Instead, he was killed in a senseless hunting accident. It's a terrible waste'.

There were nine professional hunters with whom I hunted lion in Botswana and who were employed by our company. Apart from Frank and Lionel, my partners, they comprised Doug Wright, Willie Engelbrecht, Simon Paul, Wally Johnson and Walter Johnson (his son), Bill Wixley, Mike Cawood, Cecil Riggs, and Ardel Moolman. From time to time during the later years, Kenny Kays and Bert Milne were also associated with us. All of these were successful and loyal friends. Walter, Mike, and Bill were outstanding commercially licensed aircraft pilots

who, with me, fulfilled all the flying required by the safari company, plus many surveys and mercy missions in which we were called upon to participate.

Jo Louis and her husband, John, (formerly U.S. ambassador to the U.K.) with Musioka and her trophy lion (1974).

A large part of Safari South concessions consisted of semidesert areas. They lay to the east of our headquarters in Maun on the east bank of the Botleitle River and southwards on the west bank. Between the Botleitle River and the Makarikari Depression of salt and alkali pans lay an area of huge grass plains interspersed with large sand dunes covered with thorn trees and the occasional baobab tree. In May and June in the early 1960s, these huge open areas received the vast herds of migratory animals coming from the south-west of the Kalahari, migrating to the north-east to the pans of the mopane forests and eventually to the Chobe River. Vital to this migratory route was the Botleitle River, which at this time was swelled by the flood waters that came from Angola through the swamps and out at Maun in the form of the Thamalakane River. The Thamalakane, sometimes 400 yards wide and 20 feet deep, flowed west from Maun until it most remarkably split. The right-hand stream flowed westwards to Lake Ngami over a hard ridge of rock that was the controlling feature of its flow rate. The left-hand stream turned back on itself, running south-east 130 miles south to Lake Dow. If the flood and the consequent water level was high, the Thamalakane flowed over the rocky barrier more strongly to Lake Ngami. In the 16 years I spent in Botswana, this took place almost without exception every year.

243

The Botleitle River flowing from the Okavango Swamps to Lake Dow, 20 feet deep and 200 yards across. Today, it is a dust bowl; water has not flowed for 15 years, and the game is gone. From L to R: me, Cecil Riggs, and Ann-Marie Langley, out for an afternoon's fishing. Note the Masai spear from Kenya anchoring the boat (1972).

After much negotiation with the government of Bechuanaland in the shape of the Ministry for Commerce and Industry, we succeeded in obtaining the Tsoi area on the west bank of the Botleitle River as a concession. At that time this area could be compared favourably with the national park areas of East Africa. Newly married, I took my wife, Sue, on a safari to look at the newly acquired and unexplored area. We left Maun late and camped some five miles away before we reached the Botleitle River on the side of a recently made track. We had no sleep that night in our little tent. At midnight the wildebeest migration arrived, and with it the zebra, hartebeest, and gemsbok. In the distance the lions roared incessantly. At 1.30 the first guy rope was snapped by a stampeding animal, and shortly after another was broken. Our drunken looking tent was in danger of collapse. It was very cold and windy, and the dust got in one's eyes and clothes. Creeping out of the tent, I lit a fire. Sand clogged the tea I made, and conditions in the midst of this huge concentration of animals were not ideal for humans seeking a quiet night's sleep. To us it was one of the most thrilling experiences of our lives. Simply to know that all this took place within the concession for which we were responsible was tremendously exciting and boded well for the future of our company.

Shortly afterwards we built an airstrip and hosted a government wildlife conference on the banks of the river. Whilst some hunting took place in the initial stages, I was convinced that this ought to be a national park, with our company running a fine lodge on the banks of the river. It was here that I had one of the narrowest escapes from a lion.

The lions in the area were numerous. Airstrips, for some reason, attracted them. This was all very well until the lions started playing with the smaller aircraft. First they chewed the tyres to ribbons. Then they tried to climb on the tail of the plane, which provided a slightly better view of the country. We decided to take out one or two lions, as two in particular had become so antagonistic that when chased from the aircraft's vicinity they turned the tables on their pursuers. It was only a question of time before we would experience a serious problem. A mile or so away was a ridge of sand dunes on top of which were some fair-sized thorn trees. In one of these trees was placed a bait, which had been dragged from the airstrip. My clients, Mr. and Mrs. 'Ace' Adams from Youngstown, Ohio, were happy to shoot the troublemakers.

Accordingly, leaving the car some half a mile from the spot, we stalked the bait. Our binoculars ascertained the presence of the lion there. Coming up behind a suitable tree for cover at about 100 yards, Ace, armed with a .375 Winchester Model 70 loaded with 300-grain soft points, put a shot in what he thought was the lion's shoulder. The lion growled and disappeared in the thick thorn scrub. Leaving the lion for half an hour, we commenced a circle of the sand dune. On the far side the lion had exited, heading out into sparsely bushed country and crossing the track from the river to the airstrip. We returned to the car and drove up the road till we reached the point where the tracks crossed the road. Descending from the car, I then did something that was remarkably stupid. Walking up to the tracks, I followed them for 25 yards off the road. I was intent on looking at the tracks. There was no blood. I wanted to be sure that we were about to follow the male lion and not a large female.

As I looked at the ground I saw a long piece of grass move downward toward me. Lifting my gaze from the ground, I saw there, not eight feet from me, the lion looking at me with blazing eyes. Instinctively, I moved slowly backwards.

Edward, who had been watching me, realised at once what had happened—he already had my loaded .470 double rifle in his hands. Slowly I retreated to the car. I don't think I have ever felt so relieved to feel the cold steel barrels in my hand. Taking Ace with me, I moved some yards to my left so that we had a side-on shot. Edward also knew exactly where the lion lay, but none of us could see it. Taking a stick, on my gesture, Edward lobbed it into the spot where the lion lay.

It was a direct hit. As the lion sprang up he was hit by a .375 and .470 simultaneously—no less than a total of 800 grains of soft-point bullets. He went down poleaxed, and two more shots ended it.

I took great care to retrace my steps, it being inconceivable to me that I could not have seen the lion so close to me. His camouflage in the yellow grass was perfect, and, lying flat, pressing his body against the ground, he was no more than a foot high. On examination, he proved to

Below: An extract from my 1955 Ethiopia game licence.

Bottom: Ethiopia movement permits for 1955.

be virtually unharmed prior to my nearly stepping on him. Ace's bullet had simply grazed his shoulder.

Our lion-hunting and safari activities combined successfully with a great deal of happiness for a long time. Eighteen years later when I revisited Botswana, the entire country had changed beyond recognition. The Botleitle River, once 200 yards across and 20 feet deep, had ceased to exist, its dry watercourse the only remaining evidence of its existence. Lakes Ngami and Dow, the former homes of many thousands of ducks, flamingos, and other migrating birds were dust bowls. The game migration of thousands of animals from the Kalahari in the south to the water holes and forests of the north had ceased—fences enclosing the Kalahari to protect cattle from game-borne diseases had seen to that. The Okavango Swamps, starved of their hitherto beautiful water supply, no longer flooded the vast open plains dotted with thousands of small islands—they were just half the size they once were. Inevitably, with such drastic reductions in game animals, the lions' food supply could no longer support large numbers of cats, and their numbers have very naturally declined. The big lions of the Moremi Game Reserve and Chief's Island still exist, as do the island buffalo upon which they live. Their roars are still heard, and their huge size is still seen by the few professional hunters that remain hunting with the now very much reduced quotas in the game-hunting areas of Botswana.

ETHIOPIA AND SOMALILAND

A brave man is always frightened three times by a lion.
First when he sees the tracks, secondly when he hears the lion
roar, and finally when he confronts the lion.

—A Somali proverb

Libah is the Somali word for lion, the 'ah' pronounced with an intake of breath, as though your finger is being stabbed with a needle when a blood sample is taken.

There is a considerable history of lion hunting in both Ethiopia and Somaliland. Somaliland was only a few days by sea from Bombay via Aden. Several British officers, seeking a break from their duties in India, undertook hunting safaris lasting, by today's standards, considerable periods of time—six months' leave of absence was quite normal. Foremost amongst these nimrods was Colonel H.G.C. Swayne, who gave his name to the hartebeest of that area. He describes in his book, *Seventeen Trips in*

247

One of my Somaliland firearm registration certificates.

Somaliland, his many safaris. Lord Delamere, of Kenya settler fame, walked and rode on horseback from Berbera on the coast of the Gulf of Aden to Nairobi. Lord Wolverton (who recorded shooting a 10-foot 7-inch lion), Captain A.H. Mosse, Captain F.B. Pearce, and Captain F. Melliss (afterwards Major General F. Melliss, V.C.) all hunted lion in Somaliland and wrote about it. Unusually, therefore, there was an interesting track record to study on my arrival in these parts.

A well known P.H. of the 1930s, Roger Courtney was buried outside Hargeisa, the capital of British Somaliland. He had the reputation of being somewhat of a reprobate. At Christmas it was customary to visit his grave. The stone slab covering it had a small hole where his head would be below ground, into which, at appropriate intervals, a hefty tot of gin was poured. Knowing the state of the mental attitude of some of the people who visited his grave at that time, I would not be surprised if his drinks were well and truly mixed. Alas, Roger Courtney was unaffected by hangovers.

Just as the Masai tribe in Kenya had the Wandorobo, a small offshoot clan that specialised in hunting and poaching, the Somalis had the Migdaan. In hunting operations it was essential to employ the Migdaan, who were superlative trackers and knew the country and habits of game intimately.

Some of my most memorable hunting experiences took place in Somaliland and Ethiopia. The area is vast and arid, but cut into huge sections by the rivers that drain to the south and east of the continent from the highlands of Ethiopia. The rivers—the Duwa Parma (later becoming the Juba), the Omo, the Webi Gestro, and the Ganale Doria (later the Webi Schebelli), to name the major ones—are the centres from which life emanates. Without their waters there would be nothing.

The people who inhabit these arid and semidesert areas are Somalis and their allied ethnic cousins, the Borana, the Geluba, and to the north the Danakil and several other minor tribal offshoots. The Somalis, however, are by far the most numerous, avaricious, and intractable people inhabiting this area, as recent history has so often demonstrated.

Whilst the Somalis are described in Western terms as a race, to all intents and purposes this is true in name only. Their territory covers the countries that we knew recently as British, French, and Italian Somaliland and the 'Ogaden and Haud' of south-eastern Ethiopia, together with most of the eastern section of the Northern Frontier District of Kenya. The Somali race is subdivided into clans, which in some cases are almost races in themselves. Though their language can be understood right across all the countries, their dialect and expressions are easily recognised from one area to another. These clans seldom agree with each other and are constantly bickering and fighting amongst themselves. All are devout Muslims. Amongst the larger clans, like the Aulian, Marehan, and the Mjertein, the clan or tribe has a family subdivision called *Rer*. Thus the Rer Mohammed or Rer Mellingour are subclans of the major clan, each with their residential grazing territory and water supplies but loyal to their parent clan.

There are many of us from the Western world who find the Somalis intriguing. They are certainly brave when it may pay them to be so. Occasionally, there is no doubt that the exception proves the rule, when one can be honest, respectful, and loyal, leading one's master to think well of one's race and write of it in glowing terms. However, recent events that are now history have led most of us to believe that the opposite is true.

For myself, in those exciting days of the mid-1950s, no modern tensions and disputes disturbed the pace of life whilst I was stationed at Mustahil on the Webi Schebelli River in south-eastern Ethiopia.

The Somali Youth League (S.Y.L.), with its blue and black flag, was in its early stages of activity brought about by the prospect of independence of Italian Somaliland. Captured from the Italians in the 1939-45

War in the British offensive (conducted by using Kenya as its spring-board), the whole of the Horn of Africa and Ethiopia were restored to their rightful owners. Importantly, however, this took place in 1941 when there were still four years of the war to run. There was consequently little effort or money put into governing these vast areas until sometime after the war. It was not until the mid-1950s that this began to change. I was fortunate enough to be there before much change became evident. Thus the environment was undisturbed for some 14 years from the day the Italians disappeared.

True, there was a so-called British administration of captured territories which, like many British colonial activities, worked efficiently on the principle that if you leave it alone it will not bite you! The 'uncrowned King of El Carre', as he was known, one Major Ray Mayers, had only recently departed from the district headquarters of El Carre with his tribal police decoratively dressed in their red headdresses and waistbands. There being no tsetse flies this far north, there was a mounted section of both horses and camels. Patrols did not look for trouble, and, indeed, left to their own devices, the nomadic people of the area tended to settle their own differences.

At the time I arrived in Mustahil, the Ethiopian Army and administration had just begun to take up their positions. The local population regarded them as unwelcome. They did not believe they were a conquered people, least of all by their time-honoured enemies, the Ethiopians, who lived in the highlands. The centre of the administration was chosen to be Calafo. This was 80 miles up the river from Mustahil and, like Mustahil, was graced with a beautiful concrete bridge over the Webi Schebelli River, built by the now-departed Italians. My camp that I built was within 50 yards of the bridge.

Mustahil was a very small village of perhaps 75 people. Overlooking the river on top of the cliffs on the southern side and about two miles away was the summer villa of no less a person than Marshal Graziani, the conqueror of Ethiopia in 1936. This was now a shell, but its roof, made of concrete, ensured that in the rains and floods that often hit the country below it was a good spot to which to repair in an emergency. Running south-westwards some 40 miles from the border with Somaliland and Kenya there was a rough track that was motorable by Land Rover and ran 165 miles to Dolo on the Dowa Parma River. Some 50 miles down the road from Mustahil was an Ethiopian Army post at Godere. The fort contained some 30 men and encompassed a good freshwater well. By keeping the water to themselves they preserved their isola-

Following page: Map of Mustahil and Somalia (1950).

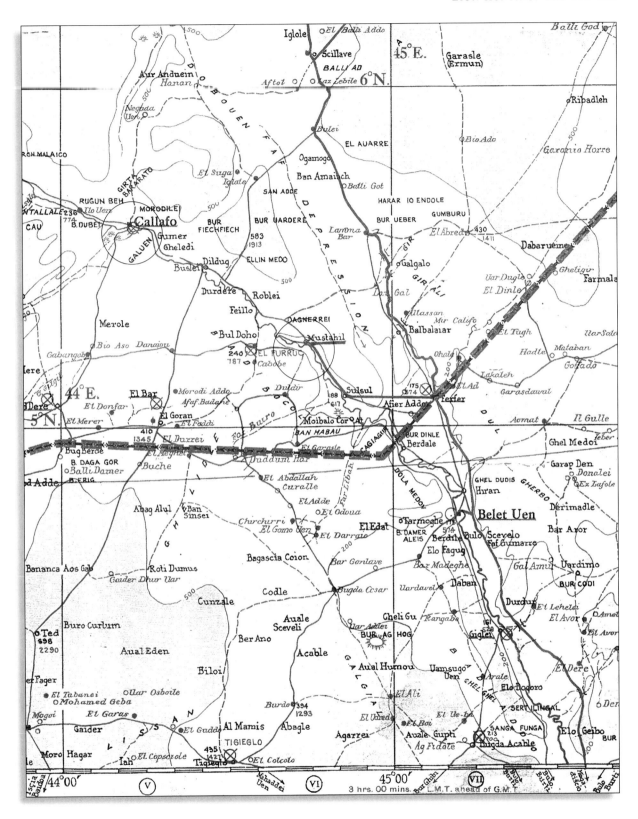

tion from the rest of the world. Once every two months they were visited with supplies and had a changeover of troops. Believing them to be likely living off game in the area, I gave them a wide berth. However, I discovered I was wrong in this belief. In fact, they were in pain of death if they fired one round of ammunition, so short were their supplies of this item. I soon made friends with them by providing them with fresh meat. I also discovered to my horror that, having no refrigeration, they happily ate rotten meat. Some of them subsequently suffered from stomach worms. Without proper medical supplies, they told me that the one positive way to get rid of the worms was to drink a small quantity of paraffin—and even petrol.

I spent a considerable time mapping this area and discovering ways of entering some of the apparently inaccessible areas of the flood plains on the south-west bank of the Webi Schebelli River. For communications I had an obsolete ex-army Model 22 radio transceiver that worked off the 12-volt battery of a car. I had a long-wheelbase Land Rover for a light vehicle and an ex-U.S. Army Dodge Power Wagon for a heavier vehicle. Both were fitted with four-wheel drive and both had winches. I built myself a nice open-plan rustic house out of dom palm trunks and fronds and made use of some old Italian road gravel dumps to give the floors some substance.

Stationed in Mustahil was a Somali assistant superintendent of police whose name was Mohammed Daud. We became good friends and did a great deal of hunting together. He became a crack shot and had considerable tactical ability, and years later he became a Somali general. The Italians had constructed a tarmac road from Mustahil to Ferfer—the border post— and thence to Belet Uen. Belet Uen was a fair-sized town, and Chianti, both red and white (together with all kinds of pasta), were plentiful there. Game meat that had been made *hallal* by a Muslim tracker was a fair swap for wine. The border guards were happy with their cut, and Daud's police made things go smoothly. The officer-in-charge of police at Belet Uen at that time was none other than the infamous latter-day Somali General Aidid, who became a national hero for throwing the United Nations out of Somalia. (He died recently, shot through the liver in an internecine fracas.)

Sommering's Gazelle

The Killers of Calafo

As I established myself at Mustahil, more and more people every day arrived to see me with their problems. Most of them came to me with cattle- and man-eating lion affairs that they felt I could settle. Knowing the Somalis as I did then, I made sure they understood that ammunition did not grow on trees and that any consideration of their problems first had to be cemented with hard cash for ammunition. This declaration tended to leave me with only the most genuine of cases.

At that time it was dry and hot, and there was not a great deal to do. I therefore decided to give the eradication of the man-eaters and stock-killers an old-fashioned try. The ensuing few months were probably one of the most exhilarating and exciting periods of my life. Looking back, I realise just how naive and foolish I must have been, and even today I physically flinch at the thought of what, on occasion, might have happened. I was very fortunate.

As my readers will see from the pictures of the vale of the Webi Schebelli River, the country to the south-west of the river was open plains, whereas to the north the 500-foot escarpment came close to the river. This tended to preclude stock from grazing on that side. Therefore, nearly all the herds of goats, camels, and some few cows were on the south-west side. A very small tribe of riverine Bantu people lived along the river banks and used hollowed out dom and borassus palm trees as canoes. One of these people, Mumia by name, became my gunbearer and tracker. He was good—his eyes saved my life on more than one occasion. The game-bird shooting was out of this world—francolin, guinea fowl, ducks, and geese abounded. My diet of game meat, game birds, pasta, and Chianti kept me well fed. The on-foot pursuit of lion and all other game ensured that I was probably fitter than at any time in my life. I could hardly wait for each new day.

Lions are somewhat lazy creatures, preferring their quarry to walk unsuspectingly into them. Not surprisingly, therefore, they mostly lay in wait in the riverine growth for the cattle and camels to come to water.

The Somalis had their regular watering and crossing places known as *mulkas*. Crossing was hazardous—the Webi Schebelli was full of enormous crocodiles, none of which had been shot for many years and all of which were bold in disposition. The game of the plains country did not drink there—oryx (beisa), Grant's gazelle, gerenuk, Clarke's gazelle, grevy zebra, and giraffe stayed well away from the river.

One morning I set off with a fly camp, two Somali guides (both complainants), and four river men in my Land Rover. For rifles I had a .318 Cogswell & Harrison (a Mauser-action rifle) and a .404 of similar manufacture and action. My .318 ammunition fitted conveniently into the clips of the wartime .303 British Army service rifle so that I was able to carry some 30 rounds very easily. Neither rifle was mounted with a telescope, open sights only. Twelve miles from Mustahil, going north-west parallel to the river and some three miles out, we came across the first lion tracks making for the river. Two miles from the river we could approach no further, the country becoming broken and pot-holed. We chose a campsite under some acacia trees and left the four men of the riverine tribe to make camp ready. I set off on foot with Mumia and the two Somalis.

We soon reached the river and began crossing numerous lion tracks as we moved upstream. Shortly we came to the carcase of a camel killed by lions the previous day. Not much was left—the hyenas and vultures had seen to that. I reasoned that with the lions well fed they would go off to find somewhere to lie up and sleep and would not start hunting again until the next day. We took up the tracks, which were made by a male, six females, and two or three young lions. After some two hours of tracking, at nearly midday the lion tracks turned away from the river and followed a watercourse, a sand river that had cut back deeply into the flood plains. On its banks grew thick patches of *mswaki* bush, the grey branches which the Somalis cut off and used to clean their teeth.

We were getting closer: a lioness had urinated not long before. Looking forward into relatively open country, I could see several likely spots in which the lions might well rest in the heat of the day. I instructed the two Somalis to sit down under a bush and not to move until I called. Mumia and I proceeded.

Mumia's eyes spotted the lions first, having seen just the faintest movement in a bush some 100 yards in front of us. Raising my binoculars I made out the head of a lioness looking away from us—the twitching of her ears had betrayed her position. Leaving Mumia with the .404 and instructions not to move unless I called, I crept forward. When I was 50 yards from the lions and on the edge of the earth bank of the watercourse that was 15 feet below me, I noticed a movement on my left in the periphery of my vision. Turning, I saw a male lion standing in the open looking towards the other lions. At that second two things happened: the lion turned his head in my direction, and the bank on which I was standing collapsed.

I fell in a maze of dust and earth to the bottom of the watercourse, ending up still clutching my gun and on my back in the sand below. As the dust cleared, I realised I was looking up at the bank from where I had fallen, and looking down at me was the male lion. Instinctively I brought the rifle to my shoulder and flipped the safety catch up and over. Lying on my back in the sand, I shot him full in the chest.

The effect was devastating. The lion jerked forward and plummeted into the sand not a foot from where I was lying. He was very dead, the bullet having taken him clean through the heart and broken his spine behind his shoulders. I was for an instant shocked and did not move, but a growl not far away brought me quickly to my senses. The lions that I had been stalking, alerted by the disappearance of their lord and master, now appeared 40 yards up the watercourse and were looking down at the lion and me in the sand. The largest lioness was growling and swishing her tail and seemed bent on coming down to investigate. Rolling over onto my stomach into a prone position, I put the second round into her chest. The angle was not so acute as with the male lion, but it nevertheless had almost the same effect, for she collapsed and slid into the watercourse, dying within seconds. The remaining lions had seen enough and left.

My excitement and shock was intense, and I found myself shaking like a leaf. The whole episode had taken less than half a minute. I decided that this was enough for the moment and called up Mumia. His eyes popped out of his head, and he was speechless for a few seconds when he saw the two lions. He told me that when he saw the dust rise from my fall he thought that I was being torn apart by the whole pride of lions! Then he heard the shots and my call.

The Somalis arrived full of smiles but, true to type, as I'd done them a favour, they refused to skin the lions unless I paid them. But I already had a plan to outwit their nonsense.

'I will pay you', I said, 'at the end of the lion hunting period'. To this they agreed. By 5.00 P.M. we were ready. Slinging the skins on a fresh cut sapling, we made the three-mile march directly to camp.

Little did the two Somalis realise that I considered the lion-hunting period as never ending.

That night the lions roared all night—the battle was on. After another week of hunting and four more lions, I felt justice had been done and returned to Mustahil to replenish supplies. However, the news had travelled by the bush telegraph, and I was swamped with entreaties to come and kill stock-killing lions. By far the most interesting application, however, came from a Somali who had walked at least 60 miles with lacerated arms from an attack on him by lions who had killed two of his companions. In order to follow up this prospect I moved and set up a temporary camp at El Behid, 70 miles due south-west toward Dolo (*behid* in Somali means oryx, so the place of oryx seemed a suitable spot). There were some wells at El Behid, but they had been poisoned by the Italians in their retreat. (An investigation of the wells revealed two large cobras

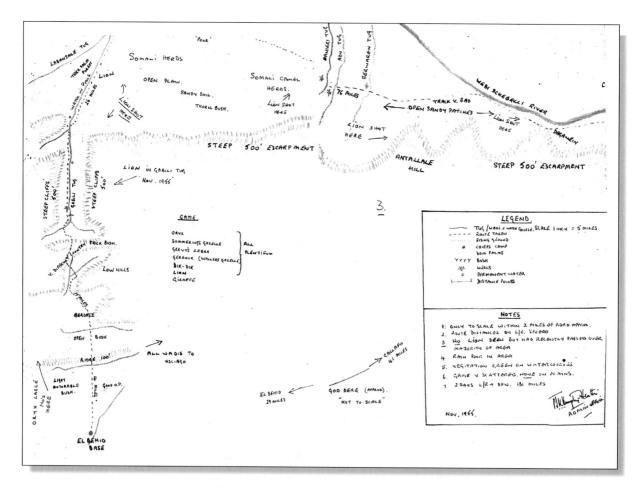

Map of Webi Schebelli River, southern Ethiopia (1955).

within the surrounding rocks. We left the wells well alone.) From El
Behid, a watercourse ran towards the Audomboi plain on the south bank
of the Webi Schebelli. Here there were large numbers of goats and camels
grazing. After two days of thirsty work making a rough track to the
plains, we found a suitable spot and camped with both vehicles. Once
again it was footwork—the terrain close to the river was too rough for
vehicles to pass. Here we disposed of 19 lions in seven days, several of
which were certainly man-eaters. I visited the cairns of stones under
which the remains of the two men who had been reported eaten by my
informant were buried. Their friend was making a good recovery thanks
to my meagre medical supplies.

On one of my days hunting I had a fortunate escape. We had located
a pride of 17 lions that were now so bold that they had begun to kill
stock in broad daylight, even when herdsmen were accompanying the
stock. The lions laid up in the riverine bush not far from the route used
by the stock to drink at the river. I decided that we would 'borrow' some

stock as guinea pigs for the experiment. This took considerable persuasion and diplomacy. However, thankfully, long conversations in the evenings by the campfire eventually bore fruit. Two camels and a herd of goats were used, accompanied by four herdsmen. Having tracked the lions to their lying-up point, the stock were driven close to them to tempt them into action.

Mumia and I stationed ourselves between the stock and the lions in a useful acacia tree. At first nothing happened, but then a short rush was made by a lion on two goats that had fed farther from the rest. The herdsmen shouted, and the lion retreated. Moving the feeding animals behind us, we were now between the lions and the stock once again. At 4.00 P.M. it looked as if nothing would happen, and the herdsmen were getting restive. Then we saw the lions moving, but their direction of approach would leave us too far on their flank. If the plan was to work we would have to descend from our perch and move into the path of the lions on the ground. We did so.

At 40 yards, I opened fire on the first three lions moving towards us through some sparse 15-foot thorn trees. I killed two and lost sight of the third. We sprinted after the others and three turned at bay. I knelt and killed two more—the third charged.

Her tail came up, and she made ground towards me very fast. I had two shots left in the magazine. Mumia, with the .404, was 20 yards away—a mistake. My first shot at her hit the ground near her left foot; the second full in her chest at 20 feet didn't stop her. As I leapt to my left out of her path, she touched the barrel of my gun and knocked it out of my hand, but she did not turn. Picking up the gun and with trembling fingers, I reloaded with two rounds. She had turned in the meantime but was hard hit. She came for me again, but not so fast, with blood dripping from her mouth—an ugly and nerve-wracking sight. My first shot missed her left foot, passing some 30 yards to Mumia's right. The second broke her neck and jaw and killed her 10 feet from me.

Mumia arrived. 'Come quickly, Bwana', he said, 'there are more over there'. Reloading and ensuring that I had one up the spout, I sprinted off after Mumia. I remember thinking with some alarm that he must have thought that I was invincible. Little did he know!

The lions were soon in sight. They were trotting off towards the river and making a half circle to cut off the stock, taking no notice of their fallen comrades. I soon saw the big male. So intent was I in pursuing him that I almost stepped on an old lioness that had decided to sit down behind a bush while the others did the work. She took off startled but

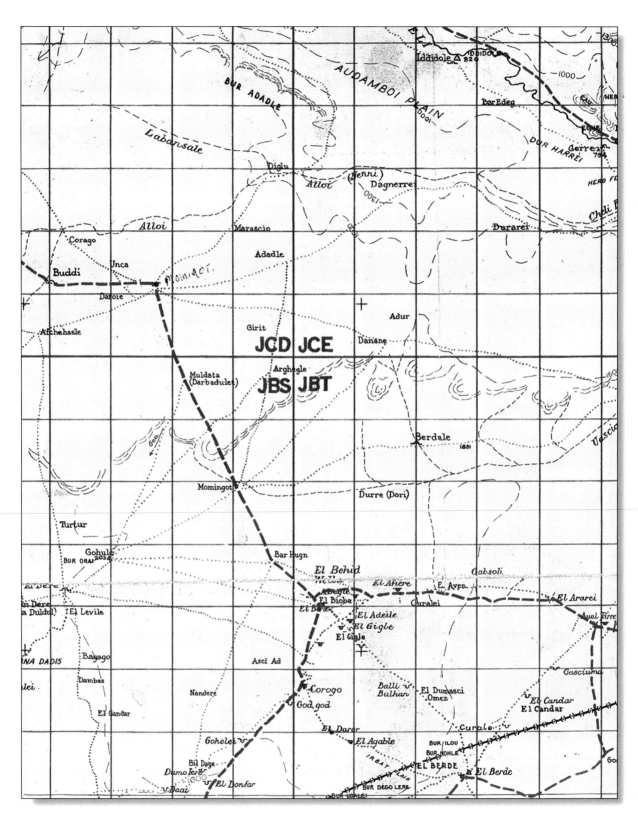

stopped, giving me an easy shot. On we ran perspiring very freely, dry mouthed with excitement. I was about done in for breath when we discovered that we were in the middle of the lions. I took the one in front of me that offered the best shot. Mumia was very close to me. 'Nyuma, nyuma' ('behind, behind'), he said in my ear. Raising the rifle and bringing it down on his shoulder, I fired at the charging lioness coming at us from behind him. She was hit well but never stopped. Before I could reload her body hit both Mumia and me, sending us sprawling but leaving us uninjured. She stood between us, her eyes glazed, as I put a finishing shot into her head. Mumia was grey, not black, at that moment.

'Pick up your gun', I said. 'Come on, we must keep going'. Automatically he responded. The lions had by this time become thoroughly alarmed and realised that they were missing some of their pride. The big male was target number one. After running about half a mile we came up with them again. The females had no heart to continue and made off, and I thought for one moment so had the male, but he must have been unsighted as to what the other lions were doing, for he walked into their tracks and stopped for an instant. Kneeling down, I put two shots into him broadside on. He left, but I felt sure he was hard hit. Reloading the .318, I took the .404 now and followed his tracks. He was hard hit—a hundred yards farther away he was lying down looking very unhappy. As he raised himself I finished him with the .404.

I don't think I have ever been so totally drained and exhausted in my life. Leaving the lions, we walked back to the tree where we met up with two of the herdsman. It was 5.45. Before long, we had some 20 people who this time were appreciative enough to cut some branches and assist in the skinning of the lions till 3.00 the next morning. Of the 17 lions in

Above: The stock killers wait by the water hole where they know the stock must come to drink (1955).

Previous page: Map of the El Behid and Audamboi Plain region—the lion area (1950).

the pride we had accounted for 10 and almost certainly those that had killed the herdsmen. The lions that escaped were young ones, barely 18 months to two years old. No doubt they would have become stock killers before long, but at this point I felt justice had been done—and an overkill was not my scene. The third lion I had shot was found dead near the other two when the rest of the lions were brought into camp.

There were several other occasions when lions were a serious problem in the areas of southern Ethiopia and Somaliland where I was stationed. It was upon one of these occasions that by chance we came across a lioness that had killed a number of stock and finally killed a herdsman. We were on our way back to camp following an old Italian road, having failed to track down the killer, when Mumia spied a huge lioness sitting on a rock just off the road. Reversing the car back down the road, I took refuge in a small watercourse and worked my way on foot towards her, killing her with one shot from the .318 at 70 yards. She turned out to be the biggest lion in length I ever shot, being 11 feet 4 inches long unskinned and standing 4 feet 6 inches at the shoulder. She was the lion we had been trailing all day, and she had made a circle around us. She was a loner and had never been seen travelling with any other lion. Daud (the police superintendent) was with me on this occasion.

I was reminded very much of Robert Browning's poem 'Youth':

> Oh, the wild joy of living; the leaping from rock to rock,
> the strong rending of boughs from the fir trees, the cool
> silver shock
> Of the plunge in the pool's living water, the hunt of the bear,
> And the sultriness showing the lion is couch'd in his lair.
> And the meal, the rich dates yellow'd over with gold dust
> divine,
> And the locust fresh steeped in the pitcher the full draught of
> wine,
> And the sleep in the dried river-channel where bulrushes tell
> That the water was wont to go warbling so softly and well.
> How good is a man's life, the mere living! How fit to employ
> All the heart and the soul and the senses for ever in joy!

Following page: L to R: Mumia, Capt. Daud, and me with the largest of the stock killers—the largest lioness I ever saw in southern Ethiopia.

All good things eventually come to an end, and in due course I moved back to Hargeisa, the capital of British Somaliland, and thence to Ethiopia and elsewhere, but that is another story. The months at Mustahil

were never to be repeated or equalled. Today Mustahil is a 'no go' area, being reputedly a drug-trafficking centre. The river floods no more, as a huge dam has been constructed some miles north of Calafo. The lions have gone—the AK-47s have seen to that.

After Mustahil, the rest of Ethiopia and British Somaliland was somewhat of an anticlimax.

There is something mystical about an African river flowing by one's camp. Somehow there is always that sense of anticipation that something out of the ordinary is about to happen. There is a concentration of wildlife activity on a river, more especially when it flows through arid, hot country. It is the life and soul of existence for everyone. Moving northwards to British Somaliland, I felt the all too familiar feeling of having lost an outstandingly good trophy. Sadness.

From Hargeisa, I was off to Las Anod and Erigavo near the coast. It was cool and dry at 5000 feet, and here among the mountains and dry watercourses there was enough water seepage to sustain lion, leopard, and a few greater kudu. Fortunately my arrival coincided with a relatively peaceful time of year, for there was no *khariff* or monsoon blowing. My headman spoke to me one morning when reporting for duty. There was a dhow sailing for the island of Socotra off Cape Guardafui, the 'horn' of Africa, and returning almost immediately. Conditioned as I was to the devious ways of the Somalis, I was lost in thought as to whether I could chance such a trip, which I would have dearly loved to have made. Glancing over my headman's shoulder, I beheld my answer, for here came a Land Rover I recognised as that of a friend of mine. The headman's back was turned to the approaching Land Rover.

'Yes', I said, 'I will go'. It was with some satisfaction that I saw the expression of joy on his face change to disappointment. My guns and kit were my primary consideration. Now I had a custodian for them. The arrangements were made and the trip successfully completed in four days. It left from and returned to Bender Cassim, the port across the border just inside Somalia. Socotra is an interesting island, blessed with a considerable sea bird population on its rocky coast of boulders. It was most surprising to see so many baobab trees there. The land birds were no different from those on the mainland. There were no antelope. The people were suspicious and villainous and reminded me of a nest of pirates—which I am sure they were—smugglers, without doubt, with faces of predominantely Arab origin. Arabic had been useful when speaking to the inhabitants. As we sailed back to the mainland, I found myself wishing that I had made the trip with Rene Babault. He loved dhows and islands.

The highlands of Erigavo were attractive. A great deal of *khat* was grown, which when chewed had the effect of Benzedrine, a stimulant. Looking closely at the pupils of the eyes, one could always see if a person was 'on'. If he was, he could be guaranteed to be unreliable, particularly if he was the driver of a vehicle.

Shortly thereafter I moved to Diredawa in eastern Ethiopia, a town on the railway line from Djibuti to Addis Abba built by the French many years previously. After taking a day or two to refit, I went down the line to a little station called Aiscia on the edge of the Danakil or Afar. Here, lodged in a derelict station building with a tame porcupine for company, I travelled extensively in the Danakil area. The fleshpots of Djibuti were not far away. I visited Djibuti only once, and that was enough for anyone. No greater example of decadent colonial power can have existed. It was a hot, torpid dump to any visitor, but a necessary evil for it had a harbour and supplies at reasonable prices. I was able to replenish my supplies of Chianti!

Striking north-west from my base, I hit the Awash River as it made its way through boulder-strewn plains, which I dubbed the 'black-rock country'. It was so hot that I physically tried the saying that 'you could have fried an egg on the bonnet of the car'. It worked—the egg fried! There was a great deal of game about, particularly Sommering's gazelle. Oryx and Waller's and Clarke's gazelle abounded. Baiting for lion and leopard brought excellent results. The lions had no manes and were much like those I had found in the N.F.D. The leopards, too, were light and rangy cats.

On one of my forays to the north-east, I caught sight of a small herd of Somali wild ass in the mirage of the heat on the depression. I should have liked to have been better equipped and then able to attempt an exploratory safari across either the north or south end of the depression, which was below sea level, striking the Red Sea coast after crossing the Assab-Diredawa Railway line, and so due north to Mersa Fatma and Massawa in Eritrea. In fact, whilst based upon Asmara in Eritrea, we reached Assab, the port on the Red Sea, by heading south from Mersa Fatma. Assab is connected to the French railway from Djibuti. The Afar and the Aoussa, the tribes who inhabit the Danakil, were fierce and warlike, and I had the impression that I was living on borrowed time, but a lion hunt that resulted in three lions shot persuaded them to tolerate me for the time being.

The Awash National Park, in the area between the Danakil and the mountains that make up the escarpment of the Ethiopian highlands to the west of Diredawa, provided a rewarding visit. In the days that I was roaming about in this area, it was a paradise and the best hunting that I found for many species of game in Ethiopia.

OTHER COUNTRIES

As mentioned in Chapter 1, I hunted Uganda on several occasions. On all occasions, if we had seen a good lion we would have attempted to shoot it, but only on two safaris did we do so. Although there were plenty about, having once hunted Tanganyika and subsequently Kenya and Bechuanaland, we were unlikely to find a lion in Uganda to match the great manes that they carried elsewhere. The best of these came from the Pian Upe and Mathineko areas. The one place that I saw a really magnificent lion was in the Kidepo, where they were protected. The lions in the Rift Valley in the areas of Lake Edward and Lake George were in wet, humid country and often in very long grass, making them more difficult to find. I never saw a great mane on any of them, although I believe that if the crater highlands of the Queen Elizabeth National Park could have been provided with a long-term water supply, which would have held the game there, the lions might well have developed into more magnificent beasts.

In the southern Sudan, where it was hot and humid, lions did not seem to be too plentiful. When they were so, their manes were poor by comparison to East Africa.

In Eritrea I shot a scruffy lion near the Setit River east of the border post at Om Oger. Here there were some open flats of grass and acacia trees and considerable numbers of herds of eland. Game, however, was in the process of being badly poached, and I saw several parties of local people around with Italian carbines. In the 1920s and 1930s the Setit had been a favourite hunting ground for big-game hunters in the Sudan. It is a formidable river. Its upper reaches, where it is called the Tacasse, drain the Semien Mountains. Its course takes it through some of the most staggering scenery in the world, the country being the home of the Abyssinian (walia) ibex. The bird life in this precipitous valley is quite wonderful. Generally speaking, Eritrea had little or no lion left at that time.

CHAPTER SIX

LEOPARD HUNTING

The Artful Dodger

GENERAL OBSERVATIONS

I have hunted leopard in all the countries covered by this book. They are by nature perhaps the most intelligent of cats. There can be no doubt that this intuitively clever cat will be a certain survivor when almost all other indigenous wildlife has disappeared. On several occasions whilst I was hidden, I have seen a leopard carefully watch the pattern of human comings and goings and then with perfect timing cross unseen into another area of human habitation. As stated in Chapter 5, I am convinced that this cat has a greater ability to perceive than a lion.

Leopards live at all altitudes, be they hot, humid, or cold, and in all types of terrain. At higher altitudes they grow more massive and have heavier pelts, and the incidence of the melanistic form—the black leopard—occurs more often. The black panther of India is no more than the melanistic form of the ordinary leopard. There have been many recordings in most countries of black leopards, and I have seen them in Tanganyika, Kenya, and Ethiopia. I well remember a respected friend and P.H. Reggie Destro, who was reported to have had his client shoot one in Maralal in northern Kenya at nearly 7000 feet. Several were regularly seen in the 1960s on the rim of Ngorongoro Crater in Tanganyika by Gordon Harvey, the warden. But by far the most prolific occurrence of black leopard was in Ethiopia, where in some areas one in every three was black. It was here that I hunted and eventually secured my only black leopard.

At last the rifle speaks,
The bullet streaks
At supersonic speed
upon its way,
The arbiter of life or
death this day.
At best the end as by
some lightning stroke,
Too swift and deadly
ever to evoke,
An apprehension, fear
or any pain,
So, squeeze the trigger
gently, or refrain.

—Lord Sheffield
'Skips' Riverdale

Suddenly I became aware that I was looking at two large yellow eyes in a black face. . . .

—J.K.-H.

Leopards are sometimes easy to shoot but are not always easy to kill. This is because a detailed understanding of their anatomy is required before the bullet can be placed in the right spot. A leopard is not a large beast, and its vitals can be measured in inches only. The average weight of a male leopard is 140 pounds. Accuracy when shooting is absolutely essential. The guns to be used on leopard, therefore, range from a .243 to a .375.

I have been asked on many occasions what my favourite dangerous animal is to hunt. As my reader will have gathered from previous chapters, I have enjoyed the greatest excitement from hunting them all. Even so, I would place leopard, elephant, and buffalo equally first, followed by lion, rhino, and hippo. I have never really appreciated shooting large numbers of animals on control, believing that, in my day, little if any proper investigation had been made of alternative methods of taking care of the problems that the animals caused. In my younger days, I was inexperienced and in no position to argue the case, being desperate for experience and my expenses to be paid. This was largely true of elephant and buffalo, and lion to a lesser extent. The control of leopard could certainly have been done by trapping and translocation, but in some parts of East Africa they were so numerous that they were classed as vermin for many years. Even today there are far more leopards about in East Africa than the multiplicity of wildlife organisations would have us believe.

The leopard is a clever animal and learns fast from experience. He is a student of human and animal behaviour, but like everyone in the world—both human and animal—he has one great failing: he does not seem to have total control of his tail! On the many occasions that I have spotted a leopard, nine times out of 10 his tail has given him away. I am sure that this telltale trait has also saved the lives of many of his would-be victims.

A leopard's intuitive intelligence is heightened by the fact that in relation to other dangerous animals it is infinitely smaller in size. Stealth and cunning are its ways of standing up for itself. I have experienced many a leopard outwitting my plans for his demise, and on more than one occasion I have found the spot a day or two later from which it had taken note of my efforts to secure its death. Many have lived to fight another day. A true hunter will admit that with leopards, one is not always successful.

So interested in leopard hunting had I become in the late 1960s that I made tentative plans to exchange a safari in East Africa for a safari in Persia. There the leopards of the hills and valleys of eastern Persia grow to a huge size, far bigger than those of the African continent. With the

Previous page top: Coming up to the bait.

Previous page bottom: In the tree.

267

Top: Essential preparations for leopard hunting—zeroing in the gun. Note the thumb under the fore-end so that the wood is insulated from the wood of the tripod, thereby decreasing jump when firing. The rifle is a .243 Winchester with Kilmorgen Optical Co. scope (1957).

Above: Finding leopard tracks. Patrolling a sand river is a good start.

overthrow of H.I.M. the Shah of Iran, my plans came to nought, but they are forever an unrealised dream. My old friend David Laylin, the promoter of Iran safaris, and more particularly Rashid Jamsheed, that incredible hunter of sheep, were my mentors. Of course, Jack O'Connor and others, too, had regaled me with their tales of that wonderful hunting country. I have never aspired to be a sheep hunter, but a huge leopard hunter, always. Interestingly, Rowland Ward's *Records of Big Game* (XX Edition) shows no entries for Persian leopard.

SOME FACTORS TO BE BORNE IN MIND WHEN BAITING

The same factors apply to leopard baiting as to in lion baiting (pages 180-182), with three exceptions:

1. Take a Tilley lamp or a kerosene or petrol lamp filled to capacity with you in the car. If you cannot see the leopard after shooting or wounding it and you are sure you have hit it, place a lamp in the direction in which the leopard disappeared. Leave it alight all night and come back at dawn next day. This is an effective way of keeping off hyena. Use two lamps if you wish. It may not always work, but it is often a great help.
2. In the case of a leopard bait, remember that lions and lionesses can climb trees to some extent; thus the leopard bait needs to lie well out on a branch and well up into the upper part of the tree. Remember also that if it is very high, you need to think about the passage of the bullet through the leopard's body in case you lose some of the damaging effect of the bullet to the angle of strike from the blind/hide.
3. Remember that leopard particularly tend to charge human voices and bright lights. Silence is golden. (See Edward G. Robinson's Leopard and *Sammy Going South* later in this chapter.)

The records of accidents with leopards involving the professional hunter fraternity are high. Most of the well-known professional hunters of recent years have all been savaged by leopards—John Sutton, Eric Rundgren, Robin Hurt, and David Ommanney, to name a few—and many of the old-timers, too. Foremost was Charles Cottar, who strangled a live leopard with his bare hands. Whilst doing so, he had one of his sons turn the handle of the movie camera! On seeing his father pouring blood from the deep scratches the leopard was inflicting upon him, his son stopped turning the handle.

Top: Sand river and bush beyond; the man pulling on the rope is in a good spot for the leopard to lie up. The impala is being hauled into the tree as bait (1961).

Middle: Building a good, strong, well-concealed blind (1966).

Bottom: The ideal result. One shot and one dead leopard in full view under the tree (1959).

269

Essential preparation for hunters wishing to shoot leopards—practice and accuracy (1970).

'Keep turning!' bellowed Cottar. I remember Donald Ker describing this incident to me. He also said that Cottar put salt on his wounds to cleanse them. That must have been painful, to say the least. It took guts and determination, of which Cottar had plenty.

As my reader will surmise from reading the account of the leopard's performance in the film *Sammy Going South*, a leopard, when wounded and cornered, does not like the noise of human voices. Likewise, at night it does not like a spotlight coupled with the noise of movement.

There are two distinct differences between lion and leopard: their methods of attack and their diets.

During the whole of the time that I was being mauled by a lion, I am absolutely convinced that nothing would have deterred or altered the complete attention of the lion upon me. My gunbearers and client came and went by my side, and yet, even when the lion was about to be shot with my broken .470 by my gunbearer—who you'll remember from the previous chapter checked the state of the gun before doing so—the lion's gaze upon me never wavered. The lion makes war upon one person, and having done so sticks to him and no other in nearly all cases.

In direct contrast is the leopard's behaviour. One seldom, if ever, hears of a leopard attacking only one person. In almost every case the leopard charges, biting, scratching, and attacking one person after another, leaving two or three people suffering from its ferocious attentions. More often than not, therefore, when a P.H. is mauled by a leopard, others are mauled at the same time. Naturally, any unwounded leopard that, of its own accord, deliberately chooses to attack one person is excepted from this observation.

Leopards have recourse to one source of food that places them as survivors long after lion have disappeared: a substantial part of a leopard's diet is fur and feathers. Young leopards, when they are learning to fend for themselves, live almost entirely on their efforts to catch birds, rabbits, and hyrax. This is an important part of the leopard's future chances of survival. Although poaching and other causes have led to the disappearance of millions of animals in Africa, over the last three decades the bird populations have suffered little. Time has become important, too, to the indigenous peoples of Africa, and many of them do not have the time to look for birds' eggs and set traps for game birds. So long as game birds and other birds continue to be left in peace, the leopard will be assisted in its survival.

Top: Ed Quinn with a big 'tom' shot near Kajaido, Kenya Masailand (1964).

Left: Ginny and John Morrill (see 'The Morrill Elephant' in Chapter 2) with one of the largest leopards we shot on safari (1968).

KENYA

Kenya abounded with leopards in the heyday of African safaris after the 1939–45 War. Though much poached and reduced in numbers today, they have survived, compared to other animals, quite well. However, leopards did not thank Jackie Kennedy when she wore a coat made of six leopard skins. Thereafter, the hunt for their skins was so intensified that they almost became an endangered species until the fashion, thankfully, died.

271

Compare Cliff Tillotson's big leopard on page 273 to a huge jaguar shot in South America by Tony Almeida's client. (Tony is second from right.) Note the jaguar's heavier body and shorter tail (early 1950s).

Leopard sizes are sometimes controversial, too. Roland Ward's *Records of Big Game* of the latest date carefully endorses its remarks: 'These are owners' measurements and cannot be verified by the author'. If the skull is in much the same position as in the record of the skin, I suppose the record must be accepted as truthful. I have seen an attempt to make a seven-foot six-inch leopard into an eight-foot one by simply tying a light rope onto the lower jaw and putting a couple of gunbearers on the tail and stretching the cat whilst a tape is put on the leopard from nose to tail. This can make a difference in measurement of up to six inches! There are long, thin leopards and short, fat ones and leopards with long tails and others with short tails. I have never seen one that

Top: A fine male leopard shot in Tanganyika by Cliff Tillotson in the Loliondo area with the author (1960).

Bottom: Lionel Palmer and me with a nice male leopard shot in the N.F.D. of Kenya in 1969.

273

Bongo

went nine feet, but I suppose it is possible. My reader will have gathered that I am a little sceptical of leopard records.

The leopard has an interesting cousin, the jaguar. Both Tony Almeida and Richard Mason—the ace jaguar hunters for more than 25 years operating in South America generally—probably have more combined experience in hunting these animals than any person alive. Jaguar are considerably heavier than leopard, but sometimes with shorter and thicker tails.

The more equable the climate, the bigger the leopard. In Kenya in the high forest of the Aberdares west of Mount Kenya, Mount Kenya itself, and in other places of similar elevation, leopards grow to their greatest size and weight. Sixteen of the leopards recorded in the 20 largest leopards in Ward's *Records of Big Game* were shot in the high mountains of Kenya and steppe land of both Kenya and Tanzania Masailand between 5500 and 6000 feet. Few of any size are seen in hot, humid, or tropical coastal areas. I recall that one of my contemporaries, Tony France, collected a huge leopard of eight feet in length and some 200 pounds in the Aberdare Mountains, which won him the Shaw & Hunter Trophy.

Very few safaris between 1950 and 1978 did not shoot a leopard if one was required and properly baited. The main reason why a safari client failed to obtain a leopard was simply a matter of time. As the price of a safari rose, the period for which the clients could afford to stay was reduced. This led the Kenya government to place restrictions on the shooting of most desirable trophies that could not be hunted in fewer than 21 days. This effectively put pressure on the P.H., as the safari period was reduced from 30 to 22 days.

On occasion leopards were seen and shot without baiting and by complete chance. Once I recall, when sitting in the car with my clients trying to decide whether to stop and camp, a huge male leopard calmly walked right across the spot in which we were proposing to camp. All the guns were packed away, with the ammunition in a steel safe behind the driving seat. Unpacking this noiselessly was impossible, but once it was undone, my client's wife and I set out to stalk the leopard in the forlorn hope that we might get a shot. Imagine our surprise when, some 300 yards later, we caught sight of him sitting on an anthill in the evening sunshine looking away from us. A convenient rest was at hand, and one clean, accurate shot got us a leopard. The decision to camp in that spot was made, and it was a

Leopard and lion shot on the same bait within a few minutes. Ace Adams with his lion, Corinne Adams with her leopard. Kajaido, Kenya (1962).

lucky safari. Interestingly, some of my contemporaries who shot huge leopards invariably shot other magnificent trophies on the same safari; one of them shot an eight-foot leopard weighing 200 pounds in the Aberdares, followed by a bull bongo with 34-inch horns shortly thereafter. Another who also collected a huge leopard then shot a 120-pound-tusked elephant. As recorded, my friends the Morrills did the same.

In the early days I did several safaris with Syd Downey, which were his last hunting safaris. Syd liked hunting leopard. The planning necessary to outwit this clever animal was a challenge, and getting it right called upon all the experience one could muster. Every hunt for a leopard was different, and no set of circumstances seemed to repeat itself.

On one particular safari we had a remarkable experience. We had baited a leopard on the Ngare Ndare River near Isiolo in the N.F.D. We had had a memorable day, having climbed Mount Lengishu and shot a greater kudu on top of the mountain and a lesser kudu at the bottom of the mountain. We had two days left, and it was time to check the leopard baits. One bait, situated on an island in the sandy watercourse of the Ngare Ndare River, had been hit. We decided to sit for it. Syd, his client, and I set out for the bait. As we approached we noticed that the sky was overcast and a huge rainstorm was approaching. Both Syd and his client took their raincoats, and I dropped them both from the car close to the blind.

There was no sign of the leopard. An hour later the first drops of rain fell, and the leopard appeared, leaping instantly into the tree and walking right up into its topmost branches, where it sat contemplating the countryside. Neither Syd nor his client could see the leopard properly to shoot, so they decided to wait and see if it would feed. Before long, I heard what at first I thought was the noise of a car. Suddenly I realised it was not a car, but the river coming down in full spate.

Not a moment was to be lost. After starting the car I made a careful approach to pick up Syd and his client before they were washed away. I was too late, but Syd was not. As the noise of the approaching water reached the leopard, it came down into the open part of the tree near the bait to see what was happening. Quickly and with only seconds to spare, one shot was used to kill the leopard stone dead. Running as fast as they could, Syd and his client just made it to the car before the water came down. Fortunately it was not a big flood, and the water did not cover the island on which the bait hung, where the leopard lay dead. An hour later, just as it was almost dark, the river had gone down enough to enable us to wade across and retrieve the leopard, with which we returned to camp triumphant. As we climbed into bed that night I said to Syd with a wry grin, 'I suppose you knew how much water was coming down that river!' The spare pillow landed on my head.

A favourite place of mine for hunting the many species of game that Kenya offered was the Kedong Valley. This ran from the southern end of Lake Naivasha, excluding Mount Logonot to the east, and took in the western side of Mount Suswa. From there it ran through a series of shelves, escarpments, and valleys falling 2000 feet to Lake Magadi and thence past Mount Stromboli to Lake Natron in Tanganyika.

The mid-1960s were busy safari times. Ker & Downey Safaris Ltd. was on a roll of popularity. Some 22 professional hunters were employed by the company at the busiest time of the year. Outfitting films, looking at the possibilities of Mozambique and Bechuanaland, plus all the other normal safari commitments made life pretty hectic. At this point Winchester decided to do a huge promotion for its firearms. The new 1964 Model 70 had arrived with a new bolt action and had to be marketed. It turned out to be unpopular, but we did not know that at the time. Whilst in the U.S.A. I had met Jim Rikoff and Scott Healey, who were the motivators of the whole Winchester promotional exercise that was to take place. A safari was planned, and of course it had to be a good one.

David Ommanney was a highly experienced P.H. and a good friend. He, like me, had accrued considerable experience in Tanganyika, where he had been working as a P.H. for Tanganyika Tours & Safaris Ltd. out of Arusha, owned by Russell Douglas. David had taken over my vehicle in Bechuanaland whilst I was in Mozambique and had preceded me in our

The massive male leopard shot by Jim Rikoff at Hell's Gate in Kenya on the Winchester safari. Note the huge muscle structure on the upper front legs (1963).

return to Kenya. He, at my suggestion, got the Winchester safari on the road. I joined him a few days later. We were camped in the Kedong Valley, where the year before I had collected the world record head of a Grant's gazelle. Here the season was exactly right—game everywhere and many different species. Scenically it was a perfect paradise for publicity pictures of an African safari. We needed lion and leopard for both Scott and Jim. John Groth, the well-known artist, had come along also but not to shoot. We had all manner of new guns.

Jim and I set out to nail a big leopard, although I knew the leopards in the area had been hunted occasionally for some 20 years. This was where Syd and many of his contemporaries had often hunted. Carefully I chose some baiting places that a leopard would have thought totally safe and from which he had ample recourse to a safe hiding spot. The extreme effort we put into it paid off handsomely. A huge leopard (one that could easily have been stretched to eight feet) came on to the bait just before dark, and Jim made no mistake. The safari was a great success, and David became 'Winchester's man in Africa' whilst I transferred my attentions farther south to Bechuanaland.

277

Until 1977, when hunting in Kenya was closed, leopard hunting was one of the most successful and satisfying experiences one could have with a client. Whilst many incidents and successful hunts for other game were well recalled, leopard hunting was best remembered for its long, drawn-out excitement and anticipatory experience. Even before hunting was closed, it was commonplace to hang five baits and to have five leopards feeding. Sadly, the Kenya Game Department found it necessary to put down poison bait in the Kedong Valley, with the result that one of my favourite spots was destroyed. This was an area where, on three occasions, my clients each shot a big leopard and fine lion on the same day. Today, overstocked with domestic animals and laced by roads, much of the game has ceased to exist.

TANGANYIKA (TANZANIA)

Having described Kenya as a country with plenty of leopard, I am bound to say that Tanganyika certainly was lousy with them. They were considered vermin for some years after my arrival there in 1949. High ground once again provided the habitat for the largest leopards, with the Loliondo area of Northern Province providing the bigger ones in the record books, but only because that was a convenient area to hunt within 120 miles of civilisation. For many years, when hunting Loliondo, I seldom shot a leopard that was less than seven feet two inches in length. There were three places in particular where I saw the largest leopards I have ever seen in my whole career. The first as described in Loliondo, the second in the far north-west corner of Tanganyika in Ibanda, and the third in the Mount Kungwe and Mahali Mountain Range on the eastern shore of Lake Tanganyika. Of the lower lying areas from 3000 to 4000 feet, the valley of the Ruaha River in the 1950s produced some whoppers. One such was shot by Bill Holmes, who also collected a 100-pound-tusked elephant on the same safari. I never shot a leopard in the Mahali Mountains, but I did take a long look at one.

I was on a long foot safari in 1949 that entailed walking up to the highlands of the Mahali Range from Lagosa on Lake Tanganyika, traversing the range southwards and descending to Kalia on the lake side. One night, after a good sleep, I awoke at five o'clock, leaving my tent at the rear to attend to the call of nature. I was about to return to my warm bed when I heard a noise at the front of my tent. Peering in the moonlight

Klipspringer

278

over the tent fly from the rear of my tent, I beheld a huge leopard calmly
taking a drink from my washbasin. I stood riveted to the spot. He was
there for a full two minutes, and then, having slaked his thirst, he
dropped back on all fours and quietly moved on into camp. Next morning, the cook complained that the leg of goat that had been hung in a
tree was gone. The leopard's tracks were very large. Enquiries revealed
that a number of goats had been lost in this area as well.

I had a similar experience in Mwanza, the port in Tanganyika on the
southern end of Lake Victoria. Here one night at 2.00 a noise awakened
me outside the window of my bedroom. Cautiously looking out of the
window from behind the curtain, I saw below me in the backyard of the
hotel a huge leopard. He had gently lifted the lid of one of the hotel
dustbins and consumed the remains of a large Nile perch that we had
had for dinner that night. He was sitting on his haunches calmly licking
his paw and washing his face just like a tabby cat at home. Slipping into
my clothes and grabbing my binoculars, I watched him until, with that
wonderful power that cats have in their back legs, he sprang up effort-
lessly onto the wall and calmly walked along it. I let myself out of the
hotel and almost at once saw him silhouetted against the sky on top of a
wall some 50 yards from the hotel. I followed him at a safe distance
through the sleeping town to the edge of the lake where he disappeared
into an area of boulders and bush. I believe this leopard was trapped
some time later and released into the Serengeti National Park. Knowing
the exceptional intelligence of these animals, I am sure he would have
lived in Mwanza for some considerable time.

There were always challenges with hunting leopard. Once when I
was on safari with the Spencer family from Dallas, we had arrived, unbe-
lievably, on the last day of the safari without a leopard. Turning to Morris
Spencer, I remarked that leopards were not shot in camp and that we
had best go out and stay out looking for one until the last possible
moment and hope that we would be lucky.

All morning we travelled up and down watercourses and likely places. At
11.30 in the morning, our luck changed. There was a zebra foal of considerable size—200 pounds—halfway up an acacia tree with its head wedged in a
crotch of the tree. There was no sign of the leopard that had killed it. If we
beat the watercourse in which the tree stood, using our gunbearers as beaters, a fleeting shot at a leopard would almost certainly bring disastrous results
too horrific to contemplate—wounded leopards and mauled people on the
last day of a safari were unthinkable. I had to have a plan.

Curiosity kills the cat, I said to myself.

'What are you going to do?' asked Morris, looking rather despondent. Briefly I explained my plan to him. We drove off onto the plain, and when we were more than a mile away, Morris and I stalked a male impala and shot it. Returning to within a few hundred yards of the leopard's kill, we split the impala in half with a *panga* (machete), exposing its innards to the sky. We sat in the car for a few moments until the sky became black with circling vultures. Then, slowly, we dragged the carcase on a slip rope attached to the car to the immediate vicinity of the zebra kill, letting go one end of the rope so that the impala carcase was left in full view of both the vultures in the sky and the leopard, had he climbed the tree to his own kill. The car dropped Morris and me behind a convenient bush downwind some 40 yards away, and we sat to await results.

An interesting sequence of events then unfolded. The vultures had seen the abandoned carcase, and they had also seen the leopard's kill in the tree. Could the leopard take care of both kills? Several vultures decided to test out the leopard. Soon the rush of their wings in descent through the air could be heard, and with a plop the first vulture landed near the impala.

'Get ready', I said to Morris. 'If anything is going to happen, it will do now'. Three more vultures landed, and many more circled slowly low overhead. Below, in the watercourse, I could well imagine the leopard lifting his head from his siesta in concern at the birds threatening his kill.

The temptation to nip up to the tree and protect his kill was great, and he yielded to that temptation, coupled with his curiosity to see exactly what was happening. He climbed the tree in full view of us. Morris had not come this far to miss a big male leopard, and his shot sent the leopard back to the bottom of the tree very dead. At this very last moment of the safari, good fortune had been with us.

Just because a leopard appeared on the bait in the tree did not necessarily mean that it was a male. Although for a long time female leopards were permitted to be shot, generally speaking, no P.H. in East Africa felt it was sporting to do so. Later, females of all species of game came to be protected. Care, therefore, had to be taken to ensure that males were shot. There were times when it was difficult to ascertain whether the leopard was a male or a female. Sitting in a blind one evening we watched no less than five leopards in and about the tree— male, female, and three cubs. The cubs went into the far upper branches of the tree while the male had the bait to himself and the mother waited patiently on another branch. We did not shoot the male, as a bigger one put in an appearance on another bait. It was thus that we hunted with a semblance of sympathy. There were, after all, plenty of leopard.

Dogs were a prime target for leopards short of food. Many a district commissioner's dog was taken when it was let out at night. *Shenzi* dogs (native mongrels) were fair game to leopard, and it was as well they were. Rabies was spread by diseased and poorly treated shenzi dogs. Peter Marcovici, a friend of mine from New York, when on a private safari of his own, shot a leopard at the moment it had killed a dog that was attempting to bay him up. Both the leopard and the dog died in each other's arms.

When on safari in the northern extension of the Serengeti National Park, Syd Downey and I witnessed an extraordinary sequence of events that involved leopard, lion, and hyena. We were driving along on the track from Kilmafeza to Kampi ya Mawe when one of the gunbearers, Ngui, who in the past had been on safari with Philip Percival and Ernest Hemingway, saw a big lion with a small pride under a tree. We drove over to have a look and almost immediately noticed a young female leopard up in the top of the tree with nowhere to go and seven lions below her on a kill. In the background were three hyenas.

When our car was added to the dimension, the leopard panicked and made a wild spring from the branches to another tree. She failed to reach it and fell to the ground. For a second she was knocked breathless, and a hyena with an eye to the main chance—and thinking that the lion on their kill would not bother with an undersized leopard as a dessert dish—made for the leopard. In an instant the big male lion grabbed the hyena and with one shake of his head broke its neck, flinging it 10 yards away. The leopard, thankful for the feline interruption, jumped up and ran away. Syd and I observed this on the same safari that we saw a big male lion, seemingly resting after a meal on a hartebeest, jump up and pursue with determination no less than three hyenas and kill them all in the same fashion.

Years later, I was reminded of the leopard's skill and stealth when moving awkward deadweight bodies over high objects. I had eight pigs in a sty when farming on the slopes of Mount Kilimanjaro. The sty was made of concrete blocks and shaded over the interior by a corrugated iron roof that rose to the top of the rear wall of the sty to a height of some 12 feet. At midnight one night, I was awakened by the Masai watchman who

This leopard killed the dog and was shot at the same moment by Peter Marcovici of New York on his own outfitted Tanzania safari.

told me that a leopard was attacking the pigs. Taking my trusty Purdey Paradox, loaded with lethal ball and heavy shot, and a flashlight, I went out to have a look at the pigs. Too late—there was blood everywhere, even on the roof. The leopard had killed a porker weighing 180 pounds and, by standing it on its rear end, had then pulled it up onto the side wall of the sty. Then, cleverly balancing it, it had slid the pig to the point where the corrugated iron met the wall. Again using the fulcrum of the pig's weight, it dragged the pig up to the apex of the corrugated iron roof and tipped it into the coffee bushes to the rear of the pig sty. Next morning we found the drag marks of the pig's carcase to the edge of the forest some 180 yards away. Part of the pig had been eaten.

By tying the pig's feet to a coffee bush and covering it with grass, it was easy enough to build a hide between some strategically growing coffee bushes, and that evening I sat down to await results. I had hardly got into the blind at 4.45 when the leopard came full of confidence to haul the pig into the forest. He failed to do so. His skin is on the back of the settee in the room in which I write this story.

Edward G. Robinson's Leopard
and *Sammy Going South*

The successful outfitting that Ker & Downey Safaris Ltd. had achieved for *Hatari* soon rubbed off on aspiring filmmakers. It was not long before Michael Balcon Productions came out from England with the idea of making a film called *Sammy Going South*, the story of a boy orphaned in the war caused by the Suez Canal seizure by the British and French forces. The story is of his determination to travel the length of Africa to his relatives in South Africa.

Chosen as the royal film premiere of 1963, the Michael Balcon production of *Sammy Going South* was made in Cinemascope and Eastman colour and was produced by Hal Mason and directed by Alexander 'Sandy' McKendrick. The film starred Edward G. Robinson with Constance Cummings, Harry H. Corbett (of *Steptoe & Son* fame), and Paul Stassino. The part of Sammy was played by Fergus McClelland. The screenplay was by Denis Cannah, taken from the book by W.H. Canaway.

Through some friends in England I got wind of this proposal, and on my way back from the U.S.A. I met Hal Mason in London and ensured his consideration of Ker & Downey Safaris Ltd. as outfitters. Not long afterwards, after correspondence with the company, Philip Shipway came out from England with his beautiful secretary on behalf of Michael Balcon Productions to tour Kenya, Tanganyika, and Uganda for likely areas where the film would be shot. This was in late 1961 and 1962. I was still recovering from being mauled by the lion, so working with Paramount was an easy task for me to perform and yet earn my living. Having started off on the Nile at Jinja in Uganda, whence the film company took over the Crested Crane Hotel, we then moved to the all too familiar site of Momella, where not long before the first unit of Paramount Pictures had shot *Hatari*. The filmmaking site had now been turned into Momella Safari Lodge and was a short distance from Momella Lake.

One afternoon we sat down to discuss shooting the part of the story where Edward G. Robinson, who took the part of an old poacher and diamond smuggler, is saved from possible death by Sammy shooting the leopard. The sequence required a live leopard charging the camera. The rest of the sequence was done with a tame leopard flown up from Lobatsi in Bechuanaland. My problem was to arrange for a charging, snarling leopard full into the camera at point-blank range and for all thereafter to be safe and happy, including the leopard.

Top: Fergus McClelland, 'Sammy' in Sammy Going South, *hears the lion-that-mauled-me story from me. I am showing him the claw and tooth kept from the lion's skin and skull.*

Right: On the set of Sammy Going South. *The scene where Edward G. Robinson is saved from a charging leopard by Sammy. I am instructing Sammy how to hold the gun. Syd Downey's retired headman, Salimu, is standing behind me (1962).*

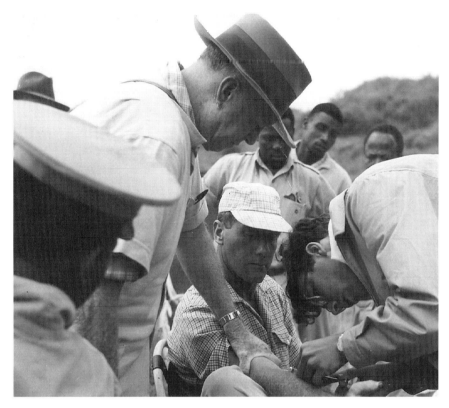

George Barrington, bitten by a puff adder in the hand, gets an intravenous injection of anti-venom from the film company doctor, watched by Eryk Ker.

I believe it fair to say that if I had not had sufficient experience at that time, I would not have come up with the answer. Even so, there was a lot to do, construct, and plan. First I obtained Hal Mason's permission to build, at the base of a rock where grew some thick bush, a cage that would accomodate the view required of the Mitchell camera. Two and a half feet above the ground at the apex of the triangle of view towards the rock, there was a small, reinforced hole where the camera lens fitted. The strong wire cage was so constructed that it was slightly larger than the view seen from the camera's lens. On the right-hand side of the camera's view, hidden in the bushes through which the wire of the cage passed, there was a small door. This was the point at which the leopard would enter the cage. All this was the easy part.

In the meantime Peter Whitehead, who had taken over as manager of Ker & Downey from Ron Stephens, was briefed that we wanted to trap a wild leopard, use it in the film, and then release it in a national park. Preferably it should be a leopard that was causing trouble. Peter was the brother-in-law of Gerry Swynerton, the former game warden of Tanganyika. He had been in the game department of Rhodesia and had many contacts in the wildlife department and knew well Ian Grimwood, then the chief game warden of Kenya. Before long, a troublesome leopard was located on the South Kinankop, on the farm of the well-known Kenya farmers, the Nightingales. A trap was set and the leopard duly caught—a huge and magnificent animal. David Williams, an old friend of many years, brought it down in a box on the back of a long-wheelbase Land Rover, arriving late in the evening in Arusha. It was parked outside the window of my bedroom no fewer than 10 feet away. (My bedroom window, however, was barred.) I did not get much sleep that night as I was convinced that the box would not last long. At 2.00 A.M. I got up, found some half-inch rope, and went out and roped the box. The leopard went berserk inside, and I have often reflected that it was sheer luck it did not burst out of it.

Next day all was set for the film. I carefully drove the Land Rover containing the box out to the site of the wire cage. There, very gingerly, the box was unloaded and left quietly at the entrance to the cage with the cage door raised. All we had to do to release the leopard was to lift up the door of the box and hope that it walked out into the cage. The problem of getting the leopard to charge was a major one, and getting it back into the box to be transported to a national park was quite another. My instructions to the Sikh contractor from Arusha were clear: as soon as the leopard was out of its box, the box was to be taken away and converted into a trap so that if we put meat inside and the leopard ate it, the door would shut behind him as a result of his grabbing the meat. It was a chance—something I had to try.

Having briefed the director, Sandy, I took him to stand with me close to the Mitchell camera and within a couple of feet of the wire. The cameraman was extremely nervous. I had with me my .470 Westley Richards loaded with 500-grain soft-points, and Edward had my Purdey Paradox loaded with lethal ball in one barrel and 12 steel shot in the other of the *cartucia gigante* type. When all was ready and silence reigned, I waved a white handkerchief for the box door to be raised. An answering wave of a handkerchief signalled that the leopard had left the box.

Nothing happened. The leopard hid in the bush at the base of the rock. After five minutes Sandy asked me if I thought the whole thing would work. It was then that I thought I had better try my one trump card. In every story of people being mauled by leopards, I had been told that the leopard, when he heard human voices, had invariably charged the spot from which the noise came. I decided to test this theory. Turning to Sandy and the cameraman, I began to discuss the matter in loud

tones, winking at them at the same time; after a second or so, extremely mystified, they played along.

A few seconds later the leopard came bald-headed for us, snarling, its tail up and showing a spine-chilling set of teeth as it threw itself into the corner where the petrified cameraman fell over backwards in fright. Sandy, totally surprised, stepped back a few paces. I did so, too, but tripped over a steel peg securing the wire cage and fell flat on my back. In a second the leopard disappeared back into the bushes from whence it came. After some surprised grins all round, Sandy asked me if it would do it again. I told him I thought it might well do so, but the cameraman was shaky. We both asked him if he could do it, and he was no person to shirk his duties—and now that he knew what was coming, he readily agreed.

'Cocky Wainwright,' the part played by Edward G. Robinson.

287

Once again we struck up a conversation in raised voices. This time there were more of us. Out came the leopard like a bat out of hell, hitting the wire, snarling and growling at us. We had retreated to a position directly behind the camera this time. Seeing the cameraman behind the camera, the leopard attacked the lens but not before the film was in the can. With a final smash of its paw with its hideous claws outstretched, it whipped the lens off the camera before retreating once again into the bush at the base of the rock. 'Sensational stuff', said Sandy.

'It's stripped the threads on the lens', said the cameraman.

A check showed that enough feet had been taken, but with a new lens on the camera we tried it once more. This time the leopard came again but not up to the camera. After stopping and snarling for a second or so, it turned back into the bush once more. Splicing this last piece of film to the first piece gave them all they needed. The box was baited and left overnight—chained to the side of the cage to be on the safe side. Next day the leopard was back in the box, and off he went to Manyara National Park to be released. His release was not, however, without incident. The door of the box was raised, fortunately by a rope from the cab of the open-backed Land Rover. The leopard, now free, jumped onto the bonnet of the Land Rover and struck repeatedly at the windscreen of the cab and snarled at the occupants, who started the engine and blew the horn. It finally made off into the forest.

The picture continued and was successfully completed. The tame-leopard shots were successfully matched, and the leopard sequence looked excellent. 'Bull', the tame leopard, had been the star of *Life* magazine when Paul Halmi, the now well-known Hollywood film director, had been a photographer for the magazine. His shots of Bull fighting and killing a big dog baboon were sensational.

Looking back on the whole experience, the maxim 'never trust a cat' was a truism. If the two people had opened the door of the box without taking refuge in the cab thinking the leopard would run away, they may not have lived to tell the tale. Discretion was certainly the better part of valour that day.

Edward G. Robinson was a prince of a man. Kind, thoughtful, and approachable, he had at that time one of the finest collections of French impressionist paintings in the world. They were his special pride and joy. I had the privilege of talking to him on many occasions and enjoyed hearing his observations on the making of the *Mr. Moto* series of films that I enjoyed in my boyhood. You would never, ever associate him with being the film industry's tough guy.

Top: The kuki cordon, Bechuanaland, running westwards to the South-West Africa border for some 120 miles.

Top left: Death on the kuki cordon (fence). An identical picture was taken 20 years earlier near this very spot. Hugh Kingsley-Heath is not happy (1990).

Bottom: The kuki cordon; no passage for wildlife (1964).

BECHUANALAND (BOTSWANA)

Leopard hunting in Botswana was divided mostly in half. There were the leopards of the Kalahari Desert and the leopards of the Okavango and northern river systems. Generally speaking, none came to baits in the manner described in East Africa. In the years that I spent

Me and Simon Paul planning new camps and roads (1970).

in Bechuanaland, few leopards were ever shot and virtually none on a bait. Leopards were where you saw them at the time—if you got a shot you were very lucky.

In the desert it was a different matter. I well remember sitting in a tree on the *kuki cordon* (fence) that prevented all animals traveling northwards from moving through the Kalahari and watching three leopards kill a red hartebeest calf using the fence to bring it down. Hartebeest were easy prey to leopards, and in the course of time a considerable number of leopards were concentrated in the area. If a bait was hung in a tree it was ignored, but we discovered that if a dead animal was hidden in a bush and covered with foliage, then there was a chance. Most safaris in Botswana had no time for leopards, as they could be obtained as part of a safari hunt elsewhere in Africa as described. Some clients had time; if the hunt had gone well in the Okavango Swamps, then a leopard became a possibility.

Hunting leopards always takes time. Many a leopard licence has never been filled because of a lack of time, and time on safari is always of the essence. A blind in most cases was made, but a longer shot than usual was planned—90 yards was about the limit. Leopards of the Kalahari were very cautious—they were meat for lions, who never hesitated to go for them if they had half a chance. On two occasions, when watching vultures dropping out of the sky onto a kill, I found the remains of a leopard surrounded by lion tracks.

The lions of the Kalahari, even more so than those in the swamps, covered their kills with sand and ground foliage. Most particularly they did this when the stomach and entrails were sucked dry of moisture. The leopards did the same. We attempted, therefore, to simulate a bona fide kill. About 40 percent of the time it worked.

Once, when we had little to do, we decided to hide the car in some trees and have lunch while we watched the bait that was 200 yards in front of us on the edge of a small open pan. Imagine our surprise when we saw no fewer than three leopards walk calmly across the pan. Halfway across the pan they got a whiff of the bait. It was obvious that the first thing they thought about was lions. It was the only time I ever saw a leopard stand on its hind legs in the open to get a better view of the surrounding country, looking as it did so like a baboon ascertaining if it was being followed. All three leopards turned and made off.

We decided to fly camp a mile or two down the fence and sit for a leopard that evening. We did so without seeing a sign of one. Next morning, leaving for town and at the safari's end, we packed up camp before it was light and set off. I suggested that we stalk the bait to the blind and give it 30 minutes.

We had just got into the blind when a nice male leopard emerged from the bush dragging a leg of a red hartebeest. He did not go much farther. One shot from a .270 Winchester made sure that he accompanied us to Maun. Seldom did this happen. Later, when access to the Kalahari from the south was permitted, the Bushman trackers that were employed tracked the leopards, and it was by this method that most of the safari clients shot them.

Many, many animals over the years were sacrificed as leopard baits, much to the chagrin of the camp staff, whose perk it was to take home all the dried meat from the safaris. Insofar as our organisation was concerned, I can only say we seemed to be as unsuccessful hunting leopard as we were successful hunting lion.

Today the situation has changed radically, and it seems a safari client has a good chance to successfully hunt a leopard in the Okavango Swamps of Botswana. One can only surmise that the contraction of the swamps, with its population of baboons, bushbuck, and many other small animals and birds, has concentrated the leopard population to such a degree that it is much easier to gain contact with them. In the old days, sitting in a leopard blind and being persecuted by tsetse flies every second of the time was not an experience to which a client wished to subject himself twice. Now the tsetse fly has gone,

Me numbering and recording trophies. Note the ink bottle.

Poached leopard? 'Where did this skin come from?' Policing concession areas, Botswana (1968).

and for both the hunting party and the leopard the irritation of the tsetse fly no longer has to be endured.

In the desert there is no change in the hunting of leopard, except that all hunting in the Kalahari is now closed but for on private land, and the populations of game animals are much reduced, as migrational routes have ceased due to the extended fencing system and the extreme drought.

Surprisingly, in view of this discourse, the biggest leopard, a record, came from the northern Okavango Swamps, shot by Jim Brophy in 1984. It was nine feet four and a half inches in length. Sadly, no skull measurement appears in the list of skull measurements in Ward's *Records of Big Game*.

ETHIOPIA AND SOMALILAND

The leopard population in Ethiopia between 1949 and 1960 may well have been one of the highest per square mile in Africa. In the south-western forests near Jimma and in the south on both sides of the Rift Valley they were most prolific, the melanistic form occurring in one out of every three leopards. All the major river systems draining these high mountains and forested areas had considerable populations that were able to prey upon not only the small antelopes, but many varieties of monkeys and birds also. In the north in the Tigre Province and in the Tacasse Valley they were numerous, but with the rapidly expanding pop-

292

ulations and the commercial interest in leopard skins, they suffered severely from poaching. Today, perhaps one of the best places to hunt them remains in the rain forests of the south west.

In the Somalilands administered by France, Britain, and Italy, leopard occurred in patches. It would be safe to say that there were none in French Somaliland in 1955. In Italian Somaliland they were mostly concentrated on the Juba and Webi Schebelli River systems, where for a time there were cover and food. However, they were poached almost to extinction by the ever-avaricious Somalis when their skins were of value in the 1960s and 1970s.

Historically British Somaliland was double the size as we knew it in the 1950s. By treaty on the 14 of May in 1897 between Britain and Ethiopia, the whole of the extreme south-east of Ethiopia, comprising the Ogaden (the clan of Somalis and their area) and part of the Haud or desert area to the south of Somaliland, was ceded to Ethiopia. Apparently Britain received nothing in return. This treaty has caused endless strife and is typical of many treaties made at the time that carved up Africa for the benefit of the European powers, without any realistic consideration of ethnic boundaries. The Ogaden has never been happily attached to Ethiopia. It is a dry and waterless area used by seminomadic people. If the U.K. was to administer British Somaliland it might just as well have administered the whole area.

Leopards occurred sporadically wherever there was water seepage and in the proximity of hills and semipermanent water. There were plenty of antelopes and gazelles, and the bird population of guinea fowl and other game birds was prolific. The leopards of this area were never large, being rangy-looking cats seldom weighing more than 135 pounds and reaching seven feet in length only occasionally. The colour of their skin was much lighter than that of the leopard of the higher elevations. I hunted a considerable number of leopards in Somaliland, particularly in the Ogaden area of southern Ethiopia and the Erigavo and Las Anod areas of British Somaliland, almost always at the behest of the local people whose stock had been ravaged. In Somalia my contemporary, Belli del'Isca, was very successful in obtaining leopards for his clients in the areas I have described. The leopards from the Juba and Webi Schebelli were darker and larger than those in the desert areas to the north and east.

Hunting the Black Leopard

I must give my reader here a little historical background. British involvement in Ethiopia dates back to 1887–88, when General Napier

*H.I.M. the Emperor of Ethiopia with
the Empress arriving at the railway
station in Jerusalem, Palestine, in
1936. He was in exile until 1941.*

was sent out from England with a military column and successfully rescued a number of hostages taken by Emperor Theodore. The hostages
were incarcerated at Magdala, and when they were liberated after a battle, Emperor Theodore committed suicide. Meantime, the Italians, desir-
ing a foothold in Africa, had taken over the port of Assab on the Red Sea.
In 1872, Ras Kassa of Tigre, Ethiopia's northern and western area, the
grandfather of my acquaintance, Ras Aserate Kassa, was crowned
Emperor Yohannes IV. He successfully defeated the Italians and
Egyptians—the former intent on subjugating the whole of Ethiopia—at
the battles of Gundet and Gura, respectively. The Italians had now seized
the port of Massawa. Emperor Yohannes IV was succeeded by Emperor

294

My uncle and General and Mrs. Makonnen at the general's house in Addis Ababa (1952).

Menelik, King of Shoa, a distant relation from the south of Ethiopia.

Menelik's prowess as an organiser and warrior was legend. In 1895 he defeated the imperial designs of Italy at Amba Alagi, the scene of the 1941 surrender of the Italian forces by the Duke of Aosta to the British General Sir William Platt, and finally and completely at the battle of Adowa in 1896. It was a phyrric victory, leaving Italy recognising Ethiopia's independence but receiving Eritrea from the Ethiopians. Eritrea, however, had always been a vassal state of Ethiopia and a problem for successive emperors to keep it so. Ethiopia was a feudal country, and when Menelik died several powerful men advanced their candidature, as his 13-year-old son was too young to rule. One of them was

Operating the ex-Army '22' radio set in southern Ethiopia.

Negus Mikael, who hailed from Harrar, one of the south-eastern provinces of Ethiopia. He was defeated by Haile Selassie at the battle of Sagale. Haile Selassie, who was known as Ras Tafari, became Regent in 1916 and was crowned emperor in 1930. In 1934 the Italians, now led by the dictator Benito Mussolini, used the Walwal border incident as an excuse and attempted to seize Ethiopia. Emperor Haile Selassie put up a stiff resistance. There was a long-standing score to settle as far as the Italians were concerned.

Ethiopia was seized by Italy and the emperor went into exile in 1936, to return with the British in 1941. His Imperial Majesty was ousted by the Marxist regime of Mengistu in 1974 and murdered in 1975. During the 1960s and 1970s, advisors on wildlife to Selassie's government were present in the form of Major John Blower, M.C., formerly chief game warden of Uganda, provided by the U.N.D.P. (United Nations Development Program), and Fred Duckworth, who had two periods in Ethiopia—two years in the 1960s and from 1970–74, leaving after surviving Mengistu's regime for a year. Thereafter the AK-47 ruled supreme, as it largely does today.

When the Emperor fled to Jerusalem in 1936, his security was placed under the control of my father, Colonel A.J. Kingsley-Heath. The Emperor came to Jerusalem with very little money but a substantial collection of jewels and precious stones. My uncle, who was the local managing director of a well-known English bank, was then called upon to handle the Emperor's finances. I well remember these events, for being a young lad at the time, my prized possessions were taken away from me to provide amusement for the Emperor's children. My feelings can well be imagined.

Time passed, and the Emperor moved to Bath in south-west England. There he lived until the beginning of the 1939–45 War. (My playthings were returned, one of which was a Diana air gun.) His finances continued to be supervised by my uncle's bank. His nephew, Ras Aserate Kassa—the *ras* being roughly equivalent in European aristocratic hierarchy to a duke—was sent to school at Monkton Combe, whence I shortly followed. Ras Aserate Kassa was a tough, adventurous boy who welcomed a challenge. He was a leader in the best Ethiopian tradition. The marks of his knife-throwing exploits were on the reverse side of the fifth form door for all to see! At the end of the war in Ethiopia against the Italians in 1941, my uncle was invited to open a bank in Addis Ababa and to advise generally on various fiscal problems that the country faced. He and my aunt visited Ethiopia from the Middle East frequently.

With this background in mind, I wrote to my uncle asking him if he might ask if I might be considered when applying for licences and permits to travel about Ethiopia. It was shortly after he wrote to the Emperor that I was called to the palace in Addis Ababa for an interview. Here I met once again Ras Aserate Kassa and the officer commanding the Ethiopian Army, General Makonnen. The Emperor and his empress were kindness itself, and I was made to feel that I asked for very little. Thus encouraged, I gave his secretary a full list of every animal I wished to hunt in Ethiopia and included several lions and leopards. In fact, I never took advantage of this, since by no stretch of the imagination could I afford to undertake a safari

My rather naive aunt at the entrance to H.I.M. the Emperor Haile Sellaise's palace with one of the guard lions (1952).

297

of such magnitude. Even so, I thought to myself if two black leopards came onto a bait, I might just need that extra licence. As far as elephants were concerned, I knew I could only afford to hunt beyond Jimma in the south-west and down to the Omo. Gambella was too inaccessible. In hindsight, I should have forgotten Jimma and the Omo and gone to Gambella. I have consoled myself with the thought ever afterwards that if I had shot a huge elephant at Gambella I would have had to sell the tusks to pay for the trip in any case.

My hunting permits secured, I then had to convince the provincial governor, known as a *djezmatch* ('lord'), that I was a bona fide person with the Emperor's permission to hunt the animals on my licence. I therefore met the secretary of the provincial or area governor, often known as a *fitaurari*. A little *hongo* was necessary: this took the form of two cases of Gilbeys gin procured from the duty-free facility at one of the embassies in Addis Ababa. The hongo paid, we were all set to travel, furnished with yet another document in Amharic, which to me was reminiscent of Sanskrit. (Amharic was the language of Ethiopia. The Amharas were an aristocratic, Christian, and intelligent people. Had they not been divided by feudal ties and consequent strife and division amongst themselves, I feel certain that Ethiopia today would have been a powerful nation. It is scenically the most fabulous country on the African continent.)

I was now eager to explore the highlands of Ethiopia, but first I needed the necessary permits for special animals. A black leopard was amongst the requirements.

I was greatly assisted in the furtherance of my plan by Ato. Adefferis Bellew (Ato. is the Amharic equivalent of Mr.), an Amhara, a senior secretary at the Ministry of Agriculture. I was also lucky to be given temporary employment whilst on leave by A. Besse & Co., which was a large and prestigious trading and shipping firm based in Aden with large offices and industrial premises in Addis Ababa. This had one important aspect that bore on my intention to hunt black leopard—the company dealt very extensively in hides and skins. In their warehouses were huge piles of leopard skins of which several hundred were black. By creating a little assistance to the registry clerk's memory of who had brought in these skins and therefore from what part of the country the skins had been obtained, I was able to piece together sufficient information as to where the greatest possibility of collecting a black leopard might occur. The south-western forests of Ethiopia on both sides of the string of lakes was undoubtedly the best spot.

As luck would have it, I was given the job of taking a convoy of trucks through the gold-mining area of Adola. This took me down the road out of Addis Ababa to Shashamane. (I also wanted to hunt mountain nyala, but that is part of another story.) At Shashamane I met up with the Italian owner of a hot-spring spa and hotel. He was a mine of information and a hunter of no mean accomplishment. It never ceased to amaze me how Italians, in spite of their turbulent history of oppression of the Ethiopian people, nevertheless aspired to survive in harmony with those who only recently had been conquered by them. This, too, in a country that had never in its entire history been subjugated by another.

There are six major lakes running north to south from Addis Ababa— Lakes Zuai, Hora Abgiata, Langanno, Scialla, Auasa, and Margherita.

The main road down which I travelled in my long-wheelbase Land Rover and seven 10-ton vehicles ran either between or nearby these lakes. Beyond them, on either side, the mountains rose to more than 12 000 feet. As I headed south, Mount Cilalo at 12 743 feet was on my left, and to the right in the distance the mountains rose to between 8000 and 9000 feet.

Shashamane was a major road junction. It seemed like a good place to start, particularly as the road was quite appalling and two of my drivers, full of the effects of khat, had turned over their trucks right in the middle of the road. Parts were needed, and whilst my Italian friend at the hot springs kept an eye on the ignition keys of the remaining vehicles, I decided to set off southwards combining hunting with a look at the difficulties of the road to come.

At Wando I took the left fork to Adola. Between Adola and Negelli there was about as impressive leopard country as could possibly be imagined. Huge forests and precipitous ravines reminded one of the slopes of Mount Kenya and the Aberdares. Local information was unmitigated in its declaration of the fact that black leopards were present.

To obtain quick results I was forced to purchase several goats. These I was assured would be taken by leopard, though I feared they might be two-legged ones. The rains broke and it was a desperately miserable experience struggling to visit four far-flung baits in the apex of the ravines I had chosen. The road was diabolical—every 100 yards had a hairpin bend overlooking an abyss.

After four days we had a strike. It was cold and the two baits I had shot way back near Dalle had not rotted. On one bait I had three large monkeys tied together like a bunch of grapes, and on another I had a live goat—it was still alive. Good blinds that had been made had fallen

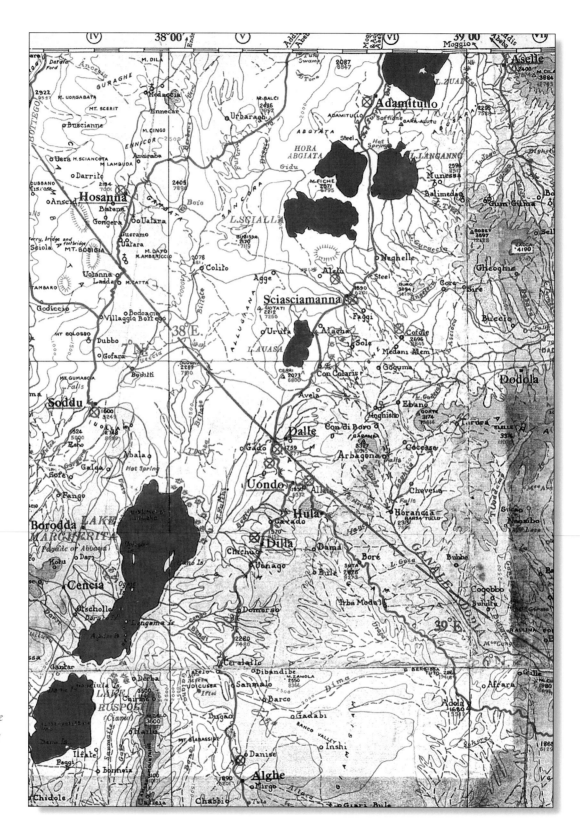

Map of the Rift Valley lakes of Ethiopia (1950).

apart, and with the heavy rain, everywhere was misty and damp. I sat at 4.00 P.M. on the one bait that had been eaten. To my great disappointment all that came was a genet cat. Day five passed and I was now concerned that I should have to return, though I hoped my new-found friend at Shashamane would commence repairs to the damaged trucks.

On day six three baits were eaten that included the monkeys, which had taken a substantial battering. For the hell of it and for no really good reason, I decided to sit on the monkeys—once more into the blind at 4.00 P.M. in the pouring rain. At 5.30 one of the monkeys started moving in the tree. Convinced that I was seeing things, I looked long and hard with my binoculars. Suddenly I became aware that I was looking at two large yellow eyes in a black face—a jet black leopard had climbed the reverse side of the tree without my seeing it move, an experience that both I and several clients have had many times since.

The leopard was cautious, lying behind the monkeys that were also black, which made it difficult to differentiate between the leopard and the monkeys' bodies.

Patience is a virtue, I said to myself. *My goodness, I have seen one*, I thought. That in itself was the sight of a lifetime. I froze and waited without the flicker of an eyelid for 10 long minutes. Then, as if satisfied, the leopard stood up on a branch and stretched itself. I was alone in the blind and the light was fading fast. Infinitely slowly, I settled the sight of the .318 on the leopard. It was big enough but not enormous, and it was very black.

The leopard turned round, and as he did so, I felt certain that he was a young male, for now he looked bigger. Another slight movement and he gave me the opportunity of a shot behind the shoulders as he looked away to his left. I must have come within an ace of pulling the trigger when he suddenly turned right round in the opposite direction. Now I was presented with the opposite angle, but the bullet would be travelling toward his rear end from his chest. He started to eat, tearing at the monkeys' flesh and spitting out the hair. As he balanced with all four feet bunched together and leaning over the meat, he gave me another chance. I took it and squeezed off nicely, feeling sure that, unless I'd been touching wood with the gun, the shot was good.

It was—he dropped like a stone. Reloading and putting on my heavy coat and gloves, I moved slowly to the spot where I had seen him fall. He was not there, and I had never heard him move. I was about to learn what a heart-shot leopard can do.

A few minutes later the local folk arrived, of which there were three.

One spoke Italian—a language in which I could make myself well under-stood—and he translated to the others. Slowly we set out on the tracks, which we soon lost as the power of the initial impetus of the leopard's flight left him. One-hundred and fifty yards later we came upon him as dead as a doornail, the shot perfectly placed. We cut a sapling and, using string, tied his paws together and slung him on the poles. It took us an hour and a half to get back to the car, for by now it was dark.

Hurriedly we gutted the leopard and set off for the long, rough ride back to Shashamane, picking up my fly camp on the way. We had not, however, reckoned with Ethiopian bureaucracy, for when we came to Adola the police would not allow us to pass the barrier—after dark no one could pass. No amount of cajoling or production of imperial passes would change their ideas. The only thing that was on my side was the cold—the leopard might keep overnight. I slept at the gate in the cab of the car.

At 7.00 in the morning the gate had still not been opened, and it was a light and sunny day for a change. At 9.00 I was sent for by the officer commanding the police, who believed that I was smuggling gold. After two hours of wasted time in which I had the greatest diffi-culty in keeping my temper, we settled for 40 rounds of ammuni-tion and I was on my way, but I still had to pass through the same barrier with the big trucks.

I got back to Shashamane just in time, not only to skin the leopard, which was a seven-foot four-inch male in rigour mortis, but also as the spares for the trucks had arrived. Our next disaster was that no salt could be found. Whilst we worked on the trucks, I had dug a shallow space beneath the stretched leopard skin that we dressed with wood ash and beneath which we placed four Tilley or petrol pressure lamps so that the hot air dried the skin, which took on the ash. It certainly worked, for when I had the skin tanned none of it slipped except a small spot about the size of a $1 bill under the back leg.

There was one disappointment, however, that I should convey to all would-be black-leopard shooters: exposed to light, the skin fades to a dirty brown colour. Never display it in direct sunlight. Fortunately I never did so, but if you look at the skin carefully you can just make out the rosettes of the pattern behind the outwardly black colour.

I was incredibly lucky to have had a black leopard strike the bait first. My journey of nightmarish proportions continued. A month later the

Mountain Nyala

302

convoy was safely delivered to Moyale on the Kenya border, and I
repaired to Mega to the welcome hospitality of John Bromley, the British
consul at Mega in the extreme south west of Ethiopia.

In my travels in Ethiopia, there was one interesting animal industry
involving cats that is worthy of record. When walking from village to village, I noticed at the back of the *tucls*, or native huts in which the
Ethiopians lived, there was a row of what appeared to be rabbit hutches
on three-foot legs. On enquiry I found that they contained civet cats.

Civet cats come in several sizes—some species can be large and
weigh as much as 20 pounds. These were of the kind about double the
size of a house cat and tabby in colour. The civet cat has one similarity to
the American skunk—it stinks when alarmed by excreting a juice from
its rear end. In the case of the civet cat, being several times the size of a
skunk, there is substantial excrement. They were trapped and incarcerated in cages. At the back of the cage was a board that hung down below
the wire floor of the cage, where there was a gourd. The excreta of the
cat was obtained by a simple method: twice a night a person with a
flashlight would approach the cage, the wire front of which was covered
with a piece of cloth. Suddenly whipping back the cloth and shining the
light in the cat's face produced the desired result—the cat performed,
and the excreta rolled down the board and into the gourd. I was shown
these cages on a number of occasions. Fortunately, though, I had lost
most of my sense of smell when I had been blown up by a land mine
during my military days. I was glad not to be able to smell very well
when I visited the cages of the incarcerated civet cats.

The next stage of the proceedings involved the use of cow horns.
These, taken from dead cows, had a convenient hollow where formerly
the bone of the skull had formed. The excreta was placed in this hollow
and the open end of the horn sealed with beeswax. The horns were then
sold in the local market and eventually made their way to the
warehouses of French merchants in Addis Ababa.

In those days there was no scientific way of creating the strength of
the *pong* of the cat's excreta. This remarkable strength of smell was taken
as the base for the production of perfume, its foul smell being successfully masked by all manner of attractive smells, but at the same time, its
property of pervading the air instantly being fully utilised. I have often

With the skin and skull of my black leopard. Unfortunately, the skin has faded to dark brown.

wondered if those beautiful and sophisticated ladies at the safari conventions have any idea, as *les dames fatales*, how much they owe to the humble civet cat. I have rarely bought my wife perfume!

UGANDA AND OTHER COUNTRIES

In the years covered by this book there was a healthy and prolific leopard population in Uganda. They were hunted on precisely the same basis as those in Tanganyika and Kenya, and they occurred less in the very tropical, hot, and humid country of long, tall grass than elsewhere. Every riverine growth, however, had a population of leopards, and it was commonplace—and still is—to see leopards in Queen Elizabeth, Murchison Falls,

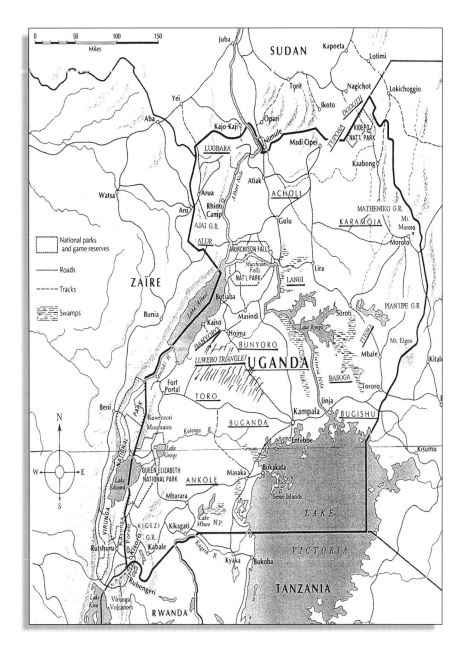

Uganda.

and Kidepo National Parks. But their numbers are dwindling—they are poached for their skins, often by the park scouts and marauding army personnel. In the heyday of the Uganda Wildlife Development Company, clients regularly and successfully shot leopards, mostly in the Pian Upe, Mathienko, and Moroto areas. Here there were sand rivers, huge rock formations, and small riverine forests which made a prime habitat for them. Moreover, these areas were well populated with game such as dik-dik,

Olive Baboon

klipspringer, and all manner of game birds and small animals, which ensured that young leopards were never short of food.

My contemporaries—Brian Herne, David Williams, Nicky Blunt, and John Northcote—were among those who were the backbone of successful hunting safaris in Uganda. In those years much of the Lake Mburo area was unsettled and here, too, great opportunities existed for successful hunting. As my reader will have noted, leopards survive longer than most animals in an African state torn by war and tribal strife. After spending two years in Uganda in recent years, I have no doubt that this species above all others could be brought back to a substantial and well-distributed population, if only a stable and honest wildlife department could be created.

In Eritrea I have no doubt that a few leopards exist, if for no other reason than that substantial game bird populations continue to manifest themselves in many areas which would normally be the habitat of the leopard. Here, too, large flocks of domestic goat and sheep are kept. Whilst it is acknowledged that the AK-47 is a deterrent often used in retaliation against the depredations made by leopards on domestic stock, darkness is on their side and their intuitive guile ensures that some, if not all, survive. The Keren Hills and the watercourses of the tributaries of the upper Setit River, many of which rise in Eritrea, most likely still harbour the occasional leopard. Farther north in the hills bordering the Red Sea near Karora, leopard, like their cousin the snow leopard, had ibex on which to prey. Alas, these are now few and far between, and I doubt that any leopard population is left here. Their skins are still of value and whilst such value lasts, they will eventually be the subject of the AK-47's attention, the infernal tool that has led to the death of so many of the world's wild animals.

CHAPTER SEVEN

HIPPOPOTAMUS HUNTING

The Canoe Crusher

GENERAL OBSERVATIONS

Whilst hippo would not be classed as a trophy hunting animal by many during the era that this book covers, nevertheless they are indeed a dangerous animal. Hippo are undoubtedly responsible for more deaths—even today—of human beings than any other wild animal in Africa. Hippos can become rogues and continually persecute human populations near their habitat. Due to the circumstances in which they live, it is difficult to dispose of a rogue hippo, because so much time has to be taken in watching for him, whereas in the case of a lion or leopard, baiting can quickly bring them to book. On Africa's waterways, where many fishermen earn a meagre living, people suffer greatly from the destructive ways of hippo—their nets are torn and their canoes savaged and upset, leaving the occupants often maimed or dead.

Hippo have survived in most parts of Africa better than any other large animal. The means to pursue them are normally lacking, boats and engines being difficult to obtain in times of war and unrest. As this means is the only hope of following and killing them, they have inevitably survived.

In this discourse it would be wrong to deal with hippos country by country, excepting to state the obvious: the greater the expanses of fresh water that occur in each country, the healthier their hippo popu-

I shot the Hippopotamus with bullets made of platinum Because if I use leaden ones his hide is sure to flatten 'em.

—Hillare Belloc
The Bad Child's Book of Beasts

The mother hippo . . . seeing the unfortunate Mervyn nearby, vented her spleen upon him by clamping her huge teeth into his backside.

—J.K.-H.

lations are likely to be. Naturally, both Botswana with the Okavango Swamps and Uganda with its numerous lakes are the major countries with large hippo populations, but Tanzania may well have the greatest hippo population of all. The Selous Game Reserve alone must account for many thousands of them.

Hippo hunting and shooting is divided into two distinct methods—the hippo in the water and the hippo on land. The type of rifle required for a water-residing hippo differs entirely from the type required for hippo on land.

A hippo met and hunted on dry land is usually one of two types of animal: a cow giving birth, wounded, or resting, or a bull sick, wounded, or resting. Either, if disturbed or given human scent, will in all probability charge.

If one is prowling along the banks of a river looking for meat for the pot or elephant tracks, then a sleeping hippo might well be mistaken for an anthill. Furthermore, they lie up in the thickest of bush. When passing such a thicket it is as well to make sure no fresh tracks of hippo have entered it. Hippo defecate in regular spots, as do rhino, so some indication of their presence is often available.

When disturbed, two tons of solid biomass will not be stopped by a .300 calibre rifle, making a heavy rifle most definitely required for hippo on land. The size and weight of a full-grown hippo bull is somewhere between that of a rhino and an elephant. Being built like a tank, with its front end covered by a huge, long, wide, and massive boned head, makes it difficult to shoot and kill efficiently. A solid heavy-calibre bullet is therefore a must for a side shot into the heart and lungs. In some cases the body of a big bull hippo is four feet thick. Penetration is therefore required, and although a soft-pointed bullet may suffice, on occasions that is not a good enough performance to ensure the optimum penetration and desired result. In short, be prepared to shoot hippo as if you were hunting elephants or rhino and use the same guns with solids.

When I first arrived in Kigoma on Lake Tanganyika in 1950 as a district officer, Mervyn Willers, who was in charge of the public works department in that district, had just suffered the misfortune of being bitten through the buttocks by a hippo. The small Kigoma Club that boasted about 30 members had enclosed a small area of sandy beach on the shore of the lake as a bathing area for members. Unbeknownst to Mervyn, a small hippo had drifted under the wire and become separated from its mother. The mother hippo made short work of the wire and,

Hippo in the fast disappearing water in pools on the Rungwa River (1951).

seeing the unfortunate Mervyn nearby, vented her spleen upon him by clamping her huge teeth into his backside. He was taken to hospital in Tabora, the principal hospital of Western Province, and made a good recovery, but I am told he walked like a sailor thereafter.

In later years, it was suggested by one of my friends in the game department (a government department always short of funds) that I could assist them and gain experience for myself if I walked the whole length of the Rungwa River and make an enumeration survey of the hippo population, from the river's source in the Rungwa Game Reserve to the point at which it entered Lake Rukwa, a distance, as the river ran, of some 250 miles. This turned out to be an interesting trip and gave me an intimate knowledge of the area, which I put to good use on later safaris. We counted some 3000 hippos in pools of varying sizes. Every day we broke camp, sending the car by road to make the next camp some 20 miles downstream, having started at roughly the source of the river where the first sizeable pool occurred.

We undertook the walk in the dry season. Each morning with a thermos of tea, some water, a packet of sandwiches, and three guns—a .404, a .318, and a 12-bore shotgun—I set out with two native fishermen plus my two gunbearers/trackers, Asumani and Juma. Each day, we hired two new fishermen who knew the area and so progressed until we eventually came to the mouth of the river where it enters Lake Rukwa. We saw a vast amount of game and huge numbers of crocodiles.

As we approached Lake Rukwa, so the concentration of both hippos and crocodiles grew more numerous. On one occasion we studied one

Top: The seventh dangerous animal—the crocodile.

Right: The Rungwa River revisited 40 years later at the spot where the river joins Lake Rukwa. My son Nigel is on the right.

crocodile that I estimated to be 20 feet long. We deliberately disturbed him and then measured the outline of his body and tail in the sand where he had been lying. He was 21 feet 9 inches long! A crocodile of this size would have weighed possibly one and a half tons and probably been capable of swallowing a live child whole. However, the river was full of barbel fish, and the crocodiles consequently fat, although I am sure they took their share of game coming to drink.

The hippo at night travelled anywhere up to five miles from the river, and their paths to and from their grazing grounds made highways upon which we could walk with comfort.

Hippo courtship is a long, drawn-out affair and invariably takes place in shallow water amidst deafening cries and snorts that are almost loud enough to wake the dead. I well remember getting little sleep on a number of occasions when camped by a pool on the river with a large number of hippo in residence.

The second method of shooting hippo necessitated their being in the water. Shooting hippo on control and for meat required a quiet approach and a high-powered small-calibre rifle of not less than 7x57 or .300. This was made much easier in later years when fitted with a 4- or 6-power scope. Almost without exception, any client I took on safari adopted the 'wait and see method' to obtain this trophy. The point being, of course, that a bull hippo had to be selected from all the hippo rising to take in air.

First a survey had to be made of the spot where the hippo was seen regularly coming up for air. A hippo has to surface at least every five minutes to replenish its oxygen supply. If we knew the rough spot that he used, the plan would be to make a hide from which we could get a rested and accurate shot at the root of his ear sideways on as he surfaced or turned his head. Hippos have good eyesight and acute hearing and can recognise in an instant if anything is abnormal in the environment surrounding them.

Prior to shooting a hippo, both my client and I would practice some dry snaps at a target about four inches square, counting to four and then letting off a shot. This represented the time that one could reasonably expect the hippo's head to be exposed. Naturally, the hippo did not always come up in exactly the same spot, so that the hide chosen needed to have a good arc of view so the firer could swing to the target either left or right. The aiming point in the base of the ear was some two inches above the water line on the hippo's head and normally killed it instantly. Usually the body sank but reappeared an hour or so later as the gasses in

the stomach floated it to the surface. Thereafter, the rather risky job of going out in a canoe and attaching a rope to a leg took place. Usually by this time a large crowd of local people had gathered offering all kinds of advice to the volunteers charged with the task of bringing the dead hippo to the shore. I well remember on two occasions a dead hippo being taken by huge crocodiles before we could get a rope on it. However, on each occasion the crocodile could not puncture its stomach fast enough, which would have made it sink again. A shot at the crocodile sent it elsewhere, and we recovered our meat supply. Hippo meat is like pork—it does not last long and rots easily. It is essential to recover the meat as soon as possible if it is to be eaten safely.

On several occasions I have made the mistake when hunting near a river (most particularly the Rungwa River) of hanging a leopard or lion bait not far from water. One morning when I came to check a leopard bait, I found the rear quarters of a hippo that I had hung in a tree besieged by five crocodiles and the leopard marooned in the tree with nowhere to go. It might well have been a variation of the *Just So Stories* by Rudyard Kipling, for the leopard knew that the crocodiles would have to return to the water. The crocodiles were not so dumb. They took turns in going to the water, keeping the meat under observation and the leopard in the tree. Whilst we watched, the leopard decided to eat. The crocodiles went mad, leaping off the ground, snapping their jaws, trying to prevent the leopard from consuming this rich prize. Insofar as we were concerned, we wished to shoot the leopard, but if we did so we were afraid that a crocodile would grab the leopard carcase and disappear into the water. We easily overcame the problem by shooting a crocodile and the leopard at the same time, as there were two clients with me. The other crocodiles scattered.

In Botswana and other countries, hippos were protected for the interesting reason that by their constant passage they kept the channels open in the swamps, so allowing the water to drain into the main rivers. During my 16 years in Bechuanaland, I noticed, however, no increase or decrease in the hippo population. As these great animals could very easily exchange their habitat to the north and east into the Chobe, Savuti, and eventually the Zambezi Rivers and swamps, it would be difficult to enumerate a resident population within the Okavango Swamps. Their presence always added a dimension to lion and buffalo hunting when one stumbled across a hippo asleep on a palm island.

There were and still are huge populations of hippo running into many thousands in Tanzania (in the Selous Game Reserve) and Uganda. More recently, when flying over Lakes George and Edward in Uganda, there still remained some 10 000 hippos. I never ceased to be surprised how, with the passage of years, the hippos and the fishermen of the enclaves within the Queen Elizabeth National Park have learned to live side by side, literally within a few yards of each other.

It was in the Queen Elizabeth National Park in Uganda many years ago that my old friend Terry Mathews had the misfortune to have his car savaged by an irate hippo. Terry was busy filming and was just about to decide to move on when a seriously disturbed hippo managed to reach the back of his Land Rover station wagon. On seeing his car when he returned to Nairobi, I asked him how the rear of his car had been crushed, as it looked to me as though a tree had fallen on it. He told me that a hippo had opened its mouth wide and bitten the back end of the car, collapsing the roof and back door.

The Canoe Crusher

A district officer's job in Tanganyika between 1949-61 consisted of a great deal of mundane and uninteresting paperwork. There was also a seemingly unending number of petty civil and criminal cases that a third class magistrate (district officer) had to adjudicate upon after having first written out in longhand every spoken word in each case.

If you were second in command to a decent district commissioner you shared the safari work. If not, he hogged the lot and left you running the office and commiserating with the local policeman, the public works foreman, and the Indian subassistant surgeon over several beers in the evening at the club. Coming as I did from a war/active army background, I found this work intensely boring. My only consoling thought was that I had to start somewhere. One of my duties was superintending the local prison.

Having served in a regiment of the Brigade of Guards of the British Household Division of the British Army, I determined to smarten up the wardens, that is, drill them and turn them into the smartest prison staff in the province. In putting this into practice I found one .303 Lee Enfield ex-1914–18 War service rifle of remarkable accuracy. I had the good fortune to kill a steinbok at 200 yards with it. I had it put carefully aside for my future use and also made sure that in my report to the provincial prison officer that I requested a further supply of ammunition with which the wardens could be put through their annual field firing exercise, which had not taken place for many years. Motivation for this course of action also came from the reports trickling into the district office of problems with rogue buffalo, elephant, hippo, and lion.

I was now armed with an accurate rifle and plenty of ammunition. The field firing exercise was a great success—all the dummy escaping prisoners concealed in the bush were shot through and through by the wardens, who thoroughly enjoyed the experience. Sergeant Musa, a great big strapping man of the Mnyamwesi tribe, had served in the King's African Rifles in the 6th Tanganyika Battalion, and his field training readily returned to him. However, there was one slight hitch: at the end of the exercise (the D.C. was on safari, naturally), a perspiring office messenger arrived on foot with a message from the Belgian trading base asking if he should evacuate the Belgian families on the next train. He thought they were under attack! That evening it cost me several bottles of good wine to return the situation to normal and ensure that the matter was forgotten before the D.C.'s return.

Gerry Swynerton, the game ranger on the station, was on long leave (six months), so game problems were on my schedule. The district commissioner had been in Tanganyika for many years and was at the end of his service. He was a striking-looking man and had a distinct resemblance to Clark Gable. He had unfortunately lost his wife some years earlier and had only recently married a woman half his age. He had one unforgettable idiosyncrasy: he chewed his handkerchief into shreds, particularly when he was reading the mail first thing in the morning. We did one safari together, on which a glance into his tent showed evidence that he had not forgotten his first wife.

I resolved to put my case for a safari of my own—to cope with the mounting wildlife problems—on Gerry's return. In this I was successful and set out with 40 porters from Ujiji. It was here, on the shores of Lake Tanganyika at the huge native village of Ujiji, where Henry M. Stanley met Dr. David Livingstone with the famous words, 'Dr. Livingstone I presume'.

Our route lay inland for some three miles from the lake shore on native paths of hard, red laterite soil. The porters were new and untried, and I wished I had Sergeant Musa to keep them going. The first day we made 10 miles. We were heading south for the spot where the Malagarasi River flowed into Lake Tanganyika. Our first task was to collect tax, the cash being stored in a large, wooden, iron-banded and encased box slung on a pole between two of the strongest porters. The second task was to kill a hippo that had apparently crushed several canoes and killed a number of people when they were ferrying themselves across the river.

The accurate .303 rifle was with me. We camped the first night near the Luiche River, crossed it in canoes the next day, and headed for Kasaba. Reedbuck and bushbuck fell into our pot, and the porters began to perform their tasks a great deal better. Our next stop was the village of Ulombolo, where we collected tax and held a *baraza* (discussion in public) with the local chief. We had some 25 miles to make next day, cutting back eastward to avoid the several mouths and small swamps of the Malagarasi River delta where it entered the lake.

By 4.00 P.M. we arrived at the river crossing. Next day was spent collecting tax and attending to the chief's problems. In 1950 it was mandatory that every family planted half an acre of cassava root. This was a famine relief measure, but as many families were wont to avoid this chore if they could, it was up to the chief, the agriculture officer, and such as myself to enforce this system. It was a good one. Tanganyika never had a famine whilst this was enforced, nor would many other countries in Africa if they had had the same system, which would have saved the Western world millions of dollars of the cost of famine relief today.

I boarded a canoe with four strong paddlers and set out for a recce of the Malagarasi Delta. On one of the many islands I climbed a tree to look out over the vast area of sand and mud flats that made up the area where the river enters the lake. At first I thought I was looking at tree debris until I realised that as far as the eye could see were any number of crocodiles basking in the sun. I don't think I have seen so many crocodiles lying in the open at any time before or since. There must have been 50 of them in sight at that moment.

At four o'clock, just half an hour before I returned to my camp, a canoe crossing not 100 yards away had been attacked by the hippo that was now the subject of our attentions. The canoe was overturned and sunk, and there was no trace of the woman on board. The man poling the canoe had escaped to dry land. The destruction of the hippo was a major priority.

Our first efforts consisted of waiting in a blind to see if he would surface. He did so a number of times but never gave me time to take an accurate aim over open sights. That night I was approached by the chief. He began by telling me it was obvious to all and sundry that the hippo was absolutely safe in the water. His suggestion was that we employ a witch doctor. At first I refused to countenance such an idea. Later, on reflection, I was sufficiently intrigued by the evidence of the past that showed that local people believed in the occult. I relented and agreed that the witch doctor should be given his chance.

It was not long before I realised that I had fallen into a religious trap, for the local schoolteacher—a Seventh Day Adventist—arrived at my tent to remonstrate. I found a well-worn governmental way out of my dilemma by inviting him also to say a prayer for the destruction of the hippo and extended my invitation to anyone of any belief to do the same. In the meantime, I had realised that the only person that was going to rid the area of the hippo was me, and that I had little time left to come up with a plan.

The witch doctor duly came with his charms, casting a mixture of chicken livers and lizard entrails into the river, which as far as I could see were soon gobbled up by the resident barbel. The Seventh Day Adventist teacher also said his prayers, as did a devout follower of the African Inland Mission and a Catholic convert of the White Father's Mission. Over a valuable beer—one of several carried on the porters heads—and in the safety of my mosquito net—for the place was alive with mosquitoes—I made a plan.

I was convinced that the hippo's attention had to be diverted by something when he surfaced. This was best done by offering him a canoe—apparently adrift but secured to a hidden anchor on the bank. With this diversion I hoped to get sufficient time to put a shot into his ear hole while he contemplated crushing the canoe. Amidst much laughter of the local population, we stuffed a maize bag with leaves and foliage to look like a person. The local schoolchildren spent all next day making a head of a man out of mud and baking it. Arms and a paddle were added and a human face painted on the baked-clay head. During one of the periods when the hippo was absent, the canoe—an old and very leaky one—was moved into a place that gave the best field of fire at the usual ferry crossing. A stake was pushed into the river mud on the downstream side that kept the canoe pointed into midstream, and a rope from the stern was secured to the bank. The dummy man was faced out of the canoe towards the spot where we expected the hippo to surface.

I had decided that I had to take a longer shot from a hide back from the steep bank. Here I was limited by the angle of the high bank that made me take a standing shot. Fate intervened. There was a huge anthill from which a good rested shot was possible. Everything was now ready, and I commenced my vigil. It was not long before I heard the familiar blow of the hippo surfacing. He was nowhere near my line of fire.

The canoe-crushing hippo.

The next time he came up he was nearer, and I correctly surmised that he was intrigued by the sight of the canoe and the dummy man. The third time he surfaced he was right in my line of fire but head on to me.

You bastard, I said to myself, *turn your bloody head*. Down he went, only to surface in almost the identical position but this time sideways on. A steady aim and a good shot told, and down he went. Running to the top of the bank, I saw the water boiling in every direction. Suddenly, out of the very centre of the cauldron, there he was glaring up at me. His mouth snapped open and he came for the bank. Into that huge mouth I fired, aiming high to hit the beginning of the spine.

The effect of the shot was sensational. The hippo turned arse over teakettle backwards! Changing my position to prone as his head cleared the surface, I gave him another shot in the ear hole that finished him. With a gurgle he sank, and all was quiet, except for the busy activities of the barbel feeding on his blood.

The village came to life. All were convinced that he was dead, but who would volunteer to put a rope on his carcase? It was four o'clock. Would the hippo's body drift downstream during the night? Would the crocodiles get him first? There was nothing for it but to organise the recovery of the hippo's body myself.

Quickly we roped two canoes together with poles so that they were some 10 feet apart. Long sticks were found and we poled into the centre of the river where the hippo sank. Within a few minutes our prodding poles had found the hippo's body in the murky waters of the Malagarasi. One native was obviously a hand who had previous experience in the

recovery of objects from the river. He soon found with his pole the hippo's leg and foot. Now came the tricky part—to loop a rope over this outstretched leg. After several attempts he succeeded in doing so.

By now a hundred or more people had assembled on both banks of the river. At last we had the hippo secured. Taking a rope to the bank with the canoes, we attempted to drag the hippo ashore. It was a dead weight submerged, and although we got it to the shore to an incline whence it could be dragged high up onto the bank, it had as yet no gasses in it to make it float. There was nothing for it but to make the rope fast and hope for the best in the morning. Next day the body was floating and was duly dragged from the river by the sterling efforts of more than 80 men. The hippo was butchered and taken away by the local population. I turned to find the witch doctor at my side.

'My medicine is strong', he said, 'the hippo is dead'.

Well-versed in the colonial government's art of diplomacy, I conceded that his power was great, as I did to the Seventh Day Adventist, the African Inland Mission follower, and the Catholic convert. With a wry smile I thought to myself, *with this track record of colonial diplomacy, I ought to make it to governor. Trouble is, they will hand out independence before that happens.*

The canoe crusher's days were over, but it had taken the combined efforts of the gods to achieve it.

In Uganda, with its huge population of hippo having recourse to innumerable safe refuges in huge expanses of papyrus swamps, there can

Desperation as the water dries up, leaving nothing but mud and the opportunity of the poacher's muzzle-loaded bullet. The Ugalla River, Tanganyika (1951).

be little doubt that many native fishermen have come to grief and perished. Few professional hunters and game wardens will disagree with me when I say that probably this animal is responsible for more deaths of the native people of Africa than any animal remaining on the continent today.

We humans have little idea of the innate strength of these huge animals.

Chapter Eight

RIFLES AND CARTRIDGES

The calibres covered in this chapter, numbering 30 if the Purdey Paradox is included, have secured the demise of more than 250 of each of the six dangerous animals covered by this book, and in some cases considerably more. It is with this experience, therefore, that I humbly submit to my reader my thoughts on their suitability to the chase.

Fate should be given no chance!

—J.K.-H.

ELEPHANT GUNS:
CALIBRES, MAKERS, AND CARTRIDGES

I have shot and killed elephants with the following calibres:

1. .243 Winchester; Model 70; pre-1964 action
2. 7x57 Mauser
3. .300 Weatherby Magnum; Model 70; pre-1964 action
4. .375 Holland & Holland Magnum*; Winchester Model 70; pre-1964 action
5. .375 Holland & Holland*; double-barrelled; Royal Grade; flanged cartridge
6. .378 Weatherby Magnum
7. .404 Jeffery*; Nitro Express
8. .416 Rigby Magnum
9. .425 Westley Richards Magnum*
10. .450/.400 Manton*; Nitro Express; double-barrelled (three-inch case)
11. .458 Winchester Magnum*; Winchester Model 70; pre-1964
12. .465/.500 Holland & Holland; Nitro Express; Royal Grade

13. .470 Westley Richards*; Nitro Express; double-barrelled; 'White Hunter' Model; box lock
14. .470 Rigby Magnum*; Nitro Express; double-barrelled
15. .500 Jeffery Rimless (based on the Schuler)
16. .505 Gibbs Magnum (one of the last made by the Gibbs Co. of Bristol, U.K.)
17. .577 Westley Richards; Nitro Express; double-barrelled (three-inch case)

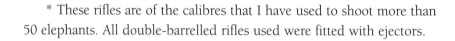

* These rifles are of the calibres that I have used to shoot more than 50 elephants. All double-barrelled rifles used were fitted with ejectors.

Note: No hand loading of any description of cartridges for these calibres should be undertaken without first referring to the rifle's manufacturer or other competent authority.

Whilst I have fired heavier calibres such as the .600 and .460 Weatherby, being mindful of the necessity to be in better shape than my quarry after the first shot has been fired, I have therefore not taken the additional risk of hunting elephants continually with these calibres. Standing 5 feet 11 inches and weighing 12 stone (168 pounds), I have never felt inclined to subscribe to the great Elmer Keith's theory of 'the bigger the bullet, the harder they fall!' This is not, in my opinion, the answer. To my mind, given a bullet that holds its shape, accuracy is all. No better example of this theory exists than the exploits of 'Karamoja' Bell with his .275 Rigby and other rifles of roughly the same calibre. Under no circumstances, however, do I recommend the shooting of dangerous animals with small-calibre rifles, no matter how accurate the hunter can be. Fate should be given no chance!

Top Right: The frontal brain shot.

Below: The side ear or brain shot (top) and the heart shot. A standing shot is preferable so as to minimize the angle upwards.

1.   **.243 Winchester; Model 70; pre-1964 action**

Acting upon the experiences of 'Karamoja' Bell, Vernon Speer of Lewiston, Idaho, made me 100x100-grain solid, tapered,

pointed bullets. At 40 yards with a 4-power scope, I shot two elephants facing across me to the left precisely in the ear hole and therefore at right angles to my line of fire and on level sight. Both dropped instantly. The bullet stopped on the far side of the brain cavity of each. The cartridges were Winchester's standard loads of powder with the soft-pointed 100-grain bullet replaced with the solid. I believe the weakest point in the elephant's armour is the earshot. Even so, the target area is a mere 2 inches x 2 inches for this small calibre, whereas the frontal brain shot is fractionally larger. However, the chance of a ricochet is greater on a brain shot, as the angle of the shot is inevitably upwards, whereas the ear shot is virtually of horizontal flight with little if any bone structure in the immediate vicinity. 'Karamoja' Bell did not have the luxury of a Redfield scope.

Essential research into the performance of each calibre and its ammunition was conducted on all varieties of game. On each safari and expedition a record was kept.

Ballistics are:
100 grain; FMJ; FL (factory loads); muzzle velocity is 2900 fps; muzzle energy is 1868 foot pounds

2. 7x57 Mauser

This calibre and make was probably the most widely distributed in the whole of Africa as a sporting rifle and a 'pot' hunter's gun. The standard solid bullet for this gun, made at the turn of the century at the time of the Boer War, readily distorted when striking bone and was not suitable for shots requiring considerable penetration. It must be remembered

L to R: Mauser action barrelled to .458 Winchester Magnum, Mauser action barrelled to .425 Westley Richards, and Mauser action barrelled to .505 Gibbs (a square-bridged magnum). Note the makeshift backsight on the .425. This is how they came back from hire! (1976).

that in those years there were no telescopic sights in general use. Vernon Speer made me some 150-grain solid tapered bullets. The load was standard with 41.5 grains of IMR 4054. I shot two elephants with this calibre, and both dropped at once, the first with an ear shot and the second with a frontal brain shot. A 4-power Redfield scope was used.

Ballistics are:

150 grain; FL; muzzle velocity is 2700 fps; muzzle energy is 2429 foot pounds

3. .300 Weatherby Magnum; Winchester Model 70; pre-1964 action

On the not unreasonable assumption that a hunter, when stalking another animal, may well become entangled with elephants and have to defend himself, I also determined to see what the likely outcome of this situation might be. One important assumption had to be made, that being that the opportunity had to occur when one had to reload with solid ammunition. Roy Weatherby was a valued friend and had been kind enough to send me a whole set of rifles to be tested and used as hire guns. I have to admit that in company with my comrades we had some disappointments with them. Fortunately, however, I was not foolish enough to disregard the great asset they had—velocity. The problem was that in the early stages the bullets did not hold together, and there were problems with the trigger and safety catch mechanism. Nosler came quickly to the rescue and solved the problem of disintegration on impact. Whilst the Weatherby Company improved the action, my old friend Richard Ayer produced a Winchester Model 70 chambered and barrelled to a .300 Weatherby, and we were in business. Without Roy Weatherby's intuition and determination, we would not have the improved rifles of today.

I shot several elephants with this rifle most efficiently also using the heart shot. Penetration was excellent. Once again Speer made me bullets with Jack O'Connor's advice. A Redfield scope was used.

The tools of the trade, 1976. L to R: 12 bore Webley Scott, 12 bore Purdey 'Paradox', .470 Westley Richards, .375 Winchester Magnum Model 70 (pre-1964 action), 7mm Magnum (Mauser action). Their adventures are recorded elsewhere.

325

Westley Richards' Accelerated Express System of ·375 Bore Magazine Rifle, for Rimless Cartridge.

THIS improved ·375 bore Rifle for Rimless Cartridge is superior to the ordinary ·375 bore. The cartridge is of the bottle neck pattern, by which perfect loading and extraction in magazine rifles are ensured. This new cartridge, adapted by Westley Richards & Co. after careful experiment, shoots a 270 grains bullet with increased velocity, *viz.*, 2,200 feet per second at muzzle, with a muzzle energy of 2,898 ft. lbs. It is arranged for the soft nosed bullet as well as the Westley Richards' patent copper capped expanding bullet. In conjunction with this latter form of bullet the weapon can be relied upon as being very effective for the larger kind of game.

THE LATEST DEVELOPMENT.

N.B.—The weight of the bullet with which the 2,200 ft. sec. velocity is obtained, should be noted. The velocity of 2,200 ft. is the highest obtainable with the 270 grs. weight of bullet in the ·375 rifle; higher velocities *which are obtained by using lighter bullets*, increase the penetration at the expense of expansion and general effectiveness, and are not to be recommended for sport.

Where a small bore rifle of higher velocity is desired, combined with sporting bullet effectiveness, the Westley Richards' ·318 bore is superior to all others.

The ·375 Rimless Cartridge Rifle, is made with the Westley Richards' patent detachable barrel, with patent solid locking lugs, which gives absolute rigidity under firing. It is the simplest and easiest form of attaching and detaching the barrel   Price **£25 0 0**

Best quality   ,,   **30 0 0**

If Fixed Barrel   ...   *less* **£2 0 0**

Price of cartridges, per 100	Solid bullet - - - -	**£1 3 0**	In Clips,
	Soft nose bullet - - - -	**1 3 6**	1/- per 100
	Copper capped bullet - - -	**1 4 6**	*extra.*

Westley Richards Patent Capped Expanding Bullet is the best extant for sporting purposes, and ensures the greatest possible shock.

326

Ballistics are:

200 grain; FMJ; FL; muzzle velocity is 2900 fps; muzzle energy is 3736 foot pounds

4. **.375. Holland & Holland Magnum; Winchester Model 70; pre-1964 action**

One could happily write a book on the .375—the gun for all seasons and all countries. In sporting terms it has probably accounted for as many elephants as all the others put together. A .375 accounted for Sundae's elephant with tusks of 180 pounds and 167 1/2 pounds, and also one with tusks of 197 pounds and 194 pounds shot in southern Tanzania by a policeman. Both of these are in my old friend Basil Reel's pictorial records. From the point of view of a hunting client, it is a gun that, if of the correct weight and design, kicks but little, and fitted with a low-power scope gives the hunter the best opportunity for accuracy at a safe distance. However, it has to be said that this does not necessarily please the professional hunter, who in all probability may be faced with a long shot with a far heavier rifle at a greater distance if the animal does not appear to be mortally wounded.

I would also describe this calibre as a 'lady's' gun. To present one of the fair sex with a .470 double-barrelled rifle to shoot an elephant is to require the lady to be of substantial proportions enough to raise and shoot accurately a heavy rifle weighing 10 pounds plus, and to take the resulting recoil. An experienced professional hunter is well able to take care of these problems, but for me I would say a hunter was under-gunned with a .375 for elephant. If he was a professional hunter he certainly would be so. In some countries the .375 is not legal on some species of dangerous game, which includes elephant. A .375 for elephant is, in my opinion, a marginal calibre for elephant and if used should be in the hands of a person with some experience. The heavier bullets and loads are best used for elephant.

Ballistics are:

300 grain; FMJ; FL; muzzle velocity is 2530 fps; muzzle energy is 4266 foot pounds

5. **.375 Holland & Holland; double-barrelled; Royal Grade; flanged cartridge**

I was once the proud possessor of a .375 double-barrelled rifle by Holland & Holland, a Royal Grade with detachable side locks and ejectors. To me, it had on game control two advantages over the .375 bolt-action rifle. Firstly, it was relatively silent on loading until two shots had been fired (even then it did not make so much noise), and it was faster on reloading. Secondly, firing at a moving target, which was often the case, was like shooting birds with a shotgun, and I was able to shoot more accurately looking down two barrels rather than one. This was particularly important when faced with shooting more than one animal. It also packed into a smaller parcel. I bought it secondhand off the British East Africa Company for £100 and sold it to my friend Dick Ayer for more. The double-barrelled .375 is a good lady's big-game gun. I never, in all my time in Africa, used a double-barrelled rifle with a scope mounted on it. To destroy the look of such an art form by the addition of a scope and its necessary fittings and removal of metal on the barrels seemed sacrilege.

I would have liked to have had a double-barrelled Westley Richards chambered to a .378 with flanged cartridges. That would be some rifle. The increased velocity and penetration would certainly make a difference. Thanks be to Roy Weatherby.

The constraints and comments made regarding the .375 H&H Magnum Winchester Model 70 also apply to this rifle.

Ballistics are:
300 grain; FMJ; FL; muzzle velocity is 2400 fps; muzzle energy is 3850 foot pounds

6. .378 Weatherby Magnum

This was Weatherby's answer to the .375 Holland & Holland Magnum, using increased cartridge space and power that drove the bullets of the same weight as the .375 Holland & Holland faster and harder. Much the same comment applies to this calibre as does to the .375. In the hands of the competent hunter it is a super plus .375. I had ample evidence of this when my friend Dr. Arnie Garza-Vale, of San Antonio, Texas, shooting a .378 Weatherby Magnum across an open stretch of water, killed a bull buffalo stone dead with one shot at 125 yards. I am not too sure this would have been the animal's fate if it had been an elephant. Three-hundred-grain bullets are desirable. The .378, in my opinion, is one of the best cartridges that Roy Weatherby produced.

Ballistics are:
300 grain; FMJ; FL; muzzle velocity is 2925 fps; muzzle energy is 5701 foot pounds

7. .404 Jeffery; Nitro Express

Many .404s were made by English gunmakers before and after the 1939–45 War. Its equivalent on the continent of Europe was the 10.75 x73mm. Its fame came from the fact that the .303 was forbidden to civil powers (being a military cartridge) and, in any case, was not of sufficient strength to combat big game. The British administration of the colonies in those days was always looking for a cheap way of solving the problem. It was able to do so in this case. Nearly all game scouts in East Africa were equipped with this rifle, which was a real workhorse. For several years before I bought a Westley Richards .425, and subsequently a .470 by the same makers, it was my right hand on all sorts of hunting expeditions and control work. The best bullets were made by D.W.M. in Germany; they distorted far less than those made by Kynoch. The Mauser action was first class and never let me down. Some were made using the larger magnum Mauser action. It is my belief that with improved modern powders and bullets, this calibre's performance could be much improved, there being plenty of room in the case for additional powder. The .404 Cogswell & Harrison was my first 'heavy' in my battery. The cost of producing these rifles was cheap, as no special wood was used in the stock, which was mass produced. Secondhand Mauser actions were two-a-penny, and barrels were cheaply and easily made.

Ballistics are:
400 grain; FL; muzzle velocity is 2150 fps; muzzle energy is 4140 foot pounds

8. .416 Rigby Magnum

Perhaps one of the most famous calibres of African big game rifles, it was used extensively by a great many professional hunters. Its ballistics, however, were not much different from those of the .425 and later the .458. It had great value, however, as a rifle, being made by John Rigby & Company with a magnum Mauser action. I owned an original one for a time and much regret not having retained it, as I have many other rifles

that I have owned. With the Mau Mau Emergency regulations in Kenya, the ownership of firearms was tightened up considerably; regretfully, it was a rifle that I sold. Therein lie some tales that must be told elsewhere. Today this calibre enjoys a highly popular renaissance, with the M77 Ruger being a fine example at a very affordable price. Ammunition has also been greatly improved by the use of Woodleigh bullets and modern powders, and it is now a rifle that has great pride of ownership in its original state.

Ballistics are:

410 grain; FMJ; FL; muzzle velocity is 2300 fps; muzzle energy is 4820 foot pounds

Note: I took a small part in the development of the modern .416 calibre. Bob Chatfield Taylor produced a .416 Taylor, and together we tested it in Africa. (See Chapter 4.)

9. .425 Westley Richards Magnum

This was certainly my favourite big-game magazine rifle, and like the .404 was widely supplied to colonial governments to equip their game department scouts. In my career I owned four of these, of which the barrels of three eventually had to be replaced. Regretfully, they were rebarrelled and chambered to .458, the .425 ammunition being impossible to obtain at that time. My Westley Richards .470 only had to have the barrels replaced once, and that was after I sold it. It is a fact that seems to escape all the pundits and gun writers of today: both before and after the war, no one of average financial capability could afford a British double rifle. There were, therefore, a very large number of magazine rifles in use. In 1955, when I bought a brand-new Westley Richards double-barrelled .470 'White Hunter' model, it cost me £185. The sum was 50 percent of my annual salary! A .425 cost £60, and that included, if you were lucky, a magnum Mauser action, added to which it had an extended magazine that gave you five in the magazine and one up the spout. More than one elephant was possible in pretty quick time, which in adversity was useful insurance. This extended magazine was not available in any other rifle at that time and was a very considerable bonus when considering the purchase of a hunting rifle for a reasonable sum of money. The price of ivory then was close to one pound to £1 sterling (£1 sterling equalled $2.83). A 100-pounder gave you one year's salary. Nearly all of my peers bought their hunting cars, rifles, and equipment out of their ivory money.

The .425 Westley Richards was easy to work and very accurate. It had a barrel length of 26 inches, and the ballistics for such a small cartridge were very impressive, producing no less than 5300 foot pounds of muzzle energy. This is what the editor of *Cartridges of the World* had to say about it in the 1996 edition:

The .425 is a poor man's Magnum. The rebated rim of the cartridge is 30 X 06 size, so any 30 X 06 or 8mm Mauser type action can be made to feed it. Take a simple Mauser action, rebarrel it to .425, have a good gunsmith rework the feed system and the result is a very good big game rifle at a very moderate cost. The .425 proved to be one of the best and most effective knockdown cartridges against dangerous game. It was very effective against elephant. Only one bullet weight of 410 gr. was made in both solid and soft types. The .425 has about the same power as the .458 Winchester Magnum.

Mauser actions continue to be available, and the profit margins of British rifle makers will remain secure so long as they offer these actions.

For myself, I have employed this method of acquiring good, reliable hunting rifles for many years and have seldom departed from the Mauser or the pre-1964 Model 70 Winchester action at any time, the strength of the action and extractor system being unbeatable during the period of my early life. I believe that more can be done with this cartridge, but my revered friend Bob Lee, who has made attempts to improve it, was disappointed with the results. Such is my respect for Bob that I am inclined to think he must be right.

An interesting feature peculiar only to the Westley Richards .425 was the cartridge guide spring fitted on either side of the bolt guide on the upper side of the magazine. Both springs were of a size that required that they be let into the stock to a small extent on either side of the magazine. The purpose of this was multifold: it steadied the bolt as it travelled forward to close and reduced the 'waggle' on the bolt common to all Mauser actions, and also reduced the noise when reloading. Further, they kept in order and proper subjection the five rounds held in the extended magazine; problems with other bolt-action rifles caused by badly feeding magazines had caused loss of life in hunting accidents.

The .425 Westley Richards was made using a number of different Mauser actions, the most common being the '98 Argentine action.

To be on the ultrasafe side, these actions, which were cheaply and mass produced, need case hardening when used with today's ammunition. A few were also made using the Belgian Brevex action and a few with the optional magnum Mauser action. The Argentine action was distinctive in that the side lever, when pushed outwards to release the bolt from the action, appeared to be part of the cartridge clip guide on the upper side of the action. In other Mausers made for sporting purposes, there was simply a small spring lever fitted to the side of the action, usually with a milled top so that the thumb and index finger of the left hand could easily push it outwards whilst removing the bolt with the right hand.

This calibre is grossly underestimated and accounted for more elephants than is generally realised.

Ballistics are:
410 grain; FMJ; FL; muzzle velocity is 2350 fps; muzzle energy is 5022 foot pounds

Note: This is what F.C. Selous said about the Westley Richards .425 on July 4, 1912: 'I can only give your .425 rifle the greatest praise. Had I only possessed such a rifle in my old elephant hunting days I am sure I could have killed four times as many elephants as I actually laid low'.

10. .450/.400 Manton; Nitro Express; double-barrelled (three-inch case)

This calibre was largely used in India, particularly in tiger hunting. As sport hunting in East Africa opened up, it was brought in mostly by those who had used it elsewhere. Though effective on big game when used accurately, it was in reality no better than a .375. From my experience, Manton & Company of England and Calcutta seemed to produce it at a lesser price than some of the other English makers. I owned one for a time and used it as a hire gun, though I shot a good deal of other game with it and often used it on elephant. Accuracy using this rifle was essential, and therefore it was better used by someone of experience. The barrels of my Manton were well set, and they grouped at one inch at 100 yards. For a double this was very accurate indeed.

Ballistics are:
400 grain; FMJ; FL by Kynoch; muzzle velocity is 2100 fps; muzzle energy is 3920 foot pounds

11. .458 Winchester Magnum; Winchester Model 70; pre-1964

As far as elephant hunting was concerned, the .458 Winchester Magnum Model 70 pre-1964 rifle was the best thing to come on the market since sliced peaches in the proverbial lunch box. It was ruggedly made, the magazine fed well, the extractor system was Mauser type, and it held three in the magazine and one up the spout. The stock was solid and unpretentious. To the hunter who proposed to use one as his 'right hand', however, it was advisable to customize a little. The sights were not of the quality or durability under bush conditions that they should have been. (Such was the popularity of this rifle that I have seen more .458 Winchesters treated like a club or a tyre lever than any other rifle. I have more than once winced at the sight of the condition of some rifles as the professional hunter disappeared into the bush with the client, but the clients all seemed to come back unscathed.)

My old friend Dick Ayer and I had several of these rifles made to look more aristocratic by clipping two inches off the barrel, burnishing the action (which improved the feed), milling the knob of the bolt, and having fitted a heavy single back sight with a good V in the middle with an inlaid white metal line to the base of the sight. The foresight had a 'pop-up' large white bead and heavy-duty sight that was covered by the white bead when it was raised. On one rifle I had the magazine lengthened in the manner of the .425 Westley Richards to take five rounds.

I enjoyed tremendous success with the rifle hunting all species of big game for many years. I would rate the .458 Winchester Magnum Model 70 pre-1964 as one of the great developments in hunting rifles in recent times. It was cost effective and an efficient gun. Nothing much could go wrong, the action being the best in the business.

Both the .338 Winchester Magnum and the .458 Winchester Magnum were constructed on the same length action. As one client put it to me, 'John', he said, 'if I had a Purdey and it was lost when sending it to Africa, I'd wait five years to get another, in which time the price would have doubled. A .458 can be bought in replacement tomorrow, probably for less than I paid for it'.

The ballistics are virtually the same as the .470 and .425, but the bullet is 70 grains heavier than the .425. The latest steel-jacketed bullets have greatly improved the performance of these calibres.

Ballistics are:
500 grain; FMJ; FL; muzzle velocity is 2040 fps; muzzle energy is 4620 foot pounds

12. .465/.500 Holland & Holland; Nitro Express; Royal Grade

As described in Chapter 1, this was my first double-barrelled rifle. Had it been in better condition when I bought it I might have become enamoured of it, but subsequent experience with it persuaded me that it was neither one thing nor the other. It was not the gun that the .470 or .458 calibres were, nor did it stand out for anything in particular on its own. It was produced as a calibre replacement early in this century when the .450 was outlawed in the Sudan, at that time a happy hunting ground for big-game hunters who had no doubt enjoyed the tales that both Sir Samuel Baker and Sir Richard Burton had to tell of that part of Africa. In a story told elsewhere (Chapter 3), I saw this bullet pass through the body of a 6-foot 2-inch human being, entering just behind the hip bone of his right-hand side and exiting just in front of the hip bone on his left-hand side. He suffered no internal damage. Was it a miracle, or did that in fact also happen when a big-game animal was shot with this rifle? I believe my opinion of this calibre is shared by other friends who have been owners of this rifle, but, interestingly, none of them own one now.

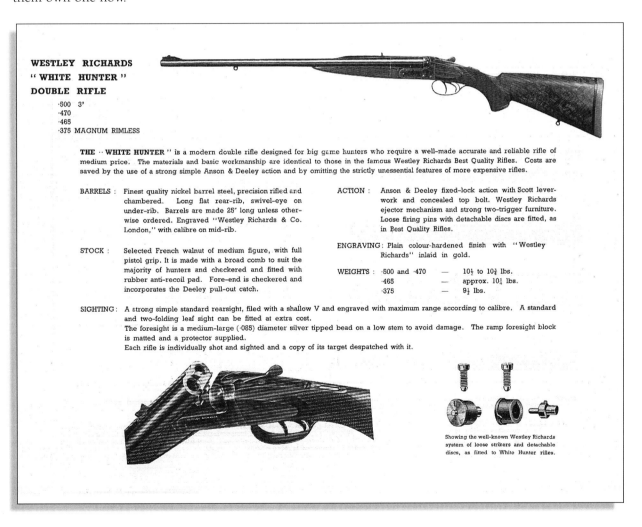

WESTLEY RICHARDS
" WHITE HUNTER "
DOUBLE RIFLE
·500 3'
·470
·465
·375 MAGNUM RIMLESS

THE " WHITE HUNTER " is a modern double rifle designed for big game hunters who require a well-made accurate and reliable rifle of medium price. The materials and basic workmanship are identical to those in the famous Westley Richards Best Quality Rifles. Costs are saved by the use of a strong simple Anson & Deeley action and by omitting the strictly unessential features of more expensive rifles.

BARRELS : Finest quality nickel barrel steel, precision rifled and chambered. Long flat rear-rib, swivel-eye on under-rib. Barrels are made 25" long unless otherwise ordered. Engraved "Westley Richards & Co. London," with calibre on mid-rib.

STOCK : Selected French walnut of medium figure, with full pistol grip. It is made with a broad comb to suit the majority of hunters and checkered and fitted with rubber anti-recoil pad. Fore-end is checkered and incorporates the Deeley pull-out catch.

ACTION : Anson & Deeley fixed-lock action with Scott lever-work and concealed top bolt. Westley Richards ejector mechanism and strong two-trigger furniture. Loose firing pins with detachable discs are fitted, as in Best Quality Rifles.

ENGRAVING : Plain colour-hardened finish with "Westley Richards" inlaid in gold.

WEIGHTS : ·500 and ·470 — 10¼ to 10¾ lbs.
·465 — approx. 10¼ lbs.
·375 — 9½ lbs.

SIGHTING : A strong simple standard rearsight, filed with a shallow V and engraved with maximum range according to calibre. A standard and two-folding leaf sight can be fitted at extra cost.
The foresight is a medium-large (·085) diameter silver tipped bead on a low stem to avoid damage. The ramp foresight block is matted and a protector supplied.
Each rifle is individually shot and sighted and a copy of its target despatched with it.

Showing the well-known Westley Richards system of loose strikers and detachable discs, as fitted to White Hunter rifles.

Ballistics are:
480 grain; FMJ; FL; muzzle velocity is 2150 fps; muzzle energy is 4930 foot pounds

13. .470 Westley Richards; Nitro Express; double-barrelled; 'White Hunter' Model; box lock

The .470 double-barrelled rifle has been made all over the world, but for me the Westley Richards I had was the best. It is without question the most successful and sought-after calibre and the one rifle that has more than held its value. I owned one made by Westley Richards most of my life. I owe my life to its reliability and its precise and simple manufacture and engineering. It has been at my right hand at nearly every tight corner in which I have found myself when hunting big game as a professional hunter. So familiar had I become with it that I have made some interesting, perhaps sensational, shots with it that will stay forever in my memory.

The 'knockdown value' of this gun just so happens to be exactly right in nearly all cases. The kick, weight, barrel length, and general handling capabilities are very comfortable, and most people can fire it accurately with relative ease. In short, it's the gun for me, and it did me proud for 40 years. No other that I owned gave me such confidence and results. God bless Westley Richards for that.

All the noted British gunmakers make this calibre, and Kynoch was, to the best of my knowledge, the only producer of reliable ammunition (although I seem to remember that in the early 1970s there was a slight hiccup when new ammunition from the factory caused the cases to stick in the chambers of rifles of much earlier manufacture).

My .470 double-barrelled Westley Richards box lock cost me £185 in 1955. It had no engraving except for the maker's name, a simple stock, no check piece, one solitary mounted back sight with a good V, and a strong, clearly white metal foresight. I must have fired upwards of 2000 rounds from it. Not being able to face the rebarrelling charges in recent times, I regretfully sold it with a letter of recommendation for $3000. An old and valued friend once said to me, 'There are no pockets in a shroud'. Whilst he is right, I would have been only too happy to have had the rifle alongside of me when I pass on, but my three sons needed education, and that is where the money went.

Ballistics are:

500 grain; FMJ; FL; muzzle velocity is 2150 fps; muzzle energy is
5130 foot pounds

14. .470 Rigby Magnum; Nitro Express; double-barrelled

When I joined Ker & Downey Safaris it had a number of these
rifles as hire guns. The fact that it survived the treatment meted out to
them as more or less common property was a tribute to their manufacture. The Rigby Company was at that time one of the first line of
British gunmakers. As the makers of the .416, .318, and .275, it had
made an unrivaled reputation. I used one of these rifles out of the company store when I was asked to do some control work on very short
notice and found this make and calibre to be all that it was commend-
ed to be.

The Rigby Company changed hands some years ago.

Ballistics are:

500 grain; FMJ; FL; muzzle velocity is 2150 fps; muzzle energy is
5130 foot pounds

15. .500 Jeffery Rimless (based on the 12.5x70mm '.500' Schuler)

Until the introduction of the .460 Weatherby, this was the most powerful and largest magazine cartridge that existed. My old friend Tony
Sanchez-Arino, the hunter of more elephants than I care to think about,
used this rifle extensively and successfully all over Africa. I once had the
opportunity of shooting an elephant in Botswana when a friend from
Rhodesia came to spend a holiday with me. He had little experience and
wounded the elephant. When we came up with it, he being somewhat
embarrassed at his poor marksmanship, asked me to finish it off. It was a
big bang and a big push. Very impressive, but for a larger man than I am.
Tony's rifle.

Ballistics are:

535 grain; FMJ; FL; muzzle velocity is 2400 fps; muzzle energy is
6800 foot pounds

The Schuler's ballistics are the same.

The "Gibbs" ·505 Big Game Magazine Rifle.

This rifle has proved a great success, and has to its credit some extraordinary achievements against Elephant and other big game in many parts of the world, including Kenya, Tanganyika, Nyasaland, Rhodesia, Angola, Portugese East Africa, India and Ceylon.

Reference to the ballistics will show it to be by far

THE MOST POWERFUL MAGAZINE RIFLE IN THE WORLD.

It is designed to take four cartridges (three in the magazine and one in the chamber).

The backsight on the Standard model has a standard and two spring leaves for 100, 200 and 300 yards, and a bead frontsight is fitted, but any other form of sighting can be supplied to suit sportmen's requirements.

Price of Rifle including anti-recoil heelplate and spare frontsight **£40 0 0**

The Gibbs ·505 Cartridge.

(Actual Size.)

Solid Hard Steel covered bullet giving great penetration.	Soft nose expanding bullet for heavy soft-skinned beasts.	Soft nose and split expanding bullet for medium sized soft-skinned beasts.
Powder Charge **90** grains. Muzzle Velocity **2,350** ft. sec.	Price of Cartridges **£4 4 0** per 100.	Weight of Bullet **525** grains. Striking Energy **6,431** ft. lbs.

16. .505 Gibbs Magnum

At the time I was living in Bechuanaland I had made for me a .505 by Gibbs of Bristol. It was one of the last rifles they made and was built on a magnum Mauser action. This huge rifle, with a 26-inch barrel and a long action, was a 'Long Tom' indeed and most unwieldy in the bush. I had the very poorest of results with it, but in fairness they might have been because the ammunition was old and infirm. Sufficient to say that on one occasion when I was shooting an elephant with no less a person than Sir William Gordon Cumming, Bt.—a kinsman of the doyen of all South African big-game hunters, Roualeyn Gordon Cumming—the bullets simply refused to penetrate, and I had no alternative but to finish off the elephant with my .470 Westley Richards double. The gun was well made and is today quite valuable, but it was abandoned to be a hire gun and subsequently sold with the company many years later. I have no doubt that today it has found a place of pride in someone's collection in the U.S.A.

Ballistics are:
525 grain; FMJ; FL; muzzle velocity is 2060 fps; muzzle energy is 4960 foot pounds

17. .577 Westley Richards; Nitro Express; double-barrelled (three-inch case)

I regret the fact that I never owned one of these rifles made by one of the most reputable British gunmakers. I shot several elephants with one with George Rushby, who was one of those redoubtable ivory hunters who had used this gun more or less exclusively in the Lado Enclave and elsewhere. Most of the ivory hunters at the turn of the century used this rifle. It enjoyed a great reputation and always held its value. For me, it was a bit too much gun. It weighed 14 pounds, and I found that often, after spending a couple of hours stalking a good bull carrying good ivory, my arms were like lead from carrying and crawling with it. Its knockdown capabilities were phenomenal. When a frontal brain shot was the target, the punch that struck the five-and-a-half-ton elephant was enough to set it back on its haunches. I have actually noted on one occasion that it shifted the entire animal six inches backwards off its feet. The elephant tracks in the dusty ground clearly showed this. The ammunition was not cheap; in fact, it was amongst the most expensive. In thick bush it had great advantages at close quarters and was an undoubted lifesaver to many of those who used it. Like no other rifle it would turn an elephant from its evil purpose at the very last moment. I would that I was a bigger man. Were I so, I would have made it my business to own one.

Ballistics are:
750 grain; FMJ; FL; muzzle velocity is 2050 fps; muzzle energy is 7010 foot pounds
Quite some performance!

Note: The doyen of all ivory hunters, Jim Sutherland, said this of his own rifle to Westley Richards on March 8, 1912: 'Two hundred and twenty-three male elephants have fallen to your .577 double hammerless rifle'.

After the use of these several calibres of rifles to hunt elephants over many years and in many different and varied countries of Africa, I am left with a few thoughts. Many years ago I met up with John 'Pondoro' Taylor of *African Rifles & Cartridges* fame. Whilst some of his stories and way of life were, shall we say, a little unusual, I agree most heartily with him in what he described as the 'knockdown value of a bullet'. In all my conversations and discussions with Warren Page, Jack O'Connor, and Elmer Keith, who were the pundits in my younger days, we all basically agreed that there was an ideal combination of bullet weight and velocity that produced the best possible effect on the animal. It is well known that Elmer favoured the larger heavier load and bullet. The advent of Roy Weatherby's cartridges and calibres with very substantially increased velocities brought up all kinds of arguments that gave gun writers of the day plenty of verbal ammunition. From my experience, I am convinced that the calibres .416, .470, .458, .425, and .577 do have the best combination of 'knockdown effect' on the largest animals—rhino, elephant, and hippo. I would add that I am sure that there are other calibres that anyone of similar experience would add to this list, namely the .500 Jeffery.

I can well remember the nights spent with Jack O'Connor round the campfire discussing this subject and with Bob Chatfield-Taylor when we did the field trials of the .416 Taylor. There is a point at which the effect of the bullet delivered is either too much or too little. The trick is to find the best combination of both that produces maximum effect. Ideally, you need to kill the animal cleanly and efficiently without its knowing that it has passed on, but in doing so you do not need to seriously impair the hunter from ever attempting to collect another trophy in the future as a result of firing a heavy rifle. Of course, there are some who are so excited at the time that the shock of recoil fails to register until later, when they notice the bruise on their shoulder.

Secondly, there are a number of cartridges that lend themselves to possible development and improvement. The .404 readily comes to mind, and some progress in this direction has been made. The .404 cartridge was never really up to scratch and there was plenty of room in the case with improved powders. The solid bullet that D.W.M. made was a really good one. With modern powders, this cartridge can be loaded up to produce much better performance than heretofore, almost matching the .416.

It is a pity a .378 double-barrelled rifle with a flanged case is not made. It would be so much better than the .375. I say flanged because the mechanism of extraction for a rebated case is so subject to dirt and consequent malfunction in African conditions that it can seriously jeopardize one's chances of obtaining the trophy sought. In my personal experiences, there were many occasions where the extractors for rebated cartridges were very frequently and necessarily checked before firing in the bush.

RHINO GUNS:
CALIBRES, MAKERS, AND CARTRIDGES

I have shot and killed rhinoceros with the following guns:

1. .375 H & H Magnum; Winchester Model 70; pre-1964 action
2. .375 H & H Magnum; double-barrelled; Royal Grade; flanged cartridge
3. .404 Jeffery; Nitro Express
4. .416 Rigby Magnum
5. .425 Westley Richards Magnum
6. .450/.400 Manton; Nitro Express; double-barrelled (three-inch case)
7. .458 Winchester Magnum; Model 70; pre-1964 action
8. .470 Westley Richards; Nitro Express; double-barrelled

According to my diaries I shot and assisted my clients in shooting some 40 rhino, of which five were on control and two in self-defence. I have made the same comments for rhino as I have for elephant, but it

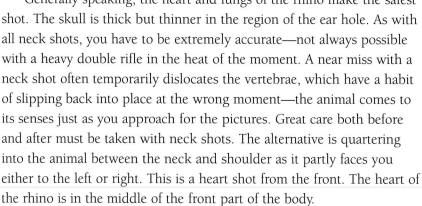

Top: From right to left, the brain shot, neck shot, and heart shot. The brain and neck shots demand great accuracy with solid bullets.

Above: The front-quarter neck shot (top) is not easy. The heart shot from the same angle, however, allows for perfect positioning. If the rhino swung its head to its left, both shots would become more difficult. You would then have to rely on a heavy calibre, solid bullet to turn the rhino.

will be recalled from the text of Chapter 3 that it is quite a different proposition to shoot a rhino, where vital parts are not all in the same place as an elephant. It should be remembered that only recently have black and white rhino been available on a licence in South Africa to sportsmen, and that in the East African era in the 1960s considerable protection was given to the now vanished species from that part of Africa. It is noteworthy also that a substantial number of visiting sportsmen of this era did not wish to shoot a rhino. If they did, and a good trophy with a horn of more than 25 inches was required, then it meant hunting the big forest areas on foot at 8000 feet where the rhino's horns were generally longer than elsewhere. In the forest on foot at that elevation it was 100 percent of the time hard work and not for the elderly or unfit. Bushbuck, leopard, and buffalo were alternatives in the same area. Had this not been the case, fewer rhino would have been shot.

Generally speaking, the heart and lungs of the rhino make the safest shot. The skull is thick but thinner in the region of the ear hole. As with all neck shots, you have to be extremely accurate—not always possible with a heavy double rifle in the heat of the moment. A near miss with a neck shot often temporarily dislocates the vertebrae, which have a habit of slipping back into place at the wrong moment—the animal comes to its senses just as you approach for the pictures. Great care both before and after must be taken with neck shots. The alternative is quartering into the animal between the neck and shoulder as it partly faces you either to the left or right. This is a heart shot from the front. The heart of the rhino is in the middle of the front part of the body.

BUFFALO GUNS:
CALIBRES, MAKERS, AND CARTRIDGES

I have shot and killed buffalo with the following guns:

1. 7x57mm Mauser (exclusively in a field trial)
2. .375 H&H Magnum; Winchester Model 70; pre-1964 action
3. .375 H&H Magnum; double-barreled; Royal Grade; flanged cartridge
4. .404 Jeffery; Nitro Express
5. .416 Rigby Magnum
6. .416 Taylor
7. .425 Westley Richards Magnum

8. .450/.400 Manton; Nitro Express; double-barrelled (three-inch case)
9. .458 Winchester Magnum; Winchester Model 70; pre-1964 action
10. .470 Westley Richards; Nitro Express; double barrelled

Being an avid buffalo hunter, which I regard as without doubt the 'sport of kings', I was careful to study the use of firearms and their application to this sometimes evilly ferocious animal. To my mind, no better example existed of 'too much gun' being used as some of those used on buffalo. There were many occasions when bullets, in reality designed for elephant, rhino, and hippo, simply cruised through a buffalo without the maximum effect of 'shock on penetration'.

Ideally the solid bullet should be found under the skin on the opposite side to its entrance. The knockdown value or shock value of the bullet is then at its maximum. Some hunters use soft-nosed bullets for buffalo. This may be suitable, but only if the buffalo is totally unaware of your presence, and even then strange things have been known to happen.

As my experience increased, I realised that this practice needed to be corrected. Jack O'Connor agreed heartily with me after his safari with me hunting buffalo in Botswana (see 'The Indestructible Buffalo' in Chapter 4).

In the course of many years of professional hunting, when at least two and sometimes four buffalo were shot on each safari, to which must be added many shot on control or for farm protection, I have shot close to 1000 buffalo.

Left: The frontal brain shot (top) and heart shot. Both shots are best taken when the buffalo is stationary, which isn't always possible.

Below: The side neck and heart shots. The neck shot requires expert knowledge of anatomy and pin-point accuracy.

The .470 Westley Richards worked well. I found the .404's performance fair but with more necessity for accuracy. This also applied to the .375 and the .450/.400, though the .375 was normally used with a scope. The smaller calibres worked well provided the target was an unsuspecting one. If one was charged by a buffalo, the question arose as to the knockdown value of the cartridge used. The gun used on a buffalo had to be a 'stopper' under all circumstances. At the top end of the scale were the .460 Weatherby and the .577 double-barrelled rifle. At the bottom was the .375. The .416 Rigby seemed a good calibre.

Large numbers of buffalo, be they cows, calves, or bulls,

Above: The 500-grain solid bullet found by chance on a log 10 yards from the buffalo it passed through (through the spine). The buffalo was shot with a .458 Winchester Magnum Model 70.

Top right: A muzzle-loaded bullet imbedded in a buffalo's horns. The horns were 44 inches in width. Note the good boss and wicked, sharp hooks (1968).

Right: A 46-inch-wide buffalo shot by Dr. Syb West in Botswana. Note the entrance hole of the bullet in the neck (1967).

were the target of poachers and legally licensed tribespeople. Very few people of this kind, if any, have the financial means to use anything other than a black-powder muzzle-loading .450/.577 Martini Henry, or something like it, with all manner of projectiles for shot. These guns make a distinctive noise and in some cases left a distinctive mark on the firer's face if the gun was loaded incorrectly. A dull *boom* was sometimes heard when we were in the middle of a stalk for a trophy. Often, when stopping local people in some remote part of the country to obtain information, one saw unmistakable signs of a breach explosion, the person's lips being badly split, the teeth missing on the right side of the jaw, and the cheek disfigured. Sometimes the eye would also be damaged. Inquiry as to how the wound occurred would normally promote a wide grin—and a laugh from the others. The grin would expose a good view of the whole damaged Draculaean image.

To sum up, I believe that on the whole a good English double-barrelled rifle was best for buffalo—if you could afford one—in calibres .470 to .577, depending on the size and weight of the firer. To those not of such financial ability, the .458 Winchester Magnum, .425 (large magazine) Westley Richards, .416 Rigby, and .404 Jeffery were good medicine, as was the .378 Weatherby. But the Weatherby, though good on frontal shots, often passed right through the buffalo without enough shock effect when shooting for the heart or neck from a sideways on position. For me, the trusty .470 double was 'mustard'.

LION GUNS:
CALIBRES, MAKERS, AND CARTRIDGES

I have shot and killed lions with the following guns:

1. 8x60 Brno
2. .318 Cogswell & Harrison; Mauser action
3. .375 Holland & Holland Magnum; Winchester Model 70; pre-1964 action
4. .375 Holland & Holland Magnum; double-barrelled; Royal Grade; flanged cartridge
5. .378 Weatherby Magnum
6. .404 Jeffery; Nitro Express; Mauser action
7. .416 Rigby Magnum; Mauser action
8. .416 Taylor; pre-1964 Winchester action
9. .425 Westley Richards Magnum; Mauser action
10. .450/.400 Manton; Nitro Express; double-barrelled (three-inch case)
11. .458 Winchester Magnum; Winchester Model 70; pre-1964 action; standard and with extended magazine and shortened barrel
12. .470 Westley Richards; Nitro Express; double-barrelled
13. 12-bore Purdey Paradox; lethal ball shot

Lord Wolverton, hunting lions in Somaliland, had this to say of the Paradox:

The frontal heart shot.

345

Above: Bob Lee with two magnificent lions shot within minutes of each other with a .270 Winchester in Angola in the 1950s.

Below: With a heavy mane, expert knowledge of anatomy and extreme accuracy is required for the side neck shot. A soft-nosed heavy bullet at the heart is the best shot.

I had only with me my 12 bore Paradox but am quite satisfied with the results for breaking cover. I hit him in the heart and he gave me no further trouble. He measured 10 feet 7 inch before skinning from nose to tail.

Guns to be used for lions require very little comment, it being quite obvious that soft-nosed ammunition is the order of the day and none other. Having said that, it is worthy of note that most professional hunters will agree that in their experience cat's meat is tougher than antelope and even buffalo meat. Buffalo hide bears no relation to lion skin's texture. Once again, more lions have probably been accounted for with .375 rifles than any other calibre. In the use of this calibre rifle, the heaviest bullet made is best—a 300-grain soft-point Nosler type. Most of the lions I shot in my early days were shot with a .318 on a Mauser action using Kynoch bullets. I never used a telescope on a rifle until 1956.

My reader will have discovered that the element of surprise is essential in lion hunting and that when this is not possible, then an upgrade to a .470 double-barrelled rifle with 500-grain soft-pointed bullets is a wise choice. As a P.H. I never had the first shot at a lion, so I seldom used a .375, unless hunting for myself or on control work. Always I backed up with a .470, .416, .425, or .450/400. Again, a .378 Weatherby is an excellent cartridge, but it may pass right through the lion unless it is raked by the shot from end to end. If I had had a .470 with me in the blind, I should not have been mauled by a lion.

Shooting a lion with a small-calibre rifle—unless in dire circumstances—is foolhardy, but if done with total surprise and accuracy, it is certainly possible. My respected friend Bob Lee achieved this in Angola with his trusty .270, killing two huge maned lions in a couple of minutes with two shots. Men of Bob Lee's ability and dedication to accuracy and discipline are not often seen. Lions, as any reader will have gathered, do not die easily and have the capacity for unbelievable tenacity for life.

No discourse on lion hunting would be complete without mention of the Paradox. For the uninformed, this was a strongly made shotgun with the last three inches of the barrels rifled. Either barrel fired lethal ball accurately up to 40 yards. All the prestigious English gunsmiths made them. Using standard shot, they were excellent for bird shooting, and with 30-inch barrels they were suitable for geese, including spurwing geese, the heaviest of African geese, weighing up to 22 pounds. I preferred and owned a Purdey Paradox 12 bore. The Purdey patented spring-loaded, self-opening action was quicker to reload (see

'The Man-Eater of Darajani' in Chapter 5). The lethal ball shot would smash anything at close quarters, and I often shot bushbuck and impala with this most useful 12-bore shotgun at 30 to 40 yards.

LEOPARD GUNS:
CALIBRES, MAKERS, AND CARTRIDGES

My reader will have to forgive me for this long discourse on my favourite weapons and trophy. I have shot a very large number of leopards solely because of the challenging shooting it offers and the extended excitement and anticipation such a hunt provides. Moreover, there are a very large number of leopards in Africa, from the top of the highest mountain to the lowest coasts of the continent, even today. It is not an endangered species.

The frontal heart shot (lower) and neck shot (top). Remember the angle upwards at which the shot is fired and make slight allowances for trajectory.

I have shot leopards with the following guns:

1. .243 Winchester; Model 70; pre-1964 action
2. 6.5x54 Mannlicher Schonauer; Model 1903 carbine
3. .264 Winchester Magnum; Model 70; pre-1964 action
4. .270 Winchester; Model 70; pre-1964 action
5. 7x57 Mauser
6. 7mm Remington Magnum; Mauser action
7. .300 Winchester Magnum; Model 70; pre-1964 action
8. .300 Weatherby Magnum; Winchester Model 70; pre-1964 action
9. .300 Winchester H&H Magnum; pre-1964 action (it is possible my reader may not have heard of this cartridge and rifle; see the details later in this section)
10. .30-06 Springfield; Winchester Model 70; pre-1964 action
11. .318 Cogswell & Harrison; Accelerated Express
12. 8x56 Mannlicher Schonauer; Model 1908
13. 8x68 Brno
14. .338 Winchester Magnum; Model 70; pre-1964 action
15. .350 Rigby Magnum; Mauser action
16. .375 H&H Magnum; Winchester Model 70; pre-1964 action

I have not included any gun that I have used to finish off a leopard, e.g., a .32-calibre pistol. Very surprisingly, only on four occasions have I had to finish off a wounded leopard, and on no occasion was it charging us. There have, however, been a number of occasions when the leopard

The side neck and heart shots. By zeroing in beforehand, all these shots become quite possible.

has been found dead next day, but never with a damaged skin or one partly eaten by hyenas or other predators. (See my leopard hunting suggestions regarding the Tilley lamp in Chapter 6.) Since I have not covered the smaller calibres in previous sections in this chapter, they are so covered now.

I have also accounted for a large number of leopards with trap guns, including my Purdey Paradox 12 bore, some during the time when leopard were considered vermin.

1. .243 Winchester; Model 70; pre-1964 action

This calibre first came on the market in 1955. Winchester was the first company to manufacture it on a Model 70 action using a necked-down .308 case. Foremost among the American gun writers in supporting this calibre was the late Warren Page, whom I often saw when visiting the Camp Fire Club in New York state with my old friend Dick Ayer. Through Dick I acquired a 'super grade', one with a 6-power Kilmorgen Optical Co. scope; it was, and still is, a very great favourite calibre. It took me 30 years to shoot out the barrel, and today I have transferred my allegiance to a Ruger .243 carbine. The .243 Winchester I had restocked by Earl Milliron, but when I sold the .243 it was back in its super grade stock. The Milliron stock now graces my .300 Winchester H&H Magnum. Quite simply, I found this calibre to be the best gun to shoot leopards from a hide. This was for several rather obvious reasons:

- It was possible to be incredibly accurate.
- There was no kick.
- The rifle was light and easy to handle when crawling into the blind.
- The magazine held five rounds.
- The cartridges could be kept in an old .303 Army service rifle clip, so there were no rattles.
- There was a choice of 80- or 100-grain bullets, and I had a supply of 100-grain solids if required.

In every attempt to shoot a dangerous animal I never had a failure with this rifle or cartridge of any sort. The nearest rival to the .243 was the British Holland & Holland .244 Belted Rimless Magnum. This was a calibre invented by David Lloyd, an Englishman. The cartridge was a

.375 Magnum necked down to .244. However, the cost of the .243 Winchester Model 70 gave its competitors no chance.

Ballistics are:
100 grain; FMJ; 42 grains of powder; muzzle velocity is 2900 fps; muzzle energy is 1868 foot pounds

2. 6.5x54 Mannlicher Schonauer; Model 1903 carbine

This little rifle is a work of art. Anyone interested in and appreciative of the art form of a rifle cannot but admire the precise workmanship of this carbine. I acquired one from a Dutch South African settler in Tanganyika in the 1950s for very little money. It was complete with a rear sight and wind gauge, and apart from a few scratches on the wood, it was in excellent shape. Unfortunately, a ham-fisted local gunsmith made a hash of fitting it with scope mounts. This resulted in the action being mauled severely. However, that did not stop me from using it without the scope as a trap gun for leopard and with a scope for shooting leopard from a blind/hide. Like the .243, it was very accurate indeed at short range, but of course its velocity and muzzle energy were relatively low, and it therefore was, as its name implies, a carbine, useful for up to 250 yards.

It had limitations. However, the feed from the rotary magazine was a joy to operate, and it never failed me. The 160-grain bullet gives it remarkable killing power. It appears to outclass its nearest rival, the .257 Roberts. One has to have a love of the art form of this gun to warrant the possesion of one, as there are better calibres and cartridges available today for shooting leopards. I have never been without a rifle of this type and still use an 8x56 Mannlicher Schonauer 1908 Model when deer shooting in Europe.

Ballistics are:
160 grain soft point; FL; muzzle velocity is 2450 fps; muzzle energy is 2140 foot pounds

3. .264 Winchester Magnum; Model 70; pre-1964 action

In 1958 when this calibre was first placed upon the market, I never

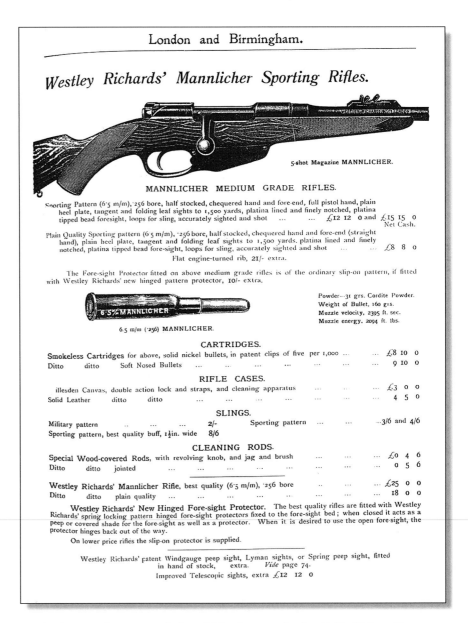

quite knew why we needed a .264 when we had a .243. This calibre was part of the velocity race that took place amongst the American arms manufacturers. Roy Weatherby produced the .257 Weatherby Magnum, and this was Winchester's apparently superior answer. The .264 bullet of 140 grains had a performance similar to that of the .257 Weatherby Magnum but with a heavier bullet and, consequently, a presumed better knockdown value. As my reader will note, this calibre was used very successfully by Jim Rikoff in his leopard-hunting experience in Kenya. One day I was in Fred Huntingdon's R.C.B.S. shop in Oroville, California,

when I chanced to see a secondhand .264 pre-1964 action Winchester in
the rack for sale for $200. I bought it and moved it safely to Africa.
Mounted with a 6 power Redfield scope, it was used as a hire gun for
clients and shot a considerable number of leopards. However, the bullet
vapourized if it touched so much as a feather on its way to the target.
Care had to be taken when shooting, and I found that Nosler bullets
were preferable.

Ballistics are:
140 grains soft point; FL; 61 grains of powder; muzzle velocity is
3100 fps; muzzle energy is 2988 foot pounds
Note: A 26-inch barrel is a normal length for this rifle.

4. .270 Winchester; Model 70; pre-1964 action

With my known and stated connection with my old friend and mentor Jack O'Connor, my reader will expect me to be a devotee of the .270.
The truth is, only to some extent. This is because I knew that if I had
fallen into the trap of putting all my eggs into the proverbial basket, I
would have denied myself the joy of trying many other rifles. The .270
is, however, a very, very useful calibre, and for leopards it is probably
just about ideal. In 1925, when Winchester first brought out this calibre
and cartridge for its Model 54 bolt-action rifle, claims for its long-range
accuracy caused considerable comment. (The cartridge was that of the
.30-06 Springfield necked down to fit the .270.) It became a sheep
hunter's rifle, and in this guise it was very successful. Its performance
could be varied by the use of 90-, 100-, 110-, 130-, 140-, or 150-grain
bullets. The flat-shooting capabilities of this rifle when used with the
100- or 110-grain bullets were impressive.

In Africa, if accuracy was given the rifle, the bullet did the job beautifully. For leopard it was quite simply 'mustard' with the 150-grain bullet. Naturally, I owned one for some 40 years but sold it at Christie's gun
sale only this year. However, do not make the mistake of trying to use
150- or 160-grain bullets at long range. If springbok was the target at
300 yards, the 110-grain Nosler, Hornaday, Speer, or Sierra was best to
retain accuracy. There are few men born who can judge two to four inches at 300 to 400 yards with consistent accuracy with a rifle that is zeroed
in to shoot a leopard the day before at 50 yards. More ammunition is
fired at targets than at animals if accuracy is to be ever present.

Ballistics are:

150 grains; FL; 52 grains of powder; muzzle velocity is 2800 fps; muzzle energy is 2612 foot pounds

5. 7x57 Mauser

The cartridge dates back to 1892, when it was first introduced by Mauser as a military cartridge. A durable cartridge and calibre to say the least, the original Model 98 Mauser actions are still much sought after by most gunsmiths. My comments on the building of custom-made guns under the .425 calibre are relative. *Mauser Bolt Rifles* by Ludwig E. Olson is the best reading on this remarkable survivor and engineering masterpiece. Model 98 Mausers were supplied in large quantities to more than 15 countries all over the world and are now being dismantled in large numbers for their actions by the custom gun trade. For those who have an interest in this aspect of Mauser guns, it is as well to remember that with modern chamber pressures it would be foolhardy not to case-harden any action that is proposed to be used in the building of a rifle for present-day use.

There must have been a huge number of leopards shot with this rifle. I used this calibre—often as a trap gun—always with 150-grain soft-pointed bullets. I bought my first 7x57 Mauser from the Van Rooyen family in Tanganyika in 1951 and only recently sold it. Van Rooyen Sr. (see Chapter 2) had purchased it new in 1899 and used it in the Boer War against the British. It was well kept, and the barrel was in good condition, though worn. My local dentist and fellow hunter, Jeremy Preston, is now its proud possessor. It has been customized and rebarrelled by John Rigby & Co. When 'Baas' Van Rooyen handed me the gun and I the cash to him, the look on his face told me that the Boer War was over or he would not have sold it—especially to an Englishman 52 years later!

Ballistics are:

150 grains; FL; 41.5 grains of powder; muzzle velocity is 2700 fps; muzzle energy is 2429 foot pounds

6. 7mm Remington Magnum; Mauser action

Remington joined the competition amongst American and European rifle manufacturers for high-velocity, flat-shooting rifles with this cartridge in 1962, when the new 700 Series of bolt-action rifles was produced. There were many wildcat cartridges of this type produced in the U.S.A., Ackley being the one that comes easily to mind. Until Remington launched it, the cartridge had been rather surprisingly overlooked. Over the years, I believe a good 40 percent of my clients came to Africa with this calibre, many on my recommendation. Using a 150-grain bullet it did all that a .30-06 Springfield would do, and better. It was flat shooting, and with Nosler bullets it did a great job with a good, solid knockdown value. It was a perfect gun for leopard and accounted for a great many for my safari clients without ever giving us a problem. However, as in the case of all leopard shooting, preparation for the vital shot was essential, and zeroing in the gun beforehand was of paramount importance.

The velocity achieved by this cartridge occasionally led to the bullet's exiting the leopard and leaving a substantial hole and some damage to the hide. Ed Quinn had once presented me with a beautiful 7mm Remington Magnum on a Model 98 Mauser action stocked by Earl Milliron. The cartridge packed a terrific punch, so much so that the shock value upon the leopard was such that if you were quick and prepared, a second shot was just possible either in or below the tree.

Ballistics are:
150 grains; soft point; FL; 62 grains of powder; muzzle velocity is 3000 fps; muzzle energy is 3198 foot pounds

7. .300 Winchester Magnum; Model 70; pre-1964 action

This calibre as an all-round gun for medium game in Africa is on a par with, and almost identical in performance to, the .300 Weatherby Magnum. As Weatherby was the precursor with velocity at that time, it was a little surprising that this calibre was not produced by Winchester till 1963, only a short time before the disappointing decision to change the Winchester action. Winchester already had the Model 70 of pre-1964 chambered to the .300 Holland & Holland Magnum. When handling the rifles, care should be taken to check the identity of each of the calibres of these guns, since Winchester did not stamp the rifle as Holland & Holland Magnum but simply as '.300 Winchester'. The earlier .300 Holland & Holland was not, therefore, the same as the later .300 Winchester Magnum.

There is a great choice of bullet weights for this rifle, from 110-grain to double the weight at 220-grain. The low weights provided altogether too much velocity for a leopard at 40 yards and simply blew a huge hole in the skin on exit, tending to give the taxidermist a problem and the client a bill and a bloody picture of the trophy. I believe the 200-grain bullet did the best job of shock and damage, and, therefore, knockdown value. Even so there were invariably exit holes. The difference in bullet weights commercially available and the remarkable performance of this rifle ensured that I had one as well as the .300 Holland & Holland Magnum.

Ballistics are:
200 grain; soft point; FL; 68 grains of powder; muzzle velocity is 2950 fps; muzzle energy is 3866 foot pounds

8. .300 Weatherby Magnum; Winchester Model 70; pre-1964 action

As described elsewhere, this cartridge more than any other revolutionized post-war thinking on African rifles and cartridges. The late Herb Klein, who was a friend for many years and with whom I shared an African campfire for many evenings, was a financial supporter and mentor of the late Roy Weatherby at the time the cartridge was developed in 1944 and came on the market in 1948. Herb had been furnished with the most beautiful set of Weatherby rifles it was possible to imagine. His favourite, 'Betsy', was the .300. It was for some time a sheep hunter's dream, and both he and George Parker from Arizona shot several grand slams of North American sheep with this calibre and make of rifle. Herb also pioneered hunting in Asia for argali and Marco Polo sheep, and here, too, the Weatherby .300 was just the rifle needed. Nosler came up with the bullets with an 'H' principle that has proved most durable. R.W.S. in Europe, with its 'H' mantle bullet developed on the same principle, was also a very successful manufacturer of bullets that held well together when sent on their way at greatly increased velocities.

In 1953, round the campfire on safari in Kenya, there sat Herb on the one hand with a Weatherby .300 and Jack O'Connor on the other with a .270. My reader requires little imagination as to the conversation, to which was added the effects of an occasional scotch.

A very large number of leopards have been shot in Africa with this calibre. The heavier bullet of 250 grains is preferable to that of 110 grains for the reasons already described for the .300 Winchester and .300 Holland & Holland Magnum. The cartridge case of the .300 Weatherby is, by the way, developed from the .300 H&H case.

Ballistics are:
250 grains; soft point; FL; 69 grains of powder; muzzle velocity is 2350 fps; muzzle energy is 3066 foot pounds

9. .300 Winchester Holland & Holland Magnum; pre-1964 action

This high-velocity cartridge first made by Holland & Holland in 1925 on a Model '98 Mauser action was known as Holland's Super '30'. For some 10 years no other rifle manufacturers picked up this cartridge. Griffin & Howe, the New York firm, played a major part in its improved popularity in the U.S.A., making a large number of them. Finally, in 1935, Winchester made a Model 70 .300 H & H Magnum, but it was not endorsed with Holland & Holland, simply .300 Magnum. Remington followed suit with a Model 721 and subsequently a Model 700. This calibre was then set as one of the most enduring and satisfactory performers yet seen and is now standard production in almost every rifle manufacturer's lists. In later years it has suffered from the advent of both the .300 Weatherby and the .300 Winchester Magnum. For leopard it is a most satisfactory gun and cartridge, and many are the settlers and farmers of Africa who have one in their armoury. I had one on safari for many years, using it for some time as a basic gun for ladies to shoot the bigger animals, such as greater kudu and eland. The heavier bullet of 220 grains I preferred for leopard for the same reasons as with the .300 Winchester Magnum and .300 Weatherby Magnum.

Ballistics are:
220 grain; soft point; FL; 63 grains of powder; muzzle velocity is 3562 fps; muzzle energy is 2700 foot pounds

10. .30-06 Springfield; Winchester Model 70; pre-1964 action

This is one of the few military cartridges that seem to have remained unimproved to any great extent. Originally made as a .300 calibre rifle by Springfield in 1906, it has always been known as the .30-06. I venture to

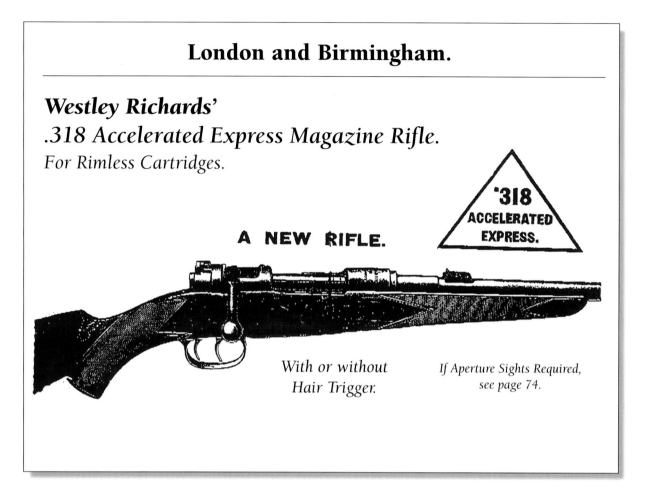

London and Birmingham.

Westley Richards'
.318 Accelerated Express Magazine Rifle.
For Rimless Cartridges.

A NEW RIFLE.

'318 ACCELERATED EXPRESS.

With or without
Hair Trigger.

If Aperture Sights Required,
see page 74.

suggest that, from my experience, one of the main reasons this calibre has survived is its ideal combination of velocity, energy, and bullet weight, which has consistently produced a reliable knockdown value. Certainly when used on leopards with a 220-grain bullet, in nearly all cases the bullet comes to rest right under the skin of the leopard on the opposite side to that from which it had entered. It must be one of the most used calibres of rifle in the world and certainly in Africa. It is indeed a tribute to its prowess and reliability that gunmakers throughout the world have failed to remove it from its place in popularity and instead, on the basis of 'if you can't beat 'em, join 'em', secured its reputation by making their guns in this calibre also. For the whole of my career as a P.H. I always had one, using it as a pot gun, trap gun, and even on one occasion in personal defence of my life. It eventually came to the end of its life with me in the auction room as a used gun. It was used most effectively on many leopards. There were many bullet weights to chose from: 110, 125, 130, 150, 165, 180, 190, 200, 220, and 250 grain. The 180 and 220 grain were preferred by most African hunters; 220 grain was the best for leopard in my experience.

Ballistics are:

220 grain; soft point; FL; muzzle velocity is 2500 fps; muzzle energy is 3054 foot pounds

11. .318 Cogswell & Harrison; Accelerated Express

This cartridge and rifle with performance similar to that of the .30-06 Springfield was developed by Westley Richards in 1910. In my early 20s I had to take note of the cost of everything down to the last detail, as my salary in Africa was equivalent to $1,000, or £350, per year. The name of Westley Richards cost approximately £10 more than Cogswell & Harrison, so Cogswell & Harrison it had to be. I used the rifle very extensively on lion (see Chapter 5). Although it had a barrel two inches longer than the .30-06, it was more accurate when used with open sights. I never used a scope on it till 1960, when I met up with Ed Hilliard, the president of Redfield Gunsight Company, who had just put Redfield on the map. The ammunition is no longer made and, regretfully, the calibre is virtually obsolete. It was always made by British gunmakers with a Mauser action and good, strong three-leafed back sights to 300 yards. For a customer this rifle is easily made today by American gunmakers in the manner described elsewhere. Such is the revival of interest in these original calibres that I am sure a private manufacturer of ammunition could be found. I shot several leopards with this rifle using open sights with 250-grain soft-pointed bullets in Ethiopia and Somaliland, including my prized black leopard.

Ballistics are:

250 grain; soft point; FL; muzzle velocity is 2400 fps; muzzle energy is 3200 foot pounds

12. 8x56 Mannlicher Schonauer; Model 1908

Mannlicher Schonauer introduced this calibre in 1908. The pride of

357

possession of this beautifully made carbine overcame any disadvantages, of which, in reality, there was only one: mounting a modern telescope on this rifle of between 4- and 6-power was not an easy task. The inevitable outcome was a scope mounted high over the action, which, for shooting from a hide/blind, had the obvious disadvantage of requiring a bigger spy hole from which to shoot. An artful leopard did not need to be given this aid to escape. In spite of this, both my clients and I used this carbine very successfully for some years. I recall its being used to shoot three leopards by three clients on one trip in Uganda. It remains in my possession today, being used on deer-culling work.

Ballistics are:

220 grain; soft point; FL by Kynoch; muzzle velocity is 2200 fps; muzzle energy is 2015 foot pounds

13. 8x68 Brno

A Brno (Mauser) was made by a Czechoslovakian company and chambered to the R.W.S. cartridge that was first produced before the 1939–45 War. This is a nifty little rifle, beautifully made on what appears at first sight to be a modern, customised Mauser action. It is a grossly underestimated cartridge in my humble opinion. Its ballistics and performance are superior to the .300 Weatherby, .300 Winchester Magnum, and .300 Holland & Holland Magnum. It has a rimless and beltless cartridge case, but only one bullet weight of 220 grains. It is in the class of performance of the .338 Winchester Magnum. I have used this gun and cartridge extensively on all game, including lion. Scope mounts are much higher set than on American-made rifles.

Ballistics are:

220 grain; soft point; FL; 67 grains of powder; muzzle velocity is 2700 fps; muzzle energy is 3562 foot pounds

14. .338 Winchester Magnum; Model 70; pre-1964 action

I did not see or handle this calibre until 1960, and when I did I saw at once that it was really a lady's .375 and her gun for all seasons and countries. It is just that fraction less fierce on you than the .375, and I feel that a 6-power scope would survive better upon it than it would on a .375. I have had one as a hire gun for many years. So successful has it been that I became quite attached to it and, though little used, have never sold it. So sorry was I to see it go that I actually bought it back out of an auction in which I had entered it! Bullet weights can be obtained from 200, 210, 225, 230, and 250 grains. Either the 230 grain or 250 grain would be excellent for leopard, and so it has proved on many occasions. I tried very hard to convince Eleanor O'Connor that she would be better off with the .338 than her .30-06, but I had little luck in that argument, much to the amusement of Jack.

Ballistics are:
225 grain; soft point; FL; muzzle velocity is 2780; muzzle energy is 3860 foot pounds

15. .350 Rigby Magnum; Mauser action

This rifle was produced by John Rigby & Co., using a rimless cartridge, shortly after the turn of the century. It was designed for medium game in Africa, Asia, and North America and was popular for a time. The rimmed case for a double-barrelled .350 was also made but failed in comparison to Holland & Holland's .375 and has not been produced for many years. Once again, Rigby was a great advocate of inexpensive Mauser actions, and virtually all .350 Rigby Magnums were made using this action. The Kynoch bullets made for this gun in 250-grain solid and soft bullets held together well. As recorded in Chapter 2, I found this gun too light—it dealt the firer some punishment! No doubt with some custom improvements of today and some assistance from a 4- to 6-power scope, it would be close to the .338 in performance. To me a .338 is a superior calibre for moving the 250-grain bullet. For leopards my comments are the same as for the .338. It is a moot question as to whether the exit hole would damage the skin altogether, but with the lower muzzle energy and muzzle velocity it may well remain on the underside of the skin on the opposite side to entry. To state the obvious, it would be better used on a bigger rather than a smaller leopard.

Ballistics are:
250 grain; FL; muzzle velocity is 2625 fps; muzzle energy is 3440 foot pounds

16. .375 Holland & Holland Magnum; Winchester Model 70; pre-1964 action

L to R: The heart, neck, and brain shots from the side.

Of course one has to mention the .375 Holland & Holland Magnum, for so many of us have described it as the one gun with which a hunter could take the world over and shoot any trophy required. This is very true, but we would all, I am sure, admit that in all honesty this is too much gun for leopard. The .375 Holland & Holland Magnum is a belted rimless cartridge and is listed as standard by the major gun manufacturers of the U.S.A.—Winchester, Remington, and Ruger, to name a few. It is probably as synonymous with African hunting as the .470 Nitro Express. It has to be the ideal calibre on the market of medium bore, not that the .378 Weatherby is not also, but the .378 would destroy a leopard, whereas the .375 would leave a great deal of it. On a cat with a pretty skin that is the trophy on which so much time, money, and effort have been spent, you do not need a .375's performance at 40 yards to kill it. For myself, if I had a big 'tom' in my sights using a .375, I might just use a 300-grain FMJ bullet to do the job, and I certainly would if I had no option but to use a .378. For leopard I do believe that with modern cartridges and bullets it is just a little too much gun. I feel that most of my peers in the P.H. fraternity would agree with me. Although the laws of most of the countries in which we have all operated as professional hunters and outfitters for many years insist that the .375 calibre is the minimum for hunting dangerous game, I doubt whether there is one of us that has not broken this regulation by shooting a leopard with a smaller calibre. I have shot leopard, and so have my clients, with the .375 Holland & Holland Magnum, but not from choice.

Ballistics are:

300 grain; soft point or FMJ; FL; muzzle velocity is 2530 fps; muzzle energy is 4265 foot pounds

HIPPO GUNS:
CALIBRES, MAKERS, AND CARTRIDGES

I have shot and killed hippopotamus with the following guns:

1.   .243 Winchester; Model 70; pre-1964 action

2. .264 Winchester Magnum; Model 70; pre-1964 action
3. .270 Winchester; Model 70; pre-1964 action
4. .300 Winchester H&H Magnum; Winchester Model 70; pre-1964 action
5. .300 Weatherby Magnum; Winchester Model 70; pre-1964 action
6. 7x57 Mauser
7. 8x60 Brno
8. .303 British Army service rifle (of 1916 vintage)
9. .318 Cogswell & Harrison
10. .350 Rigby Magnum
11. .375 Holland & Holland Magnum; double-barrelled; Royal Grade; flanged cartridge
12. .375 Winchester; Model 70; pre-1964 action
13. .378 Weatherby Magnum
14. .404 Jeffery; Nitro Express; Mauser action
15. .416 Rigby Magnum; Mauser action
16. .425 Westley Richards Magnum; Mauser action
17. .450/400 Manton; Nitro Express; double-barrelled (three-inch case)
18. .458 Winchester Magnum; Model 70; pre-1964 action
19. .470 Westley Richards; Nitro Express; double-barrelled
20. .577 Westley Richards; Nitro Express; double-barrelled

L to R: The brain (ear) shot and the neck shot (only if exposed above water).

As my reader will observe, there are 20 different calibres of guns with which I have shot hippo. Ninety percent of the hippo shot were to feed indigenous people who suffered from disturbance of their fishing activities and in some cases the destruction of canoe ferries and rice cultivation, etc. These calibre rifles probably disposed of some 400 to 500 of these huge and cantankerous animals.

A FINAL EXAMINATION OF KNOCKDOWN VALUE

During my research into my reasons for becoming so interested in firearms, the overriding factor that I came to acknowledge was the essential element of 'knockdown value', or what some people might call 'shock value'. I wanted to be sure that the animal died without suffering.

I was privileged many years ago to meet John Taylor on two occasions. For a great deal of time during these meetings we talked of his conception of knockdown value. There have been many hours of dis-

DETAIL OF STANDARD FITTINGS

FORESIGHT — the famous Westley Richards Hinged Foresight Assembly is a standard fitting. The protector is spring loaded and snaps firmly into the covered or uncovered positions. The illustration shows the enamelled folding night sight lying flush. The normal foresight has been inclined silver bead of approx. .085 in. diameter.

BACKSIGHT—Medium-wide V pattern sights. The fixed standard inclines rearward to avoid reflection, is inlaid with platinum line and regulated and marked for maximum flat—shooting range according to calibre. The two spring leaves are also lined and marked for convenient additional ranges.

TRIGGER.—A specially made modern trigger mechanism is fitted. It is adjustable for weight of pull and absolutely eliminates creep or drag.

GRIP CAP.—A steel case-hardened grip cap with spring loaded trap is fitted, and is convenient for carrying spare foresights.

DETAIL OF EXTRA FITTINGS

APERTURE SIGHT.

This retractable aperture is mounted in the bolt head, so as to allow open or telescopic sights to be used without interference. It does not interfere with the grip of the rifle as do folding apertures, and yet remains ready for instant use. The elevating disc is rotated clockwise to raise the aperture stem which clicks firmly into position at correct elevations. The various ranges for which elevation clicks are zeroed, are engraved in the face of the disc. Photograph on left shows Aperture Sight elevated for use. When an aperture sight is fitted the fixed standard open sight is removed leaving the folding leaves only, since with an aperture the foresight only should be in view.

TELESCOPIC SIGHT MOUNTING.

Westley Richards Low Detachable Mounts are available in all standard diameters for fitting to Mauser type and double barrelled rifles. Full details of the mounting and of the recommended telescopic sights are given on a separate page. This mounting allows instant removal of the telescope and leaves the top of the action clear for use of open or aperture sights. The photograph of Aperture Sight above shows the bases of the W.R. Low Detachable Mount on the Mauser action.

cussions too with Jack O'Connor, Warren Page, Roy Weatherby, Herb Klein, Bob Chatfield- Taylor, and many others on this subject. I cannot recall anyone who, with experience in big-game hunting, would not readily agree that the effect of the bullet is based upon its velocity, size, and quality relative to the weight and size of the animal at which it is launched.

For the sake of discussion, one must take for granted that if a modern firearm's bullet is aimed with accuracy at an animal for which it is suitable medicine, the animal will die instantaneously. But what happens if the firer is not quite as accurate as he should be? Then we have a wounded animal that is suffering and very dangerous. It is here that if the bullet carries the punch brought about by its weight and velocity, coupled with proper expansion of the bullet on impact—if it is so required and the form of the projectile is maintained in flight—the knockdown value is so important. Not only is the animal temporarily immobilized, but also the opportunity for a second shot to kill it cleanly is manifestly possible.

To throw a little more factual material into the discussion, I am convinced that the meat and bone consistency of elephant, rhino, buffalo, and hippo are fractionally different and totally different, respectively, from those of the cat family. I have no doubt that this can be a factor in selecting the best cartridge, velocity, bullet weight, and construction of the projectile. All the hunter asks is that if the animal is to be shot, it is killed as quickly as possible, with the absolute minimum of suffering. It is my view that the best knockdown value is when the bullet stops in the animal, preferably on the far side from the impact just under the skin.

Today's hunting fraternity's permissiveness in allowing videos to be made and sold of animals wounded and repeatedly shot has no place in the ethics of my generation of professional hunter. This merely supplies the anti-hunters with tailor-made ammunition in their efforts to discredit hunters and bring hunting and the ownership of firearms to an end.

Given my experience, it is safe to say that, barring a very few persons employed on game control, it is now very unlikely that any P.H. of today's vintage can possibly have had the experience of those of my vintage in accruing the knowledge of the true value of a bullet with the best knockdown value. Game control work that was common in my early years is now nonexistent. Most of my contemporaries had experienced shooting 20 to 30 buffalo in rough terrain and thick bush before even filling in their P.H. licence application, this being coupled with at least 15 or 20 elephant and a similar number of lions and leopards. In all cases, this took at least two or three years to achieve for virtually nothing more than the cost of food and ammunition and certainly for no profit.

EPILOGUE

If

If you can keep your head when all about you
Are losing theirs and blaming it on you,
If you can trust yourself when all men doubt you,
But make allowance for their doubting too;
If you can wait and not be tired by waiting,
Or being lied about, don't deal in lies,
Or being hated, don't give way to hating,
And yet don't fool too good, nor talk too wise.

If you can dream—and not make dreams your master;
If you can think—and not make thoughts your aim;
If you can meet with Triumph and Disaster
And treat those two impostors just the same;
If you can bear to hear the truth you've spoken
Twisted by knaves to make a trap for fools,
Or watch the things you gave your life to, broken,
And stoop and build 'em up with worn-out tools.

If you can make one heap of all your winnings
And risk it on one turn of pitch-and-toss,
And lose, and start again at your beginnings

In spite of all the problems we faced, fortunately, human nature is such that we only remember the good times.

—J.K.-H.

And never breathe a word about your loss;
If you can force your heart and nerve and sinew
To serve your turn long after they are gone,
And so hold on when there is nothing in you
Except the Will which says to them: 'Hold on!'

If you can talk with crowds and keep your virtue,
Or walk with Kings—nor lose the common touch
If neither foes nor loving friends can hurt you,
If all men count with you, but none too much;
If you can fill the unforgiving minute
With sixty seconds' worth of distance run,
Yours is the Earth and everything that's in it,
And—which is more—you'll be a Man, my son!

—Rudyard Kipling, "If"
Rewards and Fairies

In reviewing this book, I am struck by the fact that there is so much that can be told from the 146 000 feet of 16mm Kodak colour film; the 12 tin trunks of records, maps, and diaries; and the three boxes of pictures and negatives that have accumulated over nearly 50 years of travel, not only in Africa but also in the Middle East. As far as possible I have followed the hunting of the dangerous game of Africa, adding for interest's sake a little history and geography where appropriate. The opening up of the safari and tourist industry of Botswana is a story of pioneering tourism in itself. So, too, are the deprecations perpetuated upon the wildlife of East Africa, Uganda being a story on its own of particular savagery.

Behind all these experiences are the disappointments and disasters that one inevitably suffered in careers spent in this type of environment, which largely go unrecognised by those outside Africa who wish to hunt there with a P.H.'s outfitting, advice, and safe passage. Although I attended safaris in Zambia and Rhodesia (Zimbabwe), I did not at any time feel inclined to hunt there. I was not particularly interested in ranch hunting in the latter and was glad I did not participate in the former, as it had unstable wildlife policies at that time.

Amongst those who achieved considerable fame in America and made amazing collections of African wildlife were Herb Klein, George Parker, Berry Brookes, Basil Bradbury, and a host of others too numerous to name.

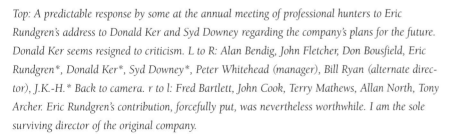

Top: A predictable response by some at the annual meeting of professional hunters to Eric Rundgren's address to Donald Ker and Syd Downey regarding the company's plans for the future. Donald Ker seems resigned to criticism. L to R: Alan Bendig, John Fletcher, Don Bousfield, Eric Rundgren*, Donald Ker*, Syd Downey*, Peter Whitehead (manager), Bill Ryan (alternate director), J.K.-H.* Back to camera. r to l: Fred Bartlett, John Cook, Terry Mathews, Allan North, Tony Archer. Eric Rundgren's contribution, forcefully put, was nevertheless worthwhile. I am the sole surviving director of the original company.

* Director

Above: What this book looked like as it was being written. Even more pandemonium ensued upon the arrival of my editor, Bob Newman. The retired U.S. Marine drank all my best scotch, too!

Above left: Essential record-keeping was conducted for all trophies for the client, game department, and company (Kenya, 1966).

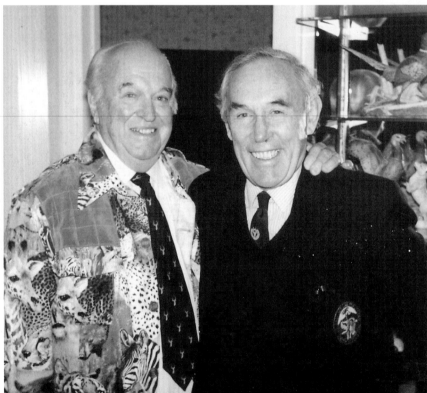

Above and right: Joel Loveridge (past president of Safari Club International) and I have shared 40 years of hunting and a wonderful friendship. Thirty-seven years separate the photos.

Many of them became good and valued friends, although they never hunted with me or any organisation with which I was involved. In all the some
700 safaris for which I was responsible with my partners for putting in the
field over 45 years, I only once had a client who bounced a cheque, of
$113, on our company! On only four occasions did I not see eye to eye with
a client. Three of the clients I had been warned about before their arrival.
On one famous occasion, after my having been insulted by a client for long
enough, he received a good hiding and was sent home. Interestingly, he
never opened his mouth about it and passed away recently.

There were enormous disappointments and financial disasters. I have
one very clear memory of setting out on the first safari that Frank Miller,
Lionel Palmer, and I did in Bechuanaland. We shook hands and looked
each other straight in the eyes, and I said, 'Well, we now have just £100
left between us. If we don't come back with a successful safari, we will be
out of business!' Failure was unacceptable. California state Senator
McAteer, our client who was also a friend, knew just how hard we had

*Top: Our safari into Bechuanaland,
1965. No road and into the
unknown. Lionel Palmer is leading,
followed by Frank Miller.*

*Bottom: Famous friends and out-
standing hunters of the 1950s and
1960s. L to R: René Babault, Herb
Klien, Berry Brooks, and Basil
Bradbury.*

369

One of my safari camps in Kenya Masailand.

worked to make the safari a success. His name still graces one of the camp-sites in the Matsibe area of the Okavango Swamps, though few, if anyone, know why it is so named. He was quite simply the first safari client to hunt there and travel into the northern sand tongue area.

The physical hardships that we endured were remarkable. Twenty-three times I drove the distance of 2158 miles from Nairobi in Kenya to Maun in Bechuanaland with trucks and Land Rovers, sometimes even with some of my hunting clients who warmed to our efforts and were happy to share our privations and experiences. On a memorable occasion when my wife and I had lost a wheel on our Land Rover, causing us to arrive late at night in Iringa in southern Tanganyika, we found our rooms had been let to others. We slept the night in the Kilimanjaro Hotel, which turned out to be a brothel! On several occasions we were held up by drunken, gun-toting policemen at roadblocks. Once, in Zambia with Georgio Verolini, we spent four hours standing up against some chain-link fencing with our fingers hooked into the wire to keep our arms in a position of surrender. Often the trucks and cars were stopped by minor customs officials looking for a bribe. If we refused to pay, the equipment was then taken apart and strewn about the road. It took hours for us to repack the vehicles.

The logistics and consequent administrative challenge, on reflection, were 50 percent of my motivation in providing the opportunity for my clients to hunt in the areas in which I had established myself. This, many years later, I summised, was a result of a reasonable education in geography, history, and economics. Added to this was my love of flying, exploration, and hunting, which became the culmination of all the effort and planning that had been put into the enterprise. Our plans, though always

well made and plausible, were often confounded by bad luck or fate. Very fortunately no mishap resulted in a mortality, but several resulted in financial loss. On many occasions my clients asked me why a safari was so expensive. When I explained all the risks and investments we endured to place them in front of a trophy buffalo, elephant, or rhino, etc., they began to understand that we followed our profession for the love of hunting and the satisfaction it gave us to overcome the difficulties that we had before us.

Only due to the weather patterns in East Africa (Kenya and Tanganyika and to some extent Uganda) could we expect to hunt for a period in excess of five months. Elsewhere for the remaining seven months there was little to do except brush up on experience and find more clients. This still left you kicking your heels for a good four months.

In spite of this, as well as the cost of living and educating one's children—which had to be done from sometimes the most inaccessible places—the major safari clubs in the U.S.A. demanded that we offer free safaris and outfitting for as much as a fifth of our income for auction at their conventions. I have always felt that this unreasonable demand upon a professional hunter, struggling to maintain himself on the smell of an oil rag, was a shabby practice. Fortunately for me, our company's reputation had little need to take notice of what was believed to be, at that time, necessary publicity. It seemed most unfair to me that a young and newly licensed professional hunter should obtain recognition only if he bought

The professional hunters and management of Ker & Downey Safaris in 1960. Probably the most successful safari company in East Africa at that time. Standing l to r: Peter Becker, Kris Aschan, Sol Rabb (company secretary), Bill Ryan, Allan North, John Cook, Fred Bartlett, George Barrington, Tony Archer, John Dugmore, Terry Mathews. Seated l to r: Roy Home, J.K.-H. (director), Syd Downey (director), Jack Block (managing director), Donald Ker (director), Eric Rundgren (director), Ronald Stephens (manager).

371

Top: We sent the truck on ahead to make camp in Lukwati, southern Tanganyika. It was one of those safaris! We had it out and running in two days (1961).

Above and right: The death of 'Dungu,' the name our staff gave to the ex-military 10-ton truck. The chassis twisted through 45 degrees. Note the two 50-gallon fuel tanks and water tanks. 'Our man in Nairobi,' Georgio Verolini, had it running again in four days. He was quite simply a mechanical genius (1968).

himself into notoriety at a hunting convention. It could also have been a self-destructive tactic, as the client who bought the hunt ran the risk of getting bottom-dollar value and the leftovers of the quotas of game available. Naturally, if the client had never been before, he hardly knew what he missed. This system does little for the hard-working agent who promotes hunting safaris and with whom any P.H. was to have an honest and long-standing relationship. It lost the agent potential clients and undermined his price structure. The incredible struggles with insecurity, bureaucracy, supplies of food, and spare parts that present-day outfitters are forced to endure make the professional hunter a candidate for financial support

Above: A gathering of "old time" professional hunters of East Africa, Botswana, Namibia, and the Republic of South Africa.

Back row:

Neville Peake (1982–1995; Botswana)*

John Kingsley-Heath (1949–1977 and 1990–1995—East Africa; 1962-1978—Botswana)

Harry Selby (1945–1961—East Africa; 1962–1995—Botswana)

Lionel Palmer (1962–1994—Botswana; 1970–1975—East Africa)

Soren Lindstrom (1965–1976—East Africa; 1977–1995—Botswana)

Peter Becker (1955–1965—East Africa; 1965–1968—Botswana)*

Willie Engelbrecht (1962–1965—East Africa; 1966–1995—Botswana)

Peter Hepburn (1975–1995—Botswana)

Mark Kyriacou (1976–1995—Botswana)

Front row:

Kevin Chadwick (1978–1995—Botswana)

Charles Williams (1976–1995—Botswana)

Daryl Dandridge (1965–1995—Botswana)

Don Lindsay (1966–1986—Botswana)

Doug Wright (1962–1995—Botswana; 1970–1975—East Africa)

Bassie Maartens (1959–1995—Namibia, Rep. of South Africa; 1962–1966—Botswana)

Cecil Riggs (1969–1995—Botswana)

Willie Phillips (1969–1995—Botswana)

* Denotes deceased

rather than a contributor to third-hand wildlife projects and the consequent employment of others with tendencies towards corruption.

In the final analysis, all the costs of every kind went into the price that the client paid. By and large, the price of a safari reflected the cost of insecurity to which the organisation was subjected by the government of the country in which it operated. Safari prices were cheaper in South Africa and more expensive as one went northwards. I proposed on several occasions that if money was needed, then an amount not exceeding an agreed percentage should be voluntarily levied on a safari that was contracted by a member of a safari club and his chosen P.H. and outfitter. In some cases clients would have been glad to match this money and duly receive tax credit. I believe this would have removed the grounds for hard feeling between all concerned, more particularly if the P.H. fraternity were allowed to be involved in the administration of the funds and, more especially, if such funds could be utilised in the country in which the P.H. operated.

There were dirt roads that were poorly maintained. Accidents were inevitable, and loss of earnings as a consequence brought us considerable hardship. No bank would lend a safari operator money on a normal business basis. None of my contemporaries were excluded from these misfortunes, and some perished in disastrous accidents. I feel certain that it was a fact that the prospective American client and the safari club to which he was wont to belong had no detailed idea of just what was involved in the upkeep and maintenance of an efficient P.H., properly equipped in the field, between 1960 and 1978.

In spite of all the problems we faced, fortunately, human nature is such that we only really remember the good times that are of such consequence that they provide the motivation for continuing to search for new experiences and new pastures.

One particularly amusing incident comes to mind when we were making the 'hell run' via Victoria Falls to Botswana in the 'Botswana bus' (Land Rover) with Syb and Joyce West, Peter and Fran Dwyer, and Peter's brother, Richard. We arrived in convoy at the bridge over Victoria Falls on the Zambia side en route to Botswana. On all three Land Rovers' front bumpers were strapped two jerricans, one on each side. We were coming into Rhodesia with fuel on board, which was not allowed. Rhodesia's surrounding African states were intent on imposing sanctions upon Rhodesia in every possible way. The officer of the customs post enquired of me as to what was contained in the jerricans on the front of the cars. (There were more in the back of the vehicles—undisclosed.)

'Petrol', I said.

'It is illegal to take this spirit into that country', he said.

'Shall I fill up the tanks?' I asked.

'No, you may not do that because the answer is the same', he replied. Calling an aide, he calmly took the fire buckets off the wall of the customs post that were filled with sand. Pouring the sand onto the ground, he then invited me to fill up the buckets with my petrol. I obliged, and we were allowed to proceed. Our straight faces exploded into laughter as we reached the Rhodesian side! Once our mirth was explained we were joined by the Rhodesian customs officers in our amusement. Such incidents are remembered, the worst thankfully forgotten.

One disaster that has materially affected the contents of this book occurred in Arusha, Tanganyika. Thieves broke through the concrete wall of the industrial premises that comprised the stores of Ker & Downey Safaris (Tanganyika) Ltd. In fact, the outside wall was also the wall of the armoury. Fortunately there were no guns or ammunition there at the time. One large box of mine was there. It contained silver given to me by my family and all my pictures of hunting in former days. The thieves took my albums of photographs, the silver, and most of my valuable papers—birth certificates, etc. The thieves and photos were never found. I have only been able to salvage some pictorial records of those days from the pictures I sent to my mother in England.

The strain upon one's marital relations was enormous. Long absences from home, lack of communications, lack of finance for home maintenance, rent, school fees, etc., all led to great sacrifices having to be made by both partners. I never knew a rich professional hunter. If there was one, he kept it a dark secret. One or two merely became rich until their marriages dissolved. This, added to other misfortunes, came to bear on their operations.

I well remember one day in Maun when I was about to sit down to lunch in my home by the bridge with my eldest son, Michael, and Dick Ayer's son, also called Dick, and there was a knock at the door. It was the police. They wished to borrow the boat to look for the body of a man whom they believed had been ritually murdered. The boys, filled with excitement, demanded that they be allowed to accompany us. We set off in my 18-foot aluminium boat with a 20-horsepower outboard motor. After some searching we found the body and towed it to the shore. The police performed the grisly task of tying the rope onto the body, which had indeed been ritually murdered and mutilated. When we returned to the house, lunch came on the table but the boys ate nothing. It was their first view of a dead human being.

Top: The arrival of new responsibilities—Nigel Kingsley-Heath.

Middle: 'Don't let him get out of the park!' Hugh Kingsley-Heath some years before his job as the artist responsible for the illustrations that grace this book.

Bottom: Nigel Kingsley-Heath catching his first big one!

The full circle—Nigel Kingsley-Heath hunting on his own in north-west Tanzania.

Prices of safaris rocketed. Not so much because of food and drink, but because of the price of insecurity in the countries in which one operated and the constant and ever-increasing greed of those who controlled the wildlife assets and the consequent *hongo* that was levied upon those who, after all, were only improving the assets of tourism within their countries. When Kenya shut down hunting in 1977, the professional hunters of East Africa lost large sums of irreplaceable cash, which in many cases was simply pocketed by the officials in charge of wildlife. Concession fees that had been paid for the coming year's operations were never returned.

I experienced one instance of good fortune when an irate client was no longer able to hunt due to the closure of hunting in Kenya and unable to obtain his deposit back most immediately due to the interminable time the Kenya foreign exchange controls took to authorise the export of U.S. dollars. He persuaded the bank in New York that the cheque made out for his deposit was in the name of the company and not me so should not have been credited to me. The bank, writing to me by sea mail, returned the money to him. In fact, his cheque was made out to both the company and me. A lawyer client of mine sued the bank on my behalf and obtained a substantial out-of-court settlement—a very welcome windfall.

In 1990 I accepted a wildlife appointment in Uganda. Over the following six years I revisited most of the areas in which I hunted, and was able to verify my information and see with my own eyes the changes in the last 20 years. In Tanzania, I returned to many of my old hunting haunts with my wife and my sons, Nigel and Hugh. Some were gone forever, and some had remained as if I was there only yesterday. My wife and sons were enthralled to see the remains of our life in Africa.

It was during this period that Harry Cornell and his wife Ann came on safari with us. Harry had been about to arrive on safari in Kenya in 1977 when hunting was banned. We never succeeded in reclaiming his deposit, which had been spent on booking hunting controlled areas. Whilst in the U.S.A. earlier in the year, I had been asked by a wealthy Tanzanian to help him form a safari company. Harry heard I was back in Africa, and he wrote to me at the home I had left 15 years earlier. The letter was forwarded, and the opportunity to visit and hunt some of the areas I had known well now occurred. I took Harry and Ann with my family to one of them. This involved my son Nigel's, coupled with the Herculean efforts of the staff (many of whom were the sons of my original team), getting the big truck and the camp over the most appalling roads and river courses to the camp in the mountains overlooking the Rift Valley. Here, on foot, we all enjoyed hunting in the old style, mostly in the hills and ravines for buffalo and leopard. We had great success and some exciting and thrilling times. Not a wheel track or footprint was to be seen in the area except our own, and I am certain that not a shot had been fired there for many, many years. It was with sadness that we all realized that when we left, there would be no return. Our presence had been sufficient advertisement to others, and poaching commenced as we packed camp and left the area. Harry and Ann, by great good fortune, had experienced the clock's being turned back for those few weeks to 1975.

My much revered friend, park warden, hunter, and flyer Myles Turner, in his book *My Serengeti Years*, had this to say: 'The time is coming when there may be no wild game left in Africa in its natural state. Then a book such as this may one day be a documentary of a wonderful world that has gone forever and give pleasure to people who will never have the chance to live the life that we led on those sunlit plains so long ago'. Amen to that.

Myles died in 1984. He was the first person to visit my home where I write this now. Together we drove down to what was then a little semi-derelict farmhouse with its antiquated telephone, huge block of granite above the fireplace, and three-foot-thick stone walls. Quietly that evening by the fire, we spoke over his whiskey and my brandy of the changes we had seen in our lifetime. As we turned and went to our beds he said to me,

'John, promise to do me a favour—write it all down'. I have willingly ful-filled a promise that, whilst I had life left in me, I was determined to keep. The depletion of the wildlife of Africa continues at an ever increasing rate.

AEROPLANES AND BUSH FLYING

High Flight:
An Airman's Ecstasy

Oh! I have slipped the surly bonds of Earth
And danced the skies on laughter-silvered wings;
Sunward I've climbed, and joined the trembling mirth
Of sun-split clouds,—and done a hundred things
You have not dreamed of—wheeled and soared and swung
High in the sunlit silence. Hov'ring there,
I've chased the shouting wind along, and flung
My eager craft through footless halls of air . . .
Up, up the long, delirious, burning blue
I've topped the windswept heights with easy grace
Where never lark nor ever eagle flew—
And while, with silent lifting mind I've trod
The high untrespassed sanctity of space,
Put out my hand, and touched the face of God.

—John Gillespie Magee Jr.

For me flying was like being a millionaire, and then being given anoth-er million! It was the icing on the cake of being a P.H. and an outfitter. Every day, whenever I could, I drove up to the airstrip and took off, climb-ing high over the swamps or desert in the early morning air, watching the sun come over the horizon in a big red ball. It was my escape, halfway to heaven—as I looked down on my world I saw my daily problems in a new light. I always returned refreshed and ready to take on the challenges and decisions of the day. Today it is the experience of flying that I miss most from my life in Africa. Flying and bush piloting added a new dimension to being a professional hunter.

I have described how aircraft supported the organisation that had to be put in place for the dangerous big game of Africa to be hunted. If one subscribed to the dangers of hunting, then hand in glove went the dan-

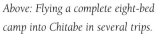

Above: Flying a complete eight-bed camp into Chitabe in several trips.

Top right: My close friend Dick Ayer, very happy flying planes and hunting buffalo in Botswana (1973).

Right: Young Dick and Norma Ayer with me in Chitabe camp with the workhorse Cessna 206.

Below right: L to R: Peter Jenkins, Ms. Green, Sarah Jenkins, Joyce West, Syb West, and Kenny Kays about to take off in 'Fox-Fox' for a look at the Okavango Swamps.

gers of flying. At no time did we ever have an accident with an aircraft. We were meticulous in our maintenance schedules, flying considerable distances to obtain the best mechanical and instrumentation services. Yet, in the best of regulated organisations, there are untoward incidents, and we experienced several.

In Botswana in 1969 we bought our first twin-engined Cessna 320 Sky Knight. In those days this was a powerful and sophisticated aircraft fitted out with oxygen and radar. It had been owned by the South African Police in Pretoria and had been used by the commandant. We needed to carry weight. The aircraft was therefore stripped of all equipment barring the necessary instruments. It already had auxiliary wing-tip tanks. Having taken a load of clients back the 524 nautical miles to Johannesburg, Walter Johnson and Willie Engelbrecht loaded the aircraft with vegetables, fresh fruit, and transport spares, and flew back to Maun. When they were 100 miles from Maun, over our desert area, the starboard engine started making a terrible noise—revs went to hell, and the engine was shut down by Walter, who was flying at 8000 feet. Walter, with not too many hours on his commercial licence, decided to try to make it to Maun rather than the desert airstrip almost below him. He had, after all, height on his side—if he could hold it. The trim of the aircraft was vital. This he managed quite well, but the aircraft continued to lose height. Jettisoning the cargo was the first aid to maintaining height, but for Willie to move about in the aircraft and even open the rear loading door in the fuselage to chuck out bags of potatoes, gem squashes, and oranges, etc., meant upsetting the trim and risking a spin.

The seats behind Willie were filled with potatoes and onions. Heaving a couple of pockets (bags) onto his lap, he began to push the vegetables one by one out of the small window let into the main window on the second pilot's side of the aircraft. Struggling with the aircraft to keep it level and at an angle of attack by which the maximum height would be maintained, Walter managed to get to the vicinity of Maun. He was down to 500 feet and still had to make his base leg turn onto the runway. There was nothing for it but to take a long shallow turn inching his way round to starboard and coming up heading down the runway. He landed safely 10 feet short of the threshold marker. This was remarkable performance for a pilot of little experience at that time, but Walter was a remarkable pilot. In the ensuing relief expressed by us all at their survival, Willie was heard to remark, 'If I catch a gemsbok eating one of those potatoes, I'll shoot the bastard!'

Above: A famous gathering of professional hunters at Game Conservation International, San Antonio, Texas (1970).

Right: Colonel Charles Askins in 1993 in his home in San Antonio, Texas, re-living some safaris enjoyed with Lionel Palmer and me in East Africa and Bechuanaland.

On another occasion, flying to Rakops with some clients, I landed at the desert strip near the corner of the kuki cordon. As the aircraft came to a stop my hand was on the throttle. I had actually begun to exert the necessary backward pressure to cut the engine when the nose of the aircraft fell forward at the same moment that the engine cut. The ground had

Together again on the sunlit plains of Africa (1995).

caved in where the nose wheel had stood—the work of spring hares! It did not take much to lift the nose out and turn the aircraft onto solid ground. An inspection of the propeller showed that it was bent. We disassembled it, having called on the radio for a new one to be sent up from Johannesburg. Taking the bent propeller to an acacia tree, we placed the blade of the propeller in a convenient crotch and bent it straight— straight enough that the human eye could see no bend. Replacing it, we flew the plane back to Maun where, next day, we had a new one fitted.

In the middle of one season the floods in the Okavango Swamps came early. The country through which one had to pass to reach the Chitabe camp was, unbeknownst to Wally Johnson Sr., flooded. The Muhohelo River—the border of Chitabe and Makwi areas—had overflowed its banks. Fearful of this situation, I decided to fly a whole camp into the swamps. The campsite was within 100 yards of the airstrip, which was short. Flying with a heavy load allowed for no mistakes.

I was using our second aircraft, a Cessna 206 with Robertson STOL and oversized gear—one of the best workhorses that Africa ever saw. First went the staff, then came an eight-cubic-foot refrigerator, beds, huge canvas tents, food, and all kinds of safari equipment. Nine trips of 40 minutes' round-trip did it, and I was able to call Wally on the radio instructing him

383

to return his truck to Maun and press on to camp, which was all ready for him. They collected some fine trophies but became completely surrounded by flood waters, and I had to fly them out.

Many of our clients and friends were pilots: my close friend Dick Ayer, the owner of a Pitt's Special, was one who flew a lot for us (whenever he could get a break from commuting to New York!), John 'The Diver' Hoynacki, Bob Chatfield-Taylor, Doug Grimm, Dick Place, and several others, to name a few. Bill Wixley was the senior pilot with his airline transport pilot's licence. He kept us running properly with his sage advice. We made—and very nearly made—mistakes with the type of aircraft we used. Once, whilst in the USA looking for clients, Bill Wixley was persuaded, against his better judgement, by John Seaman, a former P.H. in Bechuanaland and then a super salesman with Comair in Johannesburg, to purchase a Cessna 337. This aircraft had an engine in front and also one at the back of the fuselage. It was a 'push me—pull you'. Its twin-boom tail was reminiscent of the Gloster Meteor jet fighter trainer of the Royal Air Force On my return it was traded in for a Cessna 206 owned by Dick Eyton, a rancher down at Ghanzi, which was the best buy we ever made. The aircraft A2-ZFF (Fox Fox) is still flying today in Maun, 20 years later! We were also very nearly talked into buying an Aero Grand Commander, but this was just a little too grand for us. By this time the Cessna 320 Sky Knight had been sold. Chartering a DC3 brought our clients in more satisfactorily and with the minimum of investment.

There was some exciting flying when we were called upon to undertake missions of mercy for sick or wounded persons. I recall one in particular that was rather hair raising. In this case it was a South African who had been severely mauled by a lion. His two companions were with him in the aircraft to tend to his needs en route to Johannesburg, whence he was destined. This was some 500 miles south-east of Maun across very flat and featureless country. Some 150 miles from Johannesburg the country rose to some 6500 feet. In those days we had no GPS system or radar in a small Cessna 206 aircraft; compass and ADF were our navigational aides. We took off from the Maun airstrip at about 4.00 in the afternoon. There was no radio communication from Maun except for the police radio to Gaberones, the capital, some 250 miles to the south-east. Having flown the route a number of times, it was a pretty straightforward trip destined to arrive at Rand Airport.

Three hundred miles out a wicked weather front came into view. I was reminded of the poet Robert Browning's words:

Here, here's their place
where meteors shoot,
Clouds form,
Lightnings are loosened.
Stars come and go.

Thunder and lightning were all about us, and the turbulence made flying most unpleasant. I was not happy, but there was no turning back and there was no alternative. On entering the civil-aviation-controlled area of Johannesburg, there was a checkpoint over the Hartebeest Port Dam, where an ADF beacon was located. I called into Rand, and a controller referred me to Jan Smuts International Airport. Attempting to fly the plane and keep it at the proper height whilst tuning the radio was somewhat of a nightmare. It was dark, and the lights in the cockpit were poor but lit by the constant flashes of lightning. Seldom, if ever, had we been required to do any night bush flying. No advance warning of my arrival had been possible, as the interference on the radio was constant, and both airports were closed due to the bad weather and persistent electrical storms. I had little fuel and certainly none with which to fly to an alternative airport.

Finally I was able to ensure that Johannesburg air traffic control knew this: they turned on their magic! By now the cockpit was almost permanently lit by lightning. It was sheeting with rain, and visibility was nil. The radio, fortunately, at this point never faltered, although the interference necessitated that each sentence be spelled out more than once. They had us on radar and had our altimeter reading. Slowly they talked us onto the great big runway of Jan Smuts International Airport. As we lost height the runway lights came into view below us—we were over and beyond the threshold. Being used to bush strips, I was concerned that I was going to overshoot, but I need not have worried as there were several thousand feet of tarmac below, stretching out into the distance in front of me, and on either side there were almost 50 yards to the edge of the runway. It was an eerie feeling of almost landing in space until 50 feet off the ground I saw the central white markings of the runway and gently let down. The airport vehicle's flashing light guided me to the spot where an ambulance was waiting, and, my mission thus accomplished, we duly celebrated. The mauled hunter thankfully recovered. I returned to Maun outwardly unconcerned but inwardly certain that all those mauled by lions had best report for flights to Johannesburg by midday in the future!

It was a life lived to the full with some hard decisions made easier by the unremitting loyalty of my wife and the unswerving support of my partners and friends, for which I am ever grateful.

THE SHAW & HUNTER TROPHY—1955–1976

Shaw & Hunter Ltd. of Nairobi was founded by R.M. Shaw and J.A. Hunter. R. Morrison Shaw had come to Kenya as a gunsmith working for Newland & Tarleton, one of the first safari outfitters in Kenya. J.A. Hunter was an elephant hunter and game warden of considerable note at the time. Together they went into business repairing guns and selling all manner of new and second-hand rifles and their accoutrements.

By 1955 Shaw & Hunter Ltd. had changed hands. Wing Commander E. Boswell, the managing director of the company, was responsible for the idea of the competition, and as a result of discussions with the officers of the E.A.P.H.A. and the chief game warden of Kenya, the Shaw & Hunter Trophy came into being. The trophy itself, donated by Shaw & Hunter Ltd., is a silver statue of a P.H. taking aim at an unseen target. It was made by the famous London firm of silversmiths, Mappin & Webb. It is based upon a photograph of the late S.P. (Syd) Downey (who co-founded Ker & Downey Safaris Ltd.) in typical safari clothes. The rifle with which he is taking aim is a 7x57 Mauser that I well remember being in Syd Downey's possession. Several replicas in bronze casting were made by the internationally known sculptor Terry Mathews and offered to all recipients. I bought two of these, presenting one to Richard B. Ayer Jr., who shot the lesser kudu world record trophy that won me the award in 1957. I kept the second.

The award made by the E.A.P.H.A. at their annual dinner was for 'the most outstanding trophy of the year shot whilst on safari with a paying

WINNERS OF THE SHAW AND HUNTER TROPHY
1955-1976

Year	Hunter	Client	Trophy
1955	*Myles Turner +	Prince Abdorreza Pahlavi	35¾" lesser kudu
1956	*Syd Downey +	Scott W. Hayes	54¾ greater kudu
1957	*John Kingsley-Heath	R.B. Ayer	37¼ lesser kudu
1958	*David Ommanney	Russell E. Wales	56½" greater kudu
1959	*Syd Downey +	Francois Edmond-Blanc	14¼" giant forest hog
1960	*Kris Aschan +	Count C. Plessen	18⅞" bushbuck
1961	*Tony Henley +	Bill Ruger	Eastern bohor reedbuck
1962	Mike Prettejohn	Martin Anderson	33⅛" bongo
1963	John Alexander +	J.H. Collins	36½" rhino
1964	Rene Babault +	–	Sable antelope
1965	*John Sutton +	W. MacDonald	32⅞" bongo
1966	*Mohamed Iqbal +	D.K. Harris	7" oribi
1967	Edgar de Bono +	F. Mazzuchelli	31⅛" bongo
1968	Brian Herne	A. Vey on Debasien	30⅝" roan
1969	Tony France	H. Walter	A leopard 7'10" long between pegs weighing about 200 lbs.
1970	*Tony Seth-Smith	T. Havens	A huge lion
1971	*Derrick Dunn	R.M. Zimmerman	47½" sable
1972	*Derrick Dunn	P.L. Deutz	59 5/16" buffalo
1973	*Robin Hurt	Dr. F.K. Flick	54" buffalo
1974	No award		
1975	Alfredo Pelizzoli	–	25" sitatunga
1976	Lionel Hartley	James C. Midcap Jnr.	27¼" Hunters hartebeest

Because of the closure of hunting, there was no competition in 1977.

Winners of the Shaw and Hunter Trophy: 1955–76. Those with a '' were members of the firm Ker & Downey Safaries Ltd. '+' indicates deceased.*

client'. The committee of the E.A.P.H.A. appointed the judges panel, and the trophy was presented annually for 21 years.

The winner was allowed to keep the trophy for one year and also received a silver tankard. The inscription on mine reads: 'The East African Professional Hunters Association Trophy. 1958. P.J. Kingsley-Heath'. It is indeed a prized possession. Although the date on the tankard is 1958, in fact it refers to the previous year: due to the heavy rains that fell in Kenya

The Shaw & Hunter Trophy is presented annually at the end of the hunting season (beginning of June to the end of the following March) at the Annual Dinner of the East African Professional Hunter's Association. It is given to the hunter who obtains for his client a trophy judged to be the best of the year. To enter a trophy, pictures of the animal with the client, of a size approximately 9" x 6", together with a Game Department certificate certifying the measurements, and story of the hunt, have to be handed to the Secretary of the Association before the Annual General Meeting (usually in April). Normally the judges consist of a most knowledgeable and older member of the Association (usually with more than 25 years of hunting experience), a Director of National Parks, a chief Game Warden and a Taxidermist. It was presented in 1956 for the first time to Myles Turner, last year to Sydney Downey, and has never yet been won by any hunter outside Ker & Downey Safaris Limited. This is the first time that a hunter has won and also been runner-up and third.

The trophy is a solid silver statuette, most beautifully made, of a hunter in safari dress standing taking aim, and is valued at £400. It is about 9" high.

I won the Shaw & Hunter Trophy in 1957.

annually in April and May, the dinner at which the trophy was presented was always held at that time but referred to the previous year ending on 31 December.

The animals that were shot that provided the trophies were all carefully measured by the judging panel, which usually included a taxidermist, an official measurer appointed by Rowland Ward's *Records of Big Game*, and a senior member of the Kenya Game Department. Generally speaking, the panel was composed of a minimum of five persons, of which at least two were members of the E.A.P.H.A.

Note: It was extraordinary that although some of the largest-tusked elephants were shot during these years, none won this trophy.

GUN MAKERS, GUNSMITHS, AMMUNITION MAKERS, AUCTIONEERS, AND RELATED INFORMATION—1949–1978

GENERAL INFORMATION ON GUN MAKERS WHOSE GUNS HAVE BEEN USED BY THE AUTHOR IN AFRICA

1. Holland & Holland Ltd. (Roger Mitchell Esq.), Dept. G&A, 31 Bruton St., London, England W1Y 8JS
   A complete history of the company is contained in *The Shooting Field: 150 Years with Holland & Holland*.
2. Westley Richards (Simon Clode Esq.), 40 Grange Road, Bournbrook, Birmingham, England B29 OAR
   The company premises in London is referred to in *The Shooting Field*.
3. Manton & Co., London & Calcutta
   Believed to be no longer in business.
4. John Rigby & Son (Paul Roberts Esq.), Great Suffolk St., London, England
5. James Purdey & Sons Ltd., 57/58 Audley House, South Audley St., London, England W1Y 6ED
6. Cogswell & Harrison Ltd. Formerly at 168 Picadilly, London
   Believed to be no longer in business.
7. Weatherby Gun Co., 3100 El Camino Real, Atascadero, California, U.S.A. 93422
8. Mannlicher Schonauer, Austria
9. Sturm, Ruger & Co., Lacey Place, Southport, Connecticut, U.S.A. 06490
10. Mauser, Wafenbrik A/N, Oberndorf, Germany
11. Winchester Arms Co., Newport, Connecticut, U.S.A.
12. Brno Arms Co., Czechoslovakia (now Czech Republic)

Some information on Captain Selous. Courtesy of Holland & Holland.

Captain Frederick Courtenay Selous

Selous was killed in action January 1917 in German East Africa, aged sixty-six years. His death was mourned by the enemy Army Commander, General von Lettow-Vorbeck, – and even by the Kaiser who regarded the life of Selous as an example for German youth.

Between 1871 and 1890 Selous had trekked on ox waggons, on horseback and on foot all over South-Central Africa. Whilst others of his generation may have shot more elephants, lions and other dangerous game, the name of Selous became more widely known than any other hunter and remains so to this day. From reading his books one wonders how he survived all his years in Africa – for he could so easily have died through disease, been killed by hostile natives or dangerous animals and even through the inadequacy of his firearms in his early years in Africa.

Holland & Holland have compiled a list of the firearms which Selous owned (or ordered). The list given below is taken from his writings and more importantly from previously unpublished information obtained from the records of several British gunmakers.

As with other special guns or rifles made by Holland & Holland, the Company is making a donation from the sale of the Selous rifle to a wildlife conservation project.

M.C.A.L. December 1988

From published works

1871 "A small double breech-loading rifle by Reilly" – "stolen".
"A double ten muzzle-loading by Vaughan and a little gun that shot well with both shot and bullet".

1872 "A short Snider and the muzzle-loading double ten, and my little shot-gun".
He bought two smooth-bore duck guns "made by Isaac Hollis of Birmingham, weighing 12½lbs. Fired a round ball of 4oz! Cost £6 each" – "including 600 miles up country delivery!"

1873 "Bought a similar, the weight being 2lbs heavier £7.10.0".
"Used them for 3 seasons and shot seventy eight elephants, all but one shot on foot."
"Since then I have shot with very expensive large bore breech loaders with Curtis and Harvey's best powder, but I have never used or seen used a rifle which drove better than these common made old muzzle-loaders. However they were so light that, when loaded as they were by hand from a leather bag of powder slung at my side, (I find that an ordinary handful of powder is over twenty drachms), they kicked most frightfully, and in my case the punishment I received from these guns has affected my nerves to such an extent as to have materially influenced my shooting ever since, and I am heartily sorry that I ever had anything to do with them."

1874 "Armoury consisted of only the two four-bore elephant guns and a ten-bore rifle with scarcely any grooving".

1877 "Killed him (Roan Antelope) with my Martini-Henry rifle".

1879 "Carrying my little Martini shot an enormous bustard".

1880 Refers to rifle he used – "was a single 450 Express by George Gibbs of Bristol."
"my own single 10 (Whitworth rifling) and a single 450 "Express" – the latter by Gibbs of Bristol."
Referring to the Gibbs – "using an ordinary Express bullet, the hollow plugged with a peg of soft wood, and only backed by 3½ drachms of powder".
"no praise can be too high for Mr. Gibbs's admirable little Metford Express rifle."
Selous's books and illustrations establish this as a Gibbs Metford Farquharson action rifle.
"I was armed with a little double 12 smooth-bore by W. W. Greener".

From George Gibbs.

1911 "A best quality ·470 double rifle. No. 20149. Completed 6th Jan. 1911".
Millais records that Selous left for Africa January 19th 1911 to try and add to his collection a specimen of the Giant Eland of the Lower Sudan.
Gibbs's records lost in the bombing of Bristol.

From Westley Richards Gun Order Book 1908 to 1912

1911 Ordered Oct. 20 1911 "A ·425 b. Mauser actn. WR Mag. Rifle. No. 37798 dct. barrel". *Following notes read:-*
'Making and supplying 2 Ivory fsts (*foresights*) same as our platn (*platinum*) one now on rifle & 2 a little higher using his own ivory from a complete Rhinos tooth presented to us by him'.
'He tried rifle at Hendon Oct 17 1911 & was very pleased with it – used 5 ctgs only – 1/9 (*one shilling and ninepence*).' *In red ink.*
'Special memo. In our letter 3/10/11 we agreed to either charge Rifle at ½ list price to him or to lend him the turnout for his trip – (signed) A. H. Gale (*who was London Manager of Westley Richards*).

From Holland & Holland records

1904 Ordered Feb. 1904 "A ·375 bore single drop block action cordite rifle. No. 24479". *Counter Book No. 11, page 463 also records –*
'He shot and approved the rifle 15/6/1904.'
Selous arrived in England late 1903 and was busy collecting here early in 1904. He left for the Yukon 14th July 1904 to hunt caribou and moose.

1907 Ordered Jan. 17 1907 "A ·375 bore Holland Schonauer Magazine sporting rifle. No. 26044". *Counter Book No. 13, page 475 records -* 'Ready to shoot 14/5/07' – 'Replied 21/5/07 is abroad till June 16' – 'Closure date of this item 3/8/07'.
In May Selous left for Asia Minor to collect eggs, home in June and left in August (for Norway on a little hunt after reindeer. A testimonial letter in the Holland & Holland 1910-12 catalogue, reproduced opposite, relates to the above rifle.

1912 Ordered May 24, 1912 "A ·275 bore Magnum Holland Mauser Magazine rifle. No. 28014". *Counter Book No. 15, page 392 also states -* 'Do not send in a/c yet'.
Selous went to East Africa late 1911 and on March 2nd 1912 he suddenly came face to face with a big lion which dived into the forest as soon as it saw him. Quoted in The Field June 8th 1912. (*Millais*). It seems likely he returned home soon after, going by the date of the above order, and according to *Millais* spent the rest of the year at home.

1914 Ordered April 23, 1914 "A ·375 bore Magnum Mauser Magazine sporting rifle. 2 Extra foresights to shoot 3" low and 2 to shoot 6" low at 100 (yds)". *Counter Book No. 17, page 295.*
Selous was at home in April and went to Texal Island in May. During June and July busy preparing for an expedition with Abel Chapman to the Sudan and White Nile. The rifle was ready early July and August saw the start of the Great War. A note in purple crayon on the order page, adds 'Lt'. (*Lieutenant*) to name F.C. Selous and to the address adds 'Driscolls Scouts – called 3.3.15 Hold over until his return from East Africa'. Another note in pencil indicates the rifle was 'used for Capt. Colville'. With no rifle number or invoice number it is obvious Selous never took delivery.

1916 Ordered between July 7 and 13 1916 "A ·275 bore Magnum Mauser Holland Magazine rifle. No. 28339". *Counter Book No. 17, page 380* also has two entries which read:-
'Meet at 5/40 No. 8 Platform Waterloo 8/8/16' and
'8/8/16 Send a/c for rifle and ctgs. will send cheque dated now but do not pay same in till Oct 1st 16'.
Selous, having returned home in June 1916 for an operation (still bringing home with him a magnificent collection of butterflies), was only ill for twelve days and then went to his home for a short rest and in August went out again with a draft to East Africa.
From the Counter Book record, illustrated opposite, it seems Selous ordered this rifle after his operation and from the No. 8 Platform instruction knew then exactly where he was going to be on 8th August and at what time. We know the appointment seems to have been kept from the dated note above regarding the account and cheque.
A letter dated Dec. 5, 1916 sent by Selous from near Dar-es-Salaam to a periodical 'African Times' reads – "Only yesterday evening did I at last succeed in distributing the contents of five boxes of comforts you gave me at Waterloo Station to take out to our Battalion".

Note: I would like to have been able to afford guns made and engraved in the best traditions of British gun making and by Griffin & Howe and others in the U.S.A. The fact that I did not use such guns is not, of course, any reflection on their undisputed quality.

GUNSMITHS

1. Earl Milliron, Portland, Oregon, U.S.A.
2. Walter Kolouch, 14995 Orchards View Road, McMinnville, Oregon, U.S.A. 97128
3. Sterling Davenport, 9611 East Walnut Tree Drive, Tucson, Arizona, U.S.A. 85749

AMMUNITION AND BULLET MAKERS

1. Vernon Speer, Lewiston, Idaho, U.S.A.
2. Steve Hornaday, Grand Island, Nebraska, U.S.A.
3. Nosler Inc., Bend, Oregon, U.S.A.
4. D.W.M., Germany
5. Kynoch, Birmingham, England

Below Top: A .300 Winchester Magnum on a Mauser action made by Tucson's master gunsmith, Sterling Davenport.

AUCTIONEERS

1. C. Austyn, Christie's, Manson & Woods, Arms & Armour Dept., 8 King Street, St. James, London, England SW1Y 6QT
   Austyn is the author of *Modern Sporting Guns*.

Below Bottom: A fine example of the work of one of the best gunsmiths in the U.S.A.: a .425 Westley Richards on a Mauser action made by Sterling Davenport.

1996 MODERN CUSTOM-MADE GUN COSTS

I have referred to the comments made by the editor of *Cartridges of the World* in the section on the .425 Westley Richards rifle in Chapter 8. The costs of two rifles recently completed by Sterling Davenport of Tucson, Arizona, for friends of mine clearly illustrate this point.

.300 Winchester Magnum	U.S.$	.425 Westley Richards	U.S.$
1. Cost of Douglas barrel:	$120	Cost of Douglas barrel:	$120
2. Cost of stock roughly cut to fit Mauser action (ex-Fajen & Co.):	$300	Cost of stock roughly cut to fit Mauser action (ex-Fajen & Co.):	$300
3. Argentine 1909 Mauser Model 98 action, all serial numbers the same on all parts:	$150	Argentine 1909 Mauser Model 98 action, all serial numbers the same on all parts:	$150
4. Cost of making and putting together the rifle as per photo with sights, telescopic sight mounts, case-hardening action, back sight ramp, foresight, sling swivels, buffalo horn fore-end, and pistol grip caps, etc.:	$2000	Cost of making and putting together the rifle as per photo with sights, extended magazine to hold five rounds, telescopic sight mounts, case-hardening the action, back sight ramp, foresight, sling swivels, buffalo horn fore-end, and pistol grip caps:	$2250
TOTAL COST:	**$2570** (U.K. £1647)	**TOTAL COST:**	**$2820** (U.K. £1807)

By comparison, the Rigby .450 magazine rifle made on a Brno action and to all intents and purposes similarly constructed is offered to the buyer at £7000 basic and £9000 with extras. The Westley Richards .425 extended-magazine rifle is also offered at £4500–£5000. The parts comprising the gun are almost the same. In the case of the Westley Richards,

I believe the stock to be of superior quality walnut, whereas the .450 has a Brno action reminiscent of a square-bridge Mauser. In both cases the buyer is paying at least $7000 for the British name on a gun made with similar parts.

For all practical purposes today, the British-made guns become collector's items and are seldom used. I am bound to record, however, that I humbly believe that the best custom gunsmithing is in the United States of America. I find it hard, as an Englishman, to admit this, but I do honestly believe that it is now true and borne out by the picture of both rifles that are undoubtedly the best value for one's money.

My reader no doubt realizes that any .458 can be easily reworked to take the .450 Rigby cartridge by simply adjusting the feed, the face of the bolt, and the chamber, no barrel change being necessary. Some $300–$400 will achieve this. However, this should only take place if the gun is then reproofed. There is a difference of approximately 1580 foot pounds of muzzle energy between the two cartridges and some 300 feet per second of muzzle velocity with a difference of only 20 grains of bullet weight. Re-proofing is good insurance!

SELECTED PERSONS MENTIONED IN THE TEXT

It would not normally have been my practice to comment on selected persons mentioned in the text. However, I have been persuaded both by my publisher and many others that so many of these fine people who made their home and life in Africa would be lost for posterity if their presence were not recorded. They will, I hope, forgive me for being brief and recording somewhat succinctly their undoubted contribution to life in Africa, not so much for me, but for all of us who were there in those stirring times.

Adams, Ace and *Corrine*. Clients of mine from Youngstown, Ohio. Hunted many times in Kenya, Tanzania, and Botswana.

Adams, Alvin. Formally senior vice president of Pan Am. Came on safari to hunt leopard when I was mauled by a lion. His son, Nat, was working in East Africa at the time and was a good friend of mine. Greatly interested in jazz and the Sky Club on the top of the Pan Am Building in New York City. Died at age 92.

Adamson, George. The famous Kenya game warden and author of *Bwana Game* who trained lions for release back into the wild and who was tragically murdered by Somali terrorists near Kora in the N.F.D. of Kenya.

Adamson, Joy. The wife of George who became famous with her husband for the film *Born Free* starring Bill Travers and Virginia McKenna, the story of the return of captive lions to their natural environment. She was murdered by one of her staff prior to George's death.

Aidid, Mohammed Farah. Infamous Somali warlord. Police officer in charge of Belet Uen in Somalia when I was there in 1955. Died in 1996 of wounds sustained in a gunfight in Mogadishu.

Akbar, Mohammed. Shot an elephant that had tusks of 172 pounds and 164 pounds on the border of Tsavo National Park, Kenya.

Alimao, Edward. Originally an office messenger in Tanga to me when I was a district officer. Remained with me for 40 years as a gunbearer. Superb elephant tracker and most loyal of all my African staff. A Makonde by tribe, he was a gifted carver in ebony and maker of elephant-hair bracelets. Murdered on his return to his tribal area by Frelimo, the Mozambican so-called 'Independence Party'.

Allen, Anton. Younger son of Bunny Allen. P.H. for many years in Kenya. Left Kenya to live in Texas.

Allen, 'Baa'. Retired Kenya police superintendent of the N.F.D. Speared through the chest by a Somali tribesman in the Ogaden, southern Ethiopia, but survived. Retired to Lamu, Kenya coast. Younger brother of Bunny. Also a distinguished welterweight boxer. Killed in a motor accident while visiting north Wales.

Allen, 'Bunny'. Father of David and Anton Allen. One-time heavyweight boxing champion of Kenya. Long-time P.H. One of the old-timers of Kenya. Retired to Lamu, Kenya coast.

Allen, David. Older son of Bunny Allen. Game warden and P.H. for many years in Kenya, where he is still guiding safaris.

Almeida, Tony. Revered friend and famous jaguar and Asiatic buffalo hunter from South America. Hunted in Botswana as a P.H. with Safari South (Pty.) Ltd. on several safaris with his jaguar clients. English educated, superb host, and speaker of many languages. Author of *Hunting Jaguar.*

Alport, Peter. Owner and operator of Norm Thompson Ltd. (a mail order company). Hunted with Lionel Palmer and me. Rowland Ward lost all his trophies. Gifted photographer. (Deceased.)

Alukar (first name unknown). Doctor of medicine. Indian subassistant surgeon, Colonial Medical Service, Tanganyika, in 1951.

Alvensleben, Baron Werner Von. A giant in clearing poaching from the Save River for Mozambique Safarilandia Ltd. Tough German who stood for no nonsense whatsoever. Great friend of mine. Successfully escaped from custody in Rhodesia during the 1939–45 War and lived thereafter in Mozambique. His admiring compadres credit him with several exploits that he recently told me are not strictly true. He and his wife, Bibla, are now retired in Portugal. Author of *Baron in Africa.*

Amin, Idi. Former ruler of Uganda responsible for the destruction of that country's wildlife assets.

Antonidis, Mrs. C. Shot an elephant that had tusks of 153 pounds and 149 pounds on the Ugalla River, Tanganyika.

Aosta, Emmanuele Filiberto. Duke of Aosta appointed by Benito Mussolini, Viceroy of Ethiopia, in 1938. Surrendered to British forces at Amba Alagi in 1941.

Archer, Tony. Long-time P.H. with Ker & Downey Safaris Ltd. Guided many scientific expeditions, most notable being the Carnegie Museum expedition. Ornithologist. Worked tirelessly for the E.A.P.H.A. in support of ethical hunting and trophy improvement and recording.

Aschan, Kris. Swedish count. Long-time P.H. in East Africa. Senior hunter in Ker & Downey Safaris Ltd. Friend of Bror Blixen. (Deceased.)

Asche, F. Shot an elephant that had tusks of 114 pounds and 108 pounds with John Fletcher in Kenya.

Askins, Colonel Charles. Colonel in command of border patrol activities in Texas. International pistol champion. Doyen of outdoor writers. Big-game hunter and gun writer. Friend of many professional hunters and all in Safari South (Pty.) Ltd. of the 1960s and 1970s. An unforgettable character and fine sportsman. Still lives in San Antonio, Texas.

Auerbach, F. Shot an elephant with tusks of 119 pounds and 114 pounds with Reggie Destro. P.H. in Kenya.

Ayer, Norma. Wife of Richard B. Ayer. Hunted big game in East Africa and Botswana with her husband. Was expecting their first child when on their first safari in Tanganyika. Son Dick was born on my birthday. Lifelong friend of all Kingsley-Heaths.

Ayer, Richard B. Jr. 'Dick'. Close friend of mine for more than 40 years. Maker of many safaris. Pilot. A preferred buffalo hunter. Big-game hunter and winner with me of the Shaw & Hunter Trophy in 1957. Godfather to Nigel Kingsley-Heath.

Babault, 'Jo Jo'. Rene Babault's wife. Killed in a car crash in Kenya 10 years after Rene's aircraft crash.

Babault, Rene. Long-time P.H. with Hunters Africa Ltd. Very close friend of mine. Killed in an aircraft crash off the Kenya coast.

Bagnall, Stephen. Killed by a lion in Kenya in 1902.

Baker, Sir Samuel. Famous African explorer of the mid-1800s.

Balcon, Michael. One of two famous brothers in the British film industry from 1939-1970. Made the film *Sammy Going South* in Tanganyika in 1962.

Ball, Sir Hesketh. Governor of Uganda in 1905.

Barrah, Jack, O.B.E. Long-time game warden in Kenya who stayed on as a wildlife advisor for some 20 years after independence. Most approachable and kind person to all professional hunters.

Barrington, George. P.H. with Ker & Downey Safaris Ltd. One of the first to obtain a bongo for his client. Wonderful person to be with on safari. Game rancher in South Africa. Author of *One Happy Hunter.*

Bartlett, Fred. Long-time game warden and control officer in Kenya. Hunted for Ker & Downey Safaris Ltd. and Hunters Africa Ltd. in Kenya, Tanganyika, and Botswana. Probably more experienced with buffalo than anyone alive today. Author of *Shoot Straight Stay Alive.* Brother-in-law of Don Bousfield and uncle of P.H. Mike Bartlett.

Bates, George. P.H. in Botswana and owner of Oryx Safaris Ltd. Hunted extensively in the Kalahari. One of Lionel Palmer's first clients in Bechuanaland. Only brother killed in Vietnam. Killed in an aircraft crash in South Africa.

Battye, R.K.M. 'Keith'. Formerly an Indian Civil Service officer. Game ranger in Tanganyika. Killed by an elephant on the Umba River, Tanga District.

Bazzy, C. 'Chuck'. Hunted Tanganyika in the early 1950s. A noted African big-game hunter in many countries, particularly the Sudan. Founding member and area vice president of S.C.I., whose unquestioned loyalty and energy in raising funds for conservation over the last 25 years has been remarkable. He is the owner of Safari Adventures and is perhaps the longest established safari agent alive, with an enviable and ethical performance record. He and his wife, Karen, have been kind and hospitable friends for many years.

Beadnell, Surgeon Rear Admiral, C.M. Big-game hunter in the 1920s in East Africa on retirement from the Royal Navy.

Becker, Peter. Very successful hunter with Ker & Downey Safaris Ltd. Even more successful when he gave up hunting and founded Botswana Game Industries Ltd. in Botswana, where he is now semiretired living in Francistown.

Bell, W.D.M. 'Karamoja'. Most famous of all ivory hunters at the turn of the century. Much decorated in the 1914–18 War as a R.A.F. pilot. Shot several thousand elephants with small-bore calibres. Author of books on elephant hunting such as *Karamoja Safari.* (Deceased.)

Bellew, Ato. Adefferis. Senior secretary in the Ethiopian Ministry of Agriculture, 1955.

Belong. Bushman tracker with Nel and Poppleton when Poppleton and Khomba were killed near Gweta, Botswana, hunting lion.

Benbow, 'Ben'. Long-time very successful hotel operator in East Africa. A friend to all in the safari business and most helpful at all times. The Safari Hotel in Arusha, Tanganyika, was owned by him and hosted the film crew on *Hatari.*

Bennett, Tom. Railway engineer in the 1920s employed on the construction of the Mombasa-Nairobi-Uganda Railway line. Experienced the attentions of the man-eaters of Tsavo.

Bernhardt, H.R.H. Prince of the Netherlands. Shot an elephant that had tusks of 102 pounds and 101 pounds with Eric Rundgen. Ker & Downey Safaris Ltd. stationery was endorsed with 'By Appointment to H.R.H. the Prince of the Netherlands'. Most kind, helpful, and hospitable to me on many visits to Holland. Fine, ethical sportsman and conservationist.

Best, G.J. 'Geoff'. Actor and journalist, Nairobi. Travelled with me from Hargeisa, British Somaliland, to Nairobi. Still lives in Kenya.

Bindloss, Bill. Agriculture officer, Tabora, Western Province, Tanganyika. One of his parents was one of the first to be murdered by the Mau Mau, prompting my return to Kenya to join security forces sometime afterwards.

Bisletti, Count Francesco. Italian P.H. for many years in East Africa based at Lake Naivasha, Kenya. Always a kind and helpful person with exemplary manners and successful safaris. His wife, Tschuki, kept a tame leopard and took part in the filming of *Hatari* in the Serengeti when she volunteered to sit in a steel cage whilst lowered into a pride of lions feeding on a zebra kill.

Blacklaws, Jack. Early P.H. after 1939–45 War. Skilled bush pilot addicted to exploring Africa. Fine friend and most successful man. Contracted sleeping sickness in Botswana and died at Victoria Falls, Rhodesia.

Blasco, F.C. Shot a record-class buffalo at Kanga N'thole, Mozambique.

Block, Jack. His parents were long-time friends of my father and uncle. Leading businessman in tourism, hotels, and allied businesses. Managing director of Ker & Downey Safaris Ltd. Exceptionally kind to me on many occasions, and respected my confidences for many years. Died of a heart attack whilst fishing in Chile.

Blower, Major John, M.C. Chief game warden of Uganda. U.N.D.P. advisor to the Ethiopian government 1972–74 on wildlife management and development.

Blunt, Commander D.E. Game control officer in Kenya and Tanganyika before and after 1939–45 War. His book *Elephant* is a valuable classic. (Deceased.)

Blunt, 'Nicky'. Long-time P.H. Son of Commander D.E. Blunt. One of the most ethical of professional hunters, who has hunted continually in many different countries for more than 30 years and still is doing so today.

Boscovic, Z. 'Boskie'. Distinguished R.A.F. pilot in the 1939–45 War who started an air charter company of the same name at Wilson Airport in Kenya. Flew H.R.H. Princess Margaret everywhere on her visit to Kenya.

Bousfield, Don. Younger brother of Jack Bousfield. P.H. and close friend of Fred Bartlett, his brother-in-law. Game warden and control officer in Nanyuki, Kenya. P.H. for Ker & Downey Safaris Ltd. and Hunters Africa Ltd. Hunted in Kenya, Tanganyika, Botswana, and many other countries. Killed in an accident with a train at a level crossing at Karatina in Kenya.

Bousfield, Jack. Older brother of Don Bousfield. Long-time P.H. and crocodile hunter. Famous for his crocodile-harvesting operations on Lake Rukwa, Tanganyika, which appeared in *Life* magazine. Animal and bird catcher in Botswana. Shot an elephant that had tusks of 109 pounds and 103 pounds near Lake Rukwa. Best described as 'quite some character'. Good friend of mine and many others. Dense bush pilot. Killed in an aircraft crash in Botswana.

Bradbury, Basil. Notable big-game hunter who travelled the world. He hunted extensively in East Africa where he was known to many professional hunters and well liked. (Deceased.)

Branfoot, Colonel D.C. Retired from British Army. Hunted privately in Tanganyika in the years immediately after the 1939–45 War.

Brister, Bob. Well-known outdoor writer and columnist for several publications in Texas. Resident of Houston. Winner of many skeet and shotgun-shooting championships. A fine friend and companion to all with whom he hunted. An unforgettable Texan.

Bromfield, Pat. Sole game warden of Bechuanaland in early 1960s. Covered the entire territory from Francistown.

Bromley, John H.M. Consul at Mega, southern Ethiopia in 1955. A wonderful character of true British disposition. Hospitable and well liked by all who met with him. Alas, a fast-dying breed.

Brooks, Berry. A Southern gentleman from the U.S.A. of the highest standing. He was president of the Shikar Safari Club of America. Won the Weatherby Award and many other prizes. A most approachable and kind person with enormous experience in big-game hunting worldwide. A person of moral standing and integrity that is sadly missed. (Deceased.)

Brophy, Jim. Shot a record 9-foot 4 1/2-inch leopard in the northern Okavango Swamps in Botswana in 1984.

Brown, David. Formerly chief game warden of Kenya. Retired and became a magistrate in Fiji.

Bryant, John. Client of George Bates on safari in Botswana and shot an elephant with tusks of 94 pounds and 84 pounds in Okavango Swamps.

Bulpin, T.V. Author of a book on George Rushby titled *The Hunter Is Death.*

Burton, Sir Richard. Famous African explorer of the mid-1800s. Distinguished big-game hunter.

Buttons, 'Red'. Actor in *Hatari.*

Cabot, *John.* Famous American actor in *Hatari.* (Deceased.)

Caldwell, Captain Keith. Game ranger and elephant control officer in post 1939–45 War Uganda.

Cameron, Mike. P.H. in the early days of safari hunting in Bechuanaland. Worked with Eric Rundgren and the Henderson brothers. Still hunting in Zimbabwe.

Campbell, A.C. 'Alec'. A qualified, gifted, and dedicated conservationist who, as chief game warden in Botswana, brought reason and long-term planning of wildlife refuges to fruition and good use. He subsequently became the curator of the National Museum in Gaberones, Botswana, which he was also largely responsible for seeing created. Now retired in Botswana. His advice is always respected and valued.

Canaway, W.H. Author of *Sammy Going South*, which was made into a movie.

Cannah, Denis. Wrote the screenplay for *Sammy Going South.*

Card, Bob. From Cleveland, Tennessee. Client and friend of mine. Hunted in Kenya and Botswana.

Carlos, H.R.H. Prince Don. Later H.R.H. the King of Spain. Shot a record-class buffalo in the Mozambique Safarilandia concession.

Carlson, Dave. Long-time production manager of Winchester and mainly responsible for the design and manufacture of the Model 70 pre-1964 action Winchester rifles. Organizer of the manufacture of the .416 Taylor for Bob Chatfield-Taylor.

Carlyon, 'Jack'. Fellow Cornishman and good friend of mine. P.H. in Tanganyika Tours & Safaris Ltd. based in Arusha. Ethical and keen elephant hunter and conservationist. Owner of the Tregrehan Estate near St. Austell in Cornwall, U.K. Tragically killed with his gunbearer when he ran into the back of a huge stationary truck showing no lights after he was blinded by the lights of an oncoming vehicle. This took place near the Longido police post in Tanganyika just past the border post at Namanga, occurring only a few hours after he had visited me in hospital where I was recovering from being mauled by a lion in 1961.

Catchpole, Tony. P.H. killed by a buffalo he was hunting in Kenya.

Cawood, M.E.C. 'Mike'. P.H. and accomplished commercial pilot. Fourth-generation rancher at Ganna Hoek, Cape Province, Republic of South Africa (R.S.A.). Hunted Kenya with the Allen brothers in the 1960s. Loyal friend of Lionel Palmer and mine when working in Safari South (Pty.) Ltd. Died of horrific burns sustained in a gas-fire accident at his home. Wife, Pat, still runs safaris in R.S.A. at their ranch.

Challis, Tony. P.H. in Bechuanaland in early 1960s. Took Lord 'Skips' Riverdale on safari. Started oryx safaris. Both Tony and Bert Danhauser were killed with George Bates in an aircraft crash in South Africa.

Chapple, Barry. Game warden in charge at Kiboko, Kenya, on the Mombasa-Nairobi road. Killed in an aircraft crash when flying a Piper Super Cub by himself.

Chatfield-Taylor, Bob. Inventor of the .416 Taylor. Test pilot in 1939–45 War. Hunted extensively in Africa. Quite definitely an unforgettable character. He was married to Brenda Frazier. (Deceased.)

Chiavarelli, Massimo. Shot an elephant that had tusks of 97 pounds and 128 pounds in Tanganyika.

Christmas, 'Ace'. New Mexico rancher and long-time real working cowboy, crack shot, master of the lariat, and loyal friend. Hunted big game initially in Kenya with John Russell and subsequently many times with me all over Africa. (Deceased.)

Clark, J.L. 'Jim'. Famous sculptor and taxidermist of the American Museum of Natural History. His bronze castings of animals are valuable pieces today. Made many hunting expeditions to Africa. His wife was a fine shot and collected some quite outstanding lion trophies. Author of several books and papers on hunting and field taxidermy. (Deceased.)

Coates, Arthur 'Art'. Dear friend and remarkable safari companion. Was wounded in the 1914–18 War, having been hit in the chest by shrapnel, that resulted in his losing an entire lung and having a hole in his back into which a human fist would fit. Yet he was able to whistle the tunes and calls of birds so well that he made many records for music companies. Shot an elephant that had tusks weighing more than 100 pounds. Hunted Botswana and shot a huge greater kudu. He was the inventor of the spherical ball system used in the cement industry. (Deceased.)

Cohen, Sir Andrew K.C.M.G. Last British governor of Uganda, who handed over the country to Ugandan rule at independence in 1962.

Collins, Duggie. P.H., author of *A Tear for Somalia*, and a highly amusing companion. Retired to Lamu, Kenya coast.

Cook, John Soutar. Old-time hunter from before the 1939–45 War. Hunted for Ker & Downey Ltd. and was most kind and helpful to me when he joined the company. Took Their Royal Highnesses the Duke and Duchess of Gloucester on safari. Died in South Africa in 1987 in his mid-80s.

Corbett, Harry H. Starred in *Sammy Going South* as the diamond buyer and poacher with an aircraft. Famous for his long-running part in the British comedy *Steptoe & Son*.

Cornell, Harry. Chairman and CEO of Leggett & Platt Ltd., one of the 30 largest corporations in the U.S.A. He was due to come on safari to Kenya in 1977, within a few days of the ban on hunting being announced. In 1995 he finally did so in Tanzania—an adventure in itself! Both his wife, Ann, and he were the kindest and most generous clients the Kingsley-Heath family ever accompanied on safari. Affectionately known as 'Harry Mac' by all of his employees, Harry had a rare administrative ability and loyalty from all who came into contact with him. A great American, a truly remarkable person, and a more hard-working and ethical hunter it would be difficult to find.

Costillo, J. Employed on the Kenya railway construction; together with Tom Bennett arranged for one of the man-eating lions to be trapped.

Cottar, Glen. Grandson of the famous Charles Cottar and son of Mike Cottar, all of whom were professional hunters in East Africa based in Kenya. Hunted for Hunters Africa Ltd. Recreated his grandfather's company of Cottars Safari Services. Developed photographic safari camps near national parks of Kenya. Always helped anyone in difficult circumstances. Fine friend, sadly missed. Died of cancer in 1996. The company continues under the direction of his wife, Pat, and son, Calvin.

Courtney, Roger M.C. Professional hunter in East Africa before the 1939–45 War. Major in the Royal Marines. Author of *Claws of Africa*, *Palestine Policeman*, and others. Married Evelyn Cottar of the famous Cottar family. Buried at Hargeisa circa 1948.

Coyle, Eliot. Big-game hunter and investor in Holland & Holland Ltd. Met with me on many occasions when I visited Pittsburgh, where he lived. His gun collection was quite outstanding. (Deceased.)

Cumming, Alistair Gordon. Son of Sir William. Worked for Safari South Ltd. one season in Botswana.

Cumming, Roualeyn Gordon. Doyen of the big-game hunters in South Africa in the 1860s. His trophies remain at Altyre, the family estate in Scotland.

Cumming, Sir William Gordon Bt. Hunted with me in Botswana. Internationally known bird shot of great accuracy. Great-great-nephew of Roualeyn Gordon Cumming.

Cummings, Constance. Famous British actress who played a part in *Sammy Going South*.

Dangerous. Tswana gunbearer of Mike Cawood.

Dannhauser, 'Boet'. P.H. in Kenya of South African extraction. Moved back to South Africa in the mid-1960s. Was killed in an air crash in South Africa. The aircraft was piloted by George Bates.

Daud, Mohammed. Captain in the Ethiopian police. A Somali sent by the Ethiopians to control his own people. He had a difficult position but was remarkably able in carrying out his duties. Afterwards became a very senior officer in the Somalian police and army.

De Beer, Wilhem 'Willie'. A very experienced wild-game trapper in Tanganyika. Amazingly knowledgeable, with an unbelievable capability with wild animals. Worked on the film *Hatari* and many others. Moved to South Africa. (Deceased.)

De Cicco, Pat. With Fred Bartlett shot an elephant that had tusks of 110 pounds and 100 pounds in Kenya.

Delamere, Lord Hugh Cholmondley. Trekked from Somaliland to Nairobi by foot 'hunting and shooting' all the way. Famous as the leader of the Kenya settlers both before and after the 1914–1918 War. Delamere Estates Ltd. were some of the largest in Kenya. He was responsible for making an inestimable contribution over many years to Kenya's agriculture.

Del Savio, J. Big-game hunter and filmmaker who went to East Africa as a very young man, realizing intuitively that the game would not be there forever. Shot some big ivory and many other trophies. Ever a friend and loyal member of the Camp Fire Club.

Destro, Reggie. P.H. with Ker & Downey Safaris Ltd., Selby & Holmberg Safaris Ltd., and in his own business, now carried on by his son, Malcolm. Vice president of E.A.P.H.A. Intensely keen elephant hunter. (Deceased.)

Dinesen, Isak (pseudonym). Maiden name of Karen Blixen, wife of Count Bror von Blixen. Wrote *Out of Africa*, which was made into a movie filmed on location in Kenya starring Meryl Streep and Robert Redford.

Dobbie, Lieutenant Colonel William. Afterwards Lieutenant General Sir William Dobbie. Governor of Malta, G.C.

Douglas Russell Bowker. Son of a famous Kenya pioneer. Founder of Tanganyika Tours & Safaris Ltd., approximately 1950–70. Built the original Lake Manyara Hotel and was a pillar of the growing Tanganyika tourist industry after the war. P.H. of distinction for many years in both Kenya and Tanganyika. Vice chairman of the E.A.P.H.A.

Downey, S.P. 'Syd'. Founder and partner of Ker & Downey Safaris Ltd. Close and respected friend of mine. He was most kind and considerate to me over many years. Founder member of E.A.P.H.A. Took Their Royal Highnesses Prince Charles and the Princess Diana on safari in Kenya. Co-author of *Downey's Africa* and *Saving the Game* with Anthony Cullen. Probably one of the most famous and highly respected professional hunters and conservationists of all time in East Africa. (Deceased.)

Draeger, Frank. One of the nicest clients I ever had on safari. Although he has passed on, we are often in touch with his wife, Ardiebelle, who came on safari with him and who has remained a close friend. Frank was well known in California as an expert on the former Spanish boundaries of the years before California became a U.S. state. Shot a charging lion without turning a hair.

Duckworth, Fred. P.H., outfitter, game warden, and administrator on wildlife to the Ethiopian government of Emperor Haile Selassie for a total of seven years, most recently from 1970–75. Representative for all types of safaris worldwide. Staunch member of S.C.I. Based in Ravenstein, Holland.

Dugmore, John. Started safari life as a very young man in the stores of Ker & Downey Safaris Ltd. Became long-time and respected P.H. Hunted extensively in East Africa. Moved to Zimbabwe and Botswana, where he owns a company manufacturing safari equipment. Nephew of Bill Ryan.

Dunn, Derrick. Long-time P.H. in Kenya and Tanganyika. Worked for Ker & Downey Safaris Ltd. and other companies. Next-door neighbour to me when I was farming on west Kilimanjaro at Poverty Gulch. Redoubtable party goer and intuitive cattleman. With a client shot a record buffalo with horns 59 3/16 inches wide in Maswa, Tanganyika Masailand. Won Shaw & Hunter trophy twice. Retired to ranch cattle in Mexico.

Dwyer, Peter, wife, *Fran,* and brother *Richard.* From Colusa, California. Fran the hunter, Pete the traveller with a most exceptional sense of humour, Richard, a monsignor of the Catholic faith. Long-time friends of Syb and Joyce West and mine. Travelled from Kenya to Botswana in the famous 'Botswana bus' and were present at Victoria Falls in the famous 'petrol affair'.

Dyer, Tony. Doyen of the E.A.P.H.A. and president for its last 11 years before it closed down. Rancher at Timau and Ngare Ndare, Kenya. Bush pilot. Long-time and respected friend of mine. Author of several books on the history of hunting in Kenya. Hunted for Ker & Downey Safaris Ltd. immediately after 1939–45 War. Founding director of Hunters Africa Ltd. Author of *Men of All Seasons* and *The East African Hunters.*

E*arle, Georganne.* Liaison from Frank Green's office of Travel Unlimited who visited Safari South, thus keeping the information going on the latest developments to Frank, the main agent for the company in the U.S.A.

Eaton, 'Dick'. Sold Safari South the Cessna 206 with registration A2-ZFF. A third-generation rancher at Ghanzi who was an appointed member of the Botswana Legislative Assembly and later Parliament. His son Clive is a well-known and highly respected game rancher in the Ghanzi area.

Eddy, Bill. Hunted with me and his close friend Dr. Jim Walker in Tanganyika. Returned with support from the Ford Foundation to take part in educational programmes for the Tanganyika national parks. Returned to the U.S.A. after several years of this activity.

Elliot, Major Rodney. No-nonsense game warden in Kenya; for a long time responsible for the Maralal area of northern Kenya. Took part in anti-Mau Mau terrorist operations in the Mau Mau Emergency. Served with distinction in the Royal Marines during the 1939–45 War. Retired in Kenya, living on the coast.

Elton, Frederick. Early explorer of East Africa. His grave is close to the confluence of the Kisigo and Makasumbi Rivers in Central Province, Tanganyika.

Engelbrecht, Wilem 'Willie'. Travelled by native bus to Tanganyika from South Africa in the late 1950s when 18 years old, determined to become a P.H. He did so by sheer determination and presence of mind. Forced to flee the country, he met up with me with only 12 hours to spare. Joined Safari South (Pty.) Ltd. in Botswana and became famous as a P.H. His good looks and sense of fun made him a most popular member of the company and a special friend of the Kingsley-Heath family. Now a cattle rancher in the Ghanzi area of Botswana.

Ennis, 'Chuck'. Larger-than-life Texan who hunted several times with Bill Ryan. Became a good friend of many of the professional hunters of East Africa, including me, whose home he visited in the U.K. Took some remarkable still and movie pictures that are now important records of wildlife in East Africa at that time. A most welcome honorary member of the E.A.P.H.A. Great supporter of Game Coin and other wildlife charities.

*F*arson, Negley. Author of *Behind God's Back*.

Field, P.A.G. 'Sandy', O.B.E. Former district and provincial commissioner in Uganda. Chief park warden in Serengeti and Ruaha National Parks, Tanganyika. Inveterate elephant hunter. Shot an elephant in Uganda that had tusks of 134 pounds each side, donated to Powell-Cotton Museum, U.K. Killed in a plane crash in Kenya at the age of 78 whilst piloting himself in bad weather. His crashed plane was not found for several months until one of its wings appeared as a roof for a native hut on the eastern slopes of Mount Kenya.

Finch-Hatton, the Honorable Denys G., Lieutenant Colonel, D.S.O. The younger son of the Earl of Winchelsea and Nottingham, the titles created in 1681. He came to Kenya in 1911. Famed P.H. in East Africa after the 1914–18 War, in which he distinguished himself. One of the first hunter-aviators in East Africa. His liaison with Karen Blixen, the wife of Count Bror Von Blixen, (immortalized in the book and later film *Out of Africa*) brought him unwanted notoriety. In fact, he should be better remembered as a distinguished and able soldier, hunter, and pioneer aviator. He was killed when his plane crashed near Voi in Kenya on May 14, 1931. He is buried on the Ngong Hills overlooking Nairobi and the adjacent national park.

Fletcher, John. Long-time P.H. and photographer with Tanganyika Tours & Safaris Ltd. and Ker & Downey Safaris Ltd. Semiretired and living in Kenya.

Fosbrooke, F.A. Anthropologist and archaeologist to the government of Tanganyika for more than 40 years. A member of the Ngorongoro Conservation Authority. A most respected conservationist whose collection of books and information on Tanzania's history is outstanding (*Tanganyika Notes and Records*). Retired, lives overlooking Lake Daluti, Arusha, Tanzania.

Foster, Bob. Undoubtedly one of the most knowledgeable professional hunters of pre- and post-war years. Reputedly shot more than one hundred 100-pound tusked elephants in his time. A kind and fair Scottish gentleman. He was a long-time member of Hunters Africa Ltd. His brother, who died shortly after him, was a dentist in Arusha and my next-door neighbour.

Foster, Robert. Killed by a lion when hunting in 1920.

France, Tony. Well-known P.H. in Kenya in the 1960s and 1970s. Collected a huge leopard of eight feet that weighed some 200 pounds in the Aberdare Mountains of Kenya, which won him the Shaw & Hunter Trophy in 1969. Immigrated to Australia when hunting in Kenya closed in 1977.

Frazer, Peter. Born in Uganda, where his father was a forestry officer. Co-director of a large aircraft ferry company operating from Camarillo Airport, California. Flew a Cessna 206 across the Atlantic to Uganda for delivery to me. Intrepid pilot and navigator.

Frederick, A.W. Shot an elephant that had tusks of 105 pounds and 102 pounds with Mohammed Iqbal in Kenya.

French, Mrs. Marcia. Shot an elephant that had tusks of 121 pounds and 117 pounds with John Sutton in Kenya.

Friedkin, T.H. 'Tommy'. A keen and well-qualified big-game hunter who purchased Safari South from us in 1977. He did so and promised to turn the company into the paramount safari company in Africa, which he did by purchasing its main rival in Botswana of Ker, Downey & Selby. He also purchased Robin Hurt's Game Trackers in Tanzania and Ker & Downey (Tanganyika; now Tanzania) Ltd. It is my opinion that Tommy Friedkin has not received the recognition he deserves for his enormous investment in Botswana's tourist industry and that industry's enormous success, the long-term effects of which are plain to see in Maun.

Furness, Viscount. English Earl who hunted with Syd Downey before the 1939-1945 War. He was chairman of the board of the Furness Shipping Line, a long-established business in the U.K. His son, the Honorable Christopher Furness, V.C., won his V.C. serving in the Welsh Guards, the regiment in which I later served, at Arras in northern France between 17 and 24 May 1940.

Gates, C.C. President of Gates Rubber Co., Denver, Colorado. Shot an elephant that had tusks of 118 pounds and 115 pounds with John Sutton in Kenya.

Garza-Vale, Dr. 'Arnie'. Client and friend of mine. Hunted in several countries in Africa and with me in Tanzania. Prominent neurosurgeon in San Antonio, Texas.

Gilley, Dr. Wayne. Client and friend of mine. Hunted in Kenya and Botswana with Bob Card. Both came from Tennessee.

Goodall, Jane. Studied chimpanzees in Gombe Stream Game Reserve, Tanganyika. Internationally acclaimed authority on primate behaviour, author.

Goodchild, Dr. R.T.S., F.R.C.S. Ear, nose, and throat surgeon, Nairobi.

Goodrich, Mrs. B. Accommodation manager at Tabora Railway Hotel, Tanganyika. Friend of Basil Reel, 1950.

Gottwald, Bill. Hunted with Lionel Palmer in Bechuanaland. Shot a record-class buffalo and many other trophies.

Granger, Stewart. Famous English actor who played tough, macho parts. Big-game hunter once married to Jean Simmons. Hunted extensively in Africa.

Gray, Jim. Shot an elephant that had tusks of 106 pounds and 104 pounds with me in Kenya. Did a double-booking of Kenya, Tanzania, and Botswana consecutively on one safari.

Graziani. Marshal of the Italian Army who was defeated in North Africa by the British and Commonwealth Forces in 1941–42. He was also the commander of the Italian Army that conquered southern Ethiopia in 1935 by using mustard gas on the Ethiopian forces. His rest house was used as a winter residence at Mustahil by yours truly.

Grey, George. Killed by a lion when hunting in Kenya in 1904.

Grimm, Doug. From Washington state. Experienced commercial pilot with military experience. Came to help us with our flying between camps in Botswana and on the long legs to Johannesburg. He was more than happy to do so in return for a little buffalo hunting.

Grossi, Dr. Enzo. Close friend of Michele Pascucci and made two safaris with him and me. Medical doctor from Rimini, Italy. Took part in the lion hunt with Magao (mentioned in Chapter 5) hunting in the Okavango Swamps.

Groth, John. Well-known artist and illustrator from the U.S.A. Came to Kenya with Winchester promotional programme for the new Winchester rifle of 1965.

Guest, Raymond. A former American ambassador to Ireland. He was a scion of the Welsh steel family Guest. His mother was an American, a member of the Phipps family of Pittsburgh. He was three times married by 1962. When he came to Kenya on safari he was married to Princess Caroline Murat. He shot two 100-pound-tusked elephants with Tony Archer on the Thowa River in Kenya in June 1962 and next day won the Epsom Derby with his horse Larkspur. Died at age 84 in 1992.

Guest, Winston. Elder brother of Raymond. He hunted elephant in 1938 in the eastern Tsavo area of Kenya and wounded a huge elephant carrying ivory of 196 pounds and 198 pounds.

Haggard, H. Rider. Author of *Alan Quatermaine* and *King Solomon's Mines*. D.C. of Lamu, Kenya, in 1920s. Gave his name to the rare Haggard's oribi.

Halliwell, E. Administrator of deceased estates, Tanganyika, 1952.

Hambledon, Lord. English earl whose forebears founded W.H. Smith & Son, an old and long-established stationery and printing chain in the U.K. He made many safaris with Rene Babault, always exploring new territory and travelling as far as Arabia with Nairobi as a base.

Harris, Richard. With wife, Sarah Jane, and son, Boyd, came on safari to Botswana from Atlanta, Georgia. Hunted with me and Jack and Eleanor O'Connor. (Deceased.)

Hartley, Diana. Killed by a 'tame' lion whilst filming on the set of *Hatari*.

Harvey, Gordon. Most experienced and respected national park and game warden in both Kenya and

411

Tanzania. Outstandingly successful in Kenya against elephant poaching in the 1950s. Later national park warden in both Serengeti National Park and Ngorogoro Conservation Unit in Tanzania in the 1960s. A most helpful and understanding man of great integrity and a good friend. (Deceased.)

Harvill. H.L. 'Red'. Shot an elephant at Nguala with me. Pioneer in aluminium diecasting processes. (Deceased.) His son was treasurer of S.C.I. and hunted with Simon Paul in Botswana.

Hassan, S.I. Asian P.H. and outfitter. Highly successful running a first-class outfitting business based in Mombasa, Kenya.

Hawks, Howard. Director of Paramount Pictures film *Hatari.* Not an easy person with whom to work. (Deceased.)

Healy, Scott. Winchester publicity/promotions manager. Visited Kenya with Jim Rikoff on a Winchester rifle promotion scheme in 1964. (Deceased.)

Hein, Lim Po. Shot an elephant that had tusks of 115 pounds and 111 pounds with Mohammed Iqbal in Kenya.

Heinzel, Wilfred. Shot an elephant with tusks of 107 pounds and 101 pounds with Peter Becker in Kenya.

Helmick, Paul. Second-unit director on *Hatari.* Tolerant, kind, and a great understander of problems. Without him things would have been very different.

Hemingway, Ernest. Famous American author of *Green Hills of Africa, For Whom the Bell Tolls*, etc. Hunted with Philip Percival and others often in East Africa, where he survived two aircraft crashes with pilot 'Boggy' Marsh.

Hemingway, Pat. P.H. in Tanganyika (Tanzania) with Tanganyika Tours & Safaris Ltd. in the early 1960s. Son of the famed Ernest Hemingway. His brother, Greg Hemingway, was resident in Arusha and a near neighbour for a few years. Pat returned to America to pursue environmental studies and further education when nationalization of the hunting industry took place after independence.

Henderson, Ian and Allan. Brothers based in Rhodesia who outfitted their own safaris in Botswana and were joined by Eric Rundgren. Ian was badly mauled by a lion.

Henley, A.M.H. 'Tony'. Long-time P.H. and game warden, Moroto, Uganda. Respected naturalist and ornithologist. P.H. with Ker & Downey Safaris Ltd. and later Hunters Africa Ltd. After Uganda, rejoined K.D.S. in Kenya and Botswana. His wife, Pricilla, and son, Henry, are gifted wildlife artists. Died of cancer in 1996.

Herne, Brian. Very experienced P.H. Committee member and vice president of E.A.P.H.A. Owned own company in his name, hunting all over East Africa. Author of *Uganda Safari.* Now retired and living in San Diego, California.

Hilliard, Ed. President of the Redfield Gunsight Co. of Denver, Colorado. Long-time friend and supplier of rifle scopes to me. Killed in a climbing accident in the 1970s.

Hodgkinson, George. Gifted pilot of Wilken Aviation. Flew one of the Tripacers that the company first owned. Later moved back to South Africa.

Hoffman, George. American P.H. who worked in many countries in Africa. Gun nut who gave his name to the .416 Hoffman, which he developed. An accomplished machinist and a fine safari companion.

Holmberg, Andrew. Long-time Swedish hunter who hunted in Kenya during the war and with Ker & Downey Safaris Ltd. Thereafter became a partner in Selby & Holmberg Ltd. On the dissolution of Selby & Holmberg Ltd. he ran his own company with his own name. Probably the first of the East African professional hunters to hunt in Botswana. Shot a huge buffalo in Tanganyika Masailand, 58 inches in horn width. Generally regarded by most professional hunters as having the ability to judge a trophy length of horns better than anyone else alive. Retired at 70 years of age. Still lives in Kenya.

Holmes, Bill. First hunted with Roy Home and subsequently with me. Shot a 120-pound-tusked elephant near Nguala and a huge leopard and greater kudu in the Ruaha Valley, Tanganyika. Author of *Safari R.S.V.P.*

Home, Roy. Old-time P.H. Officer in a machine gun regiment in the Great War versus the Germans in East Africa. Valued friend of mine. Hunted a great deal with J.A. Hunter for ivory. Figured in a famous murder case in Kenya in the 1950s in which J.A. Hunter was a witness for the defence. Mother died at 101, Roy at 78.

Hopkins, Donald and *Marjorie.* Inveterate elephant hunters booking safaris for months at a time with Stan Lawrence-Brown. Don never did shoot one that had 150-pound tusks, but Marjorie shot several over 100 pounds a side (both deceased).

Hornaday, Steve. President of Hornaday Co., manufacturers of the best bullets available for African game hunting. Most kind in his advice and assistance to me over many years.

Howard-Williams, Mark. P.H. for Safariland Ltd., Kenya. (Deceased.)

Hoynacki, John 'The Diver'. Keen big-game hunter. Unable to finance a safari, John flew for Safari South (Pty.) Ltd. for a season and thus paid for his safari. He ran a leisure centre in the U.S.A. that specialized in scuba diving.

Hunter, J.A. Famous elephant hunter and game warden of Kenya before and after the 1939–45 War. Shot several man-eating lions in Kenya at Darajani (see 'The Man-Eater of Darajani' in Chapter 5). Author of several books, including *Hunter's Tracks* and *Hunter by Hunter*. Died at age 83 in 1963 at Hunter's Lodge, Kiboko, on the Nairobi to Mombasa Road.

Hurt, Robin. Son of Kenya game warden Lieutenant Colonel R.A. Hurt, D.S.O. He is now probably the most well-known and accomplished P.H. on the African continent. He reached a pinnacle of success in outfitting safaris and obtaining record-class trophies that is now impossible to emulate. The teamwork that was put into this achievement in the face of most appalling bureaucratic difficulties is quite remarkable. No African country where hunting was possible escaped his attention. However, his achievements would never have been so remarkable if it had not been for the most exceptional administrative ability of his former wife, Jan, who made it possible for him to pursue his hunting plans and who kept the costs and profitability of his company under strict control. He won the Shaw & Hunter Trophy in 1973 with a 54-inch buffalo shot by Dr. F.K. Flick, the CEO of Mercedes-Benz.

I*Ionides, C.J.P.* Game warden and herpetologist extraordinaire. Big-game hunter, mentor of Brian Nicholson. One of the finest naturalists in any of the game departments of East Africa. Author. (Deceased.)

Iqbal, Mohammed 'Bali'. Asian P.H. A most successful elephant hunter. Friendliest of all persons, much loved by all professional hunters in East Africa. Died of a heart attack.

Isca, Belli Del'. Well-known P.H. from Somalia based at Mogadiscio. Hunted big elephant in the coastal swamp of the Webi Schebelli River. Outfitted well-organised safaris. Retired when Somalia received independence.

Iverson, J. Shot two elephants that had tusks of 122 pounds and 119 pounds, and 133 pounds and 126 pounds with John Dugmore in Kenya.

J*Jamsheed, Rashid.* Undoubtedly one of the greatest sheep hunters the world has known to date. Played a leading role in opening up Iran to controlled hunting during the reign of the Shah. Nothing is good enough by his standards of Asian sheep hunting except a record. Left his old and aristocratic background of Persia when the Shah of Iran was deposed; now resident in the U.S.A. Long-time international director-at-large of S.C.I. Author of *Memoirs of a Sheep Hunter*, a classic depiction of a hunting sportsman's endeavour to obtain the finest trophies by the most ethical of hunting procedures.

Jenkins, Peter, M.B.E. Longest surviving original national park warden of Kenya national parks.

Dedicated conservationist and friend. Visited Botswana. Pilot and wildlife conservation advisor in East Africa. Semiretired.

Jenvey, Bill. Long-time P.H. in East Africa. Hunted for Safariland Ltd. and Ker & Downey Safaris Ltd. in both Kenya and Tanganyika. Hunter on set of *Hatari*. Retired to his native land of Australia.

Johnson, Walter Jr. Followed his father's footsteps in Mozambique and accompanied his father from an early age. P.H. and remarkably proficient commercial pilot with Safari South (Pty.) Ltd., Botswana, for many years. Close friend of the Kingsley-Heath family. Retired in California.

Johnson, Walter Sr. 'Wally'. One of the real old-timers of ivory hunting in Mozambique before the 1939–45 War. Gold miner and P.H. of many, many years' standing. Hunted with Safari South (Pty.) Ltd. at my invitation when Mozambique descended into anarchy and he lost all he had. Shot two elephants that had tusks of over 160 pounds each. (Deceased.)

Jonas Brothers. Joe Jonas Sr. founded the firm in Denver, Colorado. Four generations later, several members of the family are still in business as taxidermists and taxidermist assessors in various parts of the U.S.A.

Joubert, A. Shot an elephant that had tusks of 101 pounds and 110 pounds in Tanganyika.

K

Kaduga, Asumani. My gunbearer in Tanganyika between 1950 and 1952. Msangu by tribe.

Karmark, A. Shot an elephant that had tusks of 102 pounds and 103 pounds with Terry Mathews in Kenya.

Kassa, Ras Aserate. Head of one of the oldest aristocratic and feudal families of the Ethiopian Empire and close and loyal confidant of H.I.M. the Emperor of Ethiopia Haile Selaisse, to whom he was related. The Kassa family's menfolk were governors of Gondar Province for many years. His father and Ras Seyum were mainly responsible for defeating the Italians at the Battle of Adowa in 1896. He was at the same public school as I but before my time. He was most kind and hospitable to me when I was in Ethiopia. The Kassa family has an exceptional record of bravery in battle and has defended Ethiopia from the 7th century. Murdered by Colonel Mengistu and his fellow army officers in 1974 when the Marxist regime seized power.

Kays, Kenny. A highly knowledgeable and capable P.H., guide, and interpreter. Born in Bechuanaland, where his father arrived at the turn of the century. Worked for both Ker, Downey & Selby Safaris Ltd. and Safari South (Pty.) Ltd. and was respected by all who knew him. Died of a mysterious disease, which was never fully explained.

Kays, Ronnie. Elder brother of Kenny. Long-time owner of the only garage in Maun in the 1950s. Operator of the famous Riley's Hotel and Bottle Store. Long-time P.H. and highly reputable elder citizen of Maun.

Keith, Elmer. American gun writer. Famous for using the biggest bore on big game. Hunted extensively in Africa. Author of many books on rifles and shooting.

Ker, Donald. P.H. and director of Ker & Downey Safaris Ltd. Founder of the company with Syd Downey. Founding member of the E.A.P.H.A. (Deceased.)

Ker, Eryk. Donald Ker's brother. Long-time farmer on the Kinankop, Kenya. Conducted photographic safaris for many years for Ker & Downey Safaris Ltd. Kenya. Took part in the making of the film *Sammy Going South.*

Kiebe, Ndana. Mkamba tribesman from Kenya. Gunbearer and tracker to Myles Turner and me. Involved in saving my life when I was being mauled by a lion. Awarded Queen's Commendation for Brave Conduct. Undoubtedly a top-class tracker and spotter of game. Went off the rails and was imprisoned in Kenya. Kiebe's last name is not given, for obvious reasons.

Killick. Present-day details unknown. First secretary at British Embassy in Ethiopia in 1954. Travelled against advice during rains from Addis Ababa to Nairobi via Somaliland. Believed to have become the British ambassador to Soviet Union in after years.

King, John M. Founder and president of King Resources Ltd., a company that went into sensational receivership. Hunted with me in Kenya and, amongst other unusual activities, tried to purchase the Meru National Park as a private game reserve. His company's Lockheed Electra aircraft took 10 tons of my safari equipment from Nairobi to Johannesburg for nothing.

Kingsley-Heath, Colonel A.J., O.B.E., K.P.M. My father. Served in the Honourable Artillery Company in the 1914–1918 War. Appointed to the Palestine Police in 1921. Barrister-at-law of Grays Inn in 1931. Deputy inspector general of the Palestine Police. Commissioner of the Kenya Police. Acting attorney general of Kenya. The aircraft in which he was travelling was sabotaged by a terrorist organization who saw his appointment to return to Palestine as a serious threat to their aspirations. (Deceased.)

Kingsley-Heath, Hugh. My youngest son. His are the illustrations in this book.

Kingsley-Heath, Michael. My eldest son.

Kingsley-Heath, Nigel. My middle son.

Kingsley-Heath, Sue. My wife. Became computer literate from scratch in order to submit this book in proper manuscript form to my publisher. Demonstrated astonishing patience with J.K.-H. during this process.

Kinloch, Major B.G., M.C. Chief game warden in Tanganyika and Uganda prior to its being granted independence. Credited with major part in creating Mweka Game Management College, Tanganyika. Shot an elephant in Kenya that had tusks of 134 pounds and 131 pounds. Also chief game warden, Malawi.

Klein, 'Herb'. One of the most famous American sheep hunters of all time, having collected more than five grand slams. Supporter and investor in the Weatherby Gun Company. First Kenya safari in 1953. Hunted extensively in Africa with Elgin Gates, Jack O'Connor, and many others. His trophy room was one of the most complete and magnificent in the U.S.A. and was used for educational purposes, as was his wish. Hunted with me on the Malagarasi River in 1962 with Don Bousfield and Fred Bartlett. Author of *Lucky Bwana*. (Deceased.)

Klien, A.L. Gave his name to Klien's Camp in the northern Serengeti. Famous American P.H. of the early days. Founding member of the E.A.P.H.A. and long-time vice president (1910 to 1939) of same. Died in Nairobi in 1945.

Kolouch, Walter. Internationally known gunsmith, big-game hunter, and traveller who, with his wife, Hanni, emigrated from Austria to the U.S.A. in the late 1950s, having served his apprenticeship at Ferlach. He first worked for Paul Jaeger. His quite outstanding work was recognised by many well-known marksmen and hunters when he moved to New Rochelle, New York, to work for himself. He hunted and shot a huge lion with me in the Okavango Swamps and moved to McMinnville, Oregon, when he took a leading part in the renaissance of the A.H. Fox shotgun. A great companion on safari, he has to be one of the finest gunsmiths of present day.

Kraft, Virginia. American news writer and successful columnist. Hunted on safari in East Africa with Owen McCullum. Supporter of Game Conservation International in the 1960s.

Kriete, Richard. Shot an elephant that had tusks of 111 pounds and 105 pounds with Terry Mathews in Kenya.

Kruger, Hardy. German movie actor in *Hatari*. I got to know him well. A fine person keen on doing all himself. Bought my hunting car.

Kyriacou, Mark. The grandson of a trader who came to Botswana in the latter part of the nineteenth century. I well remember meeting him in the Kalahari as he was riding a horse bareback and looking after his father's cattle. Today he owns Bird Safaris in Botswana and owns large concessions on the eastern side of the Okavango Swamps for big-game hunting. He is the present chairman of the Botswana Outfitters and Professional Hunters' Association based in Maun.

L*angley, Ann-Marie.* My secretary in Maun for several years during the building up of Safari South (Pty.) Ltd. A loyal and hardworking person and very attractive—she was much admired by the professional hunters of the time.

Lawrence, M. St. J. Early national park warden in Kenya. Founder of Hunters Africa Ltd. Former president of E.A.P.H.A. (1959–64). Accomplished wildlife artist and cabinet maker. Long-time friend of mine. Pioneer in Bechuanaland based at Kasane.

Lawrence-Brown, Geoff. Long-time P.H. in Tanganyika, firstly representing Lawrence-Brown Safaris Ltd. and later director of Tanzania Wildlife Development Co. Took over as chairman of the Tanganyika Professional Hunters Association from me.

Lawrence-Brown, Stan. Long-time P.H. Ran his own company, Lawrence-Brown Safaris Ltd. Long-time friend of Don and Marjorie Hopkins, with whom he sometimes spent six months a year hunting elephants. (Deceased.)

Laylin, David. Played a major role in the 1950s and 1960s promoting Iran as a safari destination for sheep hunters and other Asian animals until the Shah of Iran was deposed.

Leader, Gary. Shot an elephant that had tusks of 120 pounds and 116 pounds with Mohammed Iqbal in Kenya. There was a party of unforgettable proportions to celebrate this success upon their return.

Lee, R. M. 'Bob'. Owner of Hunting World, which he founded in 1965, a chain of internationally known shops in Europe, Asia, and America with more than 100 points of sale. Partnered and co-founded Lee Expeditions Ltd. in Angola (1959–65), at the time the only American-operated safari outfitter in Africa, where he hunted in the Macusso concession areas in south-east Angola. Author of *Safari Today* and *China Safari*. Contributor to *Sporting Classics*. Meticulous in the preparation of his safaris. Famous big-game hunter who hunted extensively in Africa. Most hospitable and kind person; he is a long-time friend of Jack O'Connor and me. Highly knowledgeable in big-game rifles and cartridges of all sorts and collector of same.

Lloyd, David. Well-known and most respected English gunsmith who brought out the first .244 calibre rifle with a cartridge of .375 H&H configuration necked down to .244. The calibre was adopted by Holland & Holland and produced on a Mauser action. At Pipewell, where David Lloyd lived in comfortable circumstances, he amassed a large collection of German ex-military rifles from which he used the Mauser actions to perfect his custom-made guns of the highest quality. His boast was that the guns he made were indestructible. He was an accomplished aircraft pilot and was the senior air controller at Tangmere during the Battle of Britain in 1939–45. (Deceased.)

Louis, John. He and his wife, Jo, hunted several times with me in both Kenya and Botswana with their family of three. John was afterwards appointed U.S. ambassador to the U.K. He was a nephew of the founder of the Johnson Wax Co. (Deceased.)

Loveridge, Joel. Originally came on safari to Kenya with Art Coates. David Williams was his first P.H., and then myself in Botswana. A finer and more loyal friend could not exist. He and his wife, Pauline, became close friends of the Kingsley-Heath family. He was a great supporter of educational hunting programmes for S.C.I., and Loveridge Hall at the S.C.I. ranch in Colorado bears his name. He was a former president of S.C.I. (Deceased.)

Lucas, George. Killed by a lion in Kenya in 1906.

Lund, Peder C. Publisher of Sycamore Island Books. A former 'Green Beret' who served as a captain during America's Vietnam War, where he was wounded. Enthusiastic bird hunter and connoisseur of fine wines. A good friend who is much admired and respected by those who work for him.

Lyall, Malcolm. Managing director of Holland & Holland in the 1960s and 1970s. His astute management resulted in the company's strong marketing abilities today. Many fine rifles and shotguns owned by the maharajahs of India and the dispersal of firearms by the Kenya police from the armoury at Gilgil at the end of the Mau Mau Emergency were bought up by his company and others.

Maartens, 'Bassie'. Bassie must be credited with placing Namibia on the hunting map. Known for some years as 'Mr. Namibia', he ran an exemplary company under his own name. His many satisfied clients testify to his remarkable ability to organize an excellent safari under genuine desert conditions. A man who has always gone out of his way to be friendly and devoid of prejudice, he is presently chairman of the International Professional Hunters' Association. He has retired from Namibia and lives in South Africa.

MacGrath, Andrew 'Alex'. Hunted extensively with me in many countries of Africa. Collected a huge leopard and many other trophies. A kind and most supportive friend.

MacKendrick, Alexander 'Sandy'. Director in Los Angeles film studios, where he began as a script writer in 1946. Went on to direct satires such as *The Man in the White Suit* (1951) and *The Lady Killers* (1955). His major American credit was the biting Burt Lancaster-Tony Curtis show biz expose, *The Sweet Smell of Success* (1957). Died at age 81.

MacKenzie, Lieutenant Colonel J.W., D.S.O. Shot an elephant that had tusks of 111 and 108 pounds in Tanganyika. Known to the Kingsley-Heath family when serving in Palestine in 1936. Senior superintendent of police in charge of Southern Highlands Province, Tanganyika. Friend of George Rushby. (Deceased.)

MacNamara, Garfield and Jimmy. Fictitious names of two clients involved in 'The Hunt for Bakuli'.

Madda, Dr. Frank. Hunter and author of *Outdoor Emergency Medicine*. Father and husband to a remarkable family.

Madison, Bob. Rhodesian entrepreneur and ivory poacher who appeared to succeed in smuggling ivory out of Botswana that he shot in the Okavango Swamps. (Deceased.)

Magao. Mamakush tribesman from the centre of the Okavango Swamps, Botswana. Credited by his fellow natives with being able to contact the spirits who knew exactly where lions could be located at any given time.

Makonnen, General. Commander in chief of Ethiopian armed forces and related to Emperor Haile Selassie. Close friend of my uncle and aunt for many years.

Manners, Harry. Old-time ivory hunter from Mozambique. Shot an elephant that had tusks of 190 pounds and 189 pounds. P.H. for Mozambique Safarilandia Ltd. Lately employed by national parks of South Africa.

Mapes, Charles. Shot an elephant reputed to be Oginga Odinga that had tusks of 129 pounds and 107 pounds with P.H. Duggie Collins. The tusks were taken to Mapes Hotel in Reno, Nevada. (Deceased.)

Marcovici, Peter. Big-game hunter, gun collector, and long-time member of the Camp Fire Club in New York State. Organized his own hunting trip to Tanzania. (See the picture of the dead leopard and dog, also dead, side by side in Chapter 6.)

Martin, Richard. Shot an elephant that had tusks of 116 pounds and 119 pounds with me in Kenya.

Martinelli, Elsa. Much-perfumed actress on *Hatari*. Boyfriend was Willie Rizzo.

Masire, Dr. Kwett. President of Botswana.

Mason, Hal. Producer of *Sammy Going South*. Kind and understanding person. It was largely due to his influence that the film was so successful.

Mason, Richard. Cornishman and long-time resident of South America. Famous jaguar hunter and partner of Tony Almeida for many years. Long-time and respected friend of mine, now running a hotel in South America.

Mathews, Terry. Close friend of mine. P.H. for Ker & Downey Safaris Ltd. Now an internationally known wildlife sculptor. Highly respected by all who know him. Owner-operator of Mathews Safaris Ltd., Kenya. Lost an eye in a bird-shooting accident and was badly injured by a rhino in Nairobi National Park, Kenya. He has now made an incredible recovery, taking nine years and 50 return trips from Kenya to the U.K. for many surgeries.

Mayers, Major Ray. Member of a well known Kenya settler family who displayed a remarkable capacity for showing the flag in the time-honoured British fashion and ensuring tribal peace in the most difficult conditions. He ended the war as an administrator of former Italian-held territory in southern Ethiopia and was known as 'The Uncrowned King of El Carre', his district headquarters. On return to Kenya he was a successful cattle rancher. (Deceased.)

McClelland, Fergus. Took the part of Sammy in *Sammy Going South* at age 12 in 1962.

McCloy, J.J. Former advisor to five U.S. presidents. Chairman of the Allied Control Commission for Germany after the 1939–45 War. Was made an honorary German citizen on his 90th birthday. Highly respected U.S. statesman. Kind friend of mine with whom I hunted in Botswana. (See also *The Chairman* by Kai Bird.) Wife and daughter both named Ellen.

McCloy, John J. II. Son of J.J. McCloy. Wife, Laura. Friend and mentor of mine. Chairman of the East African Wildlife Heritage Fund Ltd.

McCullum, Owen. P.H. for Hunters Africa Ltd. and other companies. Survived many scrapes with dangerous game. Died in 1964. Father of Danny McCullum, a P.H. of long standing who is still operating today.

McKendrick, 'Sandy'. Internationally known director of many famous films. Director of *Sammy Going South.*

McShane, Dr. Brian. The doctor who flew into camp on the Ruaha-Kisigo River when I was mauled by a lion. Was also in charge of my speedy recovery. Owns one of the finest collections of Africana books imaginable. Now retired after a distinguished medical career. He remains a close friend of the Kingsley-Heath family, with whom he meets frequently.

Mecom, Miss B. Shot a record-class buffalo in Bechuanaland with Harry Selby.

Melliss, Captain F. Hunted extensively in Somaliland and many other parts of Africa. His literary work is a classic, valuable and rare. He became a British Army major general and won the Victoria Cross, the highest military honour that can be awarded, in the Ashanti wars in West Africa.

Mellon, Jay. Author of *African Hunter*, one of the classic stories of hunting in Africa. Made a safari with Bill Ryan and me. Long-time friend.

Miller, Frank. P.H. for Ker & Downey Safaris Ltd. and Tanganyika Tours & Safaris Ltd. Partner with me and Lionel Palmer in John Kingsley-Heath & Frank Miller Safaris Ltd., Nairobi, and Safari South (Pty.) Ltd., Maun, Botswana. Hunted almost exclusively in Tanganyika and probably knew the country better than anyone connected with wildlife. Loyal and respected friend of mine. Son Gerard also very successful P.H. in Tanzania. Died at age 71 in 1995 in Tanzania.

Millership, Edward 'Ted'. Estate owner and labour recruiter, Kigoma, Tanganyika.

Milne, Bert. Joined Safari South (Pty.) Ltd. as a P.H. in the late 1970s. Hunted in Rhodesia and northern Bechuanaland.

Milton, Oliver. Shot an elephant that had tusks of 162 pounds and 158 pounds in Rujewa,

Tanganyika. Originally served in Burma before joining the Tanganyika Game Department as a game warden. Left the service for the U.S.A., where the tusks were sold.

Misner, Dr. H.S. Shot an elephant that had tusks of 125 pounds and 111 pounds with John Sutton in Kenya.

Mitton, Charles Jr. Accompanied his father, Charles Mitton Sr., at the age of 20, on safari. Together they shot two 100-pound-tusked elephants, two enormous maned lions, and two 49-inch sables. Hunted Kenya, Tanganyika, and Botswana several times.

Mitton, Charles Sr. Made several safaris with me in East Africa and Botswana. Probably has finest collection of trophies obtained for him by me of any client I ever took on safari. (Deceased.)

Moolman, Ardel. Next door neighbour and long-time friend of Mike Cawood. Farmed at Trelawney near Craddock, Cape Province, R.S.A. Joined Safari South (Pty.) Ltd. and hunted very successfully for the company in the 1970s. Visited the Kingsley-Heaths in the U.K., and he and his family have remained great friends for many years.

Morchand, Denis. Came on safari with me and hunted greater kudu and other big game in the Ruaha Valley. His wife, Denise, was one of the most beautiful women ever to grace a safari camp. Presently an aircraft charter pilot in Kenya.

Morrill, John. With his wife, Ginny, made a famous safari with me in Kenya when John shot an elephant that had tusks of 134 pounds and 132 pounds, as well as an enormous leopard. We remained good friends ever since.

Mosse, A.H.E. Hunted extensively in Somaliland. Author of *My Somalia Book.*

Mothero, Khomba. Killed when accidentally shot in the back while tracking a lion near Gweta, Botswana.

Mousley, Keith. Super pilot of great ability and experience. Taught me to fly and to be careful. His parents from South Africa settled in the south-east of Kenya. Held posts of director of Ker & Downey Aviation Ltd. and sometime manager of Ker & Downey Safaris Ltd. Only elephant he ever shot was one with 100-pound tusks. Wonderful person and friend. Never suffered fools gladly. Still flying.

Mowat, Murray. Manager of the Life Assurance Department of J.H. Minet & Co., Nairobi.

Mumia. African of the riverine tribe living on the Webi Schebelli River in southern Ethiopia, who displayed remarkable ability as a gunbearer for me.

Musioka, Konye. Gunbearer and good-natured Mkamba from Kenya. Wonderful smile, showing the best set of teeth any man could have. Loyal and excellent tracker. Hunted with me in many countries in Africa. Retired and now a bus driver in Kenya.

Mustek, J.R. Shot an elephant with tusks of 110 pounds and 104 pounds with Mohammed Iqbal in Kenya.

Nassor, Ali. Shot an elephant that had tusks of 116 pounds and 110 pounds in Tanganyika.

Nassoro, Saleh. Shot an elephant that had tusks of 142 pounds and 147 pounds at Uyowa, Tanganyika.

Ndaka. A Mkamba tribesman. Assistant gunbearer and skinner in my camp on the Ruaha and was with me when I was mauled by a lion.

Ndambuki. Mkamba tribesman of Kenya. Probably the best animal skinner I ever employed.

Nell, Japie. Survived the accident in which Keith Poppleton was killed at Gweta when hunting lion. He was hit in the arm by the same bullet that killed the tracker and Poppleton before striking him.

New, Dr. Paul. Shot an elephant that had tusks of 117 pounds and 120 pounds with Roy Home in Kenya.

Newman, Bob. This book's editor and a retired U.S. Marine. Came to my home and spent two weeks there sorting through huge quantities of film, thousands of photographs, and considerable amounts of manuscript. A keen hunter and fly fisherman. Author of many books who has become a good friend.

Ngui, Mindu. Killed and eaten by a lion at Darajani, Kenya. (See 'The Man-Eater of Darajani' in Chapter 5.)

Nicholson, Brian. Game warden and conservationist to whom major credit must be given for the survival and utilisation of the Selous Game Reserve in Tanganyika. Great friend of C.J.P. Ionides, who was his mentor. Today a safari guide and wildlife consultant in Kenya.

Northcote, John. A P.H. who hunted for many years in Uganda and also in Kenya, Tanganyika, Zimbabwe, Zambia, South Africa, and Botswana. He has probably been hunting in Africa continually as long as anyone. A good companion and friendliest of persons.

O*'Connor, Bradford.* Son of Jack. Outdoor editor of *Seattle Times* and long-time friend of mine.

O'Connor, Jack. Doyen of gun writers and gun editor of *Outdoor Life*. Author of *Boom Town* (a best-selling novel) and many other books on rifles, cartridges, and the outdoors. Hunted worldwide with his wife, Eleanor, and received many awards for his hunting achievements. Client and mentor of mine for many years. Made several safaris with me between 1953 and 1970. (Deceased.)

O'Donahue, Dr. Pat, F.R.C.S. Well-known and respected surgeon in Nairobi. Operated on me after I was mauled by a lion in 1961. My ability to walk without a limp is largely due to his expert surgery. Also operated on 'Kiko' Samson Ndolo, my safari cook, for a peptic ulcer and refused payment.

O'Hara, John W. Killed by a lion in Kenya in 1899.

Olin, John. Chairman of Olin Mathieson Chemical Corporation and well-known big-game hunter. Came on safari in the 1960s with Ker & Downey Safaris Ltd. Went out with Eric Rundgren and Terry Mathews with his son-in-law and daughter, Mr. and Mrs. Pretzlaff.

Olson, Ludwig E. Author of *Mauser Bolt Rifles*, a most authoritative work on this subject with full details of all models covering many different countries.

Omari. Driver of Syd Downey's truck and long-time employee of his.

Ommanney, David. Long-time friend and P.H. in East Africa, Zambia, Sudan, Zimbabwe, and Botswana. Achieved undying fame as 'Winchester's man in Africa'. Probably knew Tanganyika in the 'old days' as well as anyone whilst working for Tanganyika Tours & Safaris Ltd. Only very recently retired to the U.S.A. after being an active P.H. for nearly 50 years.

Outram, George. Killed by a lion when hunting in Kenya in 1922.

Owen, John, O.B.E. Formerly senior political officer in Sudan Civil Service. Dynamic director of Tanganyika national parks in 1960s. Famed for raising funds for national parks. On retirement suffered ill health. (Deceased.)

P*age, Warren.* Well-known and highly respected gun editor of *Field & Stream*. Hunted many countries in Africa most successfully. Lived in close proximity to the Camp Fire Club in New York state. He was generally credited with the development of the .243 carbine. (Deceased.)

Page-Smith Captain. Senior captain with Pan American Airways. Was on safari with Jack

Blacklaws when Jack contracted sleeping sickness in Bechuanaland. Flew him in Blacklaw's aircraft to Victoria Falls.

Palleja, Jorge. Famous Spanish big-game hunter from Barcelona. He and his English wife hunted with me in East Africa and Bechuanaland.

Palmer, Lionel H. Long-time friend and partner of mine in both Botswana and Kenya. Has an unparalleled reputation for hunting lion. Super safari companion and raconteur. There is no better person. A legendary character. Lives in Maun, Botswana.

Palmer, Phyllis 'Phyl'. Managed the office of Safari South Ltd. for her husband, Lionel, and me. Undoubtedly the most devoted and loyal person that any business could possibly have and without whom we would not have done so well. Sister of Ronnie and Kenny Kays.

Papalios, Dimitri. Greek shipping magnate who hunted in Botswana with Tony Almeida on a costly whirlwind safari. Subsequently sold his entire lifetime collection of trophies from all over the world.

Parker, George. Lifelong friend of Colonel Charles Askins with whom he served in the U.S. Border Patrol. A revered African big-game hunter of international repute. He collected five 'grand slams' of North American sheep and was often accompanied by Herb Klien. Died of cancer.

Pascucci, Michele. Italian owner of large Travertino Romano quarries at Tivoli near Rome. He and his wife, Marthe, hunted with Lionel Palmer and me in both Botswana and East Africa on a number of occasions. Close friend of mine before either of us was married. He drove Ferrari cars and was the epitome of the Italian who enjoyed life. Named his son Phillipo after Phil Hill, the world champion motor racing driver at the time.

Patterson, Lieutenant Colonel J.H., D.S.O. Author of *The Maneaters of Tsavo*, the story of the lions that attacked the construction workers building the railway from Mombasa to Nairobi at the turn of the century.

Paul, Simon M. My godson. Came to Botswana from the U.K. at age 21. Became a highly reputable P.H. Shot one of the few 100-pound-tusked elephants ever shot in Botswana. Dairy farmer and businessman in Maun, Botswana.

Pearce, Captain F.B. Hunted continually in Somaliland. Author of *Rambles in Lion Land*.

Pearce, Stanley. Appointed assistant superintendent of police in Palestine, where he was personal assistant to the commissioner, Brigadier Nicol Gray, D.S.O. He transferred to Tanganyika on promotion to superintendent in 1949, was in charge of the police mobile force, and was responsible for rounding up the 'lion men of Singida' and bringing them to justice. A good friend, Stanley Pearce always had his leg pulled at his striking good looks and resemblance to the late Tyrone Power, which might have given him a career in Hollywood.

Percival, Philip Blaney. Most famous of all the Kenya-based professional hunters of the 1920s, taking on safari too many famous people to name. Accompanied Teddy Roosevelt for a period on safari. Founding member and president of the E.A.P.H.A. for many years.

Perrott, John. A Bechtel Corp. oil-pipe engineer who was on safari with me when 'the man-eater of Darajani' was shot. He has travelled the world and is now semiretired but espouses the cause of maintaining the primitive life of the Bushmen of the Kalahari.

Pettit, Ray. Long-time service with the insurance firm of J.H. Minet & Co. Became managing director of J.H. Minet East Africa and eventually managing director of the company in London. Married Sir Alfred Vincent's daughter. Sir Alfred was chairman of the board of trustees of the Royal National Parks of Kenya.

Phipps, Amy. From Pittsburgh. Mother of both Winston and Raymond Guest.

Pitman, C.R.S. Chief game warden of Uganda during and after 1939–45 War. Big-game hunter and author of *Big Game Hunter*.

Place, Dick. From Illinois. Came to fly our aircraft during the busy season's work in Botswana. He was accompanied by his attractive wife, and their help and support when we were so busy were very much appreciated.

Polaski, Stanislaus 'Stash'. Shot an elephant that had tusks of 109 pounds and 114 pounds with me in Kenya.

Pollard, Tim. Game ranger in charge at Arusha at the time *Hatari* was filmed. Was responsible for shooting the lion that killed Diana Hartley.

Poolman, Henry. One of three brothers, all hunters. His brothers were Gordon and Fred. Henry was a highly respected and successful P.H. and member of the E.A.P.H.A. Killed by a gunbearer's bullet into his neck when confronting a lion with Henry's client.

Poppleton, Keith. Owner of Gweta Safari Lodge in Botswana. Killed in a shooting accident when hunting lion in the Makarikari Depression.

Powell-Cotton, P.H.G. Shot an elephant that had tusks of 198 pounds and 174 pounds, the second largest ever recorded, in the Lado Enclave. There is a museum of his name in Kent, England, where the tusks reside together with those obtained by Sandy Field.

Preston, Jeremy. Dentist, gun nut, distinguished pistol shot, avid hunter, and kindred spirit in Cornwall, U.K. Purchased my 7x57 Mauser.

Quadros, Ruis. A gifted and hard-working P.H. with Mozambique Safarilandia Ltd.

Quinn, E.C. 'Ed'. Senior vice president of the Chrysler Corporation of America. Hunted very successfully with me. Management of Ker & Downey Safaris Ltd. upset him, and he then hunted with David Ommanney. Gave me a ride in Chrysler's experimental jet car. Most equable and generous person. Gave me two rifles stocked by Earl Milliron: a Mauser 7mm Magnum and Model 70 .243 Winchester.

Rainey, Paul. Killed by a lion when hunting in Kenya, circa 1919.

Rasmussen, Arthur. Mercedes franchise owner from Portland, Oregon. He and his friend Peter Alport hunted with Lionel Palmer and me in Kenya.

Rattray, Andrew. P.H. and game trapper. Resident near Nanyuki in the early 1930s. Distinguished himself by training wild animals to do domestic work. Crossed zebras with horses and called them zebroids. Went on the Lord Furness safari with Syd Downey.

Reed, John. Shot a record-class buffalo with Ruis Quadros in Mozambique.

Reel, Basil. Game observer with Tanganyika Veterinary Department. Kind friend to me in the early 1950s. Died at age 79.

Ricardo, Major David C. Came to Tanganyika's Southern Highlands Province after the 1939–45 War. Established himself as a cattle trader of integrity. Pioneer of the trekking of cattle through tsetse-infested bush—after being inoculated against tripanosomyasis, the disease resulting from the bites of tsetse flies—en route to market in Central Province of Tanganyika. Left the country at independence.

Ridder, Eric. Shot an elephant that had tusks of 118 pounds and 122 pounds with John Sutton in Kenya.

Riggs, Cecil. Very successful P.H. with Safari South (Pty.) Ltd. Born in Botswana. After I left Safari South, he worked for Hunters Africa Ltd.

Rikoff, Jim. Originally in charge of Winchester/Western publicity and promotion. Came to Kenya and hunted with me and David Ommanney. Director of Game Coin and subsequently chief executive officer of The Amwell Press. Big-game hunter and safari guide. A long-time friend.

Riverdale, the Right Honorable Lord Sheffield 'Skips'. Big-game hunter and author of *Squeeze the Trigger Gently*. Hunted in Bechuanaland in the early 1960s with Tony Challis.

Robinson, Edward G. Famous American actor who starred in *Sammy Going South*.

Rotibor, His Grace the Duke of. Austrian nobleman who hunted with me and Tony Archer when we were with Ker & Downey Safaris Ltd.

Royal, Charles. Kenya railway construction engineer. He was dragged from a coach and killed by the man-eaters of Tsavo near Voi in 1900. Buried at Nairobi Cemetery.

Ruck. Family killed by the Mau Mau in Kenya in 1953 in a most ghastly and depraved manner.

Ruger, Bill. Owner of Sturm, Ruger & Co., the most successful sporting arms company of modern times, and long-time friend of Jack O'Connor, Bob Chatfield-Taylor, me, and many other gun enthusiasts. Hunted extensively in East Africa with Tony Henley. Most hospitable and generous person and highly respected by all who have met him.

Rumsey, Charles. Shot an elephant that had tusks of 101 pounds and 107 pounds with Eric Rundgren in Kenya.

Rundgren, Eric. During 1939–45 War years was in charge of game control in Aberdares and on Mount Kenya. Based in Nanyuki, Kenya. Long-time P.H. with Ker & Downey Safaris Ltd. and outstandingly successful. Was responsible for film *Hatari* going to Ker & Downey Safaris Ltd. Afterwards a game rancher in South Africa with a large herd of roan antelope on his farm. Died in Australia, where his family now lives.

Rushby, George H. Ivory hunter in the Lado Enclave and friend of Jim Sutherland. Prospector, farmer, game ranger, and deputy chief game ranger, Tanganyika. Most kind and considerate to me in the early 1950s. Died at age 80 in South Africa.

Ryan, Bill. Best-known P.H. at Ker & Downey Safaris Ltd. Most entertaining of persons and universally popular. Vice president of E.A.P.H.A. Director of Ker & Downey Safaris Ltd. when I departed. Died at age 80 in Malindi, Kenya.

Saidi. Game scout who accompanied me shooting cattle-killing lions at Pawaga/Isasi, Tanganyika.

Salmon, Captain R.J.D. 'Samaki', M.V.O., M.C. Chief game warden of Uganda in 1920s and 1930s. Originally an ivory hunter and chief elephant control officer. (Deceased.)

Sanchez-Arino, Tony. Famous P.H. from Spain who hunted in just about every African country for more than 40 years. Shot many large-tusked elephants. His unsurpassed experience could hardly be repeated. A most able linguist, he is a genuine friend to everyone and particularly ethical in all his methods of hunting. He is one of the great personalities of African hunting today.

Sandford, Brigadier Dan. Distinguished soldier and long-time resident in Ethiopia from 1921 onward. A close personal friend of the Emperor Haile Selassie. He took a prominent part in organizing the Patriot Forces in the recapture of Ethiopia from the Italians in 1940–41. He farmed at Mullu outside the capital, but his family was ejected by the Mengistu regime after his death in 1972.

Santomo, Arthur. Pittsburgh businessman who hunted with me in Kenya and Botswana. Was charged repeatedly by a rhino after shooting an elephant. (Deceased.)

Sarnadas, A. Owner of the concession in Mozambique that I visited with Wally Johnson, which bordered the Kruger National Park of the R.S.A.

Savidge, John A. Formerly warden of the Murchison Falls National Park in Uganda. Retired to U.K. and now a well-known glass engraver and raptor authority.

Scheir, Keith. Long-time friend of Safari South (Pty.) Ltd. in its formative years. Hunted with Frank Miller and on occasion with Lionel Palmer. His hospitality and help to us in the U.S.A. were outstanding. He was one of our very first clients and explored the Okavango Swamps with us for the first time. Contributed photographs to this book.

Schindelar, Fritz. Killed by a lion when hunting in Kenya in 1914.

Seaman, John. One of the earliest professional hunters in Bechuanaland in 1959–60. Knew the Okavango Swamps well and shot some very large record heads of sitatunga. The most plausible salesman I ever met in my life. He sold aircraft where no one else could do so. He once sold an airship that never appeared to the British Admiralty. He was one of the unforgettable characters of Africa whom, no matter how bad the things were that he did, you could not help liking. He ran a crocodile farm near Maun until recently. He was a friend, and to his friends he was loyal. He died of cancer in 1996.

Seely, Hall. A nicer safari client you could not meet. Hailed from Roseburg, Oregon. Hunted with me and shot a huge lion in Chitabe, Botswana. Host of one very memorable party in Riley's Hotel.

Selassie, Haile, His Imperial Majesty, the Emperor of Ethiopia, Lion of Judah, King of Kings. Son of Ras Makonnen, right-hand man of the redoubtable Emperor Menelik, the victor of Adowa, to whom he was related. As Ras Tafari he fought against Negus Mikael, who represented Menelik's 12-year-old grandson, and won the battle of Sagale. The succession to Menelik, who died in 1913, went to his daughter Zauditu. In 1916 he was made regent over all other contenders. He was crowned Emperor of Ethiopia in 1930. When Ethiopia was seized by the Italians he fled first to Jerusalem in 1936 and then to England. After the defeat of the Italians in 1941 by the British and Ethiopian forces, he returned to his capital of Addis Ababa. In 1960 he crushed an attempted coup against him. The leader, Mengistu, was publicly hanged against the emperor's wishes. In 1974 the 'Derg' (army officers and an ad hoc committee) took over the government and murdered most of the royal family and some 60 leading aristocrats. It is generally believed that the leader, a ruthless and cruel man, Colonel Mengistu Haile Mariam, personally murdered the emperor at age 84 in 1975. Mengistu's regime was itself destroyed in 1993. Mengistu fled to Zimbabwe, where he lives at the pleasure of Zimbabwe's ruler, Mr. Mugabe. My uncle and father took care of the Emperor and his family when he fled to Jerusalem in 1936 and to a lesser extent in Bath, England. My uncle assisted in the setting up of the finances of Ethiopia after the war. His Imperial Majesty was most helpful to me when I wished to hunt and explore Ethiopia in the 1950s. I met the emperor's grandson, where he now lives in Washington, D.C., in 1994, who on the death of his father has succeeded to the title.

Selby, J.H. 'Harry'. Immortalised in *Something of Value* and *The Horn of the Hunter* by Robert Ruark. Originally with Ker & Downey Safaris Ltd., he left and started his own company with Andrew Holmberg of Selby & Holmberg Ltd. Later rejoined Ker & Downey Safaris Ltd., which became Ker, Downey & Selby Safaris and was subsequently bought by the owners of Safari South (Pty.) Ltd. in Botswana, where Harry was the managing director of K.D.S. Safaris Ltd. Probably the longest serving P.H. working today, he has been hunting continually for 50 years. His son, Mark, is also a P.H. in Botswana, where the Selby family resides in Maun.

Selous, F.C. 'Fred'. One of the most famous of all big-game hunters and naturalists and an international personality. Author of many books, now most valuable in first editions. Pioneer settler of Rhodesia (Zimbabwe). Personal friend of Theodore Roosevelt. Killed and buried in the Selous Game Reserve, Tanganyika, in 1917.

Shepherd, Peter. Shot an elephant that had tusks of 103 pounds and 106 pounds in Tanganyika.

Shipway, Philip. Production manager of *Sammy Going South*.

Shirley, Jim. Shot an elephant that had tusks of 112 pounds and 109 pounds with Peter Becker in Kenya.

Shivji, Mohammed. Licensed ivory dealer, Iringa, Tanganyika.

Smith, Robin F. 'Fungi'. Officer in charge of Bohotle border post, British Somaliland.

Spang, Tom. My friend from Massachusetts and a fellow writer who loves to shoot birds all over the world. He is currently writing a book about hunting birds in Africa. Introduced me to Peder C. Lund, the publisher of this book.

Speer, Vernon. Owner of Speer Bullet Co., Lewiston, Idaho.

Spencer, Morris. With his son Nelson and brother Glen hunted with Terry Mathews and me in Kenya and Tanzania in the early 1960s. Subsequently Morris returned again to hunt with me in Kenya. To us in Africa, he was one of the finest ambassadors of the U.S.A. we could wish to meet or take on safari.

Spurrell, A. Killed by an elephant. Buried at Kibaya, Tanganyika Masailand, in the 1930s.

Stanley, Henry Morton. Explorer, geographer, and reporter who set out on behalf of the *New York Times* to find Dr. David Livingstone and did so with the never-to-be-forgotten words, "Dr. Livingstone I presume", at Ujiji on the shores of Lake Tanganyika.

Stanton, N. Brother of famous P.H. George Barrington. Owner of Bushwackers Safari Hotel off the Nairobi to Mombasa Road. Owned the tame rhino believed killed by Mindu Ngui, himself killed by 'The Man-Eater of Darajani'

Stassino, Paul. Actor who starred in *Sammy Going South* as the crooked dealer who tried to obtain money for disclosing Sammy's whereabouts and lost all.

Stephens, Marlies. Wife of Ronald Stephens and senior secretary in the Ker & Downey Safari office. A most efficient and loyal person.

Stephens, Ronald 'Ronnie'. Manager of Ker & Downey Safaris Ltd. Formerly a national park warden and chemist. Arguably the best manager the company ever had.

Stuart, Walter Ernest. Killed by a lion near Machakos, Kenya, when hunting in 1911.

Summerfield, Sir John Crampton, C.B.E. Born in Nairobi. Called to the Bar of Grays Inn, U.K., and appointed crown council in the Tanganyika Legal Department, 1949. Prosecuted Julius Nyerere, afterwards president of Tanzania, for the slander of a district officer. Prosecuted the Mangati ritual murderers who dressed up as lions before killing their victims in Singida District, Tanganyika. In a long and distinguished colonial legal career, he was chief justice of Bermuda and the Cayman Islands and president of the court of appeals in Belize. He was most helpful to me as a district officer, his guidance being involved in the recording of cases of preliminary enquiry to murder. (Deceased.)

Sundae, Edward. Shot an elephant that had tusks of 180 pounds and 167 pounds in Tanganyika.

Sutherland, Jim. Most famous of all ivory hunters at the turn of the century in the Lado Enclave. Author and most respected by all who knew him. Friend of George Rushby, with whom he made several expeditions. Was lethally poisoned by a recalcitrant member of his staff. Buried on the west bank of the Nile. His grave was refurbished by Tony Sanchez-Arino.

Sutton, John. Long-time P.H. with Ker & Downey Safaris Ltd., Selby & Holmberg Ltd., and Ker, Downey & Selby Safaris Ltd. Vice president of the E.A.P.H.A. Active conservationist. Board member of A.W.L.F. and other charities.

Swayne, Colonel H.G.C., Royal Engineers. Famous Somaliland and southern Ethiopia explorer and hunter. Gave his name to hartebeest he discovered in Somaliland and southern Ethiopia. Author of *Seventeen Trips in Somaliland.*

Swynerton, G.H. 'Gerry'. Game ranger, Kigoma, Tanganyika. Afterwards chief game warden of Tanganyika. Died of the long-term effects of a car crash whilst in office.

Taylor, John Falconer. Leading personality and pilot in East African aviation circles. Flew a Tripacer on *Hatari* film. One of the first directors of Wilken Aviation. Moved to Seychelles Islands and started an air charter company there.

Taylor, John 'Pondoro'. Author of classic *African Rifles & Cartridges.* Met me in London on two occasions. Hunted for ivory for years at a time in Mozambique and anywhere he could poach them. (Deceased.)

Temple-Boreham, Major L., M.C. Former game warden of the Narok area of Kenya Masailand. Strict and stood for no nonsense. Acted as deputy chief game warden. Highly respected. (Deceased.)

Temple-Perkins, E.A. District commissioner and game warden in Uganda before and after 1939–45 War. Survived two bouts of blackwater fever. Ivory and crocodile hunter. Died at 93 at Kichwamba overlooking the Queen Elizabeth National Park.

Tennant, Lawrence, M.R.C.V.S. A veteran and also the chief game warden in Uganda and later chief game warden in Botswana from approximately 1966–74. His wise counsel was most effective in the creation of the Botswana Wildlife Department, and he was strict and effective in the control of those who sought to take advantage of embryonic wildlife policies.

Thesiger, Sir Wilfred, C.B.E., D.S.O. Born in Ethiopia in 1910. Famous explorer and naturalist. Distinguished soldier for his exploits in Ethiopia in the 1939–45 War with Major General Orde Wingate and with the S.A.S. in the deserts of Libya. Honoured author of many books on Arabia and the marsh Arabs. His awards include the Founders Medal of the Royal Geographical Society, Lawrence of Arabia Medal, Livingstone Medal of the R.G.S., Burton Memorial Medal, and Heinemann Award. Recipient of a Fellowship of the Royal Society of Literature and holder of an Honorary Doctorate of Literature of the Universities of Bath and Leicester. A Fellow of the British Academy and Honorary Fellow of Magdalen College, Oxford. Long-time acquaintance of mine from Ethiopia and Kenya days. Well known to many East African game and park wardens and professional hunters to whom he freely gave his practical help on many occasions. Knighted by H.R.H. the Queen in 1996. Now 86, he has retired and lives in Chelsea, London.

Tillotson, Clifford. My 79-year-old client who hunted Tanzania with me and John Dugmore. He said he was the manufacturer of 'after-dinner ware' (hand and lavatory basins)! At the age of 80, he bought a farm near mine on the slopes of Mount Kilimanjaro, where it was reputed that the largest-tusked elephant ever to be shot was taken. The tusker was said to have tusks of 224 pounds and 226 pounds and was supposedly shot by an Arab ivory hunter named Sunussi.

Torielli, Guilermo. Shot an elephant that had tusks of 111 pounds and 103 pounds with Eric Rundgren in Kenya.

Torrens, Kevin. P.H. who was on safari with me when I was mauled by a lion on the Kisigo River. Now a civil engineer, temporarily in Botswana.

Towson, Brenda. Senior ward sister on MacMillan Ward, Nairobi Hospital.

Trafford, Brian. Shot an elephant that had tusks of 142 pounds and 140 pounds with David Allen in Kenya.

Train, Judge Russell. Shot an elephant that had tusks of 106 pounds and 102 pounds with George Barrington. Became president of the World Wildlife Fund.

Trimmer, Lieutenant Colonel 'Bombo'. Former commander of a battalion of King's African Rifles. Warden of Murchison Falls National Park, Uganda, after the 1939–45 War.

Tuckwell, John. Battle of Britain pilot. Distinguished commercial pilot based in Nairobi. Flew many thousands of hours over East Africa and into many bush airstrips.

Turner, Myles. P.H. with Ker & Downey Safaris Ltd. and then game warden of Serengeti National Park, Tanganyika; Nyika National Park, Malawi; and Mara Game Reserve, Kenya. Long-time friend of mine. Died in the Mara Game Reserve and was buried there overlooking the Sand River and northern Serengeti.

Ungan, Singh. Killed by a lion in 1899 on the Mombasa to Nairobi railway.

Van Rooyen, Atti. Shot an elephant that had tusks of 105 pounds and 109 pounds in Tanganyika.

Van Rooyen Sr. 'Baas'. Famous P.H. and outfitter from Essimingor, 45 miles west of Arusha. He trekked up to Tanganyika from South Africa in 1919. Anti-apartheid policies drove his family out of Tanzania.

Van Rooyen, Luis. Shot an elephant that had tusks of 111 pounds and 113 pounds in Tanganyika. Friend and fellow hunter. Outfitted safaris in Tanganyika with his brother Quirce for many years both before and after the 1939–45 War.

Van Rooyen, Quirce. Shot an elephant that had tusks of 103 pounds and 105 pounds in Tanganyika.

Verolini, Franco. Owner of Light Transport Ltd., Nairobi. Born in Eritrea, where his family had business interests and a hotel at Ghinda, between Asmara and Massawa. Killed with his wife, Leslie, when a Cessna 182 crashed at Governor's Camp airstrip on the Mara Plains in Kenya.

Verolini, Georgio. Brother of Franco Verolini. Took over Light Transport Ltd. on the death of his brother and maintained my transport in Kenya. Ran a successful newspaper distribution business in

Nairobi. Travelled to Botswana with me. Retired to farm in Pietermaritzberg, R.S.A. He and his wife, Milvia, are long-time friends of the Kingsley-Heath family.

Viviers, 'Red'. One of Uganda's unforgettable characters. He was a control officer and hard-working game warden.

Walston, Vern. Shot an elephant that had tusks of 102 pounds and 100 pounds with Eric Rundgren in Kenya.

Ward, Captain Vivian. President and founder member of the E.A.P.H.A. who presented me with the Shaw & Hunter Trophy in 1957. He retired and handed the E.A.P.H.A. over to Donald Ker. (Deceased.)

Wattville, D.E. Killed by a lion circa 1914 in Kenya.

Wayne, John 'The Duke'. Famous Hollywood movie actor. Hunted privately with me whilst on the set of *Hatari*. Wonderful, natural person to be with and most happily married. (Deceased.)

Weatherby, Roy. Long-time and respected friend of mine. I tested guns for him in Africa. Founder of the famous Weatherby Rifle Company. (Deceased.)

West, Dr. R.S. 'Syb', D.D.S. A dentist from Willows in northern California and former president of the Mzuri Safari Club and its charitable wildlife foundation in San Francisco. First hunted in East Africa with Tony Henley and subsequently along with his wife, Joyce, and long-time friends Pete and Fran Dwyer, with me. Big-game hunter of great distinction who hunted with me in both East Africa and Botswana and travelled the 'hell run' in my convoy of vehicles in the 'Botswana bus'. A fine friend to many professional hunters of Africa.

Wetzel, Bill. Hunted extensively with me in East Africa and Lionel Palmer in Botswana. Fine friend and good companion. Prominent member of the Camp Fire Club of America. Member of the famous team that won the Great Eastern Skeet Championship.

Wheater, Roger, O.B.E. Former chief park warden of the Queen Elizabeth National Park in Uganda. He also served as the director of Uganda National Parks and the Edinburgh Zoo in Scotland. 'Pretty quick on his feet', was the way a fellow park warden described him.

White, Stuart Edward. Author of *African Campfires* and *The Rediscovered Country*. American big-game hunter of the 1920s and 1930s.

Whitehead, Peter. Former game warden from Rhodesia, manager of Ker & Downey Safaris Ltd.,

Nairobi. Conservationist. Prime mover in the Arabian oryx rescue scheme. Related by marriage to Gerry Swynerton, formerly chief game warden of Tanganyika. Retired to South Africa.

Wilkens, Donovan 'Don'. Master dowser (water diviner) and staunch Cornishman. Revered friend of mine. Went on safari in Kenya with the Cheffings family. Spent many pleasurable hours with me hunting and shooting in Cornwall, for which the author is indeed indebted. (Deceased.)

Willers, Mervyn. Worked for the Public Works Department of Tanganyika at Kigoma. Bitten through the buttocks by a hippo at Kigoma in 1950.

Williams, David M. Long-time friend of mine who served his apprenticeship with me on a number of famous safaris, including Jack O'Connor's. Hunted extensively in Uganda and joined Ker, Downey & Selby Safaris Ltd. on my departure. Served in southern Ethiopia in an area adjacent to mine and in Saudi Arabia. Long-time director of Ker & Downey Safaris Ltd. and successful wildlife photographer and safari guide, to this day with Ker & Downey Safaris Ltd., Nairobi, ably assisted by his remarkably efficient and able wife, Verity.

Wilson, Captain E.C.T., V.C. Won the Victoria Cross as a captain in the East Surrey Regiment in British Somamiland in 1941. District Commissioner of Tarime, Tanganyika, in 1953-54.

Wilson, Ed. Shot an elephant that had tusks of 112 pounds and 110 pounds with Fred Bartlett and Peter Becker in Kenya.

Wilson, Erwin. Shot an elephant that had tusks of 101 pounds and 110 pounds with Terry Mathews in Kenya.

Winter, W.H. 'Bill'. Served in Kenya police during the Mau Mau period. Game warden and P.H. in Kenya. Started own safari company in his name, which was very successful. Long-time friend of mine, visited me in Botswana and did safaris there. Was shot in the lower leg by accident while hunting buffalo. Now retired and living in Nairobi. Most kind and hospitable person. Great conversationalist.

Winter, W. 'Bill'. Son of W.H. Winter. Runs the best photographic camping safari in East Africa, quite simply an absolutely first-class operation, and has done so for many years. A 'chip off the old block'.

Wixley, Bill. P.H. in Safari South (Pty.) Ltd. Holder of A.L.T.P. flying licence and loyal and close friend. A strong and determined man, he joined the Selous Scouts and fought for his native Rhodesia. He was the last European to be killed in the war by a terrorist's bullet. He is survived by his wife Janice.

Wolverton, Lord. Hunted extensively in Somaliland. Author of *Sport in Somaliland*.

Wootters, John. Well-known and highly respected gun writer for American magazines. Went on safari with Lionel Palmer in Botswana and tested the .416 Taylor. Has remained a loyal friend of both Lionel Palmer and myself.

Wright, Douglas 'Doug'. Perhaps one of the most informed and knowledgeable persons about the wildlife of Botswana from the layman's point of view. Born in Nokaneng on the western side of the Okavango Swamps, he grew up speaking Tswana and the 'click' language of the Bushmen and once walked and swam across the swamps from east to west for the hell of it! He joined Lionel Palmer, Frank Miller, and me as a P.H. in 1963 and was one of the most successful, ethical, and efficient hunters with whom it was my privilege to work. He and his wife, Diane, manage and own part of a safari company in Maun, Botswana.

Yoshimoto, W.T. Famous American hunter from Hawaii. Shot an elephant that had tusks of 127 and 123 pounds and a huge buffalo in Uganda. Hunted worldwide and was awarded many distinctions in the hunting world.

Yulu. Headman in my safaris during 1970s. Instrumental in fomenting a strike in camp when he demanded double pay. Was fired and never reemployed by me.

COSTS OF SAFARIS AND PROMOTIONAL INFORMATION— 1954–1977

I t would be unnecessary to publish all the different brochures of information on safari outfitting that appeared immediately after the end of the 1939–45 War. However, that of Safariland Ltd. was at the time the most comprehensive and informative. This and other information as to game licence costs will give the reader some idea of the requirements that a prospective safari client had to undertake when taking a big-game-hunting and photographic safari in East Africa. The daily rates of charge bear little relation to today's daily rate safari charges.

Following pages: Safariland information that went out to our clients prior to their arrival.

CABLES & TELEGRAMS:
"SAFARILAND"
TELEPHONE: 23186

HEAD OFFICE
SADLER HOUSE, NAIROBI
P. O. BOX NO. 699

SPECIALISTS IN
BIG GAME HUNTING AND PHOTOGRAPHIC SAFARIS

PLANNING YOUR SAFARI

This depends largely on where your interest lies. If you are on your first safari, your ideas are likely to run in the direction of a general bag. Given ordinary luck you should be able to obtain in about 45 days, specimens of some twenty species of game, including lion, rhino, buffalo and an elephant. If you are more selective in your requirements, you must be prepared to travel longer distances, spending more time in fulfilling your ambitions, for instance, the sportsman who wants a specimen of the Greater Kudu, Sable, Roan, Situtunga and an elephant with heavy ivory. For the Kudu, Sable and Roan, he would probably go to Southern Tanganyika ; for the Situtunga to the swamps bordering on Lake Victoria ; and for the elephant to the Tana River in Kenya. On the other hand, you may not care for shooting and prefer to capture some of the vivid impressions of wild life which the photographer can always find. Many people of course, combine both shooting and photography.

What we do. In the first place we **plan** your safari, and then from the moment you arrive in Nairobi until you leave we look after your comfort and interests. In addition, we provide everything that is required for your trip, that is to say :—

An experienced white hunter.

Full African staff comprising gun-bearers, skinners, personal servants, cooks, drivers, and camp porters.

Double-fly sleeping tents, with verandah and bathroom attached. Mosquito-proof dining tents and latrine tents.

All the camp equipment required.

The best quality food.

Medicine chest.

Transport, especially designed safari hunting car, and 5-ton trucks for carrying staff, equipment and your trophies.

We recommend you stay two clear days at least in Nairobi between the day of your arrival and departure on safari. During this time you will be introduced to your professional white hunter and will have an opportunity of discussing with him any alterations in your safari plan as may be found necessary by the latest news of game movements. Further, you will be shown lists of your tentage, camp equipment and food, so that any changes can be made to suit your tastes. In addition there are game licences and clothing to be bought. Similarly, on your return, we suggest a further two days in Nairobi to wind up the safari and to give you an opportunity of instructing taxidermists in detail regarding your trophies.

Quotation. Safaris differ considerably and no two are exactly alike. It is in the planning and organising of safaris to suit individual tastes and wishes that our experience is at your disposal . As far as possible we try and give an inclusive quotation, avoiding unwelcome extras.

The following information will assist us to plan and quote for your safari :

The size and composition of your party. Relationship, affects tent accommodation.

Duration of safari.

Game required.

Territories to be hunted.

A professional white hunter escorts one or two people only. If a professional hunter is required for each client, please indicate.

Will you bring your own weapons and ammunition ? Do you want to hire weapons from us ?

Do you wish to engage a professional photographer ?

Do you require a refrigerator ?

When would it be convenient for you to come to East Africa ?

White Hunters. The services of a professional white hunter are essential on a safari, he knows the favourite haunts and habits of the various species of game, and can lead the party to the best shooting grounds without waste of time.

We have many experienced hunters on our books, men who besides their hunting proficiency, are agreeable companions and who know how to look after the comfort and welfare of safari parties.

We do not allow a professional white hunter, to take out more than two persons when shooting, this makes for good results and for safety when dealing with dangerous game.

When to come. There is no closed season for big game in Africa. The best months are from the middle of June to the end of October, and again from the beginning of December to the end of March. During April and May our long rains occur, and the short rains fall in about November. It is possible to shoot through the rains, and many sportsmen prefer this period, as tracking is easier, but some delay may be expected owing to unfavourable and generally muddy conditions.

Size of parties. We are often asked to organise large sized shooting parties in the nature of fifteen to twenty sportsmen. We do not recommend this practise as the game in any one locality would soon disperse. Large parties of the size indicated could, of course, travel together to Nairobi and then separate into small groups for shooting, limited we recommend to six at the most.

The above does not apply to game viewing safaris the numbers then being only limited to the accommodation available.

Game Viewing Safaris. Our game viewing safaris are planned for the visitor who wishes to see and photograph game in its natural haunts, but who do not want to incur the comparatively heavy expenditure of a full shooting safari.

These safaris take the visitor to the National Parks and Reserves where the animals are protected but live under natural conditions. In addition to game the visitor will see much of the Native life and scenery with which East Africa abounds. It should be understood that no shooting can be done on game viewing safaris. Details of these safaris are in a separate pamphlet.

In Conclusion. Separate literature is available which deals with our charges in detail, game licences, notes on safari life in general, arms and ammunition, customs regulations, immigration and health rules, and other matters concerning safaris, also photographs of camp life.

Even so there are sure to be matters on which you will require further information, we welcome enquiries, every one of which will receive the personal attention of an expert.

Finally we believe that a satisfied client is the best advertisement that a firm can have. Sportsmen come to us from all over the world and have been kind enough to express their willignness to give a personal reference. If you would like to have their first-hand opinions on our organisation we shall be pleased to put you in touch with them.

CABLES & TELEGRAMS:
"SAFARILAND"
TELEPHONE: 23186

HEAD OFFICE
SADLER HOUSE, NAIROBI
P. O. BOX NO. 699

SPECIALISTS IN
BIG GAME HUNTING AND PHOTOGRAPHIC SAFARIS
GENERAL NOTES ON SAFARIS

WEAPONS—With regard to weapons we advise a selection from the following:

(a) Light:	30.06 Springfield or Winchester	
	.300 Magnum	
	.275 Rigby Magnum	
(b) Medium:	.375 Holland & Holland Magnum	
	.375 Winchester	
	.350 Rigby Magnum	
	.318 Westly Richards	
(c) Heavy:	Any of the following good double barrelled:	
	.465 Holland & Holland	
	.470 Evans or other good make	
	.475	

In addition some clients like a .22 rifle, but in Kenya this weapon can only be used for killing Dik-dik or game birds. You will require a heavy rifle for elephant, rhinoceros, buffalo and possibly lion, whilst a light or medium will suffice for plains game.

We have weapons for hire and many clients prefer hiring heavy rifles from us, as they are expensive to buy and some sportsmen have little use for them after a safari. The cost of hiring heavy rifles is £12 ($34) per month.

If you are bringing you own rifles, it is wiser to let us have details of them so that we can let you know whether ammunition is available here.

AMMUNITION—The amount of ammunition required on a safari depends largely on the individual, but as an approximate guide we suggest that the following is taken for each sportsman for 30 days:

Heavy rifles	Solid 30 rounds	Soft 20 rounds
Medium rifles	Silvertip 100 rounds	Solid 40 rounds
Light rifles	200 rounds	
.22 rifles	400 rounds	
Shotgun	100 No.4	100 No. 6

N.B.—If much bird shooting is intended naturally more ammunition will be required.

CAMERAS AND FILMS—The most popular still camera for taking game photographs is the 35 mm equipped with a 13.5 cm or equivalent photolens. A tripod should be brought and a gun stock attachment for the camera is also recommended.

440

Any good make of 16 mm turret head camera with three lenses one inch, three inch and six inch lens. Again, a steady tripod is most necessary.

A reliable exposure meter should be brought.

We recommend bringing your own 16 mm film and 35 mm colour film as both are seldom available in Nairobi. As a guide about 3,000 ft. of movie and 10 rolls of still film would be required per month.

LUGGAGE—You will find it an economy if travelling by air to send arms, ammunition and personal effects by sea, but you must allow ample time to ensure their arrival, generally at least four months from the United States. If goods are sent ahead either by air or sea, they should be sent addressed to :

By Air : The Express Transport Co. Ltd.,   By Sea : The Express Transport Co. Ltd.
Nairobi, Kenya, East Africa.   Mombasa, Kenya, East Africa.
A/C. of (Owner's name)   A/C of (owner's name)
        c/o Safariland Limited,   c/o Safariland Limited,
        P.O. Box 699,   P.O. Box 699,
            Nairobi, Kenya.   Nairobi, Kenya.

Do not address packages to yourself as this involves a delay.

Bill of Lading, Insurance, Keys, Invoices and certified values should be sent to us by registered airmail. It is most essential hat the amount and make ot ammunition and the calibre, make and registered number of weapons, be sent to us, otherwise much time will be lost in clearing goods through the customs. Personal effects should NOT be packed with arms and ammunition.

CUSTOMS DUTY—

(a) **Weapons** : twenty-two per cent. duty is charged on these. If you intend to re-export them within six months, as is of course normal, this amount is refundable in full on re-export. The fact that you intend to re-export your weapons must be stated on arrival. If you send your weapons on ahead we will arrange this.

(b) **Ammunition** : Twenty-two per cent. duty is charged and is not refundable upon surplus which may remain over at the end of the safari.

(c) **Film** : A free allowance of 500 ft. of 8 and 16 mm film per week is allowed for a stay of up to one month, thereafter 1,000 ft. of this film per month, if intended for use on your safari and if brought in the baggage which accompanies you personally. **Should your film be sent ahead, twenty-two per cent. duty is charged. It is therefore better to bring film with you.**

(d) **Personal effects, cameras and binoculars** : These are allowed duty free in reasonable quantities. Duty will not be levied on alcoholic liquors or perfume not exceeding one pint of each, or on cigars, cigarettes or tobacco not exceeding over half pound in weight. The free allowances do not apply to anyone who has in his possession a quantity in excess of this allowance and duty is then leviable on the full quantity in his possession.

The above information refers to Kenya, Tanganyika and Uganda. Conditions for sportsmen visiting the Sudan, Belgian Congo and other countries are different and special information will be sent if required.

Personal effects should be packed separately to rifles, ammunition and film.

MONEY—Generally speaking money can be transferred into Kenya without difficulty. We recommend that you open a current account with the Standard Bank of South Africa, Nairobi, transferring an adequate amount to cover our charges and other expenses whilst in this country. This course is most advantageous from the exchange point of view and is less troublesome. Traveller's Cheques we suggest should be kept to the minimum required for the voyage as commission on these is comparatively high. Any balance standing to your credit not expended at the termination of your stay can be returned to the country of origin without difficulty.

IMMIGRATION REGULATIONS—Every visitor must possess a valid passport endorsed for travel to the British Empire. Visas, are also necessary, except for clients from Scandinavian countries, Holland, Switzerland and Italy.

Entry permits into Kenya are required. Full names should be sent to us so that we can obtain the permits and meet you with them on arrival.

HEALTH—We strongly recommend vaccination against smallpox and inoculation against typhoid and yellow fever. These are not compulsory for travel by air to Nairobi, but are necessary for outward travel from Nairobi ; much delay is therefore avoided if inoculations are done before your departure.

Although cases of malaria contracted by clients are very rare we recommend taking a malaria prophylactic which we provide.

CLOTHING—We recommended the following clothing for safaris :

Men :   *2 Khaki drill bush shirts and trousers
         *3 Khaki shirts
         *1 Pair mosquito boots (not essential)
         *1 Pair light canvas shoes
         *1 Sun helmet or felt hat
         1 Raincoat
         2 Pairs light but strong ankle boots
         1 Pair shoes
          Thick woollen socks
         1 Pair glare glasses
         1 Woollen pullover
        *1 Tin trunk to hold your clothing

We suggest that the articles marked with * be bought in Nairobi, where they are readily available at cheap rates. The khaki clothing can be made to measure in 24 hours and costs about £5 ($15) a suit.

If you purchase the articles suggested in Nairobi, you can travel by air with normal requisites, as suits are worn in Nairobi.

Women—We suggest similar clothing as for men. Naturally when shooting, bright colours should be avoided.

Nairobi has quite a good shopping centre, and most "last minute" requisites are available.

We recommend bringing a few cotton washable dresses for use in Nairobi and for the evenings in camp.

African servants wash clothes daily in camp so that numerous clothes are not necessary.

BINOCULARS—Good binoculars should be brought ; 7 × 50 or 8 × 40 are suitable.

LICENCES—We obtain arms and game licences on your behalf, arms licences cost Sh. 10/- ($1.40) for all your weapons whether brought personally or hired from us. The rules regarding game licences are subject to alteration, particulars regarding these, as they exist at present, are enclosed separately.

TROPHIES—Field treatment, that is to say skinning and preserving of trophies during safari, is carried out under the direction of the Professional White Hunter in charge of the safari with the assistance of an experienced native skinner, the cost of which is included in our quotation.

For the final treatment, including dipping in anti-vermin solution, clients can make their own arrangements with taxidermists in Nairobi which include Rowland Ward Ltd., and P. Zimmermann.

GAME LAWS—The professional white hunter knows the game laws, which must be strictly followed. It is essential that sportsmen should make themselves acquainted with the more important ones, as not shooting from motor cars, or within 200 yards of a vehicle and after dark.

PROFESSIONAL PHOTOGRAPHER—A competent photographer can be provided to accompany clients' safaris if required. Rates of pay vary, but the ordinary charge is about £7 ($20.00) per day or £8.10.0 ($24.00) if he provides his own cameras. Clients providing their own film.

HOTELS—The rates charged in Nairobi hotels vary but the average price for a single room with bath-room is £2 ($5 60) a day, including meals. We normally arrange hotel bookings.

DRINKS—Most kinds of drinks are readily available in Kenya. American cigarettes are most difficult to obtain.

CLIMATE— As a guide to temperature we give the following table of mean maximum and minimum temperatures at various altitudes :

Altitude	Mean Maxiumun	Mean Miniumm
Sea level	86 degrees F.	75 degrees F.
1,000 feet	85 degrees F.	72 degrees F.
2,000 feet	84 degrees F.	68 degrees F.
3,000 feet	81 degrees F.	65 degrees F.
4,000 feet	80 degrees F.	65 degrees F.
5,000 feet	78 degrees F.	57 degrees F.
6,000 feet	77 degrees F.	54 degrees F.
7,000 feet	75 degrees F.	51 degrees F.
8,000 feet	73 degrees F.	47 degrees F.

Most of the shooting, except for elephant, takes place at an altitude of 4,000 to 5,000 feet. There is little variation between the so-called winter months, *i.e.* July, August and September, and the summer months, January, February and March—at the most about 6 degrees.

NAIROBI—We recommend that you spend two clear days in Nairobi before and after your safari. There are many matters to attend to, and experience has shown that this amount of time is necessary.
We personally meet you on arrival and look after your interests and comfort until you leave.
COMMUNICATIONS—Your mail should be sent care of us, it is possible to forward it on to you from time to time.

Every safari carries a radio receiving set, and important messages (such as received by cable) can be relayed to you after the evening news from Nairobi.

LIABILITY—Safariland Limited will not be held responsible for any loss to you by way of accident, injury, sickness, permanent or temporary which may occur to you whilst on safari.

CABLES & TELEGRAMS:
"SAFARILAND"
TELEPHONE: 23186

HEAD OFFICE
SADLER HOUSE, NAIROBI
P. O. BOX NO. 699

SPECIALISTS IN
BIG GAME HUNTING AND PHOTOGRAPHIC SAFARIS

OUR CHARGES

Safaris differ considerably and no two are exactly alike.   It is in the planning and organising of safaris to suit individual tastes and wishes that our experience is at your disposal.
The cost of safaris will naturally depend on your wishes, further, much will depend on territories that you propose visiting, for instance, a safari to the Sudan costs more than one to Kenya or Tanganyika.
We give below, as a guide, our approximate charge per day for a safari of about thirty days, this daily charge would be more for shorter and proportionally less for longer safaris.

BIG GAME SAFARIS

1 CLIENT ;	1 Professional White Hunter			£35
2 CLIENTS ;	1 "	"	"	£42
2 CLIENTS ;	2 "	"	"	£66
3 CLIENTS ;	2 "	"	"	£73
4 CLIENTS ;	2 "	"	"	£78

The above quotations include the following :

(a)   The services of white hunters according to the quotation.
(b)   Full tentage, *i.e.* dining tent, double-fly sleeping tents with bathroom and verandah attached, and lavatory tents, African staff tents.
(c)   Full camp equipment, including beds, tables, chairs and long canvas baths, mosquito nets, bedding, linen, lamps, water filters, cutlery, cooking utensils, radio receiving sets, etc.
(d)   African staff, gunbearers, skinners, drivers, cooks, personal servants, waiters and porters.
(e)   Food and soft drinks for the party on a generous scale.   The list of food and stores, etc., will be shown to you before leaving on your safari for approval.
(f)   Medicine chest and first-aid outfit.
(g)   Transport. One safari hunting car is supplied with every professional white hunter.   One five-ton truck to transport tents, camp equipment, African staff, trophies, etc., for parties of one or two clients.   For three or four clients two trucks are necessary. For one month's safari we give a free mileage allowance of 1,500 miles for each hunting car and 1,000 miles for each lorry with other periods in proportion. Extra mileage is charged at Sh. 2/50 (35 cents) per mile.
(h)   Hotel accommodation charges during safari, *i.e.* en route or whilst refitting.
(i)   Treatment and preservation of trophies during your safari.

The above quotations do not include :

(a)   Cost of game licences.
(b)   Hiring of rifles.
(c)   Hotel bills in Nairobi before and after the safari.
(d)   Alcoholic drinks (which are paid for as required.)
(e)   Ammunition.
(f)   Dipping, packing and shipment of trophies.   Packing and despatching of your personal equipment.

With the exception of these items our quotations include all your expenses on safari.

Your safari starts on the day you leave Nairobi and ends on the final day you return.   Periods spent in Nairobi before and after your safari are not included in these quotations.

Regarding payment for the safari, our terms are twenty per cent, in advance at the time of booking and the balance on arrival.   If, after the deposit has been paid you cancel the safari the deposit is refunded less expenses incurred and compensation to the professional hunter and the African staff.   The payment of the deposit is also our guarantee that a definite booking has been made.

Rifles can be hired as follows :
Heavy double-barrelled rifles   .   .   .   .   .   .   at £15 per month
Light and medium rifles   .   .   .   .   .   .   at £15 per month

The following extras can also be supplied :
Refrigerator   .   .   .   .   at £15 per month

A professional Game Photographer can be provided for by special quotation.

CABES & TELEGRAMS:
"SAFARILAND"
TELEPHONE: 23186

HEAD OFFICE
SADLER HOUSE, NAIROBI
P. O. BOX NO. 699

SPECIALISTS IN
BIG GAME HUNTING AND PHOTOGRAPHIC SAFARIS

KENYA GAME LICENCES

The animals shown on this schedule may only be hunted on the appropriate game licence as set out below :—

SPECIES	MAJOR LICENCE Costing £50 Valid 1 year	MINOR LICENCE Costing £10 Valid 14 days
Lion—except Masai Extra Provincial District	1	...
Hippopotamus—but only in Lake Victoria and within 5 miles thereof	1	...
Buffalo	2	1
Zebra—Common	4	1
* Eland—Males only	1	...
* Greater Kudu—male only and only in N.F.D.	1	...
* Lesser Kudu	1	...
Bongo	1	...
Sable	1	...
Wildebeeste	3	1
Waterbuck—Defassa	1	1
Ellipsiprymnus	1	1
Oryx—Beisa	1	1
Callotis	1	1
Topi—except Uasin Gishu and Trans Nzoia District	3	1
Hartebeeste—Coke's, excluding the Nakuru and Neumann's Hartebeeste	3	1
Hunter's Antelope, Subject to special permission	1	...
Situtunga—except in Trans Nzoia District	1	...
Impala	4	2
Bushbuck	6	2
* Reedbuck—Common Ward's	1	1
* Gazelle—Grant's (1 Masai ; 3 elsewhere)	4	1‡
Peter's	2	...
Thomson's	9	3
Gerenuk	2	1
Klipspringer	1	...
Steinbuck	1	1
Oribi—Haggard's, Coast Province only	1	...
Kenya, Central Province only	1	...
Cottoni, except in Uasin Gishu District	1	1
Duiker—all species altogether, other than Yellow-backed	6	2
Dikdik—all species altogether	6	2
Pigmy Antelope	2	1

Special licences available to holder of a Major Licence

First Elephant (Ivory to exceed 25 lbs. in total)	£75	Colobus Monkey (3 only)	Shs. 20/- each
Second Elephant	£100	Leopard (1 only)	£25
Rhinoceros (1 only)	£20	Lion (Masai District)	£20 each
Giraffe (2 only) 1 N.F.D.; 1 Elsewhere	£15 each	‡Blue Monkey (3 only)	Shs. 20/- each
Ostrich (2 only)	£2 each	Grevy Zebra (1 only)	Shs. 50/- each

NOTES

1. There is also an extra charge per animal to both licences for shooting in the Masai, Maralal and Kajiado Districts.
2. The schedule and charges are liable to change by the Game Department, Kenya.
3. The shooting of birds is included in the above licences subject to closed seasons in Rift Valley and Nyanza Provinces and Kajiado District.

    * Females now Royal Game ;   ‡ Not in Coast Province or Masai.

SPECIALISTS IN
BIG GAME HUNTING AND PHOTOGRAPHIC SAFARIS

TANGANYIKA GAME LICENCES

Except where otherwise provided for in the Ordinance the animals specified in this Schedule may only be hunted on such game licences, in such numbers and upon payment of such fees as are set out below.

A. GENERAL AND SUPPLEMENTARY GAME LICENCES

For shooting in Tanganyika Territory you must take out a General Game Licence, under column A. In addition to the game allowed under A, you may take out additional licences allowing animals under column B prices for such quoted under column C. *

SPECIES	A GENERAL GAME LICENCE £ 50 ($ 140) valid one year Maximum numbers of animals	B SUPPLEMENTARY GAME LICENCE Maximum numbers of animals	C Fee per animal payable by the holder of a Visitor's Licence Shs.
Buffalo	1	1	100
Bushbuck	2	3	20
Caracal (Lynx)	—	1	30
Dikdik	2	2	10
Duiker—Abbott's True	—	1	50
Blue	2	1	20
Common	2	3	20
Red	2	1	20
Eland	1	1	200
Elephant	—	2	1,500
Gazelle—Grant's	2	1	20
Thomson's	3	2	20
Gerenuk	—	1	200
Giant Forest Hog	—	1	100
Hare	10	—	—
Hartebeest—Coke's	2	1	40
Lichtenstein's	2	1	60
Hippopotamus	2	2	100
Impala	2	1	20
Klipspringer	—	1	40
Kudu—Greater	—	1	200
Lesser	—	1	200
Leopard	—	1	500
Lion	—	1	400
Monkey—Black and white	—	2	40
Blue (Sykes')	—	2	40
Oribi	1	1	20
Oryx	—	1	200
Ostrich	—	1	200
Otter	1	—	—
Pigmy Antelope	2	1	10
Puku	1	1	40
Reedbuck—Bohor	1	1	20
Mountain	—	1	40
Southern	1	1	20

Rhinoceros		1	500
Roan Antelope	1	1	60
Rock Rabbit	—	2	10
Sable Antelope	—	1	200
Serval Cat	—	1	20
Sharpe's Grysbok	—	1	20
Sitatunga	—	1	100
Steinbuck	2	1	20
Topi	2	1	60
Tree Hyrax	—	2	20
Warthog	3	3	10
Waterbuck—Common	2	1	60
Defassa	1	1	60
Wildebeest—Nyasa	1	1	60
White-bearded	2	2	60
Zebra	3	1	60

B. BIRD LICENCES

The following birds are classified as game birds :—

	SPECIES	NUMBER THAT MAY BE HUNTED	
		All species	Unlimited
1.	Ducks and Teal	,,	,,
2.	Geese	,,	,,
3.	Button-Quails	,,	,,
4.	Francolin (including Spur-fowl), "Partridges" and "Pheasants"	,,	,,
5.	Quail	,,	,,
6.	Guinea-fowl	,,	,,
7.	Lesser Bustards	,,	,,
8.	Snipe	,,	,,
9.	Sand-grouse	,,	,,
10.	Pigeons, (including Green Pigeons and Rock Doves)	,,	,,

* Example: If you wish to shoot a lion, it will be necessary to purchase a £50 ($140) general licence and pay an additional £20 ($56).

NOTE

1. Elephants may not be shot if their tusks do not weigh twenty-two pounds or over, or eleven pounds or more in the case of an elephant having only a single tusk.
2. A bird licence alone may be bought for Shs. 20/-.
3. For general purposes to convert shillings into dollars divide by seven.

GAME LICENCES AND QUOTAS OF GAME— 1950-1977

My reader will observe that there were substantial numbers of small animals and monkeys on licence. As a rule, in 90 percent of cases, a client seldom, if ever, shot these small mammals, monkeys, or even a giraffe, as they had little or no trophy value. In my whole career I never shot a giraffe on safari: as it was the national emblem of Tanganyika/Tanzania, it would have been sacrilege to do so. For a time some clients took advantage of favourable tax exemptions when collecting for museums and so did, in fact, collect many small mammals that were on licence. Few, if any, clients shot hyenas, baboons, wild dogs, and small cats. In a few permissible cases, species such as zebra and rhino females were permitted to be shot on licence.

In reviewing this information, my reader would doubtless be interested to know that those brought to justice for hunting without a licence were, of course, poachers. The value of the trophies they poached would determine the severity of the sentence or fine. For example, poaching ivory would carry a sentence of perhaps five years in jail, a fine, and confiscation of ivory, whereas a person shooting an impala for meat would be fined £200 or, in default, be sentenced to a month's imprisonment or even road work in his district. Generally speaking, poachers were caught time and again breaking the law.

Ker & Downey Safaris Ltd.

SCHEDULE OF EAST AFRICAN GAME LICENCES AND CHARGES AND RESTRICTIONS

KENYA — E.A. £'s
- A Full Licence — 50
- A Fourteen-day Licence — 10
- A Bird Licence — 2
- Controlled area fee — 10
- (Only 2 shooting members permitted in each controlled area at one time.)

TANGANYIKA
- A Full Licence — 50
- Minor Game Licence — 2
- Bird Licence — 1
- Elephant Licence — 100

(a) Payable at the time of issue — 100

(b) Payable on registration of ivory, in respect of each pound avoirdupois of ivory obtained— (E.A. £ s.)
- (i) up to 100 pounds — Nil
- (ii) for every pound exceeding 100 pounds up to 300 pounds — £1 -
- (iii) for every pound exceeding 300 pounds — £2 10
- Controlled area fee — 10 -
- (Up to 4 shooting members permitted in each controlled area at one time.)

UGANDA
- A Full Licence — 50 -
- A Fourteen-day Licence — 5 -
- A Bird Licence — 1 -
- Controlled area fee — 10 -

GAME LICENCE FEES

KENYA

SPECIAL LICENCE (E.A. £ s.)
	£ s.
1st Elephant	75 -
2nd ,,	100 -
1 Rhino	40 -
1 Hippo	10 -
Each Buffalo	- 5
1 Eland	2 10
1 Lion (Masai)	25 -
1 Lion (Other)	2 10
1 Leopard	25 -
1 Greater Kudu	5 -
1 Bongo	2 10
1 Hunter's Antelope	5 -
1 Grevy Zebra	5 -
Each Blue Monkey	1 -
1 Ostrich	2 10

SPECIAL AREA FEES (Payable after the animal is shot) (E.A. £ s.)
	£ s.
Lion	1 10
Leopard	1 10
Oryx	1 -
Oryx	1 -
Hartebeeste	- 10
Wildebeeste	- 10
Topi	- 10
Hunter's Antelope	1 10
Buffalo	- 5
Bushbuck	- 5
Lesser Kudu	- 10
Greater Kudu	1 10
Bongo	1 -
Eland	1 -
Reedbuck (Common)	- 5

(middle column, Kenya) (E.A. £ s.)
	£ s.
Chanler's Reedbuck,	- 10
Waterbuck Defassa	- 10
Waterbuck Ellipsiprymus	- 10
Duiker (except Yellow-backed)	- 5
Pigmy Antelope	- 5
Oribi	- 10
Steinbuck	- 5
Klipspringer	- 10
Grants Gazelle	- 5
Thomson's Gazelle	- 5
Gerenuk	- 10
Impala	- 5
Dik Dik	- 5
Common Zebra	- 5
Grevy Zebra	1 -
Elephant	5 -
Rhino	5 -
Ostrich	1 -
Blue Monkey	1 -
Giant Forest Hog	- 5
Crocodile	- 5

CONTROLLED AREA FEES NAROK AND KAJIADO (£ s.)
	£ s.
Lion	10 -
Leopard	5 -
Rhinoceros	5 -
Giraffe	5 -
Bongo	3 -
Buffalo	2 10
Eland	2 -
Oryx (Callotis)	1 10

(right column, Kenya) (E.A. £ s.)
	£ s.
Grants Gazelle	1 10
Zebra	1 -
Wildebeest	1 -
Hartebeest (Cokes)	1 -
Topi	1 -
Waterbuck (Defassa)	1 -
Waterbuck (Elipsiprymus)	1 -
Lesser Kudu	1 -
Gerenuk	1 -
Klipspringer	1 -
Ostrich	1 -
Colobus Monkey	1 -
Blue Monkey	1 -
Bushbuck	- 10
Reedbuck (Common)	- 10
Impala	- 10
Thomson's Gazelle	- 10
Oribi	- 10
Steinbuck	- 10
Duiker (other than yellow-backed Duiker)	- 10
Pygmy Antelope	- 10
Dik Dik	- 10
Serval Cat	- 10
Elephant	5 -

Note: Elephant in Kenya—
The following applies:
- When total weight of both tusks is less than 140 lb. — 5 -
- When total weight of both tusks is 140 lb. but less than 200 lb. — 25 -
- When the total weight of both tusks is 200 lb. or more — 50 -

SUPPLEMENTARY LICENCES

TANGANYIKA

(left column) (E.A. £ s.)
	£ s.
Buffalo	5 -
Bushbuck, male only	1 -
Caracal (Lynx)	1 10
Dik Dik	- 10
Duiker:	
Abbott's True	2 10
Blue	1 -
Common	1 -
Red	1 -
Eland, male only	10 -
Gazelle:	
Grant's, male only	1 -
Thomson's, male only	1 -
Gerenuk, male only	10 -
Giant Forest Hog	5 -
Hare	- -
Hartebeest:	
Coke's	2 -
Lichtenstein's	3 -

(middle column) (E.A. £ s.)
	£ s.
Hippopotamus	5 -
Impala, male only	1 -
Klipspringer	2 -
Kudu:	
Greater, male only	10 -
Lesser, male only	10 -
Leopard	25 -
Lion, male only	25 -
Monkey:	
Black-and-white Colobus	2 -
Blue (Sykes's)	2 -
Oribi	1 -
Oryx	10 -
Ostrich	10 -
Otter	- -
Pigmy Antelope (Suni)	- 10
Puku, male only	2 -
Reedbuck:	
Bohor, male only	1 -

(right column) (E.A. £ s.)
	£ s.
Mountain, male only	2 -
Southern, male only	1 -
Roan Antelope	3 -
Rock Rabbit	- 10
Sable Antelope, male only	10 -
Serval Cat	1 -
Sharpe's Grysbok	1 -
Sitatunga, male only	5 -
Steinbuck	1 -
Topi	3 -
Tree Hyrax	1 -
Warthog	- 10
Waterbuck:	
Common, male only	3 -
Defassa, male only	3 -
Wildebeeste:	
Nyasa	3 -
White-bearded	3 -
Zebra	3 -

RHINO TOTALLY PROTECTED

UGANDA

(left column) (E.A. £ s.)
KATONGA AREA
	£ s.
Buffalo	5 -
Eland	5 -
Zebra	2 10
Topi	2 10
Waterbuck	2 10
Reedbuck	2 10
Bushbuck	2 10

SEMLIKI FLATS
	£ s.
Elephant	25 -
Lion	25 -
Leopard	25 -
Buffalo	5 -
Waterbuck	2 10
Jackson's Hartebeeste	2 10
Hippo	2 10
Bushbuck	2 10
Reedbuck	2 10
Giant Forest Hog	2 10

(middle column) (E.A. £ s.)
KARAMOJA AREA
	£ s.
Reedbuck	2 10
Buffalo	5 -
Eland, female and male	5 -
Grants Gazelle	2 10
Greater Kudu	10 -
Lesser Kudu	5 -
Leopard	25 -
Lion	25 -
Oryx	5 -
Roan	5 -
Waterbuck	2 10
Zebra	2 10

MASHA AREA (ANKOLE)
	£ s.
Buffalo	5 -
Bushbuck	- -
Duiker	- -
Eland	5 -
Hippo	2 10
Leopard	25 -
Sitatunga	2 10
Topi	1 5

(right column) (E.A. £ s.)
	£ s.
Waterbuck	2 10
Zebra	2

LAKE MBURO (ANKOLE)
	£ s.
Buffalo	5 -
Bushbuck	- -
Duiker	- -
Eland	5 -
Hippo	2 10
Impala	2 10
Leopard	25 -
Lion	25 -
Sitatunga	2 10
Topi	1 5
Waterbuck	2 10
Zebra	2 10

VISITOR'S SPECIAL LICENCE
	£ s.
1st Elephant	30 -
2nd ,,	60 -

RHINO TOTALLY PROTECTED

Ker & Downey fees on a per-animal basis.

JOHN KINGSLEY-HEATH SAFARIS LTD.

P.O. Box 2983, Nairobi, Kenya
Cables: "Simbatembo" Nairobi
Telephone: 29110   Radio Call: 2837
Nairobi, KENYA

GAME LICENCES — KENYA

General Licence Class "A"	$214.30
Fourteen Day Licence	71.43
Bird Licence	8.57

SPECIES:	NUMBER WHICH MAY BE HUNTED:	CONTROLLED AREA FEE:
Dik dik	2	$ 4.29
Duiker Grey	2	3.57
Gazelle, Grant's	2	5.72
Gazelle, Thompson's	2	5.72
Hartebeeste, Cokes	2	14.29
Oribi	2	5.72
Reedbuck, Bohor	2	5.72
Steinbuck	2	5.72
Warthog	2	5.72
Wildebeeste	2	7.15
Game Birds	Unlimited	Nil

ANIMALS ON SPECIAL LICENCE

SPECIES:	NUMBER ALLOWED:	LICENCE FEE:	CONTROLLED AREA FEE:
Bongo	1	$ 71.43	$ 142.87
Bongo, female	—	71.43	285.74
Buffalo	4	14.29	28.58
Bushbuck	2	4.29	8.58
Crocodile	1	10.72	21.44
Duiker, Blue	1	4.29	28.58
Duiker, Black	1	4.29	8.58
Duiker, Red	1	4.29	8.58
Eland	1	28.59	57.18
Elephant	2	285.74	See below*
Gerenuk	1	35.72	71.44
Giant Forest Hog	1	10.72	21.44
Giraffe, Common	1	107.15	214.30
Hartebeeste, Cokes	1	7.15	14.30
Impala	1	7.15	14.30
Klipspringer	1	8.57	17.14
Kudu, Greater	1	71.43	142.85
Kudu, Lesser	1	28.58	57.16
Leopard, male	1	142.86	285.72
Leopard, female	1	142.86	285.72
Lion, Masai	1	85.74	171.48
Lion, other	1	42.87	85.74
Monkey, Blue	1	4.28	8.56
Monkey, Putty Nosed	1	7.15	14.30
Monkey, Patas	1	7.15	14.30
Monkey, Colobus	1	8.57	17.14
Oryx, Fringe Eared	1	28.58	57.16
Oryx, Beisa	1	28.58	57.16
Ostrich	1	14.29	28.58
Reedbuck, Mountain	1	5.72	11.44
Rhinoceros	1	357.15	714.30
Suni	1	4.28	8.56
Topi	1	25.72	51.44
Waterbuck, Common	1	7.14	14.28
Waterbuck, Defassa	1	7.14	14.28
Zebra, Common	3	7.14	14.28
Zebra, Grevy	1	35.72	71.44

Fees charged to my clients on a per-animal basis in Kenya.

TANGANYIKA TERRITORY

Game Animals (Licences)

(Schedule III—Section 17)

The animals shown on this schedule may only be hunted on the appropriate game licence as set out below.

A.—MAJOR AND MINOR GAME LICENCES

Species	Major Licence	Minor Licence	Species	Major Licence	Minor Licence
Antelope :			Kudu :		
Pigmy	10	10	Greater (male)	2	—
Roan	3	1	Lesser (male)	2	—
Sable (male)	2	—			
			Lelwel (See Jackson's Hartebeest)		
Buffalo	10	6	Leopard	1	nil
Bushbuck	20	10	Lion	4	2
Cheetah	1	—	Monkey, Syke's	6	—
Dikdik	20	10	Oribi	4	2
Duiker :			Oryx, Fringe-eared	2	—
Abbott's (male)	1	—	Puku	4	2
Blue			Reed-buck :		
Common	20	15	Common	4	2
Harvey's			Bohor	6	4
Red			Chanler's	2	—
Eland	3	1	Sitatunga (male)	2	—
Gerenuk (male)	2	—	Steinbuck	6	4
Giant Forest Hog	2	—	Suni (see Antelope)		
Grant's Gazelle	4	2	Thomson's Gazelle	12	6
Hartebeest :			Topi	6	4
Coke's	6	3	Waterbuck :		
Jackson's	1	—	Common	4	2
Lichtenstain's	4	2	Defassa	4	2
Hippopotamus	2	1			
Impala	8	4	Wildebeest	10	5
Klipspringer	2	—	Zebra	20	10

u.P.Dem. S 58320 11 47 4000

B.—SPECIAL LICENCE

Colobus, all species	not exceeding	2	10/-
Elephant (specimens of which the tusks exceed ~~twelve~~ *Thirty* pounds in weight each)	,,	2	~~400/-~~ 600/-
Giraffe	,,	1	150/-
Tree Hyrax		2	
Ostrich	,,	1	20/-
Rock Rabbit		4	1/-
Rhinoceros	,,	2	200/-

NOTE.—Applicants for Game Licences are advised to acquaint themselves with the Game Ordinance and Regulations, a copy of which may be obtained from the Government Printer, Dar es Salaam

Right: Licence fees in Tanganyika (1956).

Following page: The Safari South (Pty.) Ltd. list of licence fees.

452

SAFARI SOUTH (PTY.) LTD.
BECHUANALAND

P.O. BOX 40   MAUN   BECHUANALAND

Enquiries to: P.O. BOX 2906   JOHANNESBURG   S. AFRICA

BECHUANALAND GAME LICENCE FEES

Animal	Package 'A' R550 or £275	Package 'B' R440 or £220	Package 'C' R330 or £165
Buffalo	4	4	Nil
Duiker	2	2	2
Eland	1	1	2
Elephant	1	1	Nil
Gemsbok	1	2	2
Red or Cape Hartebeeste	1	2	3
Impala	6	3	Nil
Greater Kudu	1	1	2
Lechwe	2	Nil	Nil
Leopard	1	1	1
Limpopo or Chobe Bushbuck	1	1	Nil
Lion	1	1	1
Ostrich	2	2	2
Roan Antelope	1	Nil	Nil
Sable Antelope	1	1	Nil
Sitatunga	1	Nil	Nil
Springbok	2	3	4
Steinbuck	1	1	2
Tsessebe	2	1	Nil
Vlei Reedbuck	1	1	Nil
Warthog	6	2	2
Waterbuck	1	Nil	Nil
Blue Wildebeeste	4	4	6
Zebra	2	2	2

Unlimited numbers of game birds, e.g. spurwing geese, ducks, francoline guineafowl, quails, sandgrouse, snipe, etc.

SUPPLEMENTARY LICENCES
(Not included in Quoted Costs)

Animal	Maximum No. which may be hunted in one season under Supplementary Game Licence	Fee per Animal £	Animal	Maximum No. which may be hunted in one season under Supplementary Game Licence	Fee per Animal £
Buffalo	4	5	Ostrich	2	1
Bush Pig	2	3	Red Hartebeeste	4	10
Duiker	4	3	Sitatunga	1	25
Elephant	2	75	Springbok	4	5
Gemsbok	1	25	Steenbuck	2	1
Impala	4	3	Tsessebe	2	10
Kudu	4	25	Vlei Reedbuck	1	10
Lechwe	1	25	Warthog	2	1
Leopard	1	25	Waterbuck	1	15
Limpopo Bushbuck	1	10	Wildebeeste	6	1
Lion	1	25	Zebra	2	10
Mountain Reedbuck	1	15			

50% of these fees in addition to the fee itself is payable as a tribal tax to the Batawana Tribe.

NOTES.
(a) Licence Package 'A' is designed to cover all aspects of hunting throughout Bechuanaland.
(b) „ „ 'B' is designed to cover Desert area hunting and partly Okavango.
(c) „ „ 'C' is designed to cover Desert area hunting particularly in the Central and Southern part of the Kalahari Desert.
(d) „ „ 'A', 'B' and 'C' is issued to "Hunter's" Safaris (See schedule of charges information.
(e) Any licence as obtained above is only included in an inclusive quotation on the understanding that the safari will be for 30 days or more.

S U D A N   S A F A R I   C H A R G E S

The charges listed below are applicable to the 1978
safari season.

4 Clients with 2 Professionals $ 275 per person per day

3 Clients with 2 Professionals $ 340 per person per day

2 Clients with 2 Professionals $ 450 per person per day

2 Clients with 1 Professional $ 315 per person per day

1 Client with 1 Professional $ 518 per person per day

24th May, 1977.

SPECIAL LICENCES.

	NO. ALLOWED	LICENCE FEE U.S.$	SHOOTING TAX EACH ANIMAL U.S.$
ELEPHANT	1	300.00	Approx. $ 16 per pound Ivory. (incl. export tax
SITUTUNGA	1	300.00	150.00
GIANT ELAND	1	600.00	300.00
NILE LECHWE	1	450.00	150.00
ORYX, BEISA	1	240.00	150.00
LION	1	300.00	150.00
KUDU, LESSER	1	195.00	150.00
KUDU, GREATER	1	300.00	225.00
HIPPO	1	300.00	150.00
GIANT FOREST HOG	1	240.00	120.00
CROCODILE	1	180.00	120.00
DUIKER, YELLOWBACKED	1	360.00	240.00
KOB, WHITE-EARED	1	300.00	150.00
ROAN ANTELOPE	1	450.00	300.00
BONGO	1	900.00	600.00
ZEBRA	1	180.00	120.00
OSTRICH	1	150.00	90.00
GIANT BUSHBUCK	1	300.00	150.00
ELAND, LESSER	1	210.00	150.00
HYENA	1	150.00	90.00
REEDBUCK, CHANDLER'S	1	150.00	90.00
AARDVARK	1	180.00	120.00
WARTHOG	1	90.00	60.00

PENALTIES.

1. PENALTY FEE FOR WOUNDING AND LOOSING AN ELEPHANT..$ 3,000.00

2. PENALTY FEE FOR KILLING AN ELEPHANT WITH TUSKS
   WEIGHING LESS THAN 15 KILOS ..$ 3,000.00

3. PENALTY FEE FOR KILLING FEMALE BONGO OR MALE
   WITH HORNS UNDER 18 INCHES ..$ 3,000.00

24th May, 1977.

S U D A N   S A F A R I   C H A R G E S

The charges listed below are applicable to the 1978 safari season.

4 Clients with 2 Professionals $ 275 per person per day

3 Clients with 2 Professionals $ 340 per person per day

2 Clients with 2 Professionals $ 450 per person per day

2 Clients with 1 Professional $ 315 per person per day

1 Client with 1 Professional $ 518 per person per day

24th May, 1977.

THE BASIC SAFARI CHARGES (DAILY RATE) DO NOT INCLUDE
THE FOLLOWING:

1.   Cost of Game Licences and Shooting Tax.

2.   Hire of Firearms and Purchase of Ammunition.

3.   Cost of Alcoholic Drinks, Aerated Waters and
        Tobacco.

4.   Packing, shipping and dipping of trophies.

5.   Charter or Schedule Flights to and from the
        Sudan.

6.   Tips to Staff.

7.   Trophy Export Fees.

8.   Hotel Bills incurred prior to or after the
        contracted period of a safari.

9.   Incidental expenses incurred during the safari
        such as postal and cable charges.

10.   Visa Fee, Firearms Permits, Customs Duty on
        Alcohol and Ammunition.

11.   Game Scout Fees

12.   Shooting Block Fees and Tourist Tax.

24th May, 1977.

EXTRA CHARGES TO THE CLIENT.

1. BIRD LICENCE   .. ..   U. S. $ 45.00

2. SHOOTING BLCOK FEES AND TOURIST
    TAX (per Client).. .. .. ..   U. S. $495.00

3. GAME SCOUT FEES .. ..   U. S. $ 9.00
    (per day)

4. VETERINARY HEALTH CERTIFICATE
    (applicable only when exporting
        trophies) .. ..   U. S. $ 10.00
    (per piece of animal)

5. EXPORT TAX ON TROPHIES
    (when exporting trophies).. ..   U. S. $ 9.00
    (per piece of animal)

N.B.

Trophies can be shipped direct from Juba, Sudan to
anywhere overseas.

The charge for this is U. S. $ 400.00 per Client. This
charge includes handling charges, packing, dipping and
documentation for airfreight.

24th May, 1977.

Appendix IV

CONVICTIONS OBTAINED IN DISTRICT COURTS FOR OFFENCES AGAINST THE FAUNA CONSERVATION ORDINANCE DURING THE PERIOD 1957–1961

Offence	Section	Number of Convictions				
		1957	1958	1959	1960	1961
Hunting in a Game Reserve	5	7	34	57	73	50
Entering a Game Reserve without a Permit	6	20	63	67	91	84
Carrying a Weapon in a Game Reserve ...	7	4	–	15	10	33
Causing a Fire or Felling Trees in a Game Reserve	8	–	–	3	13	10
Hunting in a Controlled Area without a Permit	11	38	62	58	59	40
Hunting professionally without Professional Hunters, Licence	15	–	–	–	–	1
Hunting Game Animals without a Licence	12	195	252	270	360	291
Transferring a Game Licence	13(4)	–	45	6	2	3
Hunting Unscheduled Animals without a Permit	18	5	2	1	2	6
Capturing without Permit	19(2)	–	–	2	–	–
Failure to Report Disqualification ...	21	–	3	–	1	8
Obtaining Licence while not in lawful possession of Weapon	22	–	1	11	5	9
Failure to carry a Licence while Hunting	23	5	4	4	2	12
Hunting Royal Game without a Licence...	24	16	29	16	30	48
Failure to Report Intention to hunt Dangerous Animals	26	10	2	–	11	1
Cruelty	29	–	2	–	–	–
Failure to Report Wounding a Dangerous Animal	30	2	–	3	1	–
Unlawful Loan of a Weapon	31	17	12	41	35	–
Hunting on Private Land without Permission	32	–	1	–	–	4
Hunting Young Animals	33	1	2	2	–	2
Using Unlawful Methods of Hunting ...	34	111	135	98	174	59
Hunting Protected Species without Permit	35(4)	–	–	–	–	1
Selling Game Meat without Permission ...	36	33	8	35	41	16
Dealing in Trophies without a Licence ...	37	3	2	–	1	–
Illegally importing or transferring a Trophy	40	–	3	–	4	–
Unlawful Possession of Proscribed Skins	41	1	–	1	2	6
Unlawful Transfer of Ivory	45	–	1	–	–	–
Failure to Produce a Government Trophy	48	4	32	12	4	11
Unlawful Possession of Government Trophy	49	159	157	145	304	293
Failure to Produce Licence, Obstructing of Officers, etc.	51	1	5	1	7	8
Failure to stop at Barrier when ordered to do so	52	1	2	–	–	–
Contravention of any Provision of the Ordinance	53(1)	–	–	5	–	1
Total ...		632	859	853	1,232	997

This document shows Tanganyika offences against wildlife. Game wardens were busy with many offences.

EXAMPLES OF A SAFARI COMPANY'S GAME-SHOT FIGURES AS THEY RELATED TO GOVERNMENT QUOTAS

T he figures in this appendix are given as a guide to the reader, who should be assured that the off-take of the excess animal populations was properly controlled to the best of the limited knowledge available at the time. Careful control of records was kept by all safari companies operating in these years, and it was a condition of their concession lease that these records were regularly kept and submitted to the government at the end of every season. Integral in any calculation of the value of the hunting industry that my reader might make would be the cost of licences for each animal. It may well be that the income to the government of Botswana from the utilisation of the renewable wildlife resource was published in a report. If this was so, then the concessionaires of the wildlife concessions were never given a copy, to my knowledge. Had this been done, the basis for future negotiation of the concession leases would have been very different.

WHAT THEY SHOT IN 1971

X   Denotes wanted this trophy and failed to obtain it.
-- Denotes not prepared to take this animal specifically. 50%
*   Denotes client shot previously in East Africa and came to

	BUFFALO	BUSHBUCK	BABOON	CROCODILE	DUIKER	ELAND	ELEPHANT	GEMSBOK	HARTEBEEST	HYENA	IMPALA
1.	2	--	--	--	--	--	1	1	2	--	1
2.	1	--	--	--	--	--	1	1	1	--	1
3.	2	--	--	--	1	--	1	1	1	--	2
4.	1	--	--	--	--	--	--	1	1	--	2
5.	1	--	--	--	--	--	1	1	1	--	1
6.	--	--	--	--	--	--	--	1	1	--	1
7.	1	--	--	--	--	--	--	1	--	--	1
8.	1	--	--	--	--	--	--	1	1	--	1
9.	1	--	--	--	--	--	--	1	--	--	1
10.											B I R
11.	1	--	--	--	1	--	--	1	X	--	1
12.	1	--	--	--	--	--	1	1	1	--	1
13.	2	--	--	--	--	--	1	1	--	--	1
14.	2	--	--	--	--	--	2	1	--	--	2
15.	2	--	--	--	--	--	1	1	X	--	1
16.	1	--	--	--	--	--	--	1	--	--	1
17.	--	--	--	--	--	--	--	1	X	--	--
18.	1	--	--	--	1	--	--	1	--	--	1
19.											B I R
20.	1	--	--	--	--	--	1	1	--	--	1
21.	--	--	--	--	--	1	1	1	--	--	1
22.	--	--	--	--	--	--	--	--	--	--	1
23.	2	--	--	--	--	--	1	1	X	--	1
24.	1	--	--	--	--	--	--	1	--	--	1
25.	--	--	--	--	--	--	--	1	--	--	1
26.	1	--	--	--	--	--	--	1	--	--	1
27.	1	--	--	--	--	--	--	1	1	--	1
28.	1	--	--	--	--	--	--	1	1	--	1
29.	1	--	--	--	--	--	--	--	--	--	1
30.	2	--	--	1	--	--	1	1	--	--	1
31.											B I R
32.											B I R
33.	2	--	--	--	--	--	1	--	X	--	1
34.	1	--	--	--	--	--	1	1	--	--	--
35.	1	--	--	--	1	--	--	1	X	--	2
36.	1	--	--	--	--	--	--	1	--	--	1
37.	--	--	--	--	--	--	1	1	--	--	1
38.	1	--	--	--	--	--	--	1	--	--	1
39.	1	--	--	--	--	--	1	1	1	--	1
40.	1	--	--	--	--	--	--	1	--	--	1
41.	--	--	--	--	1	--	--	--	--	--	1
42.	1	--	--	--	1	--	1	1	--	--	1
43.	--	--	--	--	--	--	--	--	--	--	1
44.	--	--	--	--	--	--	--	1	1	--	1
45.	1	--	--	--	--	--	--	--	--	1	1
46.	1	--	--	--	--	--	--	--	--	1	--
47.	1	--	--	--	1	--	--	1	1	--	1
48.	1	--	--	1	--	--	--	1	1	--	1
49.	1	--	--	--	--	--	2	1	--	--	1
50.	1	--	--	--	--	--	1	1	--	--	1
51.	1	--	--	--	--	--	1	1	1	--	1
52.	1	--	--	--	--	--	--	1	1	--	1
53.	--	--	--	--	--	--	--	--	--	--	--
54.	1	--	--	--	--	--	--	--	X	--	1
55.	1	--	--	--	--	--	--	--	--	--	1
56.	1	--	--	--	--	--	--	--	X	--	1
57.	1	--	--	1	--	--	--	1	1	--	1
58.	1	--	--	--	1	--	1	1	--	--	1
59.	1	--	--	1	--	--	1	1	--	--	1
60.	1	--	--	--	1	--	1	1	1	--	1
61.	1	--	--	--	--	--	--	1	--	1	1
62.	1	1	--	--	1	--	1	1	--	--	1
63.	1	--	--	--	--	--	--	1	--	--	1
64.	2	--	--	--	--	--	--	1	X	--	--
65.	1	--	--	--	--	--	X	1	X	--	1
66.	2	--	--	--	--	--	1	1	--	--	1
67.											B I R
68.											B I R
	62	1	--	4	10	1	27	50	18	3	60
QUOTA AVAILABLE	115	15	U	15	65	15	47	87	84	U	135

These facts can be verified with the Gar

Botswana game taken by the company in 1971.

...imal being shot if the client had seen it by the way.
...cific trophies only.

LEOPARD	LION	OSTRICH	REEDBUCK	ROAN	SABLE	SITATUNGA	SPRINGBUCK	STEINBUCK	TSESSEBE	WARTHOG	WILDEBEEST	WILD PIG	ZEBRA
—	—	—	—	—	—	—	1	1	—	1	2	—	1
—	1	—	—	—	1	—	1	1	—	1	1	—	2
—	—	1	1	1	X	—	2	2	1	2	1	—	1
—	—	—	—	—	X	—	1	1	1	1	1	—	2
X	—	1	1	—	1	1	—	1	1	1	1	—	1
X	1	1	—	—	1	1	—	1	1	1	1	—	1
X	—	—	—	—	—	—	1	1	1	—	—	—	1
1	1	1	1	—	X	—	1	1	1	1	1	—	1
—	1	—	1	1	—	—	—	1	1	—	1	—	1
	O N L Y												
X	1	1	—	1	1	—	1	—	1	1	—	—	1
X	1	—	1	—	—	—	1	1	1	1	1	—	1
X	1	—	1	1	—	—	1	1	1	1	1	—	3
X	1	—	1	—	—	—	1	—	1	1	1	—	1
X	1	—	1	1	1	—	1	1	1	1	1	—	1
X	1	1	1	—	1	—	1	1	1	1	1	—	1
X	—	—	—	—	—	—	1	1	—	—	2	—	—
X	1	1	1	—	1	—	1	1	1	1	1	—	2
	O N L Y												
X	—	—	—	—	1	—	1	—	—	1	—	—	1
X	—	—	—	—	—	1	—	—	—	—	—	—	—
—	—	—	—	—	—	—	—	—	—	—	—	—	—
1	1	2	—	—	X	—	—	1	1	1	1	—	2
X	—	1	—	—	—	—	1	1	1	1	1	—	2
X	—	—	—	—	—	—	1	1	—	1	3	—	1
X	—	—	—	—	X	—	1	1	1	1	1	—	1
X	1	—	1	—	—	—	1	1	1	1	1	—	1
—	1	—	1	—	X	—	1	1	1	1	1	—	1
X	—	—	—	—	—	—	1	—	—	1	1	—	1
—	1	1	1	1	1	—	1	—	1	1	1	—	1
	O N L Y												
	O N L Y												
X	1	—	—	—	X	—	1	—	—	—	1	—	1
X	1	—	—	1	—	—	—	—	1	—	—	—	1
X	—	1	?	—	X	—	1	1	1	1	1	—	1
X	1	1	—	—	—	—	1	1	2	1	1	—	1
1	—	1	—	—	1	—	1	2	1	1	—	—	1
1	1	—	1	—	—	—	—	—	—	—	1	—	2
1	—	1	1	—	X	—	1	1	1	1	1	—	2
—	—	1	1	—	X	—	1	1	1	1	1	—	1
X	—	—	—	—	1	—	1	1	—	1	1	—	—
—	X	—	1	—	1	—	1	1	1	1	1	—	2
X	—	—	—	—	—	—	—	—	—	1	1	—	—
—	—	1	—	1	—	X	1	1	1	—	1	—	1
X	—	1	1	—	—	—	—	1	1	—	—	—	1
X	—	1	1	1	1	—	—	1	1	—	1	—	1
—	1	—	1	1	1	—	1	1	—	1	—	—	1
1	1	—	1	1	1	—	1	1	—	1	—	—	1
—	1	—	1	—	—	—	1	—	1	1	—	—	1
X	—	—	—	—	—	—	1	1	1	1	—	—	1
X	1	1	1	X	X	—	1	1	1	1	1	—	1
—	X	1	1	1	1	—	1	1	1	1	1	—	1
X	—	—	—	—	—	—	—	—	—	1	1	—	—
—	X	—	—	1	1	—	—	—	1	1	1	—	1
—	—	—	—	—	—	—	—	1	1	—	3	—	1
1	1	1	1	—	1	—	1	1	1	1	1	—	1
1	1	1	1	1	1	—	—	1	1	1	1	—	1
1	1	—	1	1	1	—	—	1	1	1	1	—	1
X	X	1	1	—	X	—	—	1	1	1	1	—	1
X	1	1	1	1	X	—	1	1	1	1	1	—	1
X	1	—	1	1	1	—	1	1	1	1	1	—	1
X	1	—	1	1	1	—	1	1	—	1	1	—	1
X	—	—	—	—	X	—	—	—	—	1	2	—	—
X	1	—	—	—	X	—	—	—	1	1	1	—	1
1	1	1	1	1	X	—	—	—	1	1	1	—	1
	O N L Y												
	O N L Y												
10	31	26	33	20	20	2	44	46	45	49	56	—	65
16	40	30	50	27	27	25	85	70	60	165	245	5	140

...O.Box 131, Gaberones, Botswana.

JOHN KINGSLEY-HEATH'S REPORT

X Denotes wanted this trophy and failed to obtain it.
– Denotes not prepared to take this animal specifically.   50% chance of the animal being shot if the client had seen it by the way.
= Denotes client shot previously in East Africa and came to Botswana for specific trophies only.

CLIENT	BUFFALO	BUSHBUCK	CROCODILE	DUIKER	ELAND	ELEPHANT	GEMSBOK	HARTEBEEST	IMPALA	KUDU	LECHWE	LEOPARD	LION	OSTRICH	REEDBUCK	ROAN	SPRINGBOK	STEINBUCK	TSESSEBE	WARTHOG	WATERBUCK	WILDEBEEST	ZEBRA	SABLE	SITATUNGA
1.	–	–	–	–	1	1	–	1	2	–	–	1	1	–	1	1	–	–	–	2	–	1	2	–	–
2.	–	–	–	–	–	–	1	–	1	1	–	–	1	1	1	1	–	–	–	2	–	–	2	–	–
3.	2	–	–	–	–	1	–	–	1	1	–	1	1	–	1	–	–	–	–	3	–	1	2	1	–
4.	–	–	–	–	–	–	2	–	1	1	1	–	–	1	1	–	–	2	3	–	1	3	1	1
5.	1	–	–	–	–	–	1	–	1	1	–	X	1	–	1	1	2	X	1	–	–	–	3	1	1
6.	3	–	–	1	–	1	1	–	4	1	1	X	1	1	1	1	2	1	2	4	X	3	2	–	–
7.	1	–	–	–	–	–	1	–	3	1	1	–	1	1	–	–	2	1	–	3	–	–	2	1	–
8.	1	–	–	–	1	1	1	1	1	1	1	–	–	–	–	2	1	–	2	–	–	2	1	–
9.	–	–	–	–	–	–	2	1	–	1	–	X	–	–	–	–	5	–	–	–	–	2	–	–
10.	1	–	–	–	–	–	1	1	3	1	–	1	–	1	2	1	–	3	–	1	2	2	1	–
11.	3	–	–	–	–	–	1	1	3	1	1	X	1	1	1	2	1	2	2	–	2	3	3	1	–
12.	3	–	–	–	–	1	1	1	4	1	1	X	–	–	1	1	2	1	2	6	1	2	3	1	1
13.	2	–	–	X	–	1	1	2	1	1	X	1	–	1	1	2	–	2	2	–	1	2	1	–
14.	2	–	–	–	–	–	1	–	1	–	1	–	1	–	1	1	2	–	3	–	1	2	1	X
15.	3	–	–	X	1	1	–	4	1	1	X	1	1	1	1	2	1	2	3	X	3	2	–	–
16.	–	–	–	–	–	–	2	1	–	1	–	1	–	–	5	–	–	–	–	1	–	–	X
17.	3	–	–	–	1	1	–	4	1	1	X	1	1	1	1	2	1	2	6	X	3	2	1	X
18.	2	–	–	1	1	1	1	2	1	–	1	1	1	1	2	1	2	5	–	3	2	1	–
19.	2	–	–	–	1	1	1	3	1	1	–	1	–	1	2	1	2	2	–	2	2	–	–
20.	2	–	–	–	–	1	1	4	1	1	–	1	–	1	–	2	3	–	2	2	X	–
21.	–	–	–	–	–	–	–	1	–	–	X	–	–	–	–	–	–	1	–	–
22.	2	–	–	X	1	2	–	5	2	1	–	1	–	1	–	4	1	3	2	–	2	4	1	–
23.																									
24.																									
25.	1	–	–	–	–	2	–	10	2	2	X	3	–	2	1	6	1	4	5	–	2	10	?	1
26.																									
27.	1	–	–	X	1	1	–	2	1	1	–	1	–	–	1	1	1	3	–	3	2	–	–
28.	2	–	–	X	1	1	–	2	1	1	X	1	–	1	2	2	2	3	–	3	2	–	–
29.	1	–	–	X	1	1	–	2	1	1	X	1	–	1	1	2	–	1	1	–	1	2	–	–
30.	1	–	–	–	–	1	–	1	–	–	X	1	–	–	2	–	–	–	–	1	1	–	–
31.	3	–	–	X	–	1	1	4	2	1	1	1	–	1	–	2	–	2	3	–	1	2	1	–
32.	–	–	–	–	–	–	–	–	–	–	–	–	–	–	1	–	–	–	–	–
33.	3	–	–	–	1	–	1	1	X	–	1	–	–	–	1	–	–	1	–	–
34.	2	–	–	X	1	1	–	1	1	1	X	–	1	–	1	–	1	2	X	–	1	1	1	–
35.	2	–	1	–	1	–	1	2	1	1	1	1	–	1	1	2	1	–	2	–	2	2	1	–
36.	1	–	–	–	–	1	1	1	1	1	1	1	1	3	1	–	2	–	1	1	–
37.	3	–	–	X	–	1	–	3	1	1	X	X	1	1	1	2	1	2	3	–	3	4	1	–
38.	–	–	–	–	1	–	1	2	1	1	X	1	1	1	–	2	1	–	2	–	1	4	–
39.	X	–	–	–	–	1	1	1	–	1	–	1	1	–	5	1	–	1	–	2	1	–
40.	2	–	–	–	–	1	1	3	1	1	X	–	1	–	2	–	2	2	–	4	1	–
41.	1	1	–	–	1	1	–	3	1	1	1	1	1	1	1	2	1	2	2	–	1	1	–
42.	–	–	–	–	–	1	–	2	1	1	–	–	1	1	1	3	4	–	1	2	1	–
43.	2	–	–	–	–	1	1	4	1	1	–	1	1	1	1	1	3	–	1	3	1	–
44.	1	–	–	–	1	1	1	3	1	1	X	1	1	X	2	1	1	2	–	3	3	1	1
45.	2	–	–	–	–	1	1	4	1	1	X	1	1	1	2	1	–	1	–	2	4	–
46.	2	–	1	–	–	1	1	4	1	1	–	1	1	1	2	–	1	2	–	2	4	N
47.	2	–	–	–	–	1	–	2	1	1	X	1	–	X	2	–	2	2	–	2	4	O
48.	3	–	–	–	–	1	1	2	1	1	X	X	–	1	1	2	1	2	3	–	2	4	S
49.	1	–	1	–	–	1	1	1	1	1	X	–	1	1	2	–	1	2	1	–	4	H
50.	2	–	–	–	–	1	1	3	1	1	X	1	–	1	1	2	–	1	2	–	–	4	O
51.	3	X	1	1	–	–	1	1	2	1	1	1	1	–	1	2	1	2	2	–	2	3	O
52.	2	X	–	1	X	X	1	1	3	1	1	X	1	–	1	X	2	1	2	3	X	1	4	T
53.	2	–	–	–	–	1	1	1	2	1	1	X	1	–	1	–	1	1	1	X	1	4	I
54.	2	–	–	–	–	1	1	1	2	1	1	X	1	–	1	1	1	1	1	–	2	N	G
TOTALS	79	1	3	4	4	24	49	27	117	49	41	7	38	15	37	26	95	28	60	112	5	66	120	24	5
Total Quota Available	145	15	10	60	22	45	81	48	375	67	45	20	38	39	40	30	255	115	75	335	15	300	230	28	10

These facts can be verified with the Game Department: P.O. Box 131, Gaberones, Botswana.

My report on a typical season in Botswana.

RELEVANT FACTS CONCERNING THE DEPRECIATION OF WILDLIFE ASSETS

KENYA

Independence was granted from Britain in 1963. Considerable progress was made initially, for some two years, whilst British park and game wardens remained. However, by 1968 corruptive practices became rampant. Presidential cognisance and clandestine support of elephant poaching and closure of hunting in 1977 ensured the disappearance of almost 50 percent of all wildlife. The elephant population declined to 20 percent of its original total.

The human population explosion from five million in 1950 to 31 million in 1996 ensured that wildlife will never return to huge areas of Kenya. Furthermore, war and insecurity in the N.F.D. ensured the virtual eradication of elephant and wildlife of any basic value. Such game populations remaining in northern Kenya are thanks to the sterling efforts of ranch owners and local wildlife funding activities.

Masailand, now largely fenced ranches, disrupts the time-honoured migrations of game dependent on weather patterns for their existence. Huge increases in domestic stock have taken over water resources and grazing areas.

Determined efforts, initially successful, by Dr. Richard Leakey ended in his dismissal—he refused to accept corruption and land hunger of the ever-greedy politicians. He succeeded in halting elephant poaching.

Despite hundreds of millions of U.S. dollars in funding by the World Wildlife Fund and many other wildlife funding agencies over a 20- year period, very little improvement can be seen or expected. As time goes by, it is difficult to justify the fact that the administrators of wildlife funding have lived with corruption for so long. When will all agencies combine and stand out against corruption so that wildlife will cease to suffer such grievous destruction?

TANZANIA (TANGANYIKA)

Independence was granted from Britain in 1961. For the initial few years after independence, some national park and game department officers remained. With the departure of the officers, corruption and mismanagement became rife. Huge populations of elephant were poached and destroyed by Somali gangs using AK-47s. The administration of wildlife and the allocation of hunting areas became subject to bribes and other corruptive practises. Quotas of game were overshot and game laws discarded in the race to 'get what you can before it goes to hell in a handbasket', as one P.H. put it. Shooting of cats at night with spotlights and from vehicles and machans became common practice.

The advent of outside professional hunters, who knew neither the language nor the country and who were admitted almost entirely on the basis of what they could produce in U.S. dollars to both the wildlife officials and the country's economy, merely exacerbated the situation.

The director of wildlife's stock answer to those who sought to help wildlife by funding behavioural studies and protective conservation systems became, 'Give us a cheque and we will do the job'. Knowing full well what this meant, funding agencies retreated from obvious misadministration and corruption, having been denied the privilege of implanting their own financial administration.

Establishment of the Mweka Wildlife Administration Training College for senior and junior staff of the game departments of several African countries has suffered considerably from underfunding, lack of administration, and feuding amongst its teaching staff. Its future is now inevitably in question as the funding agencies, on their track records, have little inclination to continue their financial support, knowing full well that funds are inevitably misadministered.

Liaison between funding agencies and corrupt officials, so that they may continue to support research programmes and maintain a field site for students from overseas universities, has been established for some time. This inevitably involves turning a blind eye to perhaps illegal mining activities that may reduce rightful revenue to the government's economy. Very recently and significantly, the upper reaches of the Umba River have been placed within the control of the game reserve in which a wildlife conservation organisation operates.

Gemstones of East Africa by Peter C. Keller throws an interesting light on this matter:

> Tiffany & Co., principal promoters of tanzanite in the late 1960s and early 1970s, stopped promoting the gem simply because supplies dwindled and demand could not be met. Prices rose dramatically.
>
> By the late 1960s, however, the Tanzania government simply lost control of the area and tens of thousands of illegal, independent miners arrived on the scene.
>
> According to eyewitness accounts it temporarily became an area of total anarchy, murder, and totally random and dangerous mining. In 1991 the Tanzania government regained control of the area and is very carefully issuing leases. In November 1990, 150-, 240- and even 1750-carat crystals were produced.

It is interesting to note that the wildlife charity operating in this area is blatantly supported by the main retailers of gemstones in the U.S.A.

In 1996 there was a general election. The new government expressed hope that the 'bad old days' were over and that a new era of constructive endeavour to protect Tanzania's wildlife and tourism industry would now commence. It is hoped that this will have the desired and far-reaching effect, and that ethics in hunting will improve.

UGANDA

Independence was granted from Britain in 1962.

For the first few years great progress was made whilst Uganda attracted more tourism and investment based upon a bolder and more efficient eco-tourist structure than any other state in East Africa.

The advent of Idi Amin as president by military coup caused total collapse of Uganda's tourism. Huge depredations of the wildlife population took place. Dereliction of all lodges and national park roads and communications resulted. Anarchy prevailed. Every able-bodied person became the possessor of an AK-47 and used it.

The country suffered civil war until 1989. All wildlife was virtually destroyed, excluding very small populations in Queen Elizabeth, Kidepo, and Murchison Falls National Parks. Game in the Sese Islands and gorilla populations in south-west Uganda survived. The elephant population fell from approximately 50 000 to 350. The present wildlife department and national parks organisation is totally corrupt and inefficient, with little hope of any improvement. The Uganda Wildlife Heritage Fund, a U.S. charity, raised $500 000 to support my appointment as, initially, chief park warden of Queen Elizabeth National Park and subsequently as assistant director of Uganda National Parks, to help bring back the national parks to some semblance of order. Within two years the fund's aircraft was seized with all ancillary equipment. I was fortunate to escape with my life when corruption and poaching were exposed and shown to be done in collaboration with the army and wildlife officials. Due to interpolitical agreements, which held the country together after the civil war, presidential action was impossible. The seizure of the fund's equipment exposed the complete lack of support against corruption that both British and American Embassy officials gave an independent U.S. charity. The British and U.S. governments believed that their decisions not to openly oppose this corruption improved their chances to further their own causes. The general attitude and the apparent lack of moral fibre of the aforementioned officials was a disgrace and an embarrassment to all expatriates.

For a year, the E.E.C. suspended its engineering and equipment support of the maintenance of the Uganda National Parks because of a lack of security and corruption. G.T.Z. (the German overseas aid organization) followed suit. In 1994, the G.T.Z. employed as advisors a highly respected staff of expatriates with very considerable African experience in national park administration. The advisors saw little or no potential in what remained of Murchison Falls and Kidepo National Parks. In the following year, G.T.Z. employed additional expatriates who also had considerable wildlife management experience in Murchison Falls National Park. The continued lack of security and unhealthy work conditions on both the north and south banks of Murchison Falls persuaded them to relinquish their posts after a year's attempt to make some inroads into the termination of the poaching of wildlife. In fact, the whole of the north bank of the Nile and both sides of the Sudan–Uganda border have become a training ground for the use of troops who have figured prominently in the takeover of both Ruanda and Zaire by new regimes.

In spite of all this, some semblance of order remains in Queen

Elizabeth National Park under the wardenship of Mr. Latif, who is assisted by two Germans, privately funded and to some extent supported by the G.T.Z., however, such support that organizations can give is lacking in the physical muscle that the control of indiscriminate poaching demands.

No progress on the reestablishment of Uganda's wildlife will be successful until funding agencies cease their independent activities and present a united front to resist corruption by the avaricious senior officials of Uganda National Parks and other officials with whom they consort. To serve Uganda's wildlife administration without cost to Uganda, one should not have to pay $1000 per month into the German bank account of the director of national parks in order to preserve one's employment.

BOTSWANA (BECHUANALAND)

Independence was granted from Britain in 1966.

Many wildlife officials remained in office for a considerable time after independence and were wise in their judgements and control of wildlife.

The cattle policy and development of domestic stock, however, ruled the minds of Botswana's politicians. Wildlife tourism was stated to be of secondary importance to the indigenous people's aspirations.

Veterinary fences were lengthened and game populations denied access to their migratory routes, resulting in the demise of many thousands of wild animals.

The Okavango Swamps were sprayed with insecticide to kill the tsetse fly, the scourge of domestic stock. Ecosystems for birds, fish, and insects were destroyed without any attempt being made to find out what effect the insecticide would have upon their continued life. Prior to this taking place there was no consultation with game concession holders, producers of substantial revenue.

The security of wildlife was further undermined by three factors:

1. The subterranean disappearance of water from the swamps
2. The failure of rains in Angola from whence the main bulk of the water came by the Okavango River into the Okavango Swamps and thence to Lake Ngami, the Botleitle River, and Lake Dow
3. A severe drought across Botswana

The effects of these factors have resulted in the disappearance of water from Lake Ngami and the Botleitle River leading to Lake Dow, and the consequent disappearance of game and bird life normally dependent on these water resources at migrational times of the year.

To complete the misfortunes of the population, a virulent bovine lung disease became rampant in northern Botswana, necessitating more than 240 000 cattle having to be destroyed. This inevitably resulted in a minor pressure on available game meat for those now without cattle. To be fair, the aforementioned veterinary fences were, in this case, a strategic line of defence against the spread of disease, which was precisely why they were so designed.

Corruption, fortunately, is so far of very minor proportions in Botswana. However, it remains to be seen whether its powerful neighbour, the Republic of South Africa, is impervious to this endemic disease advancing from the north.

ETHIOPIA

In this independent African state ruled by H.R.H. the Emperor of Ethiopia, the hunting was reasonably controlled by the Ministry of Agriculture. There were very few anti-poaching controls.

The Emperor of Ethiopia, Haile Selassie, was assassinated and the government overthrown by the Marxist regime of Mengistu Haile Mariam (now resident in Zimbabwe). The entire royal family and many close relatives were murdered, with one or two exceptions amongst the youngest members of the family. Poaching was rife.

In a recent civil war, the Mengistu regime was defeated. A generally democratic government is now in the process of reestablishment. Poaching is widespread, with the acquisition of firearms by most of the population.

Hunting was closed for several years and was reopened in 1996 on a very limited basis, but no efficient controls seem to exist and wildlife populations remain unverified.

Nearly every able-bodied Ethiopian carries an AK-47. Game suffers daily accordingly.

ERITREA
(FORMERLY PART OF ETHIOPIA)

In the 1939–45 War, Britain, having captured Eritrea from the Italians, returned it to Emperor Haile Selassie. However, by then the people of Eritrea were determined to usurp the control of the subsequent Mengistu regime and successfully achieved independence from Ethiopia in 1993.

During these historical events and upheavals, human populations remained sparse in the low-lying areas of western Eritrea and stark mountains of the desert areas of the Red Sea littoral. In the west, until the 1950s, there were elephants, lions, leopards, and substantial populations of greater and lesser kudu and gazelles.

With the coming of war and subsequent independence, coupled with the lack of food, huge inroads were made upon the wildlife populations. Elephant and lion have all virtually disappeared. Only in the Red Sea hills could the hunting of Red Sea ibex and gazelles be possible, although greater and lesser kudu survive in the hills near Keren and westward to the Sudan border.

Today the fledgling government of Eritrea, largely supported by overseas aid, is attempting to tackle the problems of wildlife and eco-tourism as best it can. The magnificent scenery that rises from the coast at Massawa to 9000 feet on the high plateau on which stands the capital, Asmara, is largely devoid of any forest whatsoever.

The reintroduction of game by translocation and the establishment of national parks could be a real possibility for this country, together with unrivalled fishing in the Red Sea and Dhalac Archipelago, only a very short flight from Europe.

No hunting is permitted in Eritrea at this time. Attempts to conserve wildlife are embryonic and underfunded.

REPUBLIC OF SOUTH AFRICA

I am including this area because here lies the major ray of hope for African wildlife. Ranch hunting of many different species of game is increasing by leaps and bounds, supplied to a great extent by the national parks and those who preserve excess populations on private game reserves. These excess populations are then translocated to ranches at an agreed price. The precise details of each animal are recorded.

Elephants are culled in areas where populations begin to destroy too much of their own habitat, and a practical and far-reaching policy for the future is being energetically pursued.

Notably, the game-ranching industry is almost exclusively in the hands of people who have concern for wildlife and its future. The 'campfire' principles that have been blessed with great success in Zimbabwe, where an ever-increasing number of indigenous people are rapidly becoming involved in the profitable use of their renewable wildlife resource, offer a realistic hope for the future.

Recent disclosures by investigative journalists have shocked wildlife conservation authorities throughout the world. Poaching of lions out of the Kruger National Park and the sale of animals as trophies to visiting clients from excess zoo populations have caused the very gravest concern.

POPULATION AND AREA FIGURES RELEVANT TO THE REDUCTION OF WILDLIFE POPULATIONS

Kenya: The population in 1945 was 4 million. In 1996 it was 30 million. It has an area of 224 960 square miles.

Tanzania (Tanganyika): The population in 1945 was 6 million. In 1996 it was 30 million. It has an area of 275 000 square miles.

Uganda: The population of Uganda in 1945 was 3 3/4 million. In 1996 it was 11 million. It has an area of 96 081 square miles, of which 13 680 square miles are water.

Botswana (Bechuanaland): The population in 1945 was 300 000. In 1996 it was 1 million. It has an area of 275 000 square miles.

Mozambique: The population in 1945 was 6 million. In 1996 it was approximately 10 million. It has an area of 302 000 square miles.

Ethiopia: The population in 1945 was 8 million. In 1996 it was 12 million. It has an area of 350 000 square miles.

Eritrea: The population and area are combined with Ethiopia.

Somalia: The population in 1945 was 1 1/2 million. In 1996 it was 3 million. It has an area of 277 000 square miles.

Sudan: The population in 1945 was 10 1/2 million. In 1996 it was estimated at 17 million. It has an area of 967 000 square miles.

The strict enforcement of hunting ethics has never been more urgent.

BIBLIOGRAPHY

Reference for confirmation of detail and spelling has been made to the undermentioned publications.

The Adventures of an Elephant Hunter. J. Sutherland.
The Africa Safari. P. Jay Fetner.
African Hunter. James Mellon.
African Rifles & Cartridges. John Taylor.
Big Game Shooting in Africa. H.C. Maydon.
Cartridges of the World. Frank C. Barnes.
The Chairman: John J. McCloy. Kai Bird.
The Danakil Diary. Sir Wilfred Thesiger, C.B.E., D.S.O.
The East African Hunters. Anthony Dyer.
Elephant. David Blunt.
The Elephant People. Denis Holman.
Gemstones of East Africa. Peter C. Keller.
Haile Selassie's War. Anthony Mockler.
The Hunter Is Death (the life of George Rushby). T.V. Bulpin.
A Hunter's Life in South Africa. Roualeyn Gordon-Cumming.
Inside Africa. John Gunther.
Kambaku. Harry Manners.
A Life of My Choice. Sir Wilfred Thesiger, C.B.E., D.S.O.
The Lords of Poverty. Graham Hancock.
The Man-Eaters of Tsavo. J.H. Patterson.

Mauser Bolt Rifles. Ludwig E. Olson.

Men of All Seasons. Anthony Dyer.

Modern Sporting Guns. C. Austyn.

My Serengeti Years. Myles Turner.

My Somali Book. Captain A.H. Mosse.

No More the Tusker. George H. Rushby.

Outdoor Emergency Medicine. Dr. Frank Madda, M.D.

Outdoor Life. All issues, 1950 to 1978.

Records of Big Game (XX Edition). Rowland Ward.

Rediscovered Country. S.E. White.

Report on Poaching in Tsavo East National Park, Kenya, 1976. D. Sheldrick, M.B.E.

The Rifleman's Rifle. Roger C. Rule.

S.C.I. Safari Times. June, 1996.

The Scramble for Africa. Thomas Pakenham.

Scrambles in Lion Land. Captain F.B. Pearce.

Seventeen Trips in Somaliland. Colonel H.G.C. Swayne.

The Shamba Raiders. Major B.G. Kinloch, M.C.

The Shell Field Guide to the Common Trees of the Okavango Delta. Veronica Roodt.

Snakeman. C.J.P. Ionides.

Sport in Somaliland. Lord Wolverton.

Survival. Ben East.

Tanganyika Notes & Records. 1923 to 1962 (Fosbrooke collection).

Travel and Sport in Africa. A.E. Pearce.

Uganda Safari. Brian Herne.

ABOUT THE AUTHOR

John Kingsley-Heath, the son of Colonel A.J. Kingsley-Heath, O.B.E., formerly Commissioner of Police and sometime Attorney-General of Kenya, was educated at Monkton Combe School and commissioned at 18 into the Welsh Guards, subsequently passing the regular commission board. After active service in Europe and the Middle East, where he survived being blown up by a land mine, he returned to study history and law at Trinity College, Cambridge University, and economics at London University before being appointed to the Colonial Service in Tanzania and the East Africa High Commission in Kenya. In this capacity he saw service in Kenya, Tanzania, Somaliland, Ethiopia, Eritrea, Sudan, and Arabia as both an administrator and honorary game warden.

Before independence was granted to Kenya, he joined the well-known safari company in Nairobi of Ker & Downey Safaris Ltd. and was a director and shareholder for many years. He was responsible for opening the company's offices in Tanzania and making a survey of Bechuanaland and Mozambique for their wildlife potential. At this time he farmed in partnership 2000 acres on the slopes of Mount Kilimanjaro. Later, after the nationalization of tourist and farming enterprises in Tanzania, he founded Safari South (Pty.) Ltd. in Botswana with Lionel Palmer and Frank Miller, playing a major part in the development of tourism there. During these years and subsequently, John Kingsley-Heath was both an honorary national park warden and honorary game warden

The safaris continue. The Kingsley-Heaths on the Ngorongoro Crater, Tanzania, in 1997.

in several countries and made a number of wildlife publicity films. During his career, John Kingsley-Heath accompanied many famous people on safari and was responsible for the management of wildlife on the films *Hatari*, starring John Wayne, and *Sammy Going South* with Edward G. Robinson. He took John McCloy, the highly respected U.S. elder statesman, and his family on safari in both Kenya and Botswana.

He is an accomplished aircraft pilot, flying many thousands of hours over Africa's game areas. He is perhaps uniquely qualified in that not

476

only has he held high and responsible wildlife conservation appointments, but he has also been involved in the utilisation of the renewable wildlife resources as a past chairman of the Tanzania Professional Hunter's Association and an executive committee member of the East African Professional Hunter's Association. He won the Shaw & Hunter Trophy in 1957 and has held a professional hunter's licence in several African countries for more than 40 years.

John Kingsley-Heath left Africa in 1978 with his wife, Sue, to farm in England and to educate their three sons. In both these endeavours he was very successful and played a major role in introducing Texel sheep from the island of that name in Holland into the British national flock. Ten years later he was asked to return to Africa to further serve the recovery and sustainment of wildlife.

In 1991, he was appointed chief park warden of the Queen Elizabeth National Park in Uganda and later assistant director of national parks. He is presently the director of field operations of the East African Wildlife Heritage Fund, visiting both Africa and the United States in the course of his duties, which involve the financial support of chosen wildlife projects. He served for two years as an international director of Safari Club International in 1994 and 1995. He continues to take out photographic and bird-shooting safaris.